Footsteps

of a

Nomad:

Journeys to
Unpredictable Places

By Diana McLeod

For Bakari
I hope you enjoy
my crazy travel stories!
Thanks for reading

Diana McLeod

Footsteps of a Nomad

ISBN: 098833562X
ISBN-13: 9780988335622

By Diana McLeod

DEDICATION:

To the memory of my parents, Doris and Gordon Swift (Swifty).

Thank you for teaching me that an adventurous and independent life is well worth the risks involved

ACKNOWLEDGEMENTS:

to my husband David, whose unbridled enthusiasm has always taken us further than I ever dreamed possible.

to Trena Isley, Bill Everts, India Hammerslough and to all the generations of loyal employees who have worked so hard to keep the business running while we've been overseas. Without you, all of this would have been impossible. Dave and I love you all, you are our family, and we are eternally grateful.

to my editor, Susan Schader, whose expert guidance gave my stories the professional smoothness they needed

To all of my blog readers on the website, whose encouragement kept me engaged in this project

To Sarah Delia, for yet another great book cover

To Createspace.com, the best idea Amazon ever had, my thanks for supporting independent authors

To Walton, whose invaluable advice once again resolved publishing glitches

And to my cats, for keeping me company while writing

CONTENTS

FUNNY

UNIQUE SITUATIONS

NATURALLY WILD

PARANORMAL, SPOOKY AND CREEPY

SOME OF MY FAVORITE COUNTRIES

INDIA

SOME OF MY FAVORITE COUNTRIES

By Diana McLeod

Footsteps of a Nomad

By Diana McLeod

INTRODUCTION

Welcome to my travel stories! This book is an autobiography of sorts, so I'll start by introducing myself.

It all began with a love affair with *National Geographic*. When I was a child, I couldn't wait for the next issue. Every article was an introduction to the world's wonders, and the photography only widened each story's impact and made me yearn for more. I spent my childhood fascinated by the exotic destinations in the magazine, never dreaming that, someday, I would be able to embrace the nomad in myself and experience so many of the world's wonders. One picture of the Taj Mahal became permanently imprinted on me. The sheer perfection of its poetic beauty made my imagination soar and instilled in me a lifelong appreciation of art. I have now been lucky enough to see this fabulous monument in the glow of sunset and even by moonlight, and I was not disappointed.

At age seven, at month-long family summer camp, I met Miss Padma Shakya Narayan, a lovely thirty-year-old from India who became my friend. I was instantly infatuated with her; her exotic beauty, her shimmering silk saris and fabulous jewelry, her lilting accent and musical laugh. She taught me how much fun it is to meet people from other countries and other cultures.

Books transported me to new and wondrous places. Rudyard Kipling's *The Jungle Book* swept me away to childhood adventures deep in the wilds of India. Tales of China and Japan were hauntingly romantic. Knowing that one of my ancestors was a clipper ship captain who sailed to these exotic destinations made me aware that the spirit of exploration was part of my family DNA. True stories of intrepid travelers like Richard Haliburton and Roy Chapman Andrews filled my expanding library with daring exploits.

I started adventuring at a young age, thanks in large part to my parents, who loved sailing. Dad was a master-craftsman and a builder of wooden boats. He custom-built us a twenty-six-foot wooden sloop, just big enough for our family—my parents and my sister and I—to live aboard. We sailed around the coast of Maine every summer. We loved anchoring off uninhabited islands along the Maine coast, exploring secret coves, abandoned homesteads and decaying World War Two watchtowers and tunnels on places like Jewel Island.

Life on the water was unpredictable. My parents battled squalls, gale-force winds, violent waves and dangerous conditions on the open sea. Watching them meet challenges head-on was a valuable lesson for me. I learned early how to read charts, plot a course and how to navigate in rough conditions. Once, we even sailed on the heels of a hurricane, using the fierce winds to shove us easterly on a night-long thrill ride, riding the big ocean rollers like a surfboard. I spent most of that night at the helm, out of sight of land, sailing by compass, with a

1

thermos full of coffee, while my parents and my sister took turns trying to sleep below.

At school, I took a memorable anthropology class at Exeter and several side courses at Middlebury that have been invaluable to me. An Asian art class, chosen just to get some easy credits, became one of the most useful subjects from my college career. Comparative religion and a compelling course on Zen Buddhism, taught by Stephen Rockefeller, gave me the foundations of an understanding of Eastern Religions, and opened a spiritual awakening within me.

My husband Dave was already a veteran solo traveler when we met. He hitchhiked and hopped freight trains all over New England and Quebec. In our late twenties, we traveled together by rail for the first time, and I was instantly hooked. My first boxcar ride was on the Crawford Notch line on the Maine Central. This scenic journey took us right through the heart of the White Mountains, and over the breathtakingly steep "Frankenstein's Trestle." Our next trip was riding the rails across America—we took passenger trains to Denver and then hopped freight trains across the American West. The experience of riding in open boxcars was dangerous but exhilarating! One day in Utah, we were in a boxcar, waiting for our train to depart, when three other hobos jumped in with us. I remember them well; an older gent with few teeth, a tough young black guy who was carrying a two-foot-long machete, and (no, I'm *not* making this up) a scar-faced mute Native American who had evidently lost his ability to speak during a knife fight. We rode for a whole day with these guys, and despite my initial panic, they were excellent companions.

Next, Dave wanted to hop freight trains across the Canadian Rockies, but I was worried about freezing to death, grizzly bears, and a few other minor inconveniences, so I was looking for an alternative destination. One day we were playing music, singing the James Taylor song "Oh, Mexico, sounds so simple I just have to go..." when the words just hit me. I lobbied hard for warmer climates, and we spent the next several years (1983-85) exploring Mexico and Guatemala.

Traveling to India, Nepal, and Thailand in 1990 changed our lives. This trip ultimately convinced us to combine our passion for travel with business. We decided to open Tradewinds, our own imported jewelry and handicraft emporium. Ever since then, we've been traveling to Asia for business every year. We buy silver jewelry, haggle for gemstones, and visit famous markets where we search out handcrafted goods. Tradewinds has also made it possible for us to vacation far from home each year, exploring about forty-eight countries so far. About ten years ago, we started an on-line store and I began a travel blog for our customers to read. This book is a collection of my favorite travel stories, some of which are inspired by those original blog posts.

By Diana McLeod

I've organized the book into three sections:

DOING BUSINESS IN STRANGE PLACES—about the beginning of Tradewinds, the buying of gemstones, and the challenge of shopping in markets around the world.

UNIQUE SITUATIONS—funny stories, dangerous adventures, tales of the unexpected, wildlife encounters, near-death experiences, and much more.

MY FAVORITE COUNTRIES—extraordinary memories from some of the places I've been.

Some stories will end with a recommended Google search, so my readers can enjoy pictures of unique places on the Internet. (for best results, always use Google, other search engines have different results).

I hope this book will encourage you to take your own journeys around our wonderful planet. Or, if travel is impossible for you at present, I hope that I can be your eyes and ears, allowing you to walk in my footsteps, bringing you closer to places you've always wanted to go.

Enjoy!

PART 1: DOING BUSINESS IN STRANGE PLACES

BORN IN A REVOLUTION: HOW OUR BUSINESS BEGAN

We had just finished eating dinner at our favorite restaurant in Kathmandu when the first rocks came flying through the windows. Outside, an angry mob of demonstrators shouted and beat at the closed doors with sticks. Inside, we dove under the tables, dodging shattered glass shards, while workers scurried to turn out the lights and close the shutters. Our waiter served us our chocolate cake under the table (which we ate anyway; no point in wasting perfectly good cake). As soon as the rioters stormed past, we paid our bill and were led out through the kitchen to the relative safety of the back alley.

It was not the best timing for our trip to Nepal. Soon after we arrived, the Nepalese pro-democracy movement turned violent. The people were tired of suffering under an absolute monarchy. The Royal family had greedily siphoned off money from corruption—enough to make the King the sixth richest man in the world! Everybody wanted freedom desperately. By the winter of 1990, they were willing to take to the streets to get it.

We got caught in the crossfire. Every time we tried to leave the tourist district of Kathmandu, Dave and I were in danger of being swept up in violent demonstrations. There were nightly riots. Once, we had to wait until after midnight to get back into our hotel because a confrontation was taking place right on the front doorstep! The owner, who was a friend, wound up at the hospital with a concussion that night.

There were some pretty dramatic moments. As we were walking down one main street, people came running towards us, fleeing riot police. Hearing what sounded like gunfire, we ran inside a travel agency office and alerted the terrified agents to the danger. Everyone cowered behind a heavy metal desk until the confrontation was over.

We kept a map of the back alleys in our heads and flashlights in our pockets, with alternate escape routes always in mind. One day, as we walked up to an intersection, an army truck, bristling with riot police and soldiers, headed straight towards us. From the other direction, a large mob of protesters surged angrily forward, ready to clash with the police. Caught right in the middle were two terrified British tourists, too panicked to react. We ran up and tackled them, dragging them into an alley to get them out of harm's way.

By Diana McLeod

Our flight dates were non-transferable, so Dave and I were stuck in the city. Because of the unrest, we couldn't visit the historic districts, or the temples, or even leave town for three long weeks. The five-block radius of Thamel (the tourist district) was the only relatively safe place to be, and there was nothing to do there but the usual touristy things: bars, restaurants, and shopping. So, we went shopping.

We did it very slowly, getting to know each shopkeeper—chatting at length, and drinking cup after cup of chai (Nepalese spiced milk tea). It did not take long for us to notice just how remarkably beautiful the silver jewelry was. One guy impressed us. His work was exquisite, his stones were all genuine, and his price for wholesale purchases was reasonable. Eventually, we decided to make a modest investment, which we hoped would help pay for some of our travel expenses. And that was supposed to be the end of it.

By the time we left Nepal, the revolution was successful. The King gave up absolute rule, and a parliamentary system of government began. The airport reopened and we were able to catch our flight home as scheduled.

When we got back to Wilmington, Vermont, a strange twist of fate occurred. We had been professional musicians, working for a booking agent who had been finding us steady gigs in Connecticut and Northern Massachusetts for several years. On our arrival home, we expected to have work lined up, but our agent had mysteriously disappeared. His office was abandoned overnight, all the phones were disconnected, and he'd left no forwarding address. His home number was cut off, too. We've always wondered—and speculated—about what became of him. Some of the owners of the hotels and clubs he'd booked us in made us uneasy. They gave us the impression that we might have been employed in shady money-laundering operations for mobsters. Had our agent disappeared into the witness protection program?

We never learned the truth. But whatever happened to him left Dave and I suddenly unemployed. It also left us quite unsettled. We'd been musicians for fourteen years, but our voices were wearing out, and we were tired of schlepping half a ton of instruments and sound equipment around everywhere we went.

Worst of all, as paid entertainers, we were learning songs straight off the radio. Original or unusual material was frowned upon in the venues that paid well. Music wasn't taking us to where we really wanted to go, anymore.

Meanwhile, the little order of Nepalese silver that we carried home sold like crazy. Local store owners snapped it up at bargain wholesale prices. The hand of Karma was giving us a gentle shove! We took the hint. And that's how it all began.

Footsteps of a Nomad

We needed capital to get started. It took some nerve to ask Dave's dad for our first big loan. We had no real "business plan," only that Dave would use the money to return to Kathmandu to buy jewelry and "some other cool stuff" and we would find someplace to sell it during the Christmas season. His dad was so anxious to get us out of the music business that he agreed to lend us the money—with interest, of course.

Dave's first business trip was successful, but by August we still didn't have anything to show for it yet, because the goods all had to be shipped. Business in Asia is mostly conducted with handshakes and blind trust. There are no legal contracts, no signatures, and no guarantees. I nearly died of anxiety waiting for our first shipments to arrive! It was quite a relief when the goods all appeared as promised!

Our next hurdle was finding a place to sell our goods. We were promised one of those aisle "carts" in a chic mall in New Hampshire, in a restored brick factory, but the deal fell through just two weeks before we were scheduled to open. Dave got on the phone and contacted every shopping mall in New England. All of them turned us down. Then, at the last minute, the downtown mall in Burlington Vermont offered us a seasonal rental in a derelict ice cream shop. And that is how we settled in Burlington. (Again, karma and plain dumb luck.)

That first shop was pretty cheesy, with homemade displays and no cash registers, but we made it work. I built a full-sized, flat, painted, plywood mannequin of a woman and outfitted her with one of our hand-knit yak-wool sweaters, hat and gloves. We put our jewelry displays on fabric-covered sawhorses. One day three football players came into our shop and when they all leaned on the main display, it took all of my strength to keep the whole thing from falling over. We added up sales on pocket calculators. But business was good, and we did well. We felt very lucky that we wound up in Burlington, a beautiful city with several colleges, a university and a thriving downtown that is a big tourist attraction. I remember leaving Burlington that year with one single cardboard box of unsold merchandise. And Dad got paid back—with interest.

Back in Asia, we worked to expand our contacts. The first two years, we concentrated on Nepal. I went from shop to shop in Kathmandu, taking notes and asking about wholesale prices until I discovered just who the true players were. Next, we added Thailand. It took us quite a bit of time to get up the nerve to tackle intimidating India, but we did, and some of the contacts we made there have been supplying us for years.

After three years of selling things at summer flea markets and holiday seasonal rentals, while still playing some music on the side, the Mall sat us down and informed us that it was time we signed a real lease and opened a full-time business. It was difficult choice in a way, because we knew that we would have to get serious. We would need

By Diana McLeod

employees; we would have to set up an actual bookkeeping system, and we would be committed to a long-term lease and all of the responsibility that goes with it. And, we would need to move to Burlington permanently.

Were we ready to try our hands at a real business? The idea was scary, but tempting. We knew we would have to work harder than we had ever worked in our lives. The vagabond lifestyle we had enjoyed in our twenties would be a thing of the past. In the end, we left music behind and signed that lease. I've never looked back with regret, and I don't think Dave has either. We love the daily challenges of what we do, and I, for one, am not ready to retire—not yet!

Starting out, we made plenty of missteps. Import/export is not an easy business, and there are no "how to" manuals out there. First-hand experience with each country's culture and customs is a job requirement, one that we're still learning. Shipping is always a challenge, government paperwork requirements are byzantine, and we've learned hard lessons in quality control and buying choices. Doing business in Asia is like peeling an onion. You strip off layer after layer until you find the actual wholesale prices of products and the best suppliers. It's an acquired skill to separate serious business people from tourist hustlers. I always wonder: if it hadn't been for the revolution, which scared away so many foreigners, would our original connection in Nepal have ever offered us a genuine business price in the first place?

Over the years, we have evolved, and today, we buy most of our gemstones and produce many of our exclusive designs. Dave has become quite an innovative jewelry designer. (If anyone had told me, back in our musician days, that Dave was going to have his own successful line of jewelry designs, I would have been incredulous. He had no interest in jewelry back then!) We also import handcrafted goods and artwork, and we've cultivated friendships with individual artisans in many countries. The next chapter will be about gemstones because jewelry buying is one of the most fascinating aspects of our business.

Author's Note: this story was about our business, not the revolution itself. For that, turn to page 173)

7

GEMSTONE ADVENTURES

GEM LESSONS WITH THE GODFATHER

During the early years of Tradewinds, when I was buying in Kathmandu, I decided to look for a gem teacher. It was time to learn the tricks of the trade and to gain some hands-on experience learning how to assess the relative value of gemstones. It was especially important to learn from an Indian family, rather than a Nepalese family, because the Indians have been in the business of cutting gemstones (and fleecing tourists) for literally thousands of years. And it's always best to learn from the experts.

I cased out various jewelers, looking for somebody with real knowledge of stones. One shop belonged to an elderly Muslim gentleman who had been a gem trader all his life. Both his son Raj and his "nephew" Satish spoke decent English and had lots of experience dealing with foreigners. It was the situation I was searching for.

The next day, I went in and made my pitch. "Here's my proposal," I said. "I want to learn about gems, especially the actual wholesale value of various stones, and I'll pay you American hourly wages to teach me to evaluate and price them. I'll come in first thing in the morning before most tourists begin to browse. As long as the shop isn't busy, you can teach me. When a customer walks in, I'll sit quietly in the corner and not let my face reveal anything of what I am thinking. Afterward, you can tell me if the tourist was overcharged, and by how much. This way, I'll learn. The most important part of this deal is that I will *never* buy any stones from this shop. Not now, and not ever. So, now that you know that, there is no reason not to teach me the exact truth about prices and values."

The men were taken aback by my proposition. They had to think about it. The money was very tempting, but they had never taught anyone their trade secrets. The elderly fellow, who was over seventy, was the hardest one to persuade. No woman had ever ventured into his professional domain before. The very idea was somewhat shocking to him, I'm sure. He was a very conservative Muslim from Jaipur, India, and he had been cutting stones since he was five years old. He was exactly the teacher I wanted. I just had to convince him to let me into his world.

One of the younger guys took me aside. Satish knew that the payment I was offering would seriously boost the shop's revenues, and he wanted to help me sway the old man. He told me about an old custom in India, that a beginning student must present a teacher with three items: two rupees, a coconut, and a hat. The act of finding and offering these "gifts" might soften up the shop owner. He also told me the gentleman's favorite nickname. Everyone called him "The Godfather," in English, which was probably a joke based on the movie. He was the absolute head of the family. His word was law, and he

8

commanded the utmost respect. But this Godfather was not a criminal; he was a scrupulously honorable and God-fearing man.

I liked this method of breaking the ice, but finding the three items proved challenging. The money was easy—I had two rupees in my pocket. The coconut was much harder. There are no coconut palms anywhere near Kathmandu. I had to scour the market to find one, but finally, I had my coconut. The hardest challenge was finding the hat. There were tons of hats in Kathmandu, but they were all made for tourists. I didn't want to insult the man! The locals wore *topis* (the traditional Nepalese cap, which is inappropriate for a Jaipuri). There were also Tibetan styles, but these were also ethnically out of the question. On many days, the Godfather wore a traditional white Muslim skullcap. As a female non-believer, I couldn't possibly purchase him one of those! No, I needed a dignified and extraordinary hat. Yet there was nothing around. I began to despair.

Then the owner of my hotel told me about a shop called the "Kathmandu Hat Shopper," and I went there immediately. Here, at last, was an interesting hat shop. They had lots of antiques and rare finds. They had British pith helmets and military hats and ethnic curiosities—even an old Scottish clan cap—but nothing quite worked for me. Chatting with the owner, I described my situation. He told me he might have something for me, but warned that it would be expensive. He went into the back and pulled out a dusty box. Inside was a treasure! It was a genuine folding top-hat, made of real beaver skin, in mint condition. It was very costly, but I knew it was perfect. The Godfather would look fabulous in it—a dashing Jaipuri Fred Astaire!

I couldn't wait to get back to the shop. I greeted my teacher, presented my rupees and my coconut, and then.... The Godfather opened the box and his eyes widened. He was old enough to remember such hats from the days of British rule in India. He popped the beaver skin open with almost childlike delight and put it on his head. It fit him perfectly! It matched his gray hair, aquiline nose and chiseled features so well that he looked ready for a black tie dinner anywhere in the world. He knew it, too. He couldn't resist running to the mirror to take a good look.

He had already been softening up on the idea of teaching me. With the presentation of the hat, I sufficiently demonstrated my resourcefulness and my determination. I was accepted! I began to study stones in earnest with the family.

Godfather was a proficient and creative teacher who managed to train me well, despite his very limited English. His "nephew" Satish was also a skillful instructor. Unlike the Godfather, whose honesty sometimes got in the way of good profits, Satish had no such scruples. His English was excellent, and he could squeeze every last rupee out of a tourist. (He would have made a great car salesman in the U.S.) I also got to know Raj, the Godfather's real son. He always called his dad

"Godfather," just like everyone else. The name somehow fit the man perfectly.

Ultimately, I believe I was accepted into the family (as much as a foreign woman could be). I was invited to dinner at their house in Nepal, and the Godfather himself prepared the meal. I think he enjoyed our sessions together as much as I did. He soon realized that I was really committed to learning, and not simply some rich American who was paying him on a passing whim. Godfather was, in a very real sense, my Godfather. He passed away a few years back, and I miss him very much. I wish he could see our shop now to see how valuable his lessons were and how his teachings helped our business succeed.

PRACTICE MAKES PERFECT: The most important skill I learned at the Godfather's shop was how to grade stones. He would bring out packets of gems (often borrowed from other, wealthier shops, I think) and we would spread them out and line them up from best to worst. Determining the value of stones involves four key factors: color, cut, clarity and carats. Easy to say, but not so easy to learn!

Each stone has rules about color. Peridot is not desirable when it is very dark. It should be bright green, the livelier, the better, although too much yellow lowers its quality. On the other hand, the best color of amethyst is dark. African stones with full-bodied, saturated intensity have more value than lighter stones from Brazil. But they should also be clear, not opaque or cloudy.

To complicate matters, there is the cutting. A well-cut stone is superior to a poorly cut one. A gem that is too shallow doesn't refract the light properly, and you can see straight through it. If a stone is cut too deep, it may look fabulous all by itself, but it's impossible to set it attractively. Many first-time buyers mistakenly choose stones cut in this manner because they may exhibit extra brilliance. In the Indian trade, they are referred to as "Qutab Minar" stones (the Qutab Minar being a monumentally tall tower spire in Delhi.)

Next, there is the clarity factor. Stones with inclusions (little fissures, lines, cloudiness, air pockets, pieces of carbon, crystals of another mineral, etc.) are less desirable. Different stones have various levels of inclusions, and learning what is "acceptable" is part of the process. Inclusions in emeralds are virtually unavoidable, while visible inclusions in citrine are never tolerated.

Then, there is a fifth factor—the one that Godfather always emphasized—the fire. If a stone has no life to it, it is no good. Fire is the most important quality. A gem with brilliance and questionable cutting is more valuable than one with perfect cutting and no fire.

All of these factors work together when you are grading stones and matching pairs. Choices have to be based on a balance of these principles. I practiced for hours to get it right, lining up the stones as carefully as I could while Godfather waited patiently. Then he would show me why one choice was better (or worse) than another. We spent days on this single task, and those lessons have stood by me ever since. Even today, as I sort gems, I still ask myself, "What would Godfather say?"

Godfather employed some very clever teaching techniques. One of my favorites was the "Lapis Rosary." He made me a strand of lapis lazuli beads, some of which were dyed, and some of which were natural. It was my job to do the rosary, announcing "dyed" or "natural" as I counted each bead. This was not an easy task! It was hard to tell by eye, but I gradually learned there is always something of a dull quality to dyed lapis. It does not have quite the same luster of naturally colored material. Around and around that rosary I went, trying to get it right. It took a lot of time, but I finally got it.

The next phase of my training involved my very own "undercover" mission. The buzz around town was that somebody in Bangkok was producing ruby doublets and passing them off as the real thing. A doublet is a two-part "stone" with a genuine natural stone cap over a manufactured or altered base. Doublets are made by cementing the two layers together. When you look only at the top of the gem, it can be nearly impossible to tell a well-made doublet from a normal stone. You must examine the side of it to be sure. This is one of many reasons why Tradewinds designs and produces our own gemstone jewelry. We do not buy high-end colored stones pre-set (except for opals and pearls). Not only do we reap a price advantage that we can pass on to our customers, but we can guard against doublets and synthetics in this way.

The Godfather got his hands on one of the ruby doublets. The top was real ruby and the bottom was garnet. It was so well made that you could only see the line at an oblique angle and by using specific types of lighting (indirect daylight was best). It was easier to see with the naked eye than with the loupe (magnifier), but it took many practice sessions before I could spot the doublet line easily. I carried the stone with me for days and studied it again and again.

Finally, I was ready for my "exam." The Godfather told me to go to specific jewelry stores in Kathmandu and pretend to be an innocent tourist. First, I would show them the "ruby," telling them that I purchased it in Bangkok. Then I was told to request another one "just like it" for earrings. My "undercover mission" was to discover which of the stores on my list had the real thing, and which had the doublets.

This challenge was a lot of fun! Acting like a clueless tourist was amusing, and the prices quoted at some of the stores were beyond belief. Everyone carefully tilted my stone, looking for the doublet line, while pretending to inspect the cutting. I'm sure all of them knew it was a fake, but nobody told me the truth. People at the honest shops didn't want to hurt my feelings, and the dishonest ones saw an opportunity to fleece me again. It was revealing to watch the salesmen at work. There was only one person who gave me a reasonable tourist price for a genuine ruby. To match the depth of color in the doublet, he had to show me a very valuable gemstone. The price was the highest I was quoted, but it also had the most integrity. If I had been an ignorant shopper, I would have happily bought another doublet instead of paying for the real deal. In the tourist gem trade, it is hard to be honest, because often your competition isn't.

Afterward, when I returned and revealed my findings to the Godfather, I am pleased to say I was right on every count. I told him some of the prices I was quoted, and the B.S. I had listened to, and we both had a good laugh. Ever since then, whenever I want to have some fun, I wander into one of these shops and get the salesmen started...

I ALMOST GOT MY HANDS ON THE ROYAL CROWN JEWELS

One morning, the Godfather and I were at his shop, having chai tea with a couple of his friends in the jewelry trade. A Tibetan antique dealer came in and asked if Godfather would be willing to look at something special. When we saw what emerged from his silk brocade pouch, our eyes grew wide with astonishment.

We were looking at a massive brooch. It was a gold circle, about five inches in diameter, and studded with prong-set gemstones arranged in a starburst and cross pattern. The heavy, 24k gold setting held over a hundred and fifty stones—diamonds, rubies, and emeralds—each one over half a carat in size. The brooch was passed around the room, and everyone got to have a good, close look. The Tibetan claimed it had belonged to the royal family, and was part of the Royal Crown Jewels collection. The Rana family sold many of these assets off in the last days of the monarchy, and the money was sent to Swiss bank accounts.

The brooch was one of the ugliest pieces of jewelry I had ever seen! It was clunky, gaudy, and the color combination was pretty hideous. It was made to call attention to royal wealth and power, and it certainly did that!

The Godfather looked it over very carefully and pronounced the stones to be genuine and of average to decent quality (which, given those precious gems, meant that the brooch was worth a small fortune). The Tibetan asked him for a frank appraisal of its value.

Godfather replied that the piece was worth a great deal for its historical value alone. The stones were worth more than he knew how to calculate at first glance. He smiled and shrugged. "Priceless," he said. "Maybe someone in Durbar Marg or a museum curator can give you a better answer."

The trader nodded and wrapped up his treasure. And that, I thought, was the last time I would ever encounter the Royal Crown Jewels.

By Diana McLeod

I was wrong. Two days later, I was thumbing through a guidebook, looking at the section on Nepalese history. Several old photographs from the nineteenth century had been reproduced, and one was a Royal portrait. The King, the Queen, and several Princesses were posed in all their finery. A shiver ran down my spine when I realized that the Queen was wearing a matched pair of brooches, which were holding royal sashes in place over her sari. There was no doubt about it—the starburst/cross pattern of the stones matched the brooch we had just seen! It had to be a photo of the same piece of jewelry I had held in my hands two days earlier!!!

I couldn't wait to show Godfather the picture. He was impressed. Again, I thought the story was over, but there is one more chapter left to tell...

Several days passed. I was wandering around a funky curio shop, peering into a glass case full of random old stuff. Most of the items were of little or no value. But, in the back corner, dusty and thrown in with everything else, I spotted, astoundingly, the mate to the brooch we had seen only days before.

My heart started pounding. I glanced at the old shopkeeper with sudden keen interest. Did he not know what he had? Was there a chance I could possess a piece of the Royal Crown Jewels? Could I get it for a bargain price? If so, what would we do with it? Legally, it could never be taken out of the country. (If I were ever caught with something like that in my luggage, no bribe would ever be big enough to get me out of trouble). If it was broken up, the stones could be reset, but that would be unethical because its antique value would be lost forever. But the stones themselves were worth so much, and the gold could be melted. Besides, the darned thing was hideously ugly and utterly unusable in the modern world.

I decided to try to get my hands on it first and then wrestle with my conscience later. Approaching the shopkeeper with the blandest facial expression I could muster, I greeted him with a smile and a cheerful "*Namaste.*" I inquired about a couple of things I wasn't interested in, and received a fair starting tourist price (still way too high, but a good place from which to start haggling.) Then I went for the brooch.

"My grandmother likes big costume jewelry like that," I said casually, pointing to the Royal piece. "What are you asking for that big pin in the case there?"

A moment later, my fantasy was over. "Oh," the gentleman replied, "that one is not costume jewelry. That is special. If you are interested, we will have to take it for a professional appraisal."

I grinned sheepishly at him. One look in his eyes and I knew that he knew exactly what he had. His eyes narrowed; he suspected I wasn't buying it for my grandmother. I eventually told him the whole story of the mate to the brooch and about the picture in the guidebook, and I wished him good luck in selling it someday.

That was my closest encounter with a royal treasure.

THE SAPPHIRE THAT GOT AWAY

One day, The Godfather offered to show me one of his favorite stones: a gorgeous sapphire. Its color was the highly prized, rich, saturated, royal blue that only a high quality gem can deliver. As the Godfather had taught me, the most important quality a gemstone can have is its fire. This stone was radiant! Godfather proudly called it his "Kashmiri Sapphire."

Godfather told me that, in the old days, sapphires from Kashmir were considered the best Asian specimens. These stones were a deeper blue than most of the Sri Lankan stones, yet brighter and less green than Thai Kanchanaburi gems. Gemologists will tell you that there are no more Kashmiri stones available. The area is played out. Still, Godfather insisted his stone was an authentic Kashmiri sapphire, worth between one thousand to fifteen hundred U.S. dollars wholesale. I never knew him to brag or exaggerate, so I assumed his estimate of its value was accurate.

It was a fabulous stone. Holding it in a pair of long gem tweezers, I admired its beauty for several minutes. At the time, I was learning how to examine stones using the long, specialized tweezers, so I used every opportunity to practice my technique.

Unfortunately, I was not very skilled with gem tweezers. They twisted in my hand and snapped closed, and the precious sapphire went flying. It all happened so fast that none of us saw where the stone landed. It didn't matter. We *had* to find it, even if it took all day.

We looked everywhere. Soon, we were all on our hands and knees on the linoleum floor of the shop, searching every inch of it. When that failed to turn up the elusive stone, I decided there was a remote possibility the stone might have rolled right out of the shop's front door. Squatting on the front steps, I sifted through the dirt and gravel outside until my clothes were filthy and I was thoroughly panicked. If the stone went missing, I would have to do the honorable thing and pay for it. I could just imagine what Dave would say!

At last we took a break. The Godfather ordered some *chai* tea, and I tried to apply reason to the situation. My briefcase was sitting on the counter, about five feet from where we had been sitting. We had dismissed it because it was zipped up. There was only the tiniest bit of open zipper at the very end, barely wide enough for the stone to fit through. Could it be in there? I thought immediately of the famous quote from the Sherlock Holmes novels: "When you have eliminated the impossible, whatever remains, however improbable, must be the truth."

I dumped the bag out carefully. When it was empty, I held it upside down and shook it. No luck. Then, just as I was about to give up, out popped the elusive sapphire! What a relief it was to find it at last! The Godfather, Satish, and one of the Godfather's young sons began conversing in rapid Hindi. I couldn't understand them, but I knew the conversation was about me. They were wondering if I had done this little magic trick on purpose.

And I'm sure, the minute I left the shop that day, they were busy checking the stone with a jeweler's loupe, making sure I hadn't tricked them with a swapped fake!

NOT FOR THE FAINT OF HEART: HAGGLING FOR GEMSTONES IN INDIA

India is the center of the gem universe. More colored stones are cut in the old "Pink City" of Jaipur than almost anywhere else in the world, and the buying and selling of gemstones is an age-old business. We work with a "buyer's broker," Sudarshan, who has now become a very dear friend. His workshops produce a lot of silver jewelry for Tradewinds. Here's how deals go down in Jaipur.

OK, it's not a Maharajah's palace. It's only an office. But imagine an office desk glittering with hundreds of strands of gemstone beads. Vibrant colors scintillate as the facets reflect the light. The jewel tones are rainbow bright. Gems, like flowers, look great, no matter how many hues mingle together.

Confronted with all this beauty, I am of two minds. In a sparkling mass, all the gemstone beads look beautiful! The woman in me wants to fall in love and adorn herself with them all. The buyer in me is less impressed, especially when I start examining the strands to begin the rejection process. So many *but*s! Dishwater color, lousy cutting, too many inclusions, not the right size, not the best shapes, some decent quality in one batch, but we already have those in stock. Much of the prettiness disappears into the dirty canvas bag from whence it came.

Looking around the room, I size up the players. Dave, maintaining the position of boss, has taken the big leather chair. Our friend Sudarshan, who owns this office, is our paid professional haggler. He is nicely dressed, looking almost Italian after spending years selling his own jewelry line in Italy. On the other side of the table are the sellers' stone brokers. They've been summoned to this office because word is out that a buyer is looking for merchandise they might have in their satchels. These guys are a very colorful crew. Most are in Western dress these days, but the older Muslim dealers sometimes show up in elegant white pyjama-like garments and crocheted skullcaps. One guy

15

is wearing a Rajasthani embroidered vest and a red velvet hat. All of them have heavy bags loaded with gems (prompting me to think that a thief in Jaipur should consider a career as a man-purse snatcher).

And then the games begin. Sudarshan is a perfect gentleman: warm and generous, utterly trustworthy, with an endearing personality and loads of charm. These attributes are not always useful in the gem business! Usually you want someone with an aggressive, trial lawyer's personality. But in a world where nice guys usually finish last, Sudarshan somehow manages to be gentlemanly even when he's squeezing the stone seller hard for that last rupee of discount. In this market, he's a pit bull, albeit with a lovely smile even when he growls. The funny thing is that these brokers are often old friends or good acquaintances. They've known each other for years. But that becomes irrelevant when they sit on opposite sides of the desk. When the haggling begins, it's not for the faint of heart. Disputes can go on for hours.

It all starts off amiably enough. First, we reject about 90% of what we see. Then the initial price process begins. Sudarshan inquires as to the asking price. Prices are rarely quoted out loud because of the other dealers. Sellers do not want to get into a bidding war against each other. In the old days, the buyer and the seller would hold hands under a white cloth, and the price would be quoted using a traditional form of touch sign language known only to gem dealers. Today, most dealers type an amount onto a pocket calculator and show it only to the other party. Older dealers occasionally still insist on using the ancient method of communication—and Sudarshan knows it well.

As soon as he gets the asking price, his eyebrows go up, and he goes on the attack. He spreads the stones out, pointing out problems with the color, the cutting, the clarity or all three. He says he'll relay the price to his client, but that it probably won't be accepted.

Then it's Dave's turn. As soon as he gets into Sudarshan's office, it's his job to look intimidating, bored, unimpressed by the merchandise, and unlikely to buy anything unless it's simply too cheap to refuse. He puts a disdainful, sourpuss expression on his face and somehow manages to keep it there all day long. The more he wants something, the more disinterested he acts. It's a bit hard for me to watch my husband turn into an insufferable *Sahib*, but it's all part of the game.

Sudarshan explains, in Hindi, that his buyer is unenthusiastic (and a terrible cheapskate). He makes a counter offer.

Now it's the seller's turn to get angry. "*Nay nay nay nay nay NAY!*" he yells emphatically. (You guessed it: "nay" means no.) A stream of invectives follows. I can only imagine what they're saying, but I'm sure it goes something like this: "This is the best quality in all of Jaipur! How dare you suggest that insultingly low a price! What are you doing, starving my children? I thought you were *my* friend, not his!"

This verbal swordplay goes back and forth, faster and louder as it gets heated. Beneath the thrust and parry, Sudarshan is wearing them down. If it's not going fast enough, he turns to Dave and says, in English (which all can understand), "David, this man will not go below his price." Then he says, under his breath, *"Fare la finta,"* an Italian phrase he taught us that means, "Make a fake show." In this case, he means "Make like you're angry."

Dave responds with the appropriate hostility. "Well, gentlemen, it seems you are just wasting my valuable time. Isn't there something else we can look at today?"

Sometimes things will escalate. On more than one occasion, sellers have stormed out of the office, slamming the door theatrically behind them. More than once, Dave has turned to Sudarshan and said, "That's a pity, I wanted to buy those." And Sudarshan will reply, "Don't worry, my dear, you just bought them." And we are left trying to puzzle out when, in the middle of all that yelling and door slamming, the deal actually took place. Not only that, we often don't even know the final price we "agreed" to pay. All we know is that Sudarshan would never have agreed if it weren't a decent deal. He has his pride and reputation to consider, as do the dealers. Most of them will only come down to a reasonable price after time and effort (and yelling). But in the end, nobody agrees to anything unless it is to their advantage to do so. We usually wind up with an excellent local price, and the dealers get their commissions, too. Sudarshan makes sure it's all fair. He knows when the seller has reached his bottom line, and he will not push below what he deems to be equitable.

Most of the time, however, the deal doesn't go down quite so unceremoniously. It often proceeds with something like this: First, Sudarshan picks up a single gemstone, grabs Dave's hand, and places the stone in it. Then he pulls the dealer's hand over and puts his hand on top of Dave's. Other dealers add their hands to the pile by way of encouragement. Then, Sudarshan will place his hand on top of all the hands with a gentle slap, saying, "For good luck, 25 rupees a carat!" This sounds like an agreement, but it is usually the cue for one more round of histrionics. If the seller thinks it's too low, he'll yank his hand away, yelling *"Nay nay nay NAY NAY!"* Or Dave might do the yelling, after which he'll turn to Sudarshan and give him a hard time, demanding to know whose side he's really on. Hands can be yanked away several times during this process.

Now Sudarshan shows his other skills. Sensing he's close to a deal, he turns on the charm. His voice becomes soothing, almost hypnotic, and he cajoles, smoothing over the differences, assuring the reluctant party that this is to their best advantage. He patiently pulls all the hands together, until everyone grudgingly agrees. Sometimes, other dealers or their associates add more physical persuasion. I've seen deals done in which four or five guys forcibly shove the seller's hand or body forward. One fellow, anxious to close his friend's deal so that he could sell his own stones, even dragged his buddy forward by the cheek, painfully yanking him back to the table. At long last, with a flourish of his palm over the pile of other hands, Sudarshan seals the deal triumphantly.

It doesn't always work out that way, either. Sometimes the deal is put "on ice." Sudarshan shoves the packet of gems into his desk drawer.

"What's happening?" Dave will ask.

"We are cooking the curry," Sudarshan explains. "We'll give the seller a day or two to come down to our price."

Sometimes, Dave is fed up with all the fighting and he is ready to cave in.

"No, no, no!" Sudarshan will say. "We can get it for a few rupees less!" He's like a determined terrier. He just can't let go.

It's not just a war of words. It's a war of gestures, poker faces, body language and head waggles. Sudarshan is a master of hand gestures, half of which are Hindi and half of which are Italian. (Sudarshan speaks fluent Italian, and he has picked up many Italian traits). His fingers move with eloquence and grace. In one singularly Italian gesture, his fingers touch his thumb, the hand moves back and forth at the wrist several times, and then the fingers open fast like a splash, for emphasis.

Unfortunately, I don't have much of a part to play. It took me some time to realize that whenever I get too assertive, I undermine Dave in the eyes of the Indian men. I usually have to channel the nervous, whiny wife who is nagging Dave not to spend too much money. It's the only role that some of the traders believe. India is still a man's world. An Indian woman would probably never even be offered a seat at this table. I have to remind myself that, a mere seventy years ago, high caste Indian ladies were kept out of sight of male guests, hidden behind latticed screens. They were never allowed out of the house, except in curtained palanquins with armed guards protecting their virtue. Considering that, and knowing that most of these men would never dream of bringing their wives into their workplace, I don't do that badly, I suppose. My friend Maria, from Florida, who was recently divorced, has it better than me. As a solo haggler, she can assume the male role on her own behalf. She does fairly well at it, too, and Sudarshan has been coaching her behind the scenes.

So I sit quietly and match pairs of stones while Dave does the heavy lifting. It's all right. He has a better memory for last year's prices than I do. Instead, I get to play with our acquisitions. And they are beautiful!!! Ethiopian opals, sparkling tourmalines, Golden Madeira citrine, Orissa garnet, peridot from Pakistan, tanzanite from Africa, rich emeralds, rubies, Brazilian amethyst. I am filled with inspiration, trying to decide what to do with all these glittering little treasures. And it's suddenly worth all the time and effort.

By Diana McLeod

DAZZLING! THE HONG KONG GEM SHOW

DINNER IN KOWLOON: Goose intestine soup. Pigs' knuckles. Beef fat slices. Fish head stew. Fried jellied eel. These tasty items and more were listed on the menu of the Hing Fat Restaurant in downtown Kowloon. We eventually ordered a baked chicken dish with shallots, onions and wolfberries, and a plate of Chinese vegetables in garlic chili sauce. The chicken, when it arrived, was quite different than the boneless, sanitized white meat we get at home in the U.S. Instead, we got all of the other chicken parts, from chopped-up pieces of neck to the feet (mercifully served without the toenails). In real, authentic Chinese cuisine, they waste nothing, especially big chunks of fat and skin, which the Chinese regard as the best parts of the animal. It was almost enough to turn me vegetarian, except that a purist would starve to death in China. Even the vegetable dishes are served with a dollop of pork fat for flavor.

We were the only foreigners eating at the restaurant filled with Chinese families, businessmen and local workers, all seated casually at diner-style Formica tables. The walls were plastered with backlit photos of regional dishes, and the crowd was lively, noisy and enthusiastic. Our waitress remembered Dave from previous encounters and gave him a well-deserved dose of friendly teasing. If you are a "regular" at a diner, there's a magical camaraderie, a unique chemistry that occurs between a talented diner waitress and her clientele, and that interaction always makes the customer feel right at home, even when they're halfway around the world.

Kowloon is on the funky, Chinese side of Hong Kong harbor. At night, a forest of neon street signs compete for our attention in a blur of glaring Chinese characters. Restaurant hustlers thrust pictures of whole, roasted suckling pigs at tourists. We strolled past traditional medicine shops full of old wooden cabinets, offering mysterious ground-up herbs and powders as prescribed by ancient recipes. They advertised many specialized (and some internationally illegal) remedies. Local street food vendors tended huge baskets of steamed buns and barbecued mystery meat on sticks, right on the sidewalks. The neighborhood bakery tempted us with almond-paste cookies and dessert treats called "coconut rocks." They're a bit hard but tasty.

The next morning, we took the ferry to Hong Kong Island. The Star Ferries are charming, historic, old ships that deliver people across the harbor quickly and efficiently, and in a much more pleasant way than on the subway. These handsome, classic ferries have been running since the 1930s, and they have become quite an institution, moving tens of thousands of people every day. Once out of the ferry terminal, we were in Hong Kong proper, home of ultramodern skyscrapers, high finance, and world-famous international shopping. It was almost like entering another country. We disembarked right beside the gigantic Hong Kong Convention Center, all six floors of which were stuffed with gems and fabulous jewelry collections. It's one of the world's largest shows, and it's only open to trade professionals—like us! I couldn't wait to go shopping.

AT THE HONG KONG GEM SHOW: I often feel out of place at world-class gem and jewelry trade shows, where millions of dollars of diamonds, pearls, colored stones and finished jewelry are out on display. No, I'm probably wrong. Given the hundreds, maybe even thousands of exhibitors, there are probably *billions* of dollars worth of products here. This year there are so many exhibitors, they stuff both of Hong Kong's massive convention centers. Most booths have stones that are worth tens of thousands of U.S. dollars each—wholesale! Rubies glow with inner fire. Emeralds, as big as pigeons' eggs, sparkle greener than a sunlit, tropical rainforest. Giant tanzanites are shot with neon-purple or violet-blue, depending on where the viewer stands. Aquamarine crystals of impossible size, color and clarity defy me to even inquire about their price.

Numerous dealers have velvet boxes of perfectly matched sets of gemstones for the kind of multi-million-dollar necklaces that would have made even Elizabeth Taylor green with envy. Many of these collections represent a lifetime of discovery, cutting and matching. How many years did the cutters have to wait, searching for that last perfectly colored, perfectly sized stone to complete the set? And then, how many shows would they have to come to, waiting for that one obsessed buyer willing to take the whole group? How many carats of diamonds would it take to surround and caress each fabulous ruby, emerald or sapphire in the manner it deserves? Would the buyer continue directly to the diamond dealers and purchase three or four-point diamonds right out of the glittering trays by the scoopful? The logistics of such a deal boggle my mind. How, for example, do they pay for this one necklace? Many of the big buyers have airline-style wheeled carry-on bags with them. Some are very high tech, with sophisticated combination locks. Are they full of stacks of Ben Franklins? How many stacks would it take to stuff one satchel full of extraordinary gems? And who are the real players here? Are they the guys in the hand-tailored suits, or do the serious players deliberately keep a lower profile?

I watch one Texan in a Hawaiian shirt and khakis. He looks like an aging hippie, but his gem loupe has seen years of service. He's assessing a collection of large, high-quality Columbian emeralds. The booth owner knows him. They chat like old friends, and a deal is going down. When they begin to haggle in earnest, suddenly I'm too close for comfort. He glances sideways at me, and I politely move on to the next booth.

I'm glad I did, because I'm now drooling over Australian opals. The flaming colors in these giant chunks of solid opal are to die for! I gasp at price tags. Eighteen thousand dollars wholesale for this pretty purple one; thirteen thousand for the vibrant teal stone shot with green fires. These are only two of several hundred such choices offered at one booth. There are at least ten opal specialists on this one floor. Heaven knows how many opal dealers there are in the whole show! Moreover,

By Diana McLeod

each vendor has buckets full of stones stashed under their counters, chock-full of more affordable goodies. Dave and I love to dig through such bins! We spend hours at these shows rummaging through stock boxes.

I move on and find myself in the hall of pearl vendors. Row after row of tables is piled high with lustrous pearls of all kinds. There are thousands and thousands of strands, from bargain freshwater necklaces to the finest natural South Sea beauties valued at thousands of dollars per string. Most of the freshwater pearl vendors come from China, but the majority of the cultured ocean pearls are sold by Japanese, Australian and Tahitian companies.

And then there is the finished jewelry. The biggest collections in this show cater to Chinese and Asian tastes. The Chinese adore large, colored stones surrounded by diamonds. Sometimes they stick to a simple sparkling border, but more often, they surround the featured stone with gaudy sprays of smaller colored stones. Most of it is much too busy for my taste. The jewelry is ostentatious, yet at the same time the designs feel old-fashioned to me. The glitter and the intensity of the lighting are almost painfully bright at times, and the Transitions lenses in my glasses darken as if I was out in the sun.

And what are we walking away with? Our biggest buy is opals. We've selected some nicely matched pairs of Australian doublet and some solid white Australian opal. We've found some fabulous matched pairs of malachite-azurite from Peru. What gorgeous earrings we will make from these! My satchel is filling with charoite, some sapphires, seraphinite, chrysocolla, sugilite, lapis, and jade. We didn't buy any finished jewelry except pearls, set in gold, and some stylish leather and steel bracelets for our male customers.

The most intriguing stone we're taking home is called "Swedish blue." This gem is actually a one-thousand-year-old man-made "artifact" from the Vikings. Back in the Middle Ages, Viking warriors developed primitive steelmaking capability. When the armories poured off the molten slag and discarded it, the slag formed into a type of "volcanic" glass. Given the cobalt present in the soil, the hardened "stone" became blue, very much like the natural volcanic material we know as larimar. But this variety has a moderate, mid-range color; less turquoise than larimar. It is quite rare!

As the Star Ferry chugs across the harbor, its antique wooden interior reminds me of a "Dr. Who" phone booth, transporting us from one amazing universe to another. I wonder what dining adventures await us tonight in the alleys of Kowloon?

recommended Google search: Kowloon street Images

BIZARRE BAZAARS

BLACK AND WHITE MAGIC: The Bangkok amulet market

Bangkok is an intimidating modern city, but it is easy to find quiet amidst the chaos if you know just where to look. You can turn a corner, slip through a doorway or into an alley, and find yourself in another world.

The temple of Wat Ratchanada is such a place. To get to this Buddhist site, I have to cross an insanely busy six-lane avenue on foot. When I finally make it through the traffic tsunami, I breathe a sigh of relief. Beside the boulevard are the formal gardens and golden pavilions of a royal ceremonial audience hall. Thai dignitaries often formally greet foreign diplomats in this elegant setting. The open-aired pagodas shimmer in the sunlight, and I feel as though I have stepped out of traffic and into a scene from a fairy tale. Behind this area, there is an old door, usually left ajar, on the back wall, through which one enters into the sacred grounds of the Wat.

Highway noise disappears inside the temple walls. The main meditation hall soars seventy feet into the air. Its multi-level pagoda roofs are decorated with gold, matching the gleam of the massive Buddha statue inside. Today, regretfully, I must pass by quickly because my destination is on the far side of the compound. I am heading for the ramshackle bazaar that houses one of the oldest amulet markets in Bangkok.

This bustling shopping mecca is devoted entirely to religious imagery and art, and it reflects the diversity of Thailand's population. The overwhelming majority of the offerings are Thai Buddhist, of course, but you can also find Khmer and Chinese themes. The Indian expat population is served by Hindu vendors. Some of the merchandise is hideously tacky; gold-covered plastic with flashing lights, tinsel, and fake jewels. Visually, it is such a jumble that the eye cannot absorb it easily. Shops are crammed to the rafters, and it's hard to squeeze my way between the browsers and the statuettes. The glitzy stuff amuses me, but my main area of interest is elsewhere: the serious bronze shops.

Here, timeless images of the Buddha crowd the cramped stalls, illuminated by slanting rays of light beaming in from gaps in the overlapping tin roofs. Incense smoke and dust motes swirl in the afternoon heat, adding mystery to each gently smiling face. These are lost-wax castings, made using ancient techniques at least five thousand years old. At first, the image is sculpted by hand in wax. A mold of clay is then applied. Afterward, molten metal is poured into the mold, burning away the wax original to create the finished product. Each image is a unique sculpture; and exact copies of each mold can't be reproduced, so no two of these Buddhas are ever exactly alike. I pick out a few of these iconic pieces every year.

Monks love to wander around here. They usually don't buy much, maybe a strand of prayer beads or an amulet, but I think some of them come just to see so many images of the Buddha. Others are sent by their monastery to fetch something like a cast bronze bell for their temple, or a significant Buddha statue for a new shrine.

A group of Thai men are bargaining for amulets at one stall. The world of Thai amulets is arcane and almost incomprehensible to anyone outside of Thai culture. These Buddhist religious pendants can be made of cheap stamped metal, or elaborate clay tablets with a Buddha image on them, housed in handwrought lockets made of genuine 24k gold with glass covers. Old and rare pieces can be worth thousands of dollars, especially when the clay actually contains cremated remains of Buddhist monks or saints. These icons are reverently worn by many Thais, both male and female. It is illegal to export them, even as gifts, unless you're Thai.

I watch the haggling, fascinated. One man carefully examines each item with a magnifying glass. Another fellow has a copy of a trade magazine devoted entirely to Thai amulets, and shows the vendor a page in it as he bargains for an item. After that, the dealer appears to cave in, and a wad of Thai baht is counted out. It's a lot of money to spend on one tiny piece of clay.

I head for my favorite stall, where Mama, perched on a stool behind a case of inexpensive metal amulets, reads the newspaper and chats with buyers. She greets me warmly and goes back to the paper. No high-pressure sales tactics here! I like it this way. I get behind the counter, grab a basket, and start helping myself.

The little stall is heaped high with piles of metal statuettes. I start digging in the stacks, and soon there are stern-faced Thai Buddhas, fat Chinese Buddhas, Kwan Yins, and various Hindu gods in my basket. I also select little animals—bronze dragons, frogs, turtles, and more. My hands are filthy from handling the merchandise. Squatting, I borrow a little water from the washing bucket in the corner.

The daughter shows up, bringing me a smile and a Coca-Cola. I know I shouldn't drink this stuff, but it's not polite to refuse, and besides, the heat and the humidity are starting to get to me. She gets right to work on my bill, and we smile and joke as we organize things. I never worry about the prices here, because they always give me a fair deal. We only see each other a few minutes each year, but, after fifteen years, she treats me like any other old and familiar customer. I feel truly welcome, and more than just another *farang* (foreigner).

With the daughter's help, I check out any new or unfamiliar items. This stall also sells ancient folk magic charms and remedies. There are love potions—unidentifiable chunks of herbs and plastic dolls floating in tiny bottles filled with mystery liquid—and other items of "black magic" (so-called, because the monks disapprove). Bundles of carved wooden phalluses hang from the ceiling, from tiny pocket penises to gigantic ones that are painted bright red. These are simple fertility talismans, to be offered up to the ancient sea goddess. There are a lot of them! They must sell frequently. Also on display are dried roots and other nasty looking things that defy the daughter's English vocabulary to explain. We laugh at our inability to communicate. There are also many charms and magic elixirs for money and "for lucky."

My parcels are small, but they weigh up to 20kg. The bronze statues I have already purchased weigh much more. I borrow the market's tip-dolly to get my goods to the roadside where I can hail a taxi. We say goodbye again for another year. Mama gives me her blessing, smiling like a benevolent Buddha herself, and the daughter gives me a quick *do wai* (bow with hands together) and I sincerely return the gesture. I am grateful for the familiarity and intimacy of this place, and hope that, next time, mother and daughter will still be there—a startlingly familiar and reassuring presence in such a foreign urban environment.

(Sadly, in 2014, the Thai military seized power following a period of civil unrest. Conservatives have changed the interpretation of existing laws regarding all Buddha images, and they can no longer be exported. I will not be visiting this market again, unless the government changes, or I take an hour off of work just to say hello to mother and daughter.)

RAINBOW ALLEY: THE KATHMANDU BEAD MARKET

Asantole Chowk is an ancient, five-cornered intersection in the heart of Kathmandu. A magnificently restored Hindu temple dominates the little square. It is a busy junction with no traffic signs whatsoever, so I have to dodge motorcycles, bicycle rickshaws, cars, porters, cows, and hundreds of pedestrians all trying to make their way around a rickety brass shrine that is, unfortunately, taking up the center of the road.

I step out of the traffic stream and into a back eddy. Two more steps and I am in another world. I'm in a tiny alley, sandwiched between two decrepit temples. The alley is so small its entrance feels almost like a secret doorway. I have entered the diminutive and dazzling world of the Kathmandu bead dealers.

Most of the shops are smaller than the average American closet. In them, the proprietor sits cross-legged on a raised platform, several feet above the street, in a stall that may be as small as four feet wide by five feet high. Curtains of shimmering glass beads surround each seller. From his pillows he can reach most of his stock without effort.

The merchandise is so appealing, I want everything! Thousands of strands of seed beads in endless variations of every color and texture merge into rainbow waterfalls. My favorites are the fancy iridescent beads imported from Japan. They shimmer like butterfly wings.

By Diana McLeod

I try to peel my eyes away from the beads and instead focus my curiosity on the shopkeepers. They are an interesting bunch. Most are Muslim, with long scraggly beards and white caps. I observe one fellow winding the knot that will be the final loop of a necklace clasp. He works very fast, using an ancient technique that involves a bobbin of thread on the end of a stick. Smiling to myself, I realize my father used the same knot to secure the loops at the end of boat ropes: make a loop parallel to the rope, wrap the rope many, many times around the length of the loop, pull it through, tie it off. Knots are the same the world over. Technology will change, humanity will adapt, and the world of the future will be virtually unrecognizable to us today, but knots are knots, and they will always be the same. There is some comfort in that.

I leave the knots alone and check out the intricacy of the workmanship. How can they produce such exquisite lacy little patterns with such tiny little seed beads? They string them into delicate little chokers and bracelets in an infinite variety of colors and patterns. I ask about one complex design. How much at wholesale price? They tell me, and I am amazed. How can they manage to sell these products for such bargain prices? So much skill! So much detail! I can't help but imagine myself doing the work; it would take me days to make only one necklace. And what happens when the bead-maker's eyesight begins to go? Is his business finished? No, that is why the family is so important here. The oldest children are already learning, spending time working with papa when they come home from school. By the time he retires, one of them will take over the trade, and the little shop will have a new keeper. It is a time-honored tradition. After talking to one very young man, I learn that he has just been given the family store. His pride in his business is evident in his eyes.

And who buys these creations? Tourists? People like me? Yes, but the typical customer for these shimmering necklaces is local. In many areas throughout Nepal, women wear these beads as marriage necklaces. A woman's jewelry is a sign of her status. At the center, there is often a tubular, decorative metal bead. Most are brass, but the better ones are gold-plated. Occasionally, you will see one that is 24 karat. Wives value gold over bank accounts in this part of the world.

Custom dictates that most of the marriage strands are red, which is why the stalls blaze with shades of crimson. Another favorite color is green. If I ever saw a local lady wearing purple or blue, I would know that women were finally daring to be different in this tradition-bound society. It hasn't happened yet. But the little girls buy every color in the world for bracelets.

It's hard for me to walk away from this sparkling world. The little girl in me wants to stay and play with all the glittering creations, but I have work to do. So I square my shoulders and head out, back through the secret door. Leaving "rainbow alley" behind, I venture back into the traffic and the crowds of the main street once again.

recommended Google search: Kathmandu Bead Market Images

MY PECULIAR WORKDAY IN KATHMANDU

What's it like to be a jewelry buyer in one of the most exotic cities in the world? Here's the story of one particular day in 2006.

I awaken to sunlight streaming into my hotel room. The Nepalese quilts are suddenly too hot, and I must take advantage of this good light. I grope for the TV remote. (Yes, I know, shame on me, but it is so nice to get BBC news broadcasts in a foreign land). Damn, the satellite is out, so only local channels are available. Fuzzy images of Hindu priests singing Vedic chants do not appeal to me.

I turn off the TV and go downstairs in search of breakfast. No shower, not yet. Hot water here is solar-generated, so it is smart to shower later in the day. In other words, no sun, no shower! (unless you're desperate). To be fair, my guesthouse provides electric hot water in the mornings, powered by a gas generator, but why abuse resources in a land where there's not enough gas or electricity to go around? Besides, those generators waste fuel and cause an unbelievable amount of pollution.

My morning work begins with specialty gems selected from our stock. I work in my hotel, choosing the stones to be used for specific pieces. It can be demanding work. For a link bracelet, you need seven or eight gemstones of the same color, cut, and height. I will have to set up forty or fifty pieces, all at exactly the same angle, and inspect them carefully to make my selections. For gold, only the most perfect specimens will do. When each little group is complete, it goes into a little paper packet for delivery to the silversmiths.

Today I have to go to Durbar Marg (a main commercial district) to reconfirm my air ticket. The system here is archaic. I must show up at the airline office in person, with my paper ticket in hand, and get it specially stamped. Along the way, I pass by the King's Palace. What an ugly building! It has been painted an unfortunate salmon pink color. Ten-foot fences make it look more like a prison than a palace. The new King is highly unpopular here, and civil unrest is picking up steam. It is only a matter of time before the population revolts...

(Two months later massive demonstrations forced the King into an even more ceremonial role. Shortly afterward, they did away with the monarchy altogether. Today, the palace is a museum.)

At 11 A.M., I have a bank appointment with Rajendra, a silver wholesaler. From Durbar Marg, the route is unfamiliar to me, so I expect to get a bit lost in the maze of medieval alleys, which is half the fun. The architecture here is fascinating! Strolling past ancient, tilting brick buildings with intricately carved windows and wooden balconies, I peer into five-foot tall passageways leading into secret inner courtyards, full of statues and shrines that are works of fine art. I wish I could ask to visit these historic apartment blocks, but the inhabitants might be embarrassed by the crumbling interiors and by the lack of modern plumbing. I hope the locals appreciate the beauty of this old city as much as I do. I never tire of exploring its historic districts.

By Diana McLeod

While heading for Asantole market, I'm struck by the number of micro-businesses that people have created in Nepal. Of course, there are plenty of farmers bringing crops to market. The raspberry harvest has just come in, and many women have only a single basketful to sell, because the berries are so small. "Bicycle businesses" are everywhere. You can sell anything from a flat basket mounted on the back of an old bike: fruit, vegetables, underwear, knockoff Rayban sunglasses, flower garlands for worship at the temples, plastic flip-flops. One guy had nothing but oil-lamp wicks of all sizes—an important commodity in a land of constant power shortages.

The "stores" in the market are not much bigger. This area is home to some of Kathmandu's oldest buildings. These historic treasures are still in use every day, even though many of them are collapsing faster than they can be propped up. Tiny doorways of defunct temples now house little stores full of brassware, spices, hardware, and clothing. Five-hundred-year-old houses with pagoda roofs and delicate wooden balconies now house a jumble of plastic vendors, rice shops, and sari stores.

I duck through a doorway and stop in at a classic Newari temple. Nestled in a sheltered courtyard, it is a world apart from the tumult of the street. The traditional pagoda rooflines are ridiculously picturesque, with carved birds and figurines on every corner. Incense smoke curls lazily up from a brazier, filling the air with fragrance. Spirit bells toll as each worshiper enters or exits the temple. Several ladies are doing *puja* (worshipping) in front of the entrance of a shrine, their colorful silk saris brightening the scene.

The courtyard is full of little stone statues and pigeons. The birds are all over the place, taking advantage of offerings of rice set out this morning. I want to go closer to see the spectacular brass artwork around the temple doors, but I'm reluctant to take my shoes off (a requirement) and walk barefoot on the dirty flagstones. Never mind, there's no time, Rajendra is waiting.

AT THE NEPAL BANK: Rajendra's silver shop is just around the corner. I'm meeting him there, to make our annual trip to the bank. Rajendra needs a deposit so he can purchase the silver for our order. He brings his special embossed seal, his official stamp and a copy of the required paperwork.

The Bank of Nepal should be a banking museum. It is 2006, well into the twenty-first century, but in these hallowed and dowdy halls, things are done the old-fashioned way. Neither computers nor calculators exist here. Everything is written into oversized old ledgers. Each entry is made entirely by hand. Columns are actually calculated by people who still know how to add and subtract. Even more stunning, I have, in the past, seen abacuses still in use at this bank! Tall stacks of ledgers adorn each desk, piling up in teetering heaps. With dog-eared edges and fraying bindings, they contain records of hundreds, maybe thousands, of accounts. Woe to the employee who spills his or her *chai* on these precious documents!

Surprisingly, ladies are working here! In this incredibly male-dominated society, and this bastion of banking conservatism, it is wonderful to see that women have landed many of the jobs in the head offices. In the Foreign Exchange Department, about a third of the workforce is female.

Rajendra and I have to do laps around the bank to get the deposit made. First, we visit the department head to get initial approval. Then we go from desk to desk, where, if required, we sign papers. Notes are written into ledgers, the seal and stamp are witnessed, paperwork is checked, and my passport is inspected. Stacks of documents and records are carried from place to place by male workers whose sole job is to ferry them around. The whole thing takes at least an hour.

Making this deposit is like running an obstacle course! Making a withdrawal is even more challenging. Crowds of frustrated customers go from desk to desk to desk, clutching metal bank tokens to mark their transaction, before they are allowed to approach the cashier. The spiders, weaving thick webs on the chains that hold up the flyspecked fluorescent ceiling lights, are far more efficient than the bankers!

But, as maddeningly amusing as this archaic system is, it usually works. We often send funds electronically to this bank, and they somehow get to Rajendra's account. Once, a transfer got lost, and the American banks couldn't trace the money. When we inquired in Kathmandu, they were able to find it again using their ratty old ledgers. The funds were stuck in a bank in New York, in an account that the Bank of Nepal maintains there. The antiquated bank succeeded after the slickest financial system in America failed.

(In 2007, when we went back to the bank's headquarters, it had been completely renovated and utterly modernized. I was torn between relief and disappointment. I almost missed the old dinosaur...)

CREDIT KARMA: The most amazing thing about the Nepalese banking system happened years ago when we began importing. We planned to set up a "letter of credit," which is a legal means of protecting both parties in international shipments. This procedure is usually managed by a financial institution.

I visited the head offices of the bank and asked the manager how companies set up a "letter of credit" system in Nepal. He looked puzzled, then replied, "I am sorry, Madam, but we simply do not do that here."

"Really?" I said, "Then how is it done?"

"You just send the money, and they will send the goods."

"And everyone does it that way? Even large companies? What if someone just keeps the money and never sends the goods?"

"Madam," he smiled patiently, "this is Nepal. It is our culture. We all believe in karma. None of us would ever do such a thing because it would result in our being reborn into a most terrible reincarnation."

I have never forgotten that conversation. What a stunning difference between the West and the Indian Subcontinent! We place all our faith in signatures, contractual obligations, and lawyers, but we seldom rely on basic ethics. They trust in karma. In Nepal, it has proven to be true. You just send the money. They will send the goods. Of course, it is still important to scope out your business connections very carefully, too, because their karmic obligations do not necessarily extend to quality control...

RAJENDRA'S SILVER SHOP: It's a hot day, so it is a relief to return to Rajendra's shop. His place is a bit deceptive. On the outside, it looks just like all the other little silver shops in town. There is a dusty window display and a counter with tiny little wooden stools to sit on while you survey the goods. Rajendra's office is a different story. A few years ago, after hearing complaints (mostly from my husband, I'm sure) about those nasty little wooden stools, he had the place rebuilt. He now has a big, wide desk with padded office chairs and air conditioning. It's a very comfortable place in which to work. Those comfy seats are particularly dangerous. They make me want to stay longer and buy more than I need to.

Rajendra's desk is chock-full of silver, and so are the cupboards behind it. His sales method is to show me style after style. He is the most innovative of all the Nepalese silversmiths we work with. Unfortunately, the jewelry is designed and crafted by men, so most pieces tend to be too heavy-handed. We must drive Rajendra a bit crazy sometimes because I turn down so many designs!

It gets worse when I have to reject good designs. This year, Rajendra has been perfecting his Indian styles of chandelier earrings. The new ones are gorgeous! Unfortunately, we bought too many of his older, heavier models, and the look is already on its way out in the U.S. It's heartbreaking to see these people working so hard to follow American fads only to get stuck with perfectly good stock when the fashion shifts abruptly. In such a traditional country, it must be bewildering for them to see how fast Western tastes can change.

Our order is complete, but Rajendra wants me to buy more, so he offers me lunch: some tasty hot *samosas*. Of course this bribe will work—it's my last chance to enjoy these deep-fried spicy snacks this year.

Rajendra is ordering from a new samosa shop. The old one, which was the Kathmandu equivalent of the most famous deli in New York, was shut down after it was rumored that a baby mouse had been found in one of the *samosas*. It could have been true, or it could be an urban myth. Set up in an open courtyard, that "shop" made samosas on the grandest scale. We used to get there by ducking into a tiny alleyway, beneath the Tip-Top Tailor sign. Inside, it was a chaotic scene. The cooking was done right on the spot, with ingredients (potatoes, veggies, onions, and spices) prepared in giant mixing bowls. Sweating "chefs" hurried to fold them into crusts and fry them in enormous vats of boiling oil. These bathtub-sized cast iron cauldrons were kept constantly bubbling, right in the middle of the open area. Patrons would crowd the sales counter in pushing, shoving multitudes, vying for fresh hot treats straight out of the vat. I used to bring fellow foreigners there all the time for a real taste of local flavor, a lunchtime "must do" when touring Kathmandu. That shop was so busy that I doubt a mouse would have ever braved the crowds.

It is Rajendra's contention that somebody from another shop started the rumor out of jealousy, which is probably the most plausible explanation for the scandal. But I notice that he is still ordering from the new shop, even though the old landmark has been completely refurbished and reopened for business. And none of us can resist making jokes *about "so-mouse-as."*

The samosas from the new shop are delicious. Wiping the tamarind sauce off my fingers, I hand Rajendra the last few packets of specialty stones I have prepared, and then it is time to say goodbye. It is a heartfelt handshake. We have known each other for a long time, and I've watched his business grow and change. He emails me digital photos now, and invoices are electronic spreadsheets and not handwritten scrawls sent by fax.. His son has grown up and is taking over more of the business. It's been enjoyable watching father and son doing business together, shifting roles and responsibilities over time. We are old friends now.

THE ART OF THE HAGGLE: The weather is rapidly deteriorating as I leave Rajendra's shop. Black clouds are moving in from the East, and the air has that leaden, sullen feeling that precedes a downpour. Rain is a dismal affair in Kathmandu. Many of the streets are unpaved and the drains back up, so everything turns into a muddy mess. I might be able to dodge a soaking if I take a bicycle rickshaw.

These are bizarre-looking contraptions. In front, they look like typical bikes, with handlebars and a standard seat. The rear flares out into a two-person cushioned loveseat with a little platform below for passengers' feet. Two oversized rear wheels power these charming little rattletraps. Most rickshaws in Kathmandu are elaborately decorated. Scenic paintings and colorful flowers often adorn the exterior. The canvas canopy is usually painted and fringed with pom-poms or tinsel. Some drivers "pimp out" their ride with pinwheels or plastic flowers taped to their handlebars. The rickshaws' red rubber bike horns sound like angry ducks.

As soon as I get near enough, the rickshaw boys spot me. "Rickshaw, madam? Very cheap! Nepalese helicopter? Where you go?" There are five of them, all vying for my attention. These drivers all speak some English, which is why they cruise this district. Rajendra's shop is near a famous series of temples.

Usually, I just grin and wave them off, but today I have already decided to take one. First, there is the haggling. If I am not careful, I will pay ten to fifteen times what the locals pay. If I am lucky, and I work hard, I will get a decent tourist price, which is still probably only two or three times what the locals pay.

30

I try the fellow with the most engaging grin. "How many million rupees will you charge to take me to the Tibet guesthouse?"

The guys approve of my approach. "Two million!" he declares.

"Only one million!" cries another.

Now that we've established the fact that they *are* going to overcharge me, I get down to business. Turning back to the first bidder, I ask, "How about fifty?"

"Million?"

"No, rupees. Fifty rupees."

His face falls. "Madam, we get two hundred and fifty. Sometimes three hundred."

"Are you crazy? I could go all the way to Bhaktapur for that! And back again!"

He shrugs. "Two hundred."

"Do I look like a first-time tourist to you? Sixty."

"One hundred fifty. Last price."

While I roll my eyes, I glance at the sky. It is looking worse. I need to close this deal quickly. When the raindrops begin to fall, prices will rise as if by magic. Supply and demand. He might not take less than a hundred right now because he knows it, too. I try my favorite trick. Luckily, I have been careful to count and arrange my money in advance. "Seventy-two," I say.

"Excuse me, Madam?"

"Seventy-two. Last price. Any takers?"

They look confused but impressed. This technique, which was developed by my husband Dave, really throws them off their game. It indicates I'm not a regular tourist (because they always haggle in large numbers). I know the value of a rupee, and I am haggling more like a local.

"One hundred twenty-five."

"Seventy-two. That's what I have in my pocket. You and I both know that's still too much."

I pull out my rupees and he can't resist. He has never met a foreigner who knows exactly how many rupees they have in their pocket. That simple fact wins him over. I hop in, and off we go.

Of course, I paid almost double the going local rate. Foreigners always do. It's O.K. These young men are struggling to make a living. Most are from the countryside. Somewhere in the hills, they have a family to support, and the rickshaws are usually rented. They often have to sleep in their rickshaws as protection from theft. It is a hard first job for most of these guys.

Footsteps of a Nomad

My philosophy about haggling is that a smart foreigner should avoid the extremes. Don't throw money at people. It makes you look stupid and disgustingly rich (which you *are* even if you are traveling on the cheap). It teaches people that tourists are ripe for overcharging, which encourages scams, theft and other problems. Vendors learn to lie about what things actually cost. It may ease your conscience to give too much, but it does great harm to the community in the long run. Instead, educate yourself about what the locals expect to pay. Then give a bit more, but not a ludicrous amount.

On the other hand, don't knock people down too far. It's a buyer's market. Sometimes vendors will even sell goods or services below cost because there's been no business that day, and they need money to buy food for the family table.

The "middle path" is best. If you feel guilty about haggling at all, don't be. It is expected of you. Find ways to keep it lighthearted and not confrontational, and it will be a pleasant experience. Channel your guilt elsewhere. Ask around for recommendations for a local charity and make a donation. Your money will be spent on people who truly need it. Then, do your haggling in good conscience.

THE RICKSHAW RIDE: My chariot awaits! The rain is starting, so I have secured my lift just in time. Twilight is coming on, and soft lights are illuminating the shops on either side of the street. Bright silks in the sari store windows streak past in rainbows of brilliant colors.

Passing the Shrine of the Toothache God, (yes, there really is a tiny street shrine to the Toothache God in Kathmandu) I notice one huddled figure standing in front of it, praying for relief. He will probably wind up at the horrendous "dentist's offices" nearby. Hopefully, his prayers will be answered—without complications.

When the rain intensifies, the driver sets up an umbrella for himself, tugs open the canopy for me and throws a piece of transparent plastic over everything. We roll down the street in a bubble. What a relief to have avoided the muddy walk home!

When we arrive at my guesthouse, I tip him. His eyebrows go up—he doesn't often get tips. He is amused that I have suddenly found more rupees in my other pocket. Grinning back at me, he waves as he circles to leave.

It's always nice to get back to my hotel at the end of a long day. "Honey, I'm home!" I call to our friend Tsering, who's behind the front desk. "*Namaste*, darling!" he replies, giggling. It's an old joke. Dave and I have been lobbing silly endearments at the staff for years now, and our banter makes the Tibet Guest House feel a bit like home and family.

By Diana McLeod

HAND-CARVED BALINESE MASTERPIECES AT
SUKAWATI MARKET

As soon as they see him coming, the wisecracks begin. Dave is a well-known character at Sukawati market. Vendors there love him, not only because he is a steady customer, but also because of his deep appreciation for quality and workmanship. Most of all, they adore him because he has learned how to speak the national language well enough to crack jokes and make people laugh. These days, Dave does all of our business in Indonesian. They really appreciate that, and he gets treated quite differently than most foreigners. Many of the sellers are now old friends, and we've been invited to peoples' houses, temple ceremonies, and even to a wedding. The Balinese are lovely, generous people, always ready to greet newcomers with welcoming smiles.

The market in Sukawati is quite diversified, with "districts" that appeal to entirely different groups of people. Locals go north of the main road, where fruit, vegetables, fish, chickens and household goods are sold. Ramshackle market stalls sell everything from motorcycle parts to temple offerings and ceremonial items.

The other side of the main road is for travelers. Clothing shops cater to Indonesian tourists, offering colorful yet modest Muslim headscarf/dress combinations for the Javanese ladies and garish, Hawaiian-style shirts for the men. Chinese tour groups head for the tacky souvenir shops where most items sell for less than a dollar. Large, brightly painted kites, paintings, ceramics, incense and batik purses are sold in specialty stores.

The minute our car squeezes into the market's crowded parking lot, we're bombarded by ladies selling sarongs, jewelry or floppy hats. Their "store" is a basket balanced on top of the head, so they can beeline straight at incoming shoppers. I turn them down every day, but they still chase me around like a hungry swarm of mosquitoes. Luckily, another car pulls in, so they instantly abandon me and target the fresh meat. Their persistence is amusing, and reminds me of an Indonesian saying: "Damana ada gulah, ada samut," which means, "Where there is sugar, there are ants."

Our favorite market street has a series of woodcarving shops displaying spectacular workmanship, from tiny wooden animals to six-foot statues of Hindu gods. The intricacy of the detail is amazing, as is their ability to evoke realistic emotion in the sculptures. The Buddhas look utterly blissful, glowing with inner peace and subtle, hinted-at smiles. Kwan Yins gaze serenely ahead, their lovely faces full of compassion. Heroic Hindu Gods ride in highly detailed three-dimensional chariots, or on the shoulders of the fierce Eagle-God Garuda. Elephants and horses seem ready to gallop right off the shelves. Even after decades of buying, we're still in awe of the Balinese carvers' skills and creativity.

33

Footsteps of a Nomad

Unfortunately, there are fewer master carvers these days. The old guys are retiring, and young men can make much more money working on construction jobs. Huge hotels are going up, siphoning off most of the workers. Seasoned hardwood is expensive, hard to get, and prices are rising. We are buying extra pieces now to ensure we'll have enough in the future.

When the day's business begins, it's a struggle for me to follow Dave's discussions with the vendors, but I'm gradually picking up vocabulary. He has the advantage of over twenty years of practice. (He used to do the annual Bali trip solo).

In fact, all of us are speaking a second language. *Bahasa Indonesia* is not Balinese. It was cobbled together by the Dutch when they colonized this huge chain of islands. They realized the only way to unify tens of thousands of islands into one country was to create a single language. Using Malay, Javanese, and Dutch words, they built a new national parlance. Every Indonesian child learns it in school, and they are fluent in it. Today, it's the language used for business, all over Indonesia. At home, with family, these guys speak traditional Balinese.

Once the choosing is over, the haggling begins. Dave turns it all into a big joke, and he is a master of the sight-gag response. When he is told the asking price, he often pretends to stagger or swoon. Sometimes he places his hand under his shirt to mimic heart palpitations. Or, he sticks one finger in his ear and shakes it. "I think there must be something wrong with my ears," he says, looking puzzled. "I could have sworn that you said two million. That can't be right! You couldn't possibly mean that much! Where is a doctor? I need to get my hearing checked."

(In case you were wondering, two million Indonesian Rupiah is about $150.00 US at the moment.)

Another price is mentioned, and Dave slaps his forehead. "Oh," he says, "I must be stupid! I thought this was only a woodcarving! I didn't realize it was made of solid gold!

The more outrageous it gets, the more they laugh. Dave points out a gigantic carved wooden penis in the corner. "Are you sure you're not trying to sell me this instead?" he quips. "Or, are you just trying to get me to sit on it? You'd like that, wouldn't you, you bad man! Come to think of it, maybe I should walk over to your friend's shop and buy from him instead. *He* doesn't treat me *this* badly," Dave says, to the giggling proprietor. "He's a nice man, unlike *certain* people..."

The guys adore all these jokes, and they come right back at Dave with more banter, as good-natured insults zing back and forth. Haggling like this is fun. The guys love being able to fool around with a customer and drop polite formality for once. I know Dave gets special deals others never get because he approaches the dealers with kindness and tomfoolery, not confrontation. In the end, we get excellent prices in a way that is equitable and fair for all parties. In addition, Dave gets real honesty as well. I've even seen them dealers tell him not to buy a piece because the wood is still a bit green and it might crack.

34

After hours of choosing, haggling and invoicing, we head over to our favorite *warung* (local restaurant) for *Ayam betutu* (smoked chicken) and *Taliwang* (chicken done Lombock style - super spicy!). Both are served with homegrown rice, veggies and water spinach. Our hostess proudly tells Dave she is serving us a special chicken today, one raised right at her home. Our meals cost us only about $6.00 for two people. It's a delicious end to the day.

recommended Google search: Bali wood carvers images

THE FABULOUS GRAND BAZAAR OF ISTANBUL

I've wanted to write about the Grand Bazaar, ever since we visited it in 2008, but the assignment has been challenging for me. On the one hand, it is one of the most legendary markets in the world. The glamor and excitement of the Kapali Çarşi have been extolled so often (and deservedly so) that I would be remiss if I didn't treat my readers to a thrilling exploration of its exotic grandeur. On the other hand, I am a seasoned professional buyer. It would be deceitful if I didn't reveal my honest opinions of the merchandise. So, here I am, the starry-eyed romantic vs. the cynical critic, penning an essay that is sure to get me diagnosed with a serious personality disorder!

THE MAGIC OF THE MARKETPLACE: The Grand Bazaar certainly lives up to its name. When you first enter the medieval gates of the historic covered market and get your first glimpse down the first aisle, the colors dazzle the eye, and the arched corridors of the market draw you irresistibly in. There is simply too much to look at!

The gold shops were virtually afire with ostentatious gemstones and the gleam of precious pearls. Window shopping, we gawked at curios, antiques and unique treasures. Emerald crystals as big as a spool of thread especially caught my eye. Our favorite shops were owned by dealers who venture into the wild interior of Asia to buy antique tribal jewelry. These artifacts were very exotic: from Afghanistan, Azerbaijan, Turkmenistan, and Uzbekistan. Fabulous wedding necklaces, headdresses, bracelets and other treasures from the East enchanted us both.

What beautiful lamp shops! Turkey produces a large variety of hand-blown glass lamps and chandeliers in vivid colors. Most of these were hanging lanterns, so each shop had clusters of ornate creations dangling from the ceiling. The overall effect was like looking at a finely detailed stained glass window. Traditional designs evoked stories of the "Arabian Nights." A thousand and one lights—perfect decor for any palace seraglio.

Oh, the silk vendors! Lovely shawls and scarves of every imaginable shape and hue were draped or folded in color palettes that delighted my eye. There were belly dancer costumes, spangled with sequins or little coins, bedspreads, brocaded pillows with red tassels, vintage

Ottoman style clothing and slippers in silk velvet. I fell in love with fabrics all over again.

Turkey is famed for its unique and lovely style of pottery, from tiny candy jars to large bowls and urns. Each piece was highly detailed in bright yellow or blue, with delicate floral patterns in pleasing arabesques. The quality and the style drew me in, and I considered buying some as gifts.

I won't forget the rug shops. The leading merchants in the Grand Bazaar undoubtedly sell the best of the best of Turkish carpets—if you know how to spot them. It was impossible to walk past without pausing to admire, and smiling carpet salesmen instantly caught me looking. These handsome young men sure can work wonders on a gal's self-esteem! The flirtatious banter that followed was undoubtedly worth enduring the sales pitch!

There was more to see down every corridor. We visited the gold sellers, the diamond aisle, the leather district, and the antique shops. Inlaid boxes and chessboards from Syria, "evil eyes" (the blue glass suncatchers that supposedly protect the home from evil), typical souvenirs and tee shirts were jumbled together. Exploring the depths of the market, where fewer tourists go, could take days. And of course, we were invited upstairs to view a couple of special collections. They welcomed us with traditional Turkish hospitality and served sweet apple tea in little pear-shaped glasses. Truly, the Grand Bazaar deserves to be called one of the best tourist attractions in all of Turkey!

BUYER, BEWARE! As I said before, I would be remiss if I did not reveal the other side of my personality. I will now, in all honesty, debunk the Grand Bazaar. Here goes:

The more that we looked at jewelry shops, the more frustrated we became. Dave and I were hoping to find good quality local jewelry we could bring home to sell. Sadly, the silver shops held almost nothing that was honestly Turkish, or even from the region. Most came from Thailand! I also saw plenty of poorly made gemstone pieces from India, some with plastic "lapis" and fake "turquoise." Prices on decent jewelry items were much higher than in our shop in Vermont. The only local products that had any appeal were pendants with Islamic calligraphy done in silver. They were well made, but not even remotely marketable at home.

The gold shops were no better. Prices were absurd, and the fake, man-made or dreadfully poor quality gemstones being fobbed off on innocent tourists were pretty shameless. Of course, that is unfortunately typical in a place like this. I wouldn't shop this market without carrying a gold tester and a gram scale with me!

The silk and clothing stores were beyond annoying. The salesmen kept insisting that everything was pure silk and Turkish. What

By Diana McLeod

nonsense! Most of the stuff was factory-made using polyester or rayon fibers. I can buy it all in Delhi, and, believe me, so did they—even the "Turkish" belly dancing outfits! Don't get me wrong; I adore Indian fabrics, even some of the synthetic ones. I just love them at Indian wholesale prices.

The pottery shops were most exciting—until I told one shopkeeper I had a lead test kit with me. He finally confessed that all of his beautiful ceramics were made using a lead-based glaze. Using them for food or drink of any kind can lead to lead poisoning! I worried about the thousands, maybe millions, of people who bring this stuff home with them. How many people use it or give it as gifts? (One buyer-beware tip: always carry a lead test kit with you if you plan to buy pottery overseas in markets. Don't fall victim to toxic pottery! (Or toxic lead paint in toys!) Tradewinds only sells pottery with official international lead-free certification.

Carpet shops in tourist traps like the Grand Bazaar should be avoided at all costs. First of all, unless you're in the know, don't buy anything because you will pay too much. You may even wind up with a machine-made Chinese carpet you could have bought at Overstock.com. Besides, even if you were lucky enough to find the most honest and most moderately priced shop in the entire Grand Bazaar, you are still guaranteed to pay far too much. Why? Because renting a shop at the Grand bazaar is astronomical! One dealer whose silver shop was eight feet by six feet square, was paying the equivalent of $5,000 U.S. dollars per month for that tiny space. Just imagine what a large carpet shop must pay! They have no choice and thus must jack their prices up to pay the horrendous rent. (Location, location, location...)

In the end, Dave and I left without buying anything except for one souvenir tee shirt for a family member who likes those things. We haggled over the price and took care to snag it just at closing time, when vendors just want to make one more quick sale before going home. I also took home memories the famous and fabulous *Kapali Çarşi* which for me are the most priceless of souvenirs. It was quite an exciting and enlightening experience —for both sides of me!

recommended Google search: Grand Bazaar Istanbul images

PART II
UNIQUE SITUATIONS

UNEXPECTED MOMENTS

"DOCTOR OF THE STONES"

This adventure took place in Jaipur, India, back in the days when they still ran steam engines on Indian Railways. My husband David is a rail fan, and riding steam trains is just about his favorite thing to do. He wanted to ride an all-stops local, just for the fun of it.

We went to the railway station and bought tickets to a large village about thirty miles outside Jaipur where we would spend an hour and then return to the city. Although the line of passenger cars was ready to board, Dave and I walked down the tracks to photograph the locomotive, which was not yet attached to the train.

I'm not really a rail fan, but there is something special about steam engines. They chuff and pant like impatient horses. Steam brings them alive. The engine crew was hard at work, stoking the firebox for the journey. When they saw Dave and his camera, they immediately invited us to climb aboard. Dave quickly charmed them into letting us ride in the locomotive all the way out to our destination. The engineer showed me how to blow the whistle and how to throw the reversing gear to back us up to attach the engine to the train. (Yes, I was driving a locomotive, on a track full of loaded passenger cars.) (No, safety rules are not strictly followed in India.)

The cab of a steam locomotive is a tiny, noisy, and filthy environment, but it is exciting. The two-man crew is kept busy. The fireman's job is to stoke the fire and to maintain the steam at just the right pressure. It is just like a giant teakettle, which must be kept at a controlled boil at all times. Dave had a huge grin on his face as the crew drove the train forward, picking up steam as we left the station. I hung out at the side of the engine, watching the Rajasthani villages roll past. The few villagers who saw my face were astounded to see a white woman riding in the locomotive of a local train.

When we arrived at our destination, the population greeted us like rock stars. News of our arrival spread throughout the town, and everyone turned out to gawk at us. Foreigners rarely, if ever, go to outlying districts. We were the most exciting thing anyone in this area had seen in months! Everywhere we went, the crowd ringed us like paparazzi. We hung out with the villagers for a while, attempting to communicate without a common language. My collection of Vermont postcards got passed around, and people were incredulous when they saw the snow-covered scenes. I don't think many of them believed the pictures were real. Most of these desert dwellers had only seen it rain a few times in their entire lives.

At last the train was ready to return to the city. It was getting hotter by the minute—well over a hundred degrees—and I couldn't bear the roaring flames of the locomotive firebox on top of the desert heat. I asked Dave if we could ride further back where it would be cooler, and we climbed into one of the regular passenger cars.

The seats were packed with locals, almost all of them men. This train was strictly third-class—the kind tourists usually avoid—decrepit and dirty, with hard wooden benches and no restrooms. It was going to be a bumpy ride.

Most of the men on the train wore simple cotton shirts and dhotis (a male sarong sometimes worn like a skirt, and sometimes tied like a diaper), but one gentleman was outlandishly attired. He was draped in a sequined fringed cloak of brilliant green, and sported a turban adorned with fake jewels and a peacock feather. His wrinkled face was a character study of a desert-born personality. He could have been a Mogul prince or a minor sultan with his regal, hawk-like nose and his impressively curled mustaches. He smiled at us, and our conversation began.

The gentleman was a self-professed "Doctor of the Stones," a traveling carny man and miracle-cure salesman who went from village to village, peddling stones and their "healing powers." For a small fee, he would diagnose whatever ailed you and prescribe a cure. He showed us some of his stones. He had a small sack of tumbled polished gemstones, mostly quartz, malachite, and lapis, and he explained their healing attributes. I learned, for example, that malachite was excellent for kidney problems, and it was especially auspicious to purchase a hand-picked malachite with a kidney-shaped color pattern.

He kept us entertained for quite some time, but the astounding part of this story was yet to come. Other men in the railroad car crowded tightly around us, listening to our conversation. Every square inch of space near us was soon jammed with people, standing, squatting, or sitting, almost on each other's laps. All of them were gawking at us, just like the villagers had done. (Indians have absolutely no notion of what we call "personal space.")

The Doctor leaned in towards me. "Do you like stones, madam?" he asked.

"I enjoy looking at them," I replied offhandedly. "Gems are beautiful." (I did not mention I was in the jewelry business, which might have been dangerous information to reveal under the circumstances. We wanted to be seen as the kind of backpacker tourists who had just enough money to get to India, and not a penny more.)

Despite my unenthusiastic response, a murmur went through the crowd. Hands reached into pockets, little white packets were produced and opened, and dozens of them were thrust into my face. Each folded paper was full of glittering gemstones. I looked at my fellow passengers in amazement.

Of course! This village was one of the famous gem cutting villages around Jaipur. Rajasthan has the largest population of skilled gem cutters in the world. Most of the world's colored gemstones pass through Jaipur on their way to market. If you have gemstone jewelry in your home, it's highly likely some of those stones were cut and polished around Jaipur. It was, after all, why we were there.

Almost every guy on this train was a cutter. These fellows were the employees of the big gem dealers in the city. Here's how it works: Wholesalers present the cutters with the rough material. The cutters take the stones back to their homes where they spend days carefully faceting and polishing them into individual gemstones. They have few modern tools or equipment and employ centuries-old techniques. This craft is passed down from father to son, and is the pride of Rajasthan.

These cutters were riding the train back to the city to get paid for their finished stones and to pick up their next sacks of rough material.

The fruits of their labor were in their hands. I was impressed. I looked around at the little gem papers, seeing every color of the rainbow. I did not see diamonds (that trade goes to Mumbai) but I saw everything else.

"Madam, look! Rubies!"

"Here are garnets!"

"I have Sri Lankan sapphires! Very cheap!"

"Moonstones! Citrines!"

"Lovely peridot from Pakistan!"

"Amethysts from Brazil! Emeralds from Colombia!"

There were enough stones on that old, third-class train that I almost began to consider a career in train robbery. A *dacoit* (bandit) with a gun would have made a killing! That dowdy little train probably had more jewels on it than the Orient Express had in its heyday!

Of course, we couldn't buy any stones on the spot. Flashing money around in such a situation would have been most unwise and wouldn't have done us any good anyway. You can't inspect and select gems on a moving train! Besides, I would still have to deal with the stones' actual owners back in Jaipur.

At last, we arrived back in the fabled "Pink City." I thanked the "Doctor" and said goodbye to all the cutters. As I watched them melt into the crowds at the Jaipur station, I wondered if we would soon be haggling with the dealers for the very stones I had just seen.

recommended Google search: Rajasthan street India Images

By Diana McLeod

EMBRACING BUDDHISM

It had rained so hard that the streets of Kathmandu flooded. Torrents of mucky stormwater flowed six inches deep over the road. On one side of the street, a seven-inch-wide concrete slab at the edge of the buildings remained above water. Hugging the wall carefully, I inched my way forward, balancing on the narrow sill. On the other side of the street, in a dry spot provided by a restaurant awning, a crowd of young men huddled.

They began to laugh and point at me, and I couldn't understand why. Rounding a corner, I saw the problem. A middle-aged Buddhist monk, also tiptoeing along the concrete slab, approached me from the opposite direction.

He and I both saw the dilemma. A monk is never, ever supposed to touch a woman! If one of us had to backtrack, it would take a considerable amount of time and effort. We looked at the sewage-laden slop and then at each other. Neither of us wished to step into the disgusting mess. If we tried to pass each other, we would have to embrace. The young men across the street whistled and made rude kissing noises at us.

I knew it was up to me to backtrack. I waved at the monk and tried to turn around, but he disagreed, gesturing for me to come closer. He was not afraid of breaking the rules of his order, although he and I both knew this decision would challenge his monastic discipline, and it would have been easier for him to avoid the issue. One single instant of eye contact told me all this. Nonetheless, he opened up his arms and hugged me tightly to his chest. He lifted me up easily, swung me out over the water, and set me down on the other side.

I smiled and thanked him, using an honorary Buddhist gesture, and we both went our separate ways, while trying to ignore the rude jeers of the crowd.

I was a bit red-faced but also amused. I couldn't help but think of an old Chinese story about two Buddhist monks. It goes like this:

Two monks were traveling together. When they came to a stream, they met a young woman who needed to get across. One monk picked up the lady and carried her on his back as he waded through the water.

The other monk was outraged. He couldn't believe his fellow monk had broken his vows so easily and touched a woman! His indignation grew until he felt he had to speak up. Turning to his companion, he angrily expressed his feelings.

The other monk listened and smiled. He replied: "I set that woman down at the edge of the river. Why are you still carrying her around?"

I had just lived that story....

ACCUSED!

One day in Kathmandu, Nepal, Dave and I decided to take an afternoon trip outside of the city to visit the Chobar Gorge. This scenic spot is a series of rock chasms in the hills, with lovely waterfalls tumbling through them.

We had gone out there on our own, riding a local bus. After a pleasant day, we flagged down another bus for the return trip to Kathmandu. It is unusual for foreigners to ride local buses in Nepal. Most travelers opt for chartered tourist buses. Dave and I prefer riding with local people for short distances. It can be cramped and dirty, and the seats are hard (if you even get one), but you can come away with a memorable travel experience.

We checked out our fellow bus passengers, and they stared right back at us! Most of them were coming into town from the countryside, and they had never seen foreigners up close before. They studied us with fascination, from our boots to our jackets. Many were amused by Dave's earring. Various ladies came right up to him and poked at it, smiling broadly.

My rings got special attention. One man, who spoke in halting English, told us the women would like to try on my rings. I agreed and handed them over. One was a puzzle ring. (For those of you who don't know what a puzzle ring is, it is a four or six-part ring that can come partially apart when you take it off. The pieces can only be reassembled by a person who knows the trick to it. They are not easy to do!)

The rings were passed around the bus, and people got to try them on. It did not take too long for the puzzle ring to slide apart. The lady who had accidentally separated the bands looked at me with alarm. I told my "translator" to explain that the ring was not broken. He conveyed my words to the crowd, and everyone beamed with relief. Then I had an idea. I asked the man to announce that anyone who could figure out how to put my ring back together could keep it for themselves, as a present.

My challenge went through the bus like wildfire. Everyone wanted to try. It was fun to watch them work at it. Even the men tried to do it with their big, calloused farmer's fingers. People shouted suggestions and ideas at each other in excited Nepalese. Everyone made an attempt, and some demanded a second go at it. It was a wonderful way to entertain all of us on the long bus ride into the city.

At last, they all admitted defeat. Nobody could solve the puzzle. Reluctantly, they handed the ring back to me. There was a lot of heated discussion in Nepalese. My translator told me that people thought it was broken after all.

I just smiled. As the owner of a jewelry store that sells puzzle rings, I must confess I am something of an expert with them. They only take me about a minute to do. I quickly reassembled the ring and stuck it on my finger.

There was a moment of astonished silence, and then everyone began talking at once. One lady jumped up out of her seat, pointed a finger at me, and yelled something in Nepalese. Several others joined her. Everyone suddenly looked uncomfortable.

I turned to my translator and asked him what they had said.

"Madam, they are accusing you of witchcraft," he said sheepishly.

Dave and I burst out laughing, which convinced most of the people on the bus that we were not witches or sorcerers. I took the ring off and demonstrated it again, slowly. I also told my translator to tell everyone it had taken me days of practice to learn how to reassemble a puzzle ring quickly. But for the rest of the ride, we saw a few people watching us superstitiously. Several of the villagers muttered warding charms against evil. Others reached for amulets worn as pendants beneath their clothing.

As for us, we did our very best to dispel our sinister new reputation with friendly, open smiles.

THE RUNNING OF THE BULLS IN VARANASI

One beautiful day in Varanasi India, I was walking through the commercial district with two Canadian friends. Suddenly, a disturbance erupted in the marketplace. Two Brahmin Bulls were locking horns, right in the middle of the street. (In India cattle are allowed to roam wherever they please. In a land where cows are considered sacred, they can do as they like. I've seen them lounging in the middle of three-lane highways, stealing brazenly from vegetable vendors and blocking the busiest downtown traffic intersections.)

Usually Brahmin cattle are quite placid. Even the bulls are not normally a menace, although it is prudent to be aware of them at all times. I have often seen them wandering through heavy pedestrian street traffic in India. Being within the range of those horns is unnerving!

On this occasion, the two bulls were not behaving well at all. Both were posturing and displaying signs of aggression. They snorted and chuffed at each other, stamping their feet, and lowering their heads. After a couple of minutes of bluffing, they began to fight in earnest. They banged their foreheads together, locked horns and shoved each other sideways, knocking over a vendor's table, sending his fruit rolling across the street. Other terrified farmers hid behind their vegetable stands. More merchandise hit the dirt as the bulls clashed repeatedly. People yelled at them, which only made them more aggressive.

The two animals started chasing each other around the marketplace. As they headed our way, one of them spotted my friend's bright red tee shirt. That bull immediately changed course and headed straight for us. The other one followed suit and charged right after the first one. Suddenly, we became the target of their aggression. The next thing we knew, we were running for our lives! Both bulls were after us now, horns down and coming on fast!

As we fled down the road, we came to a traffic island virtually covered with a jumble of parked bicycle rickshaws. At first we ran around the circle, but the bulls just kept chasing us, around and around, getting closer and closer. Then one changed course and headed the opposite way, trapping us right between them! In desperation, we jumped up onto the bicycle rickshaws and scrambled to the very center of the heap as quickly as we could. The bulls made a couple of halfhearted attempts to plow into the rickshaws, but, not wanting to lock horns with a tangled pile of metal bicycles, they soon decided we were out of reach.

In the end, the local population came to our rescue. Merchants brought out buckets of water and threw them on the animals to cool them off and to distract them from us. A taxi driver nudged them with his taxi, and a local cop brandished his club at them. Others brought out brooms and mops. The bulls finally got the hint and sullenly lumbered away down an alley. I'm sure they were headed for more trouble in another part of town.

As for us, we got out of that area as quickly as we could. I must say, I know the city of Varanasi is one of the most unusual places on earth, and we expected to see strange things there, but I never expected it to be the Pamplona of the East! *Olé!*

INDIA WILL ALWAYS ASTOUND YOU

It was our fourth or fifth trip to India. On arrival, we caught a taxi into Delhi from the airport. As we rode along, Dave and I remarked to each other how we were becoming accustomed to India's day-to-day chaos. Roadside squatters in ragged tents, cows wandering everywhere, strange temples, the barrage of good and bad smells—nothing had that initial "shock value" anymore.

One minute later, we were gawking like first-timers. We were on the modern highway that connects the airport to the city when, suddenly, there was a big traffic snarl. Three lanes were being forced to merge into one. What was it? A terrible accident? (These are far too common). As we approached, we could see that it was a religious procession. Pilgrims dressed in white walked abreast, blocking the passing lanes. They were playing musical instruments and chanting. In front of them, a man, stretched out full length on the asphalt, was *rolling* down the road, dressed only in a loincloth. His long, dreadlocked hair was bound up in another cloth, and dirty bandages cushioned his elbows and knees.

Dave and I reasoned he must be a *Sadhu*, a Hindu holy man. These ascetics dedicate their lives to their religion, abandoning their families and wandering as mendicants around India. They commonly beg for food, and they will give you a *tikka* mark on your forehead as a blessing in return for small donations.

Sometimes these holy men will take strange vows to prove their ability to stick to their ascetic ideals. One yogi took an oath to stand on one leg for five years. Another vowed to hold his arm up for eight years, as a salute to the gods. When it came time for him to lower his arm, he couldn't move it—it was stuck! The more outlandish the pledge is, the more devotees a Sadhu will attract. These followers support the ascetics when they are in the midst of their vow. Slings are made to keep these guys in position when they are sleeping. They have to be fed and cared for. In return, the *Sadhu* will deliver religious sermons and wisdom to his followers.

Our taxi driver was as astonished by this strange scene as we were. The ragged little holy man was rolling down the tarmac, virtually shutting down a major urban artery. Only in India! We marveled at his ability to perform this insane stunt on the broiling hot pavement. His limbs had sores on them, and his face was pressed right onto the dirty roadway. Did he do this on dirt roads, too? How could he stand to roll around in the choking dry dust and dung of India?

Later, back in Vermont, we saw a TV documentary about the very same yogi we had encountered. He was known as the Lotan Baba. He had actually promised to roll all the way from South India to a holy ice cave on the edge of a Himalayan glacier. According to Hindu legend, the God Shiva had visited that cavern himself. The distance the *sadhu* covered was over 2,000 kilometers! We apparently saw the Lotan Baba when he was over halfway to fulfilling his vow. On his day of triumph, when he finally reached the famous shrine, thousands of people celebrated with him. He had been rolling for months.

Back in the taxi, Dave grinned at me and winked. "Now *that's* what I call a 'holy roller!'" he chuckled.

This is what I love most about India. Whenever it seems "predictable," watch out—India will always astound you!

recommended internet video search: Youtube: Lotan Baba

A NIGHT IN A GENUINE HILL TRIBE VILLAGE

In Chiang Mai, in northern Thailand, I often visit a famous market called the Night Bazaar, open from six p.m. until midnight. There, small family-run businesses sell handcrafted goods made in their homes. Many set up shop right on the sidewalks. We've been buying from some of the same people for years.

One couple sold cast statuettes. Each year, I would find them and place an order. On one visit, they suggested I go with them to their village in the hills. The next day, they would drive me back into town, along with my goods. I was being invited to spend the night with the family!

This was a great honor, and I knew I had to accept. *Farang* (foreigners) almost never get asked into people's' homes. Besides, these people weren't Thais; they were Hmong people. The Hmong are one of the distinct ethnic groups who live in Northern Thailand. They have their own language, culture and customs. I was excited about this chance to see a genuine Hmong village and the inner workings of a tribal house. On the other hand, there could be problems. I would be going into the mountains, at night, with a family I could barely communicate with. We didn't know each other well. I might have to leave, and in a hurry if things went badly. I knew I'd best pack carefully.

After shopping for the expedition, I stuffed a small knapsack with jungle clothes and trekking boots, bug spray, lots of safe drinking water, a decent map of the area (in case I had to find my own way home) a compass, a flashlight, a Thai phrase book, some cash, and emergency rations. Then I added gifts for the family: fresh strawberries, cookies, baked goods, chocolate, and of course, the obligatory small bottle of Mekong whiskey.

At 11:30 p.m., I helped the couple pack up their stall for the night. The husband went off to get their ride, which turned out to be a shiny new Japanese pickup truck with four-wheel drive. (Wow, my friends lived in a tribal village, but their vehicle was newer than mine at home!) About eight people squeezed into the truck. We stacked the unsold goods in the back, and crammed ourselves in behind the boxes for the open-air ride, which was delightful in the warm night.

We drove for about an hour. I actually knew most of the route, because we passed a famous temple, Doi Suthep, along the way. The road snaked up along a mountain ridge, and I could see the airport lights glittering far below in the distance. Following the contours of the mountainside, the ride got rougher as we left pavement behind. Those of us seated in the back shared smiles in the moonlight as we hit bump after bump.

Finally we reached the village, which had no electricity. We passed small wooden houses, lit here and there by hearth fires. In the darkness, the candlelit cottages were charming. The truck pulled up to

46

a large, barn-like building—the family longhouse, in which multiple generations slept under one roof. Inside, there was a central fire pit and a main room with a dirt floor. On either side of the central area, there were raised sleeping lofts with plank floors, separated into little bedrooms. At night, each set of parents had privacy. Kids slept in groups, separated by sex. Cloth curtains were strung across the access to the central room.

I presented my gifts, which were graciously accepted. Nobody touched the whiskey, but I knew they would all enjoy it at a later date. It was now 12:30 a.m. and we were all tired. My hosts indicated I would share a room with two of the teenage girls. I took my shoes off and crawled into the compartment. We all stretched out on a big sleeping pallet and got under the coverlet. I was now part of the family. It was a decent night's sleep, except for some occasional strange thumping sounds outside.

I awoke to voices and crowing roosters. It was about 7 a.m. and everyone was already up. Large family groups were congregating in the kitchen, which was a smoky little shed on one end of the longhouse. Women were preparing breakfast—a sweet rice porridge. I took my toothbrush and went out to find the outhouse.

By daylight, the village was stunningly beautiful. Even the outhouse was cute, and extremely tidy. A little mountain stream trickled down the hill, supplying each homestead with clean, fresh water. Every dwelling had well-tended flower and herb gardens. Mountain trails led from house to house. It was all picture-postcard perfect.

Back inside, breakfast was ready. We shared their food and mine. Family members sat around a crude plank table, while others grabbed food on the run as they took care of the children. I did my best to be an entertaining guest, even though we had no language in common. I played with the children, dandled a baby, and passed around my postcards of Vermont. These were a big hit, especially the pictures of the moose and the snowy winter scenery.

The young children were all dressed in full Hmong costume. Each tribal group in Northern Thailand has distinctive traditional clothing, often covered in elaborate embroideries and fancy quilted fabrics. The kids also wore the traditional collar necklaces, bracelets, anklets and decorated hats of their ethnic group. They looked so cute in their finery!

A bit puzzling was the fact that most of the adults wore Western clothing. Usually, the older generation clings to traditional dress while the little kids run around in tee shirts with bare bums. I was beginning to get the idea that something was peculiar here...

After breakfast, they invited me on a tour of the village. The school and the clinic were really fancy for a small town. This place was prospering! Were they all making a living from opium production? If so, the place seemed too tidy. Usually, where there's opium, there's also addiction, which leads to ramshackle villages with no work ethic at all.

We went back up the path, and hiked over the hill to a truly picturesque spot. A lovely waterfall was flowing down into a man-made fishpond, surrounded by beautiful gardens. On one side of this little park, picnic tables were placed carefully on well-groomed lawns. Somebody had gone to a lot of effort to make this area attractive...

Circling back along the road, I finally solved the mystery. I was standing just inside the entrance gates of a village that tourists pay to see! If I had come here on a bus, it would have cost me $3.00 just to walk around town!

Eager Japanese tourists, bristling with cameras, were pouring off a tour bus, and the little children from my family group were starting their work day—posing for photos for money. They hammed it up in front of the cameras, capitalizing on cuteness. Already seasoned professionals, they smiled and waved at me, and went right back to work. Their lovely costumes made perfect sense to me now.

Rows and rows of souvenir stands were set up in a little mini-bazaar on the road back to the bus park, and local families were prospering from the crowds. My friends had a large stall here, and business was brisk. The bus parking lot was already full, and the incoming tourist tide was a bit overwhelming.

I found my way back to the house and settled up my order. My friend loaded the truck and said he would drive me back to my hotel. I thanked the family profusely for a very enlightening experience. As we left, I finally solved the last mystery. The guilty party who had disturbed my sleep was chained up on a ledge right outside my room— the family rooster!

My feelings were mixed as we descended the mountain. The shameless marketing of their ethnicity was disturbing, and I was abashed to have been a part of the gawking crowd. On the other hand, this was a golden opportunity for a tribal village to prosper without opium. I thought about the school and the quality of the teachers this town could afford. Young people could remain here, with their families, instead of fleeing to the cities for employment.

In the end, I found it all pretty amusing. After all, I live in a tourist town, too.

recommended Google search: Hmong culture images

By Diana McLeod

THE TESTIMONIAL BOOK

On our first trip to India in 1990, we gradually became accustomed to Delhi's chaotic atmosphere. One day, we were in the little park above the Palika Bazaar. (Palika Bazaar was one of India's first attempts at a Western-style shopping mall. The bazaar was built entirely underground, beneath the central plaza in the very heart of the city.) Dave and I knew that if we sat down in the park, we would get hustled. Vendors would zero in on us like cash-seeking missiles. As an experiment, we decided to entertain ourselves by counting the number of items or services on offer. I soon lost track because there were so many! Food sellers were out in force, hawking bananas, pineapple, coconuts, *samosas*, gum, mystery snacks wrapped up in banana leaves, betel nut, peanuts, *namkins* (spicy chips) Indian ice cream (unpasteurized and utterly unsafe at the time), water, soft drinks, "frooties" fruit drinks and more.

Interspersed among the food sellers were the souvenir people. They had everything you could imagine that could come from India or Nepal: costume jewelry, Kama Sutra picture books, bedspreads, shawls, postcards, incense, flutes, drums, paintings of Mughal Emperors, pictures of Hindu Gods, jingly anklets, bangles, and other items I can't remember. It was as if they had emptied out the entire underground bazaar just for us.

Last, but not least, were the people who offered services. We met fortune-tellers, masseurs, palm readers, musicians, sketch artists, henna painters, and sellers of Ayurvedic healing remedies. Most of these folks had testimonial books in which previous customers had written nice things about them. (This was in the ancient times before Internet reviews). One fellow was a professional ear cleaner. He showed us his kit: a scoop to clean out the ear wax, scary-looking pointed tools, which looked perfectly capable of permanently damaging ear drums, and a pair of tweezers for pulling hairs. His testimonial book had a commendation supposedly written by Margaret Thatcher, the British Prime Minister at the time. Dave and I had a good laugh at that.

But the best was yet to come. A scrawny, unattractive fellow in a loincloth squatted down beside me, while Dave was engaged with another vendor.

"What is the name of your good country?" the guy inquired.

"USA," I replied. He waggled his head in the peculiar Indian way and began to thumb through his testimonial book, looking for an endorsement from America. He searched for quite a long time as I became impatient. He wasn't telling me what he was selling, and whatever he was selling, I certainly wasn't buying. The book was very long, and there were a lot of entries. Just as I was about to tell him to get lost, he finally found one from the U.S. He handed me the book, and I began to read...

"I can't believe I said yes..." the entry began. Then it went on to graphically describe the best sex the writer—a young woman —ever had.

My first reaction was shocked disbelief. Somebody had faked this. I glanced over at the wiry little fellow, who was nobody's first choice on the dance floor. Surely this was preposterous. But then I stopped reading the shocking text and stared at the handwriting. The glowing accolade was written by a girl who had obviously taken middle-school cursive classes in America. No boy could fake that distinctive feminine style. Was somebody an expert forger? No again! Only an American would know the slang words and the idioms.

So I turned the page. Page after page of entries. Women from England, France, (I can read French pretty well) Italy, New Zealand, Spain, Israel (how was he faking Hebrew?) Ireland, Australia, Singapore... There were entries in Chinese, loads of Japanese, and even Korean, and given the variety of handwriting styles, they were almost undoubtedly written by native speakers of each language. And everything I could read confirmed that this guy was some kind of magician in bed. There were details... way too many details! There were things in that book my conservative New England upbringing had never prepared me for. It was astonishing!

I tore my gaze away from the book and back to the guy. I tossed it back to him, huffing scornfully, "I am a married woman! This is my husband!" I gestured at Dave, who was sitting right beside me, chatting with someone else.

The man's only response was to gaze directly and intently into my eyes, while giving me another of these famous Indian head waggles. "Yes, well, so?" he said, as if Dave was completely irrelevant.

Disgusted, I got up and stomped away indignantly, dragging Dave beside me. It was only afterward that I wondered: was he was offering a free service or was he actually getting women to pay for sex with him? If so, how much was he charging? And I regret that I didn't cut a deal to borrow that extraordinary testimonial book and photocopy it while I had the chance!

By Diana McLeod

BOOKSTORE SURPRISE

KATHMANDU, NEPAL: One afternoon, I was shopping in a little local English-language bookstore with the hijacked name of "Waldenbooks." I was looking at information about Buddhist art when I heard rustling sounds beneath the shelves. As I browsed, I noticed it again. Eventually, a rat emerged, darting past my feet as it crossed the aisle.

I thought this was a matter the management of the store might want to do something about, to keep customers from screaming and running away, so I approached the bookstore owner.

"Do you know there is a large rodent in here?" I asked.

The man smiled happily. "Oh yes!" he nodded. "He is Ganesh's little friend. We are honored to have him in our store. He is our good luck. We feed him every day."

It would never have occurred to me to have a rodent as a mascot. But the rat is the honored companion of the Hindu God Ganesh— the most auspicious of all the gods—who brings good luck and removes obstacles.

I nodded, trying to look at things from a brand new perspective. What a classic culture clash! I could respect their feelings, as long as their "friend" didn't try climbing up my skirt. I'm not sure that most English-language shoppers would feel the same way...

DANGEROUS

LOST! ON A TINY ISLAND, 1,000 KILOMETERS AWAY...

We could have done it the easy way, flying from a major airport. But Dave noticed these cheap flights to Jakarta from a little island off the coast of Singapore. At the Garuda Airline office in Bangkok, Dave showed the young ticket seller exactly where we wanted to go, pointing it out on their wall map. "Tanjung Pinang to Jakarta," he repeated, speaking slowly and carefully. We got the tickets and then booked a three-day train trip down from Thailand, through Malaysia, and into Singapore.

When we got to Singapore, we were feeling a bit disappointed by the trip. Malaysia was pleasant, but a bit ho-hum. We did all the usual tourist things and saw the big cities, but nothing struck us exciting or truly memorable. We were experiencing a bit of travel fatigue. It was not challenging enough. That was all about to change...

The ferry ride to the island was quite pleasant. The boat pulled up to the docks of a decrepit fishing village. Buildings in the tiny hamlet were almost entirely built on stilts, perched over the water. When a perky young man approached and asked what we were doing in his town, we told him we were there to catch the Garuda flight.

"There is no Garuda flight from this island," he frowned.

We did not agree. He looked concerned and said, "Come meet my friend. He's a travel agent who can help you. His English is very good."

We decided to go with him to check on our tickets. The travel agent puzzled over them for a minute, then he shook his head. "There is a mistake," he explained. "I'm very sorry. These tickets are from Tanjung Pandang, not Tanjung Pinang. Tanjung Pandang is over 1,000 kilometers away from here. This flight is for tomorrow morning. You would have to get to a Garuda office before the flight in order to fix these. There is one on the next island, but it's a long way from here. It is already 2:15. The office closes at 4:30. You'll never get there in time. I'm afraid you will lose these tickets and have to find another way to get to Jakarta."

Bummer! This was early in our career, and we didn't have the financial resources to cover big mistakes. Would we have to return to expensive Singapore and spend a fortune booking a flight at the last minute?

Our young friend suddenly got a flash of inspiration. "I have an idea!" he cried. "You may be lucky after all! I'll need about twenty U.S. dollars in order to try. Do you trust me?"

By Diana McLeod

Here it was—the age-old question. If it had been a big city, we would have said no. But out here... We were about to throw away $200 worth of airline tickets, and lose a big chunk of time out of our trip. For $20 more, we might possibly save them. We took the gamble and gave the kid the cash. He flashed us a brilliant grin and disappeared.

We waited for about ten anxious minutes until he came trotting triumphantly back.

"It's arranged!" he crowed, as he grabbed most of our luggage and took off running. We followed, jumping carefully across the raised bamboo platforms. There, at the end of the pier, was a swanky new sixteen-foot speedboat with a gigantic rack of engines. And at the wheel—a young man whose face was covered by a black wool mask with holes only for his eyes and mouth. He looked like a terrorist.

Our luggage was thrown into the boat.

Our friend spoke very quickly. "He'll take you to the next island. There will be a taxi waiting for you. Tell the driver to take you to the Garuda office, and promise him a good tip for driving fast. I paid this boat driver. Goodbye!"

We were now in the hands of "the terrorist." He took off with the speed and G's of an amusement park ride, while we crouched in the back, desperately holding onto the luggage and the rail. Soon we were out of the harbor and into the high surf. Leaping and pounding like a caught fish, the boat hydroplaned off the waves. The hull shuddered under the pressure as the power of the ocean met the thrust of the throttle head on.

Dave and I were terrified as our pilot gunned the engine harder. He didn't turn to look at us, so even if we had yelled at him to slow down, he never would have heard. I think he was enjoying this chance to prove his new boat's worth. His mask made sense to me now because the sea spray, at this reckless speed, stung quite a bit.

It got worse. The waves died down, but only because we were now over a shallow reef. All around us, jagged rocks pierced the water's surface, while submerged dangers lurked just below. Our guide never slowed down; he just threw the wheel violently from side to side. We hung on as he executed hairpin turns through the coral minefield like a man with an active death wish. If we had hit that coral, it would have been all over.

But we didn't crash. The reef was his world, and he knew it well. To our relief, we finally entered deep water. A squall was brewing. The sky darkened ominously as we passed some tiny islets, lightning forked across the sky on both sides of us, and the wind was picking up.

Our destination slowly materialized out of the blue haze. I noticed, with alarm, that the land we were heading for showed absolutely no sign of civilization—not a house or a boat in sight, only mangroves as far as the eye could see. The entire island was a snake-infested swamp. Where were we being taken? It didn't get better as we got closer.

53

Was he was going to dump us here? He pulled up to a mud flat and began to throw our luggage out of the boat.

Jungle, nothing but jungle! Were we about to be abandoned in the wilderness? What should we do? The faceless man behind the mask pointed and gestured for us to get out. Through the tangle of mangrove roots we saw an opening that might be a footpath...

With hand signals, we made signs for him to wait. He didn't. As soon as we were out, he gunned the engine and shot away, leaving us alone with the crabs and the mangroves and who knew what else. We picked up our bags and headed through the muck. Yes, it looked like it might be a path...

My panicked brain was busily thinking about jungle survival techniques, but the little path continued. And then, tire tracks! And then, the taxi! It really was here, out in the jungle, waiting! I have never been so relieved in all my life!

The driver was half asleep. "Get to the Garuda office as fast as you can!" we yelled. He saw the color of our money and took off, driving almost as madly as the speedboat "terrorist."

It was now nearly 4:00 p.m., and we were still in the depths of the mangrove swamp. The dirt track went for a long way before we hit a real road. Sure enough, all of the development was on the other side of the island. What a welcome sight! The taxi screamed through the town, our driver ignoring traffic rules and going as fast as he could. We checked our watches every few minutes. 4:10, 4:15, 4:20... We were rapidly losing hope. Ten minutes left...

At 4:25 there it was! The Garuda office! Some of the workers were already leaving as we ran in. Luckily, one lady inside spoke decent English. Using our map, we showed her how the Bangkok office had messed up. She smiled as she checked the computer. "No problem! We have a flight to Jakarta at 7:30 a.m. tomorrow, and I have seats. We can switch these tickets."

"I was about to lock the door," she laughed, "You're lucky you got here!"

That was an understatement! Dave and I left the office in triumph. We knew it could have gone badly for us, but it didn't. Our instinct to be suspicious of strangers had been overruled by the sincerity of one young man. Trusting him had been the right decision.

Dave looked at me and grinned. "You know, I was feeling a bit bored by travel," he confessed. "I think I had Malaysian Malaise."

"Me, too," I agreed.

"Well, I'm over it. I'm psyched to travel again."

"Me, too!"

Does that make us a bit crazy? You be the judge...

By Diana McLeod

ESCAPE TO FREEDOM

Author's note: We should never forget the value and the importance of the freedoms we often take for granted. Here is an example of how much liberty means to a person who has none. This story was told to me by a young man who lives in T1b 't. I've deliberately misspelled this word to circumvent the censorship machines of the country that conquered his homeland. You will see other misspellings in this chapter because we don't want to be denied permission to travel to that country in the future. When we entered T1b 't, we had to sign papers swearing we were not journalists, and publishing this biography will undoubtedly violate that rule. In E-book format, my writing is still vulnerable to review.

To bring this story out of T1b 't, I had to promise my friend that I would rewrite my notes into a "safe format." He was concerned that they could be dangerous, both for him and for me. Tourists have been arrested for less. After the interview, I faithfully rewrote the whole thing into the form of a fairytale, complete with evil wizards, fanciful characters, and Harry Potter references, and I tore up my original notes before leaving our hotel that night. Could you imagine having to do such a thing in our country? Let us all guard our civil rights carefully!

THE STORY OF RED BULL: We met him at a restaurant, on our way to Everest Basecamp. When the conversation turned to the Himalayan mountains, his friend volunteered the information that Red once made it over one of the high passes when he was only twelve years old. We bought them both drinks, hoping to hear about his ascent and the reasons behind it. He ordered a Red Bull (hence the nickname I gave him). At first, he was very reluctant to trust us, but when we promised him that his narrative would make it safely to the U.S, he agreed. Glancing around, he decided that the large group of T' Jaineze at the next table was too boisterously drunk to take notice. I discreetly took out my notebook, hid it in a menu, and we talked late into the night.

It took great courage for him to tell me his story. Even though the events happened a long time ago, he still risked being jailed as a dissident. Anyone who has ever fled the regime is considered a threat, a marked man for the rest of his life. Red Bull also knew even foreigners could be recruited as government spies. The internal police are well known for such tricks as hiring friendly, fake T1b 'tan monks to catch dissenters at the monasteries. Even tourists are under surveillance; I also took a risk talking to Red Bull. Our guide and driver both warned us about this repeatedly.

Red Bull is only twenty-seven years old. He is tall and rather thin, but he is well muscled, more like a kung-fu fighter than an ex-monk. His face is very animated and easily brought to laughter. When something amuses him, his whole face lights up. Remembering his past, his expression shifts, and he looks older and more somber. Little lines track along the sides of his mouth, marking him with years of sorrow and painful memories. I liked him and trusted him straight away, and was flattered and grateful he felt the same towards us.

Red's parents were simple farmers in a tiny village in T1b 't. Yearning to become a Buddhist monk like his eldest brother, Red left the farm at age twelve to enter the monastery. His hopes were denied. The T 'Jaineze put strict limits on new devotees because monks and nuns were in the vanguard of protest against the regime. The waiting lists were very long, and he was too impatient.

At that moment, Red realized he had three choices in life. The first was to remain in his village and become a farmer like his father. Or he could go to a T ' Jaineze school. It would be an education by rote, more propaganda than actual knowledge. He would also have to learn to read in T 'Jaineze (10,000 printed characters that would have to be memorized, one by one). The consequences of such an education weren't worth it. The third option was to wait until he could get into the monastery, which might take years. In the meantime, he was spending his time in the city, bored, and idle, and he was falling in with a bad crowd of street kids. Unwilling to return to the farm, and unwilling to join his country's oppressors, he instinctively knew that his punk friends were a danger all their own. And so, at twelve years old, Red made a momentous decision. Rejecting all three paths, he chose to escape to India.

Red knew his family would never support his decision. Concerned for their safety, he told no one of his plans. He stole a hefty sum of money from his brother and ran away. The cash gave him enough bargaining power to get an older companion, a forty-year-old man who also wanted to escape. Together, they hired a "coyote" (in this case, a Nepalese guide skilled in smuggling people) to take them over a pass near the flank of Mt. Everest and into Nepal. Knowing the high passes wouldn't be watched in the wintertime, they left in January.

ESCAPE OVER THE MOUNTAINS: The guide cost all of Red's money. The two escapees had no special mountaineering gear, no special clothes, no tent, and no food except *tsampa* (a paste made of barley flour), and they attempted the dangerous ascent wearing only old sneakers. Red took nothing to remind him of his family or his previous life. Nearing the pass, their guide drove them to walk 20-22 hours a day, because if they slept too long, they would freeze to death. The air at high altitude was dangerously thin, even for T1b 'tans, and they had to fight altitude sickness. The terrain was cruel as well; T1b 'tan hills are made of very crumbly stone, and many dangerous scree fields had to be traversed. Feet sank deeply into the slanted banks of loose pebbles, dust clouds choked the lungs, and avalanche was a constant threat.

At high altitude, they encountered deep snow for four days. At times it was up above their knees. The guide poked the ground ahead with a stick, checking for hidden crevasses. When the three of them roped together for safety on the ice fields, they began to encounter frozen corpses. Thousands of people had attempted to escape during the first cruel days of occupation, and many never made it. Red said he personally saw between ten and fifteen unburied dead people up there. As he told me this, his face sobered and he paused, remembering. He was still haunted by mental images of those frozen faces.

When fuel for their camp stove ran out, they had to melt snow for the water with which to make the *tsampa*, or they would have had neither food nor water. Their guide decided to burn the rubber soles off of his spare hiking boots, creating enough heat for them to survive.

Red began to have trouble with frostbite. At age twelve, he was not quite able to keep up. He was lucky; the older man took pity on him and carried him part of the way. When he was carried, the frostbite got worse, and he soon realized it was safer to keep walking despite the pain. Red thought he was going to die, and that fear increased when they encountered two avalanches. The second one came down right above them, and they ran for their lives.

At last, the mountain pass was behind them, and the trail descended into a vast forest. One night, their camp was surrounded by wolves in the darkness. Luckily, when they flashed flashlights and shouted, the predators shied away. As they descended, they began to spot Nepalese villages, but Red and his friend were afraid to approach. It was known that such places held informers who were paid by the T 'Jaineze, and they didn't want to risk being turned in.

Food became a huge issue. The *tsampa* had run out, and Red and his companion were starving. Their Nepalese guide had his own food, but he refused to share. In desperation, they raided fields at night, and got their hands on some potatoes. Eventually, stumbling with exhaustion, they made their way to Kathmandu, Nepal.

The "Free" T1b't Em* b @ssy took them in. The T1b'tan refugee community takes superb care of its own people. Red was fed, clothed, and given enough money to go to India and get the education he had always dreamed of. When he got to Dh @rams @la, India, the D @lai L@* ma's government in exile paid for everything and sent him to a good school. He was never asked to pay any of the money back. He told me that his experience in India really cemented his faith in Buddhism. While he was there, he went to many religious events and he saw the D.L. in person. (The D.L is considered a living Buddha by people of that faith.)

Red spent twelve years in India. He applied himself to the study of English, since his education would be conducted in that language, and he enrolled in school. Still, although he was living his dream, he missed his family, especially during holidays. His classmates went home during the summer months while he remained at the empty school. He couldn't contact his family, because none of them had a phone number; the family farm never even had a mailing address.

Then, something happened that changed Red's destiny. Two of his aunts showed up in Dh @rams @la. They brought posters and old photos of him, which were posted on bulletin boards at the reception center for T1b'tan refugees. Somebody there identified him, and Red was given his brother's phone number. The exiled teenager suddenly felt a very intense desire to reconnect with his family, so he made the call.

His brother was thoroughly convinced that Red was dead. It took ten days of lengthy phone calls and shared memories to persuade him that Red was not a T' Jainese imposter. When his brother was finally sure Red was alive, he pleaded with him to come home. At first, the young man was very reluctant, but the yearning to be reunited with to his family was also strong. He couldn't concentrate on his studies.

In the end, he quit school, got a job, and began to earn money for the trip home. He couldn't enter T1b't legally, so he hired another "coyote" to take him across the border. This time, the trip was far easier. There are not many people who choose to enter T1b't illegally, so the T'Jaineze are not as concerned about the border from that side. Red and his guide used an area near a main highway, and the crossing took only eight hours at night.

Red spent four nights hiding in a border hotel, waiting for his brother to come, bringing papers so that Red could pass the nearby police checkpoint. They traveled to his brother's home and spent a whole month getting to know each other. Sadly, Red's brother had been kicked out of his monastery for wearing a little pin of the original T1b'tan flag. The T' Jaineze regard all symbols of the previous regime as acts of rebellion. This symbolic defiance cost Red's brother his religious freedom. He was banned from all monasteries for life, and he was devastated. (His brother was one of the lucky ones. In the beginning of the occupation, he would probably have been executed.) It took a long time for Red's brother to accept his fate, but Red said he has learned to make the best of it. He now has a job, a wife, and children. Physically, he has a very good life. Mentally, it has been difficult.

When Red was ready, his brother took him to see his parents for the first time in twelve years. They were completely convinced he was dead, and did not recognize their own son. Even with his brother's help, it took a long time to persuade them that he was their long lost boy. When the family finally began to believe their good fortune, it became a joyous and tearful reunion.

Red has successfully reintegrated back into T1b'tan society. He has a decent job and he has his family back, but he still has no freedom of religion, and he is careful to hide his past. His story is one that would land him in jail as a dissident if the T' Jaineze were to find out about it. He told me: "I am a black man." When I asked him what he meant, he said he is treated in the same way blacks have been treated in America.

By Diana McLeod

He is repressed and discriminated against. He will never have access to the same economic opportunities the T' Jaineze do unless he joins them and assists them in exploiting his native land. He will also have a black mark on his name forever. Having experienced Indian democracy and religious tolerance, he is therefore a dangerous criminal. When I asked him what the T' Jaineze would do if they ever found out what he had done, he said, "They will jail me for sure, and put a virus in my brain or something."

Red is not content with his life. The close family ties he has regained have kept him in Tlb't thus far, but he is uncertain about his future. When asked if he was more pessimistic or more optimistic, he admitted he leans towards optimism. Dave and I sincerely wish him our best. Perhaps he will help his countrymen and women by teaching English to others. Not everything in English on the Internet can be censored.

This was written in 2007, just before the unrest that preceded the 2008 Bay-gin Olympics. Tlb'tans strongly objected to the carrying of the torch through their land. Security tightened up, and the situation worsened once again.

TAXI DANGERS

Taxis can be dangerous overseas, and the savvy traveler should be aware of taxi scams around the world. Female travelers are particularly vulnerable.

One Mexican scam is well known. The driver takes the foreigner to a prearranged intersection, where the car is suddenly surrounded by gang members. The foreigner is taken out and robbed (or worse). The taxi drives away, and the victim seldom thinks to question the driver's innocence. They never remember his ID number.

I got an airport taxi at the Mexico City airport while traveling with a fellow (female) employee. No sooner had we left the airport than the driver stopped to pick up a "friend." I knew what was up, and I was prepared. Before I even got in the car, I wrote down the license plate number. The driver's identification plaque was hanging up inside the car.

I got out a phone and pretended to call a friend. I carefully read out the license, and the driver's name, address, and airport taxi number to my "friend". Then I explained where I was going, and that, if I didn't call back in twenty minutes, they were to call the authorities.

The men in the front seat listened carefully. Afterward, the driver's "buddy" actually turned around and told my employee, in English, "Your friend, she is very smart."

The two of them dropped us at our destination, unharmed, and went off in search of fresher meat.

NEVER ANNOY TRIBESMEN CARRYING MACHINE GUNS

ETHIOPIA, 2013. We were deep in the tribal outback, in the southern part of the country. The people there are still herders and hunters, and they live pretty much they've lived for centuries, holding on tightly to their unique customs and languages. They don't interact much with the outside world, but they do have a few modern conveniences, including machine guns. Almost every adult male has one.

On market day, one community was teeming with people of various tribes, eager to trade. Most were decked out in traditional costume, and they were busily buying or selling local agricultural products. It was a spectacularly target-rich environment for candid photos of people, and Dave was snapping away as fast as he could.

After about an hour, we left the vegetable market and wandered over to the livestock market area. *Bana, Hamrar* and *Tsamai* tribesmen were crowded into groups, bidding on cattle. Dave waded right into the action, and I (reluctantly) followed. One market official voiced his displeasure that we were there. Perhaps he just didn't want tourists interfering, or maybe he disapproved because I was a woman. (There wasn't another woman in sight, although the place was crowded with men.) Undaunted, Dave shrugged and grinned, acting like he couldn't understand that the fellow wanted us to leave. Eventually, he gave in and let us stay.

Dave got right into the bargaining sessions, photographing fierce-looking tribesmen in traditional dress (each with an automatic weapon slung across his back.) It didn't take too long before Dave got into one guy's face a little too closely. The man tensed and gave him a strange look, which was apparently designed to intimidate. The pupils of his eyes jiggled from side to side. Everyone caught the meaning of his threat, and the market came to a standstill as the locals waited for our response. Tension rippled through the crowd as the message of the challenge to fight was delivered. But Dave didn't flinch. Instead, he did the unexpected—he grinned, pursed his lips, and made a wet, smacking, kissing sound.

My stomach lurched uncontrollably. For a split second, it could have gone either way. Dave could have been beaten to a pulp, or killed outright if they took his gesture as a homosexual advance.

Dave's antagonist blinked in astonishment and his eyes narrowed. Then he burst out laughing. The whole group joined him, appreciating the disarming joke. The warrior threw his arm around Dave's shoulders and shook his hand. Everyone respected my husband's fearless and humorous response to the challenge, and he got to take all the pictures he wanted. It was all in good fun, and we lived to tell the tale.

By Diana McLeod

PRISONERS IN PARADISE

This is the only story in this book that is not our own. It was told to me, in about 1995, by two young British kids. They were a charming, sincere young couple, fresh out of university, who had decided to bicycle across northern Thailand. It is such an extraordinary tale that I have remembered it all these years, and I simply must share it with you.

Thailand is a popular tourist destination because it is well known as one of the safest environments in the developing world. Crime is low, and travel is relatively effortless, as long as travelers avoid political strife. However, in Northern Thailand, when you get off the beaten track and out into the countryside, there are areas where opium is cultivated. Among the poppy fields, things can become a lot less civilized...

My British friends were partway through their bicycle trek when they encountered armed men beside the road. Although the Brits smiled, waved, and tried to pass, automatic weapons were aimed at them. They were taken hostage, blindfolded, and loaded into a jeep. They were terrified for their lives.

The jeep drove for a long time up a rough mountain road. When it stopped, the blindfolds were removed, and my friends gasped in amazement. They were at a magnificent mountain estate comprised of a stunningly beautiful mansion, a swimming pool in which children were happily playing, manicured lawns, and an outdoor bar. Smiling servants brought the two hostages chilled drinks and carried their luggage to the mansion. The bicycles were taken away.

Servants ushered the hostages into the presence of the wealthy owner of the estate. The Thai gentleman smiled and gestured for them sit down. He introduced himself in English, giving himself an English nickname. I can't remember now what they said he called himself, but I think it was "Jimmie."

"Welcome to my home," Jimmie said graciously. "You are my guests. Relax and enjoy yourselves! If there is anything you need, anything at all, please do not hesitate to ask. I must tell you, however, not to attempt to leave, or to stroll too close to the perimeter fence, because there are armed guards. After dusk, you must remain inside the house, for your safety. We will be serving dinner at 7 p.m. Please come to the dining room and join the family. My servant will show you up to the guest suite. I'm sure you will find it quite comfortable."

The young hostages spent a week in their luxury prison. Everything at the mansion was beautiful, and their guest suite was magnificent. They discovered a library with some English titles, a well-stocked bar, several big screen TVs with an extensive collection of

American movies, and an exercise room. A masseuse was on call. There was no Internet access at that time, nor could they use the phone. They were cut off from the outside world. Their camera was missing from their luggage.

Mealtimes and most of each day were spent with the family. Their host was gregarious, and they soon began to relax. The cuisine was world-class and the mansion's wine cellar was impressive. The Brits enjoyed playing with the kids. They would have been perfectly at home if it weren't for the lack of freedom.

Then, as suddenly as it began, it was over. "Jimmie" said goodbye, and a helicopter swooped in to pick up the whole family. The Brits were escorted back down to the perimeter fence where their bicycles and knapsacks were already loaded into a jeep. Blindfolded again, they were driven back down the mountain, right to the spot where they were first taken hostage. The jeep driver took off their blindfolds and indicated they could continue on their bicycle trip. Then he drove away. Later that night, when they went through their bags, they found that the camera had been returned.

The Brits were astounded by this experience. It had never occurred to them they might have been riding right into the drug harvest. Their host obviously did not relish the idea of tourists visiting his production fields right at the critical time. They could have seen things that they shouldn't have seen, or worse, they could have photographed them. Worse still, they could have been shot by a trigger-happy guard. If that had happened, it would have turned into an international incident, and the Thai Federal government would have been forced to act. Local officials, who were all probably getting a cut of the profits, might have turned on their drug lord buddy. British and American DEA agents would descend on the area like a swarm of locusts. Any incident involving foreigners would have been deeply embarrassing. Thus, their Thai host decided that the best course of action would be to keep the couple locked up where he could keep them out of danger. Besides, it sounded as though he thoroughly enjoyed showing off and making "friends." When the young couple thought about reporting their detention to local police, they realized their story would sound unbelievable—particularly without any evidence. So they never even tried to report it.

This kind of thing can happen in the backcountry of Northern Thailand. Dave and I once decided to take a stroll outside a mountain village. A gunman carrying an automatic weapon popped out of the long grass and told us to turn back. And we did. Quickly.

Is Thailand safe? It is. It's safer than our country, given our proclivity for gun violence. In Thailand, tourists are treated delicately. People who want to see the countryside usually go on organized treks, which carefully skirt problem areas. But if you ever wander off on your own, out into the fields, and somebody tells you to turn around, I strongly advise you to obey them.

By Diana McLeod

DETAINED IN PAKISTAN

This incident happened early in our travels when Dave was always searching for the cheapest flights to Asia. One year, he booked me on Pakistani Airlines to fly to Germany, then on to Karachi, Pakistan, and after an eight-hour layover, another flight to Kathmandu.

The trip started well, although I noticed that the only airline safety video was a short film of an Islamic Imam blessing the aircraft. The problem occurred when we landed in Karachi where gun-toting soldiers detained all of the transit passengers. Nobody spoke to us. Gesturing with their rifles, the soldiers herded us into a large, empty room, where a stern-looking turbaned official sat behind a desk. He demanded our boarding passes for our next flights.

My fellow passengers were all beginning to look at each other nervously. There were about twenty of us, mostly Europeans, and none of us had a clue about what was going on.

The official took all of the boarding passes and wrote all the names down on a piece of paper. Then he handed us back our boarding passes and demanded our passports. Our names and passport numbers were written on another piece of paper, and the passports were stacked up and put in a box. The officer handed the first list to a Bangladeshi businessman who was a member of our group. Instructions were given in a language they both understood. Then came directions in English. They were terse. We were bluntly told to "follow that man."

List in hand, the Bangladeshi businessman left the room and headed for the immigration counters. We tailed him anxiously. He was the only person who could identify any of us, and he had the only proof that our passports were in some unnamed official's custody. We were all terrified.

Our group passed straight through immigration. Now we were officially on Pakistani soil—with no personal identification. When our "leader" left the airport terminal and got on an empty bus, we all gaped at each other, wide-eyed. Were we really supposed to follow him onto a bus? In the end, we all sheepishly got on board, unwilling to be left behind in the street. Somebody tried to ask him what he was doing, but none of us could understand him.

Footsteps of a Nomad

The bus left the airport grounds and pulled into a hotel. We all went inside and were given rooms— for free! We were finally told what was going on. The airport was remodeling, and the departure lounge was temporarily unavailable, so Pakistani Airlines was supplying hotel rooms to all international passengers with long layovers. We had pleasant rooms, long showers, refreshing naps, and an excellent buffet lunch. Everyone was smiling when we met again at dinnertime.

Despite the generous treatment, our lingering anguish about our passports was not quite over. Seven hours later, the bus came to pick us up. The Bangladeshi guy got us all back through immigration, and we were taken to a large open area where several hundred people were jostling each other to get close to a raised "pulpit" in the center. An official was standing above the crowd, holding up one passport at a time and reading out the names. When somebody in the huge crowd raised their hand to claim their passport, the officer threw the passport into the air, in the general direction of the passenger who claimed it. Many passports failed to make it all the way back to their owner. They were grabbed by the crowd and passed, hand-over-hand, through the mob.

When they called my name, I put up my hand to identify myself, but I was way at the back of the throng. My passport was tossed in my direction, but it fell about ten people short of me and disappeared. My heart sank. In a desperately impoverished nation, surrounded by many other struggling lands, an American passport was worth a fortune! It would have been so easy for somebody to pocket it. I had visions of being all alone in Karachi, Pakistan, with no I.D., and no proof I had brought a passport with me. The thought terrified me.

But then, I saw it coming, from the hands of locals in turbans to the hands of Hajis (Muslim pilgrims dressed in white, on their way to Mecca), to hands in worn, frayed shirtsleeves. When it finally came into my own, I hugged it to my chest like a long-lost friend, murmuring *"Shukran, Dyanabad"* ("Thank you!" in Arabic and Hindi) to my neighbors in the crowd.

Pakistani Airlines had done everything right, but they *really* needed to improve their communication skills. I do not have such kind words for the Pakistani immigration authorities.

By Diana McLeod

NEAR DEATH EXPERIENCES
a series of scary experiences over the years

WHITE WATER: A three-day whitewater rafting expedition in Sulawesi, Indonesia sounded like fun. It was our very first rafting excursion, on a river that had both Class III and IV rapids. A highly experienced rafting team was guiding us, and they were very well trained in every respect. There were two rafts, fully equipped with all of the supplies we would need on a three-day river trip through remote, unpopulated jungles. On the first day, all went smoothly. Probably, looking back at it, we should have been more afraid than we were, but we felt confident enough.

It must have rained hard up in the mountains during the night, because, the next morning, the river seemed rougher and faster than before. An incoming branch added to the flow. We did well until about mid-afternoon. Suddenly, our guide shouted out, yelling for us to get down into the bottom of the raft. Dave and I had been trained to do this whenever there was particularly rough water. We wound up going over a small waterfall. The raft fell about five feet and landed precisely in a circular "hole" in the river as the waterfall emptied into a deep well. As the water surged back up from the bottom, it actually *flowed backward* when it hit the stones along the front edge of the basin.

Astoundingly, we were stuck! The river hydraulics prevented us from moving forward! The fall had sheared off both aluminum steering oars, so our guide was helpless to budge us out of the hole. And since we were no longer moving with the current, the terrifying power of the river was overwhelming. Not only that, but the waterfall was pounding on the back edge of the raft. I had, unfortunately, watched a video about the dangers of rafting, and I knew our situation was dire. If the raft shifted backward, even a few inches, the waterfall's strength would swamp us, causing the raft to flip, throwing us directly under the waterfall. We would be sucked down, almost undoubtedly drowning in the churning chaos of the hydraulics. Our bones would roll endlessly down there, never to be seen again. When I looked at our captain, I saw sheer panic on his face. His eyes met mine, and he signaled me to stay perfectly still. I yelled to Dave not to move.

The guides on the second raft had seen our situation and had turned back, paddling desperately against the powerful current. They tried in vain to throw us a line, but it was no use. They couldn't get anywhere near us. We were stuck, in imminent danger of death, and with no apparent solution to our situation.

For about five minutes, we sat there, immobilized. Our guide eventually got the idea of throwing his body weight against the "downhill" side of the raft. At first, it didn't seem to make any difference, but then each forward thrust nudged us a tiny bit away from the dangerous waterfall. Suddenly, we gained traction, and the raft jerked as the current sucked us violently back into its flow.

65

We shot forward, popped like a cork out of a bottle. Dave and I resumed paddling, and eventually we were able to meet up with the other raft. To my immense relief, they had packed a spare pair of steering oars, so we were soon back on our way, with our guide back in control of the raft.

That evening as we camped, the crew produced some homemade alcohol, and we all had a couple of belts to calm our nerves. Our guides confessed that we'd been in the most dangerous situation they'd ever seen on the river in the seven years they'd been rafting. They had all been terrified. The waterfall and the "hole" below it were completely new and unexpected. The river had shifted during the couple of weeks since they had last seen it. We were all lucky to have survived.

I still have dreams about those five perilous minutes.

— — — —

THE FLAMINGO HOTEL: In 1983 we were in Colima, Mexico. Dave and our friend Jean were on the rooftop of our hotel, admiring the sunset view of the twelve-thousand-foot smoking volcano near town.

Dave was leaning on the railing when suddenly, it gave way. Seconds later, he was upside down, clinging to the broken metal, dangling four stories above the busy street! The railing was hanging by one single bolt, and it was about to pull out of the wall entirely. Jean reached out, as far as she could, and managed to grab one belt loop of his pants. She slowly hauled him back, praying that the stitching would hold. Dave barely made it to the roof's edge before the straining metal collapsed.

Needless to say, Dave had a couple of extra *cervesas* that night, to calm down. So did I, when I found out what had happened. And, ever since then, we always look before we lean.

— — — — —

THE FLIGHT THAT TURNED BACK: Dave was flying to Kathmandu, Nepal from Delhi. I was at home when he telephoned to tell me his plane had turned back due to severe turbulence from storms over the mountains. Ten minutes later, my friend Jean also telephoned. (Yes, this is the same Jean who saved him in Colima, Mexico.)

Jean, who is quite an amazing natural psychic, somehow knew that Dave was flying that day, on the other side of the world. She barely greeted me before she blurted out, in a panicked voice, that she was worried about him. I put her at ease, explaining that I had just spoken to him from India. Her relief was evident, even over the phone. She then told me that she had had a powerful clairvoyant vision. She was sure, she said, her voice shaking, "If that plane had not turned back, it would have crashed into those mountains."

By Diana McLeod

Since I hadn't spoken to Jean for six months, and she had no idea of when or where Dave was flying, yet she was certain he would have perished in a plane crash that particular morning, I consider this to be a near-death experience. Later that year, two flights plowed into the foothills near Kathmandu, killing all on board.

— — — —

TAXI FROM HELL: India's highways are always crazy and dangerous, but one incident stands out. We were in Delhi, on our way to the airport, when the driver became angry at the traffic. He suddenly swerved and intentionally started driving down the wrong side of the divided highway! Three full lanes of rush hour traffic came straight at us at sixty miles an hour, on a collision course, with no breakdown lanes. Somehow, we survived our death-defying encounters with trucks, buses and cargo vans. Horns screamed in protest as our driver jerked us back and forth between lanes, sometimes with only inches to spare. At a break in the action, we flashed a wad of cash at him and we told him we would tip him if he would PLEASE drive on the other side of the road.

The promise of a tip worked, but we had to wait for several more white-knuckled minutes before he was finally able to slip through a break in the concrete barriers. In the meantime, he engaged in more death-defying stunts, playing high-speed chicken with everybody else on the road.

When we finally got to the airport, we, of course, did *not* tip him! Instead, we yelled at him and refused to pay him at all for risking our lives so stupidly.

— — — —

TIGHT SQUEEZE: We rented a motorbike on Phú Quốc, an island in Vietnam. Dave is an experienced and prudent driver, but no matter how careful one is, sometimes circumstances just get in the way. We came around a corner on a dirt road and met an oncoming bus, which was hogging most of the right-of-way. On the other side stood a big male water buffalo with large, pointed horns. Just as we came close to the bus, the buffalo sauntered right in front of us. We "threaded the needle" between his horns and the bus, with only about two inches to spare on each side! That was a very close call!

FUNNY

HAMAMS – TURKISH PUBLIC STEAM BATHS:

–THE GOOD, THE BAD, AND THE UGLY!

My friend Sandra from Amsterdam took me to a real Turkish steam bath in Istanbul, and it was a delightful experience. Cemberlitas Hamam and Spa is in a historic neighborhood, and has been operating since the 1500's. After we paid, we were given thin cloth towels and storage lockers for our things. Sandra and I stripped down and headed for the steam room. The Ladies' side consisted of a circular, domed room with little marble sinks off to the sides where you could douse yourself with water at the temperature of your choice. In the center of the misty, sauna-like atmosphere was a huge marble slab. Women were stretched out all over it, enjoying the warm moisture radiating from the heated stone. Lying still with their eyes shut, they looked like contented turtles, sunning themselves on a river rock on a hot summer's day.

Sandra had paid for the full treatment. I did not. (I'll explain my reasons later). I simply enjoyed the relaxing heat of the slab, watching as she received the attentions of the spa staff. First, female attendants lathered her down from neck to toe, using a special soap that turned into a thick bubbly froth when squeezed through a muslin bag. Then they scrubbed her with a slightly rough cloth, exfoliating her skin. After that, she was sent to the massage room for a luxurious rubdown. When she came back, she stretched out on the marble and absorbed the warmth with a blissful smile.

I decided to forgo the spa treatment for two reasons. One was that the famous Istanbul hamam was really expensive. The whole package would have cost me close to $75, which would have thrown our daily budget for a loop. The second reason was because I had already had an unforgettable scrubdown at a steam bath in Morocco—an experience that I never want to duplicate!

MOROCCO 1993: My haman misadventure took place in the city of Fez. We made friends with Mohammed, a guy who offered to "help" us shop for our store, claiming to know just where to get the best wholesale prices. (It turned out later that he was just another hustler, making his living by taking advantage of foreigners. Still new to the business, we got sucked in.)

By Diana McLeod

Mohammed decided to entertain us in order to win our trust and increase his profit, so he offered to treat us to the local hamam. He sent me off to the ladies' hamam, accompanied by his sister, who really didn't speak English, while Dave went with him to the men's side. He paid a bit extra for us to get full scrub downs and massages. Unfortunately, in Morocco, that "treatment" was really rough! In my case, it was a nightmare...

Inside the steam room, Mohammed's sister dumped me immediately, and went to hang out with her friends. I was the solo foreigner, surrounded by naked, middle-aged Moroccan housewives. They were a noisy, exuberant bunch, much more comfortable in their own skins than we insecure Americans will ever be. Looking around, I realized the hamam was the one place in Muslim society where these women could escape from the male-dominated rules they all had to live under, and simply be themselves.

The hamam attendant sought me out. She was an overweight old crone with long, greasy, grey hair, a few remarkably rotten teeth, and an obvious dislike of foreign infidels. Clad in only in panties, she sat me down on the slab, reached out, and grabbed the back of my head. Before I could comprehend what she was doing, she shoved my face right into her upper belly, wedged in between her massive, pendulous old breasts, and proceeded to rip the flesh right off my back with something that felt like extremely coarse sandpaper. It was horrible! For one thing, I couldn't breathe at all, stuffed as I was between her sweaty bosom and her repulsive belly rolls. Her hand gripped me tightly by the hair, so I couldn't push away or even protest. I thought I would suffocate! And, while she tortured me, those heavy breasts swung back and forth, slapping my cheeks and boxing my ears until they rang.

Finally, she released me. As I lay there, gasping like a spent runner, she tore the flesh off the other side of me. Next, she gave me a spine-twisting, neck-crunching pummeling form of torture she probably thought of as massage. (Yeah, in Guantanamo Bay!) The old hag expected a tip, too, and was angry when she didn't get one. I was amazed that she expected I would have money for her—I was naked in a steam room!

Needless to say, given that memory, I was very reluctant to accept the "full treatment" in Istanbul. At first I was really glad I had refused it since the spa attendants were all muscle-bound Eastern European women who looked like they'd been doping up for the Soviet-era Bulgarian swim team! But Sandra looked very pleased. When she returned to the slab, she was grinning like the Cheshire Cat. *Hmm...* I thought. *Maybe I shouldn't judge all hamams by the one in Fez. Next time, I'll give it another try.*

UGRUP, TURKEY: I got my second chance in a pleasant little town in the heart of Cappadocia. The hamam was an unusual one, since it had a unisex steam room. Men and women could use the same slab, at the same time! We thought this was an unbelievably liberal policy for a

Muslim culture. On Tuesdays and Saturdays, the hamam was reserved for women only. I'm sure most of the village women planned their spa visits on those days, and only the oldest married ladies, accompanied by their husbands, would use it when the men were there. The spa was in a big tourist area, so the men were obviously used to foreign females in their steam room. The policy was certainly good for business. It was a very popular spa.

Dave and I went with friends from our hotel, Felix and Veronique, a young couple from Quebec, and Osan, a Turkish man who lived in Germany and was touring his native country. Veronique and I wore our bathing suits for modesty's sake since we were going to the hamam on the unisex day. It was odd to be in the baths with local men, who were wearing only towels, but the guys were quite blasé towards us, and we were treated with respect. All of the attendants were also male, which meant that they would be soaping and massaging us. Veronique and I made sure that our husbands were watching when it was our turn!

This time the experience was great! Our masseurs were perfectly professional and did a fabulous job. They lathered us up with soap bubbles and gently scrubbed us until our skin felt like it was brand new. The massages eased the knots out of our tired muscles (sore from hiking), and restored us back to perfect condition. Afterwards, we all went back onto the slab and "blissed out" in the steam, until it was time to go. At the end, after we were dressed, we were served glasses of Turkish apple tea.

The verdict: if you ever get a chance to try a Turkish bath, try it! Most of the time, you'll probably have a wonderful experience. If not, you'll at least walk away with a funny story to tell!

recommended Google search: Hamams Istanbul Images

By Diana McLeod

A MONKEY, SOME HOLY MEN, AND ONE FOOLISH TOURIST

Kathmandu, Nepal is home to a large number of *Sadhus*. These men are followers of Shiva, the Hindu God of destruction and regeneration. Some are genuine Hindu mystics. They wear simple robes, grow their hair into amazingly long dreadlocks, paint their foreheads and go barefoot, even in the Himalayan winter. Leaving their homes and families behind, these mendicants adopt the religious life—sleeping at temples and making pilgrimages from holy site to holy site. Their days are spent begging for food, preaching, or deep in meditation.

Sadhus do have a funny side. They are legally allowed to smoke *ganja* (marijuana) as an important part of their religious practice, and many of them indulge in this habit daily. This "sacrament" supposedly helps them meditate. Occasionally, it provokes a severe case of the giggles. I recall one hilarious scene involving a group of *Sadhus*, which took place during my visit to the Pashupatinath temple (the main Hindu temple in Kathmandu).

I had brought an orange for lunch and sat down to enjoy it outdoors on the temple terrace. Unfortunately, a large male monkey was determined to take it away from me. He was a full-grown male macaque, almost two feet tall and quite aggressive. On most days I would have simply given up and tossed him the orange. On this afternoon, for some reason, I was not in the mood to capitulate to a bully. The orange was my only lunch. Besides, it was about time somebody stood up to the monkey mafia. (This was incredibly stupid on my part. Monkey bites can be extremely dangerous). I took off my shoe to use as a weapon, and prepared to do battle.

The monkey advanced, and I retreated. Then I charged him, jumping, yelling, hissing, waving my arms, baring my teeth monkey-style and brandishing the shoe. He fearfully backed up. Then he threatened me again, and I backed up. Back and forth we went. The fight went on for several minutes. It must have looked ridiculous—the monkey and the middle-aged foreign woman squaring off. In the end, I won. My instincts were correct. This monkey was willing to bluff but was not prepared to take me on for real. He ran away, and I claimed victory.

As soon as he fled, I became aware of a lot of noise coming from a nearby stonewall. The *Sadhus* of Pashupatinath had come to watch me fight the monkey. Half of them were clapping and cheering. The rest of them were so convulsed with laughter they were falling over, holding their stomachs, and crying like babies. I was apparently the funniest thing they had ever seen. When I gave them an annoyed look, they all flew into new fits of hysterical giggles. The guffaws continued while I attempted to regain my dignity and enjoy my lunch. Every time I glanced over at them, they simply started laughing all over again.

71

The holy men of Pashupatinath are a remarkable group. Foreign tourists come from all over the world to see and photograph them. But, for the *Sadhus* themselves, I suspect *I* will become a legendary character, a story to pass down from generation to generation of young *Sadhus*. I only wish I could be there to watch them "ape" me.

recommended google search: Pashupatinath Kathmandu images WARNING: this search will show very disturbing images of human cremations, (which take place at this temple) but it also has pictures of some of my giggling friends and the temple itself

ALL BETS ARE OFF

It was late at night in Kathmandu, Nepal, and I was walking back to my guesthouse. All the streets were empty and the shops had closed. Only the strains of distant music wafting from the tourist bars — Bob Marley, of course — kept me company as I turned my flashlight on.

Rounding a dark corner, I came across an unexpected throng of locals, mobbing a small Ganesh shrine. (Ganesh is the Hindu God of Good Luck and Remover of Obstacles.) All of the worshippers were men. The late hour seemed highly unusual, so I asked them what was going on.

"Excuse me, is there some special *puja* ceremony happening tonight?" I inquired.

"No, Madam. Horse racing day is tomorrow, Madam," came the reply. "We are praying to Ganesh for the success of our bets."

Hmmmm, maybe they need a few Ganesh shrines in Vegas...

By Diana McLeod

TERROR IN GUATEMALA

In 1985 the country was being torn by civil strife. Whole villages were getting massacred by rogue army factions. So when people in army uniforms stopped our bus and ordered everyone to get off and march fifty feet into the jungle, we naturally thought we were next. These men were wearing gas masks and carrying odd-looking weapons that reminded me of small bazookas. As we stood there trembling, some of them got back on the bus ...and started spraying for Mediterranean Fruit Flies! The "bazookas" turned out to be for agricultural pest control.

----- ----- ----- ------

Antigua is Guatemala's most romantic colonial city. Despite ongoing civil disturbances in the countryside, we were enjoying our stay there. One day, while walking along a busy downtown boulevard, we realized the street was deserted. The local population had utterly vanished, making us very uneasy. As we looked around anxiously, we suddenly heard loud gunfire. Dave and I hit the dirt, hoping not to get killed. Then, strangely, we heard music playing. We timidly raised our faces from the street and saw a marching band appear around the corner, followed by a colorful parade. Fireworks exploded overhead, and the street came alive with onlookers. As I brushed clouds of dust from my clothes, I looked up in amazement at a flower-laden parade float covered with girls in shimmering evening gowns. They flashed beauty pageant smiles at us, waved graciously and blew us kisses with gloved hands, while we tried not to look like complete idiots.

JOKES FOR THE JOHN

Asian bathrooms are different from ours. The toilets are challenging. Many are simply porcelain holes in the floor with two raised foot pads. Americans are not accustomed to this at all, but after all these years, Dave and I now prefer a modified Asian style. Here are a few select vignettes about toilets. Don't worry, these stories have been "sanitized" for your protection.

THAILAND: There was one foreigner we met who encountered his first squat toilet in Thailand. He came out of his hotel room, exclaiming, "There's no crapper in the bathroom! But they have this awesome foot washer..."

Footsteps of a Nomad

NEPAL: Lloyd, our longtime Aussie friend, runs a charity project in a remote village in Nepal. Whenever he visits, he is treated like a rock star because many people in that region have never seen a foreigner before. When Lloyd went to one village meeting, a few curious children followed him everywhere, even on a visit to the outhouse. It was a relief when he was able to shut the door and get a little privacy. He was still in full squat when the decrepit door simply fell off its hinges. Lloyd looked up and realized, to his horror, that his audience had grown. The entire village had gathered outside, and they were all elbowing each other for the best view of his very white butt.

VIETNAM: While visiting Vietnam, we rented a motorbike to tour around the countryside. Somewhere outside of Nha Trang, we blew a tire. There was a little hut beside the road, and the inhabitants were not surprised to see us stranded. In a land where every tire is worn down to treadlessness, a good living can be made by those with a few repair tools.

One member of the family patched our tire while the lady of the house made coffee. (The Vietnamese make fabulous coffee.) Dave wandered around the back of the house looking for the outhouse. He never found one. Coming back, he encountered Grandpa.

"Toilet?" Dave inquired.

The old gentleman grinned toothlessly. He raised one eyebrow and gave him a smirk and a wink as his skinny arm waved across the countryside. "Vietnam!" he cackled.

We guessed he was not much of a patriot....

JAPAN: In 2008 the airline put us up in a Tokyo hotel on a long layover. The bathroom made me feel like I was a visitor from a poor, developing country. The toilet didn't have a flush lever or toilet paper. Instead, on one side of the throne, there was a small handheld computerized keypad. It was all in Japanese, so I just started pushing buttons.

Amazing things happened. It was like a car wash for the human body. I was steamed, washed, and blown dry automatically. Water pressure, direction, and temperature controls were at my fingertips. Everything was automated, including the flush. I'd never seen a toilet with a remote before! It was like a video game. They are beginning to market these wonders in America now. I'm waiting for the price to come down....

NEPAL, 1990: Here's a wonder of a different sort. High in the Himalayas, the mountain village of Chomrong is a five-day hike from anywhere. To get there, we faced steep uphill climbs of over 2,000 feet at a time, followed by exhausting downhill treks into deep chasms, and right back up again. It was incredibly beautiful, but an extreme physical challenge. After days on the trail, we came to this little village. It was pristine and utterly traditional, with no electricity or any other conveniences of the modern world. We stayed in an inn that seemed as old as the mountains themselves. Its walls were constructed of hand-cut stone, built in the traditional way, without mortar. The beds were hand-hewn planks topped with crude, funky mattresses, and the furniture was all handmade, often using pegs instead of nails.

We went to the outdoor toilets, expecting a typical outhouse. When I opened the door, I gasped in astonishment. There, in all its splendor, was a genuine porcelain squat toilet, set into a real cement floor. There was one for the ladies and one for the gents. Porters had carried those toilets, on their backs, for a week, up and down mountains, just for the convenience of we finicky Westerners! And others had carried all those bags of cement! All the way back, as I huffed and puffed along the trail, I kept thinking about those toilets...

WHEN LETTERS FALL OFF HOTEL SIGNS:

NATURAL SWIMMING FOOL

FREE POO

THE STRANGEST MENU WE EVER READ

Misspelled and garbled English used to be common in Asia. Dinnertime became entertaining, especially in restaurants, simply by reading the menu. In many areas, this is no longer true. English is now very widely spoken. Kids are taught English in school, and they're eager to learn it. There are also plenty of foreign English teachers around who can spell-check menus in return for a free meal. Computers also correct many a mistake. English rapidly is becoming the universal language. We are all fortunate to be born English speakers!

China is the one place where you can still find some amusingly rogue English translation attempts. Lately, this has been made even funnier by poorly written computer programs that translate one word at a time, with no correct context. Below are the best examples of this we've ever seen. These actual dish names were all copied from one unique restaurant menu in Guangzhou China. Bon Appétit!

Baptist puffy fish slide

Foot Chess club

Picked up the beef

Braised codfish rooting pillar

U.S. great intestinal first

Mexican beef stone

Crispy fried ketchup

Iron gel gel pork

Thai fans bacteria Baptist bass

Sandy Sticks bamboo pothead

Baptist eel pieces of ice

Thai capsules of bone

Bamboo fungus gall

Food money

Rugby Cornish broken to force the beans dry

Gold ring ding tape

Do not pull all kinds of intestinal

Cabbage grain porridge

Burned bones

French tart baked department

Salt corner

Thai fans bacteria diphead

(And my all-time favorite:) Winter is really unfair bass Thai dip

By Diana McLeod

DAVE WAS IN THE DOG HOUSE - IN CHIHUAHUA!

MEXICO, 1985: A night that will live in infamy....

It was our last night in Mexico. We had tickets on the 6:00 a.m. express train across the border to El Paso, Texas. If we missed that train, we would miss our flight home. Dave and I were dead broke, with only about $6.00 left in our wallets, and this was in the days before we owned credit cards. If we were late, we would be stranded in Mexico, hungry and penniless.

We were staying at a small guesthouse. I was feeling a bit ill, so I went directly to our room. Dave wanted to hang out in the park and play the guitar he had purchased in Patzcuaro. He promised to come back in about half an hour, just at nightfall.

I dozed off. When I awoke, it was the middle of the night, and he still hadn't returned. My clock said 2:00 a.m. I thought it must be wrong, so I wandered out to the hotel's front desk.

Their clock said 3:00 a.m. Even worse! Their clock was incorrect, it later turned out, but at the time, it threw me into full panic mode. I was convinced something terrible must have happened to Dave. Somebody had rolled him for the guitar and thrown his lifeless body into the bushes. After all, Dave bought the tickets for the 6 a.m. train. He couldn't possibly have chosen to stay out that late... Shaking with dread, I had the desk clerk call the police.

Two Mexican cops arrived quickly. Crying and utterly freaked out, I tried to explain my emergency in Spanish.

The cops just laughed at me. "Oh, no, no, Señora," they said patronizingly, "A thousand to one, your husband is drunk. We see this kind of thing all the time. Don't waste our time! Call us back if he doesn't show up in the morning."

"Impossible!" I said. I begged them to listen, and I was trying to explain about the train, when Dave came stumbling in, drunk, on the arms of two Mexican guys. They were all singing. The cops just looked at them, sniggered, and rolled their eyes at me. They shot me disgusted, pitying glances as if this was all my fault.

The Mexican guys took one look at the cops and the outraged, panicked wife, and dumped Dave like a hot tamale. They took off quickly before the cops turned their attention on them.

Dave realized what was happening as soon as he saw the police. In fact, it was a good thing the cops were there because I was about ready to murder him myself. He knew he had been very irresponsible and was apologetic, but he was in the doghouse for quite a long time. I certainly had no pity for his morning hangover!

It turned out that he had been having an excellent time. The two local guys had invited him to the El Presidenté Hotel, Chihuahua's fanciest new high-rise, which had a swanky rooftop bar. Dave was called up to the stage to entertain the crowd. He was well received, and he got many free drinks. He was having so much fun that he was surprised when "last call" was announced at two a.m.

We made the train early the next morning. But ever since then, whenever I hear the word "Chihuahua" I think of those two cops and a very, very small but serious doghouse!

MEXICAN STYLE

Mexico City built a new airport in about 2008. Despite all of the up-to-date equipment and technology, the old Mexican mañana attitude still prevails.

Later that year, after we checked in for our return flight to the U.S., we searched for our information on the airport monitors. It wasn't listed. Puzzled, Dave asked an airline official, who told him, with a very solemn, matter-of-fact tone, "Oh no, Señor, those are yesterday's flights. We put this morning's flights up this afternoon."

WORST TOURIST ATTRACTION EVER

Guatemala, 1985: On our second trip to Latin America, we visited the famous Mayan ruins of Tikal. On the way, we stopped at the lakeside town of Flores and we took a boat tour around the lake that afternoon. Our captain stopped at several points of interest, including an abandoned water park. Fancy concrete waterslides had recently been built, but then were left to decay in the advancing jungle.

Our boatman offered to haul water up so that we could enjoy the slides. Other locals were also willing to help. They were incredibly friendly. They had several large buckets, which they filled and carried on their shoulders while they climbed the high steps, just for us, which we thought was astonishingly kind.

The boys poured the water so that we could slide down the chutes into the lake. We both had several runs down the biggest waterslides, which was a lot of fun, and we enjoyed ourselves very much. The villagers seemed to take great pleasure in our amusement. Afterward, we thanked them profusely for their help.

Only later did we find out the truth about the water park closure. A crocodile had devoured a young patron. Apparently, our new "friends" were hoping for a repeat performance—with Gringos as bait!

By Diana McLeod

A "SKIMPY" TALE

Sometimes, you just can't help it. No matter how careful you are as a tourist, you can find yourself in situations where you are just inappropriate, or in the wrong place at the wrong time.

On our last day in Malaysia, we decided to pamper ourselves. Dave and I spent two nights at the "Sama-Sama" luxury hotel at the airport in Kuala Lumpur since we were starting the ordeal of flying home the following day, and we wanted to get the best night's sleep possible.

That morning, I planned to sunbathe at the gorgeous pool, which was located on the bottom floor of the hotel, one floor below the lobby. After breakfast, I donned my swimsuit, wrapped a semi-transparent scarf around my bare shoulders and back, and headed for the elevator. I thought that my long "skirtini" with the modesty scarf would be suitable enough for the elevator, even in a conservative country, so off I went.

The elevator opened into the conference hall of the hotel. The pool entrance was off to the right, on one side of the ballroom. When the doors pinged open, I was surprised to see that the venue was packed, despite the early hour. Several hundred people were seated facing the elevators, and every eye was on me.

To my horror, I realized that I had innocently walked right into a Muslim prayer convention in my bathing suit. Every man wore a stark black robe and a white Muslim prayer cap. Every woman was fully veiled. And there I was, the brazenly overexposed American...

Sidestepping, I headed for the pool with all the dignity I could muster. Talk about being underdressed for the occasion!

HOW TO SPELL CORN FLAKES

corn flacks
corn flicks
corn flags
corn flecks
corn fakes

STRANGE SIGNS OVERSEAS:

from a Christmas card sent by a supplier in Nepal: Beast wishes!

The unfortunate name of a small sandwich shop: TITBITS

A laundry sign: Drop your pants here!

A sign in an Indian railway station: DO NOT SPIT
                                           HERE AND THERE

A sign at a border checkpoint:

    Let us not produe, perfuse or peculate narcotig druks!

"Better service than you'd expect"

Delhi Police; Better late than never!

Humpty Dumpy Kids School

the Believe B.S. Gem Company

Antiques made to Order

Handicrap

MORE MENU OPTIONS

stubborn farm vegetables	noodies
Shrimp tales	Sauteed Lamp
chicken spit with peanut sauce	Coca Coal
fish cutelet	river soup
humburger	pigtails stewed
banana flammable	Fried crap
Pain cakes	Wild Bacteria Soup
slices of hum	Cantaloop
filet mingo	Fried Selfish
fanatic chicken	Chinese bumpling
mind soup	Fried bean crud
Three big Bombs	Wanton Soup
Oyster sauce explodes the duck	Chicken with herpe
Tomatoes cooked with species	

By Diana McLeod

UNIQUE SITUATIONS

YOUNG, NAIVE AND STUPID!

THE DUMBEST SITUATION I HAVE EVER GOTTEN MYSELF INTO (AND OUT OF)

HOLY CRAP! I was on a fishing boat, in Mexico, down in the cabin with the brawny, mustachioed captain. He grabbed me, stuck me on his lap, and wouldn't let go. When I pushed him away, he just grinned. I was alone and defenseless. Fighting him was out of the question—he would have simply roared with laughter. No, I was going to have to talk my way out of this situation. But how could I possibly do that? I had only been studying Spanish for two weeks!

OK, let me back up and explain how I could possibly have gotten myself into this much trouble. It was on our very first trip outside of the U.S. We were staying at the beachside village of San Blas, Mexico, and we planned to have a beach barbeque with some friends. Unfortunately, when we went into town for supplies, the market was already closed for the day. Dave sent me down to the pier, all by myself, to see if I could get fish from the boats while he went to buy the beer. I protested, arguing that down by the docks wasn't the safest place for a woman, but Dave assured me I'd be fine. And, because I was young, naive, and on my first foreign adventure, I believed him.

I encountered a young man who spoke a little English and asked him if any of the boats had brought in shrimp. He asked several fishermen, who pointed out one boat that had just returned with a catch. It was lashed to several others. I was going to have to climb over three other boats in order to get out there. My "guide" helped me cross the slimy, stinky decks and step aboard.

My "friend" hollered down below, and the captain, who was a husky, handsome devil, invited us in. I explained that I needed to buy shrimp. He took one look at me, swept me into his arms, sat me on his lap, and said something that might have translated to, "But there is no need to buy any fish. You're welcome to have dinner with me, my dear."

The captain gestured to a large pot boiling away on his greasy stove with unnamable tentacles, fins and fish heads squelching around inside it. He winked at the other guy. I panicked as I realized what they were thinking: I was the catch of the day, and they were going to share me, along with the stew.

This pirate was built like a tank. If I had struggled, he would have found it adorable. Talking my way out of this mess was the only solution, but I only knew about two hundred Spanish words! I said a quick prayer to the God of Spanish vocabulary.

Luckily for me, he asked how old I was, which gave me an idea. I told him. Then I counted the years and did some quick mental calculations. *"Tengo siete niños"* I sighed. (I have seven children.) *"Tienen hambre."* (They are hungry). I also told him that I was *Católica* (another bald-faced lie, but I hoped Jesus would forgive and protect me from randy sea captains) To add emphasis, I waggled my finger under his nose and said, "No no no no NO!" (I did not tell him that my "children" were really a bunch of traveling hippies having a decadent beach party.)

His mustachios drooped in disappointment. In Mexico, where family always comes first, being a "mother" changed everything. He set me down reluctantly. *"No hay camarones,"* he said, *"pero hay mucho pescados."* (I don't have shrimp, but there are lots of fish). He opened the hold and—holy mackerel, there were a lot of mackerel in there.

"That would be perfect, thank you," I said. He got out a very large plastic bag and stuffed it with at least two kilos of mackerel.

"How much do I owe you, sir?" I asked.

"There is no need to pay me," he smiled.

"But I have money. I'll be glad to pay you!"

He considered this, smiling. "No," he finally said. "This is for the children. But you may pay me with one kiss, (he pointed demurely at his cheek), one kiss for my friend, and the flowers from your hair."

I pulled out the little sprig of wildflowers I'd been wearing and handed it to him. He sniffed them and sighed theatrically, and we all laughed. I gave him his kiss, and the one for his friend, then got the hell out of there before they could change their minds.

As I left, he gave a great belly laugh and called something out after me, which I couldn't understand. I think he was trying to tell me that I was "the one who got away."

The mackerel were delicious. The "children" enjoyed them.

Ladies, don't ever, ever, do anything this stupid when you travel. If I hadn't come up with the right B.S., I'd still be on that boat!

By Diana McLeod

THE DAY I GOT IN TROUBLE AT THE KATHMANDU AIRPORT

Dave and I bought a cache of old coins at an antique dealer's shop in Kathmandu. There were over two thousand of them. Most were in denominations of one rupee, now out of date and no longer legal tender. I thought they would make fun gifts for our customers. The dealer told us a few coins in the collection were considerably more valuable than others, but we could buy the whole pile for two rupees each. (I should also explain I had no way of knowing the exact age of the coins because the dates were stamped in Nepalese numerals.)

When I packed for the flight home, I threw the coins in my big knapsack, right on top. I knew they would set off the metal detector at the airport, so I placed them where I could retrieve them easily. I even remember thinking that the coins would draw attention away from some other potentially more sensitive objects stashed in the bottom of my knapsack.

Sure enough, they did set off the metal detector and a customs officer was summoned, a serious-looking older gentleman who acted like an official of high rank. He pawed through my coins while I waited impatiently.

He grabbed one coin and inspected it carefully. His eyes narrowed, and he gave me a chillingly stern look. "Madam," he said imperiously, "this coin is over one hundred years old. It is worth up to a thousand dollars to collectors. It is forbidden to take antiques out of Nepal. You, Madam, are a coin smuggler!"

At his words, armed guards around the customs area perked up and raised their weapons. Too late, I remembered the dealer's comments about the age and value of some of the coins. I was in trouble. The question was, how to handle the situation?

I had my *baksheesh* money handy. (*Baksheesh* is the term in Asia for bribes.) Ninety-five percent of officials in these countries live on bribery. It is expected that an officer will overlook a minor transgression as long as there is enough money dangled in front of his nose. You can even haggle with them over the amount to pay. Would that plan work now?

The official was looking me straight in the eye, trying to determine if I was an innocent tourist or a criminal smuggler. He must have seen the genuine expression of bewilderment on my face when he found the valuable antique. I gazed back at him, trying to size him up. I decided that this was the one official in all of Kathmandu too patriotic and proud to take a bribe. He would throw the book at me if I tried.

I could not play the part of the stupid tourist, either. He would see through that. So I started to laugh. I explained to him why I had bought the coins. I said I found them in the old section of Kathmandu, at a market notorious for tourist rip-offs, and that I never dreamed I had bought anything worth real money.

"Didn't the dealer tell you that some of the coins were old?" he asked.

"Sure!" I answered. "The dealer swore they were. 'Oh yes, madam, very very old, from mountain, from Tibet!'" (This is a classic B.S. line.) "Of course, I didn't believe a word the guy said!"

I chuckled, trying to relax and look amused. "Do you mean to tell me that I actually met an honest dealer in Basantapur Market, who sold me something that was really worth something?" I asked. "I had no idea! I even thought half of these coins were repros. I can't believe it is possible to buy anything valuable at Basantapur! Look, I didn't mean to break the law. I truly did pay only two rupees each for them. If they are a hassle, I don't want them; you can have them."

A few of the security officers lowered their guns and snickered. The old man hesitated for one more moment, as my heart nearly seized up in my chest. Then he relaxed and nodded. He believed me! My cynicism was credible. Next, he revealed his own honesty. "Madam, you can keep most of these coins," he said. "There are only a few that cannot, by law, leave the country. They are too old. But they are still your property. Is there someone you could call, who can come to the airport and pick them up for you?"

I was impressed. Most customs officers would have confiscated them—right into their own pockets. I didn't want to bother any of my Nepalese friends with these coins. They might actually be valuable, but I had no idea what to do with them. Also, time was getting short. I did not want to miss my plane!

"I would be happy to donate these coins to the Chhatrapati Free Medical Clinic," I said with a smile. "I don't know if they can sell them or not, but I know they could use the money."

The official beamed back at me. Now, we were friends. "It shall be done!" he agreed. "I will see to it personally. But now, we must pick out the coins."

I glanced at my watch. "I appreciate that, sir, but there isn't time. I will have to leave them all or I may miss my flight."

"Nonsense!" he cried. "These coins are your rightful property, and you shall have them. Besides," he stated proudly, "I am the Chief of Customs at this airport. I have the authority to hold the plane!"

I cringed at the prospect of holding up a whole jet full of people just because of my stupid coins, but it was no use arguing with him. He was determined. He snapped his fingers and subordinates came running. Security guards put down their guns and sorted coins. I was also allowed to help. I soon learned the difference between the newer coins and the old ones. In the end, only about fifteen coins were culled from the group, and the rest were back in my bag.

The official shook my hand, and I bowed to him gratefully, murmuring "Namaskar," which is the special form of the greeting "Namaste." It is reserved only for honored individuals and very high officials. In this case, I sincerely meant it.

By Diana McLeod

THE COLOMBIAN BIMBO

Here's one of the weirdest airport situations I have ever encountered. It took place in about 1993. I was flying solo to Bangkok, with an unbearably long layover in Seoul, Korea. I was in the transit lounge when a curious English announcement over the P.A. system caught my attention:

"If you speak Spanish, please contact the agent at the information booth. We need your help."

I needed a diversion, so I wandered over to the information counter to see what was going on. I confessed that my Spanish wasn't proficient, but nobody cared—I was the only person who had responded to their call. They sent me over to immigration where two harried officers were trying to deal with a crazy woman from South America.

What a piece of work she was; a bleached blonde, with a figure that had been surgically enhanced in strategic places. She was wearing all of the streetwalker classics: a leopard-print skin-tight mini dress with a plunging neckline, a rabbit fur vest, and a pair of six-inch, bedazzled Lucite platform high heels. Her purse was a very costly designer brand, and her jewelry was a combination of tawdry rhinestone chandelier junk and genuine gold chains.

I had about two seconds to take all this in before she started yelling at me in rapid-fire Spanish. It took some time to get her calmed down while I explained how terrible my Spanish was. I then had to persuade her to be quiet while I talked to the two officials.

One spoke some halting English. He explained the situation. She had flown to Korea, unaware that people from her country couldn't enter Korea without a visa. She didn't even seem to understand what a visa was.

"What country is she from?" I asked.

"Colombia," came the answer.

Great, I thought, *I'm probably dealing with Pablo Escobar's girlfriend!* She looked like just the type a drug lord would keep around, and that would explain the way she was acting. In Colombia she would be able to bribe or threaten her way past any legal inconvenience. But in conservative Korea, her very presence was causing an uproar. People were staring at her, openmouthed, as they walked past us.

The poor immigration official bore the brunt of her wrath. Luckily, he was mercifully oblivious to the meaning of all of her Colombian swear words. He said he could not offer her a standard visa, but he could issue her a temporary stamp if the police in her country confirmed that she didn't have a criminal record. He wanted to put me on the phone with the Medellin police headquarters!

It took about a half an hour to establish a phone connection. In the meantime, she talked my ear off. Although she spoke too quickly for me to understand everything, I think she said she'd first tried to bribe the officers and was insulted when they wouldn't take her money. I kept trying to tell her she would have a better chance of success with them if she would shut up and behave herself.

At last, the operator contacted the Medellin police. The phone connection was terrible, with a severe echo, and I struggled with the Colombian accent. I read them her name and passport number, but I'm not sure they understood or believed me at all. Did they even recognize that Korea was a nation? In the end, it seemed this woman didn't have a criminal record, but I couldn't be sure. She did not present a security risk to Korea as far as I could tell, so I decided my best guess at translation was good enough.

The officials beamed in relief when I told them the news, and they granted her the seventy-two-hour visa. I told her she could stay in Korea for three days but NO LONGER. I could tell she wasn't listening to my warning, and was thankful I would be long gone when she overstayed her welcome and set off another crisis.

As for Miss Colombia, she sailed off through Immigration without acknowledging my help or thanking the two officials who had so clearly bent the rules for her. The men were quite embarrassed, and thanked me profusely by bowing repeatedly. As for me, it made a boring layover quite entertaining, and I was glad to help those poor guys get rid of such an embarrassing problem!

HAPPY DRUNKEN EASTER!

SULAWESI, INDONESIA, about 1998. We were really out in the boondocks! Our destination was the Tancoco Nature Preserve, in the far corner of the island of Sulawesi, where we hoped to see Tarsiers (the world's smallest primates) in their natural jungle habitat. The only "civilization" near the park was a small fishing village at the end of a long dirt road, and the only way to get there by "public transportation" was in the back of the daily fish truck.

As we were waiting for our glorious transport, an epic Indonesian monsoonal rainstorm began. It was like having a bucket dumped over our heads. Some local men noticed how drenched we were, and invited us to take shelter at their house across the street. It was Easter Sunday, and they were Christians who were taking the day off. (I suspect their wives had all gone to church while they stayed home.) We quickly made friends, and it didn't take long before they decided to turn our chance encounter into a party. One of them jumped on a motorbike, zoomed off, and returned triumphantly with an unmarked bottle of *arak* rice liquor. *Arak* is homemade moonshine, and it goes down like liquid sandpaper mixed with kerosene. Consuming this stuff first thing in the morning is not recommended!

By Diana McLeod

Despite our protests, our hosts insisted we join them. Reluctantly, we took one drink, out of politeness, and the devastatingly potent stuff did its evil work.

Dave then made a nearly fatal mistake. He discovered that our host, who was quite a character, was ethnically part Chinese; his family had come to Indonesia sometime in the distant past. Dave taught him how to say the Mandarin toast "*Ganbei,*" which means "bottoms up." You can't make this toast without downing the entire glass. Our friend, seizing on the knowledge, repeatedly refilled our glasses, yelling "*Ganbei!*" Since we were the idiots who taught it to him, we couldn't refuse his generosity. We toasted each other, downed our shots, and steeled ourselves for the inevitable consequences.

I was soon hoping for something to put in our stomachs besides alcohol. Lunch arrived, steaming hot, from the kitchen: spicy barbecued dog meat smothered in hot chilies.

Oh dear! I had seen these dogs for sale in the market. People in Sulawesi eat many things that would horrify most Americans. At least they didn't serve up stewed fruit bat, which is rumored to be vile beyond belief. My revulsion for eating dog clashed with my good manners. Our new friends were very hospitable and we did not wish to embarrass them. I reminded myself firmly that these were wild dogs, not somebody's pets, and that we eat plenty of other domestic animals and think nothing of it.

In the end, I took a few bites and I found it terrible. It tasted like bear meat—greasy, gamey and gross. I excused myself from eating more because the chilies were too spicy for me (also true), and I downed some more *arak* to get the taste out of my mouth.

By the time the fish truck arrived, Dave and I were thoroughly wasted. We grabbed our backpacks and climbed onto the back of the truck with about ten locals. The open-backed truck was loaded with large barrels full of fish and very fishy seawater. Planks were placed across the tops of the open casks for people to sit on. It was the funkiest mode of public transportation we had ever taken, especially since the stinking water sloshed all over us every time the truck hit a bump. I remember singing, guffawing, and nearly falling off the truck as we lurched wildly along the rough dirt road. Dave and I were the morning's entertainment for our fellow riders.

It took at least fourteen woozy hours for us to finally sober up. Tancoco, when we finally got there, was amazing, but we never did see a Tarsier. We were simply too hung over to get up before dawn, when the nocturnal creatures usually come out of hiding.

What a crazy Easter Sunday morning!

TEA FOR TWO—A CURIOUS TALE OF THE INDIAN EMBASSY

KATHMANDU, 2003. Getting a visa stamp for India in your passport is a real pain in the ass. Even here in America, if you try to call the Indian Embassy, you get stuck on hold while you listen to raised voices shouting in Hindi. Then, after twenty minutes of waiting, they hang up on you. If you need to get your visa in Nepal, you have to slog all the way over to the Indian Embassy and wait in line for hours. It is an infuriating process. After filling out reams of papers, you stand in line "A" for several hours, while the queue creeps infinitesimally slowly forward, only to be told, when you get to the front, that you have to wait in line B *before* you stand in line A.

People get frustrated and angry, but the Indians never change. They do things their way, and there is nothing, absolutely nothing, anyone can do to speed up the ordeal.

One year in Kathmandu, I was yet again a victim of this process. I bemoaned my fate but had no choice. Arriving at the Embassy, the queues were already growing long. By the time I had made it to line A, things were moving even slower than usual. A couple of hotheaded Australians in the line behind me were making loud, rude comments. Looking at my watch, I became afraid that soon the Indians would break for their usual two-hour lunch.

At last I got to the head of the line. Sitting down at the official's desk, I hoped for a quick stamp. He stared at my passport; then he stared at me. "Madam," he said dubiously, "you do not look your age. Not at all. This passport says that you are 48 years old! There are no wrinkles on your face. Not one!" (It was the truth; my face didn't wrinkle until I was in my mid-fifties).

This was bad. Was the official implying that my passport had been altered? Did he think I was presenting a faked document? My stomach churned with sudden nervousness. I needed that visa!

He rang a little bell, and a steward appeared. "We will take tea," he ordered.

I sat uncomfortably while he asked me a few casual questions about my travel experiences. The tea service appeared, and the servant poured while the official offered me a little plate of cookies. Politely accepting one, I tried to keep the look of bewilderment off my face. I felt a bit like Alice in Wonderland, who, having fallen down the rabbit hole, was having tea with the Mad Hatter.

The officer took a sip of his tea and then leaned in towards me. "My wife is obsessed with wrinkles," he explained. "Please tell me; what is your beauty secret? I would very much like to ask your advice."

I was stunned. Glancing surreptitiously at the line behind me, I felt the wrath of three dozen sets of eyes. (They could all see me having tea). Most of the visa applicants had been waiting in the hot sun for hours, without food or drink. I'd better think of something to say, and quickly! But I had no secrets! Most beauty products seem to me to not be worth the rigamarole and expense cosmetic companies con women into.

Taking a sip of tea, I told him one suggestion I have long believed. "The best way to avoid wrinkles is to use a small amount of soap. It is a harsh substance that dries out the skin. Tell your wife to use as little as possible, and only on those areas that really need it. Leave the natural oils on the face, where they belong."

He clapped his hands with delight. "This is wonderful," he cried. "You are right! Too much soap! And my wife buys all these moisturizers to keep her face from drying out. What marvelous advice! I can't thank you enough! The best part is that your beauty secret is free," he crowed, giving me a dazzling smile. "Everyone else's advice is expensive. Thank you so much!"

I wanted to ask him for my visa stamp right away, but I was afraid to be impolite. So I sat there, squirming in my chair while he offered me seconds on tea and cakes. When I declined, he insisted, so I accepted. He chatted quite candidly about his marriage, which was a happy one, although his wife must have been completely neurotic about aging. He asked me what I thought of his country, and I gave India a rave review (of course). I left out my opinion of Indian bureaucracy, which was getting lower by the minute!

At last, the tea service was cleared away, and we were back to business. My treasured visa was stamped in my passport. The official gave me a vigorous handshake and sent me on my way. Sheepishly making my way down the length of that angry line of foreigners, I half expected them to start throwing rocks at me. Next time, I decided, I would bring a basketful of drinks and snacks to share with my fellow applicants!

Starting in 2016, India finally put a visa-on-arrival application form on-line. While this may seem like an improvement, it took a friend of mine fifty-two attempts to get hers approved.

MEXICAN ROCK AND ROLL

SAN BLAS, MEXICO, 1983. Electric guitar and drums pulsed through the languid tropical night. Dave and I had to investigate. Why were we hearing live rock music, on a weekday evening, on the backstreets of a sleepy little Mexican fishing village?

It was easy to find the band, which was rehearsing in an open garage. We introduced ourselves as fellow musicians, and our new friends warmly welcomed us to join the jam session. (This was back in the days when we were eking out a living playing in a bar band in Vermont. We hadn't started Tradewinds yet.)

Musicians everywhere have a "language" all their own. Soon we were all catching the groove and sharing songs and guitar riffs. The bandleader even invited us to a party on Friday night. It sounded cool, and we were always up for a musical adventure. He said he would pick us up.

Right on time, on Friday, a ramshackle old truck, piled high with sound equipment and band members, pulled into the driveway of our hotel. We scrambled into the back of the truck, along with everyone else, and headed out of town. On the way, they made a brief stop at a local gas station where one of the guys did a furtive deal with somebody. We were suddenly nervous. Drugs? No, the item being purchased was a large jerry can of gasoline, which was promptly loaded into the back with everything else.

After cruising down the coastal highway for about ten miles, the truck turned and headed up into the hills, bouncing along a narrow dirt road. Where were we going? What if we were driving so far we would end up needing extra gasoline? The bandleader explained everything, but our Spanish was too weak at that time to get the gist of everything he said.

We finally reached a scruffy little village called Las Palmas (the palms). It was barely big enough to have a village *zócalo* (town square) with a modest church and a couple of little shops bordering it. The truck stopped right in the middle of the plaza, and the band members began to unload sound equipment. Puzzled, I asked them about the party. (I had assumed it would be at someone's house).

"*Si, si,*" replied our friend. "*Es una Fiesta.*"

Another bystander observed my confusion. He smiled and said, in English, "You Americans rock-and-rollers are going to play for the town." He pointed to a poster tacked to the side of a light pole. It wasn't going to be just a party after all. It was going to be a Fiesta with a capital F. And Dave and I were the featured act!

Oh. We were going to have one interesting evening!

The band set up the equipment. This "rock concert" was going to be held in the most unlikely of places. Chickens were wandering casually through the square. On one corner of the plaza, a little mountain

By Diana McLeod

rivulet was flowing over the cobblestones, slowly eroding the main street. People squatted beside the water, washing their dinner dishes. Nearby bushes were draped with people's laundry laid out to dry. The electricity was a bare wire coming out of a tree. One band member gingerly grabbed the live ends and attached them to other bare wires on a funky-looking homemade junction box. We were going to be lucky if we survived this gig!

Our "audience" consisted of a half dozen old men in sombreros and serapes, village women draped in shawls, and little bare-assed kids. Was this a rock and roll crowd? What was going on here? Later, as we neared "show time," people began to turn out. Somebody had been out doing some advertising. Vehicles crammed with eager teenagers from adjoining communities appeared, and I began to relax. Maybe this would be a real dance after all.

The five-gallon jerry can reappeared. As it turned out, it was not full of gasoline —it was full of party juice. The furtive "deal" had been to purchase illegal homemade coconut alcohol. This stuff was rocket fuel! Grown men gasped as they swallowed their shots. One guy filled his cup, ran for the bushes, retched, came back out, and got right back in line for more!

By the time the local band had finished their first set, the young men were sufficiently lubricated to lose some of their inhibitions, and they were asking the women to dance. Young girls wearing scandalously tight jeans and high heels teetered around on the broken cobblestones with their drunken partners.

Little kids danced with each other. Whenever the band played a slow song, older couples joined in. Almost everyone enjoyed the music, except for a couple of diehard old coots in the back row.

Then Dave and I were on. We found ourselves challenged by the funky instruments, a drummer whose ability to follow cues was less than optimal, and the squealing pig who ran through the sound equipment, almost knocking over the mike stands. I'm sure we had been advertised as American pop stars (ridiculous). Of course, we didn't meet the high expectations, but we pulled out a few rocking classics the Mexicans loved. One young girl in astoundingly tall high-heeled shoes came up to Dave to make a request. *"Disculpé Señor,"* she asked politely, *"Conocé usted,* 'Another One Bites the Dust'?"

The party swelled until the *zócalo* was packed with dancers (and dogs and chickens, who seemed right at home in the middle of the gyrating crowd). The devastating effect of the firewater on some of the partygoers was growing increasingly obvious. A tin cup was shoved in my face. "Hey, try this, Señorita!" one of our musician friends grinned. I was dubious but my drunken amigo insisted. He explained that if the stuff was heavily cut with warm coconut milk, it was safe "for girls." I have to say it was one of the most delicious drinks I have ever tasted.

At the end of their second set, the band put us back on "stage." Now it was their turn to hit the jerry can. By the time we wrapped up the show at midnight, only a few dancers were still on their feet. The band had disappeared (probably sleeping it off at someone's house). The driver of the truck was obviously not going anywhere. He was sprawled across the front seat, deep in an alcoholic coma. How in hell were we going to get back to town?

We had to get back to San Blas; not only did we have an early bus to catch, but our friend Jean had no idea where we were. She would panic in the morning if we weren't there. Out of options, we decided to walk down the mountain road, even though we were about twenty kilometers from our hotel. The full moon streamed through the jungle, providing me just enough light to see the coral snake I almost stepped on! It took half an hour to reach the main highway on foot, and it was already well past midnight. If we couldn't flag down a passing vehicle, it was going to be a long, miserable hike.

In the end, we managed to get a ride, but our driver had been to another party. He veered into the ditch at forty miles an hour and nearly got us all killed. Luckily, he somehow miraculously managed to regain control of his vehicle and steer it back out onto the road. Crossing himself solemnly, he slowed down after that.

If this story has a moral, it is this: if you're going with locals to an unknown place or event, be sure to pack survival gear: a flashlight, water ...and aspirin. Hitchhiking is always dangerous ...but the adventure is often worth the risk.

By Diana McLeod

NATURALLY WILD

THE ZIPLOCK MONKEY AND OTHER MONKEY BUSINESS

Monkeys in Asia are very smart, very bold, and occasionally vicious. We usually spot them in forested areas, but many monkey troops these days have adapted perfectly to urban environments. We've even been cautioned not to leave our windows unlocked—on the sixth floor!!

Indian cities are plagued with them. Roving gangs of street-smart monkeys fearlessly invade urban neighborhoods. They swarm over the rooftops, shimmy across power lines, and steal everything that isn't nailed down. I've seen an hour-long T.V. special on one of the Jaipur tribes, which showed monkeys breaking into a restaurant that often supplies us with lunch. The famous old LMB Hotel bakery was practically torn to shreds by the marauders, and the culprits were caught red-handed on video, gulping sweets and making one hell of a mess.

IN THE WILD. We visited a rainforest sanctuary in Sulawesi, Indonesia. Our jungle guide had just completed a stint as a hired observer for a three-month university study. A large troop of Crested Black Macaques up in the forest canopy recognized him right away and came out of the trees to greet him. He offered them some food and let them borrow a little piece of mirror. The monkeys were intrigued with their own images. They tried to sniff the monkey in the mirror and groped behind the glass, to touch the phantom ape.

Dave and I took tons of pictures as the troop came right up to us. We flipped the video camera screen around so that the monkeys could watch themselves on T.V. They loved it. Several of them even reached out to touch the camera, running their fingers along the edge of the screen, and even delicately adjusting the viewing angle so they could see better. We were very nervous about having wild creatures handle our expensive equipment, but they treated it (and us) with gentle respect and courtesy. (These monkeys were a different breed from the destructive Rhesus Macaques in India. I would never allow *them* near my gear!)

THE ZIPLOCK MONKEY STORY. Here's my favorite monkey story of all time: Trena (our manager) and I visited Kathmandu together on her first trip to Asia when she was only twenty-one. I took her to see Swayambhunath (A.K.A. the monkey temple of Kathmandu.) The temple and its grounds always swarm with big Rhesus Macaques, and we've had several encounters with them over the years. One monkey even stole Dave's eyeglasses right off his face. (He wrestled them back.)

While Trena and I were walking around the temples, she paused to change the film on her old SLR camera. She set her bag of the finished film down just for a moment, and a big male Macaque came along and swiped it. He climbed to the top of a temple *chorten* (a type of shrine) and sat down near the pinnacle to enjoy his prize.

Trena was devastated. All of her treasured pictures and memories were gone! I, however, wasn't about to give up so easily, not without a fight.

Monkey fighting is a mostly a matter of bluff and bluster. Usually it only gets dangerous between rival males. I did my best to be intimidating. I fluffed up my hair and stood as tall as I could, lifting my arms high in the air to show off my claws. I curled back my lips forcefully to fully bare my canine teeth, and hissed loudly. I must have looked ridiculous.

But not to the Macaque. He looked me over appraisingly, seeing an obviously inferior species of monkey, but one who was much larger than he was. He flinched as I jumped up onto the base of the *chorten,* trying to demonstrate my prowess.

He was quite close to me now and I could see the wheels turning in his little monkey brain. Fight or flee? That was the question. But first, what was he actually fighting for? He turned the ziplock over in his hands, trying in vain to determine its contents. When he failed to identify his prize, he swiftly unzipped the plastic zipper (he had apparently opened them before) and stuck his nose in the bag. The smell of camera film did not impress him in the slightest. My adversary gave me a marvelous expression of pure disdain mingled with pity since only a dimwitted ape would desire the contents of the bag. He re-zipped the plastic zipper and dismissively tossed it back to me. The loot wasn't worth the hassle after all. I became human again, thanked him politely, and returned to the ground where I belonged.

Trena gave me a huge smile when I returned victorious, but in this case, not necessarily superior. I must have looked pretty silly climbing monkey-style up the temple *chorten*!

THE SHOESTRING MONKEY. A Russian girl was visiting the famous monkeys of Monkey Forest in Ubud, Bali. As she entered the park, her bright pink sneakers caught the eye of a newborn baby macaque. It jumped away from its mother's arms and went to investigate. As the Russian person stopped to watch, the infant monkey eyed her sneakers and shoelaces curiously. Then he reached out his tiny fingers and, in two astoundingly rapid motions, triumphantly untied both of her shoes.

MONKEY POOL. The famous snow monkeys of Japan are not the only simians that have learned to swim. Macaques in Bali are expert divers and underwater swimmers. It's delightful to watch the little ones disappear underwater, only to emerge on the other side of the pond to ambush their friends. I've seen splashing parties, "cannonballs" and crazy leaps, as youngsters try to shove each other into the water. Older Macaques search for food along the riverbed, surfacing with freshwater clams, which they break open on the rocks.

By Diana McLeod

Calm ocean tide pools attract just many swimmers as freshwater swimming holes. Near Pemuteran, Bali, a large troupe of macaques often swarm the beach at low tide. "Babysitters" supervise as the young ones play in the pool while adults forage for food along the beach. Macaque daycare!

recommended Google search: swimming monkey Bali Images

MY UNDERWATER FRIEND

It is always lovely to be befriended by someone. When that "someone" is a wild, underwater creature, it is a rare and extraordinary event.

This encounter took place years ago in Jamaica where Dave and I were vacationing with friends. Carol and I went snorkeling together, beneath the edge of some cliffs. We were cruising along, in about twenty feet of water, when we saw a five-foot stingray, half buried in sand, on the bottom. When he spotted us, he shook himself off and floated away.

To our surprise, he rose up directly beneath us and followed us as we swam. He maintained our pace, turning as we turned. I remember his wingspan being a bit wider than my outstretched arms. Soon, he was directly beneath me, so near that, if I had reached down, I could have put my hands on his shoulders and taken a ride. The further we went, the surer I became that he wanted me to do this. I wanted to—it was tempting—but I knew this creature has a painful stinger, and I did not want to risk it. He shadowed me for a while longer, and then swam off, disappointed. I realized he must have befriended some local person, and was thus accustomed to interacting with humans and giving them rides.

Carol and I swam off to explore a little sea cave beneath a cliff that had been hollowed out by the surf. We were in water so shallow that we had to be very cautious of running into something sharp or dangerous as the waves sloshed us back and forth between the rocks and the corals. Suddenly, I heard Carol shriek into her snorkel. I turned around and was confronted by a massive eyeball! It was our stingray friend. He had followed us into the cave, at considerable risk to himself, and was within touching distance, watching us. I couldn't imagine this area was part of his normal territory. He had come to find us, and to hang out with us. It was an extraordinary experience!

95

ON THE TRAIL OF THE WILD RHINOCEROS

Chitwan National Park in Nepal is a wild jungle where you can see tigers, rhinoceros and sloth bears in their natural environment. All of those creatures are amazing, but they can easily kill you. In Kathmandu, I encountered a young couple who had just visited the park. Here is their story, followed by my own.

"We didn't have enough money to hire elephants," the couple told me, "so we went deep into the jungle on foot, with a single guide. He told us that, if we saw a rhinoceros, he would throw down his coat. The rhinoceros would stop to sniff it, to identify the unfamiliar smell, because their eyesight isn't very good, which would give us enough time to climb a tree before the rhinoceros charged."

"We didn't take the warning very seriously," the woman added. "We actually thought the guy was just kidding, trying to scare us. But then a rhino came charging out of the underbrush, straight at us! Sure enough, the guide threw down his jacket, and we took off, running for our lives. I've never climbed a tree so fast in my entire life."

"Yeah," her husband agreed, "the rhino soon lost interest in the coat, and he came after us. My wife's butt was only about one foot away from that horn as she scrambled up into the tree."

"We clung to that tree for about an hour, terrified, waiting until the beast went away! He did his best to push it over, too!"

After hearing their story, I vowed that, if we ever visited Chitwan, we would do it only when we had enough money to hire elephants. I booked a tour with an outfit that promised lots of jungle action with guaranteed elephants, and Trena and I went off for a jungle adventure. (Trena is our store manager.)

After a six-hour bus ride halfway across Nepal, we saw a small group of farm animals right beside the road. I almost missed the fact that half of them were wild rhinos! They were grazing among domesticated water buffaloes. We were delighted! We hadn't even left the bus yet, and already we had seen big game.

The park rangers ferried us across the river on small boats. Guides brought us to our bungalows, and then they took us out for our first jungle adventure. But we did not get elephants! Our group was overlapping with another tour, and *they* got the elephants! We went on foot, right into the jungle, just like those other tourists I said I would never imitate....

I was extremely nervous. The guides carried bamboo sticks, which would never stop a rhino or a sloth bear. I scanned the underbrush warily, and I always had several trees picked out, just in case. I began to wonder how many tourists are gored every year. Fortunately, we sighted nothing except a few Siberian Geese. After dinner, we were strictly cautioned to stay on the designated walkways after dark and never roam around the jungle by ourselves. Our guides warned us that tigers occasionally hunted nearby at night.

By Diana McLeod

As the sun went down, silhouetting the trees on the other side of the river, we watched a monkey family settling down for the night in the branches. The littlest ones were still making mischief, munching on flowers and chasing each other around the disgruntled adults. Older animals sat in groups of two or three, quietly grooming each other and socializing. The river was peaceful and still, and it was a lovely place to watch the last light fade as the stars came out. When darkness came, we crowded around the outdoor riverside bar, listening to the inevitable strains of Bob Marley. As I sipped my beer, enjoying the pleasant scene, I thought again about the monkeys in the trees just across the river. Were they studying our social behavior just as we had studied theirs?

The next morning, we took our first elephant ride. The tour company had built a ten-foot tall loading platform for the tourists. We all climbed the stairs, and were boarded onto little square platforms on the elephants' backs. Each person took a side, and we sat back to back, with our legs dangling over the edge of the platform. There was a low railing to prevent anyone from falling off.

As soon as we were seated, each elephant lumbered off in a different direction. The mahouts planned to get as far apart as possible so each could search for wildlife. Our elephant crossed one small stream and moved into an open meadow full of tall elephant grass— prime tiger hunting territory. Our guide spotted an eagle up in a nearby tree. Then we went back to our island, and into the dense jungle, visiting a hidden lily pond that was a watering hole for all the local wild game. Our guide pointed out various animal tracks left in the mud that morning. Unfortunately, when we got there, the pond was deserted. We did not see any big game on that ride, although a few of the other groups did.

We fared a bit better on our river excursion. They took us out in dugout canoes, which were very thin, just barely wide enough for our large tourist butts. Trena and I shared a boat with an older couple, whose combined weight helped to push the sides of the dugout only inches from the water. This was a bit unnerving; Trena had already researched this area on-line and we knew there were marsh mugger crocodiles in the waters around the park. (Marsh mugger crocodiles can grow up to sixteen feet long, and they can become man-eaters). I noticed that our guides did not mention the muggers to the tourists. I was even more surprised when they allowed one woman to stand up in her canoe to take pictures! She could easily have lost her balance and dumped the whole lot of them into the river. I wondered how fast she would have sat down if she had known about the muggers.

We were lucky enough to spot a Gharial, a critically endangered species of crocodile indigenous to India and Nepal. The Gharial has a very distinctively narrow snout, quite unlike a mugger. He was sunning himself on the riverbank, enjoying a warm bed of sand. About eight to ten feet long, he was not quite imposing enough to persuade that silly tourist to sit down.

SWIMMING WITH ELEPHANTS: The next afternoon, after our morning safari, we tourists were invited to go down to the river where the guides washed the elephants. We were told we could wear our bathing suits and swim with the elephants in a secluded, croc-free pool.

Trena was one of the first ones in. She rode into the water, bareback, while I got out the video camera and filmed the whole thing. It was great! Four elephants took the plunge, each with a tourist on board. They got partway into the water, then turned to face the spectators (and the cameras) lining the bank. Lifting up their trunks, they fire-hosed their foreign riders right in the face while everyone else cheered and applauded. Trena got a fine shower. After that, it was a general melee, with elephants shooting water at each other, and at the neighboring riders. There was a mad splashing contest, and then the real fun began. On the command of the mahouts (the elephants' trainers) each elephant waded deep into the river, and casually rolled onto its side. One by one, the hapless tourists slid off right into the water. It was so much fun to watch! The tourists swam around and climbed back on, while the elephants did their best to knock them gently off again. I got the whole thing on video, although I had to duck when one elephant decided to fire-hose me! Luckily, I got the video camera out of the way just in time.

My turn was next. It was a bit odd, feeling my bare legs against the scratchy back of the elephant. It didn't seem like the most stable perch. Trena got on the bank with the camera to document the soaking and dunking that was about to take place.

I got a particularly playful elephant. She sprayed me, first in my face, and then from above. Then she waded into the water and shrugged me off. I swam around and climbed back on again, only to have her gently grab me by the foot and tug me off the other way. The third time was a bit scary for a minute because she rolled onto her side, intending to toss me off her back. But I slid the wrong way and wound up between her legs as she struggled to right herself. I got the heck out of there as fast as I could swim. I didn't want to get kicked by those massive legs! But the mahout, who was with her the whole time, giving her commands, wasn't concerned at all. He trusted her to be gentle, no matter what.

I was struck by how much the elephants enjoyed themselves. They weren't just obeying orders; they were improvising and playing their own games, intelligently interacting with us. The tourist dunking was obviously the high point of their day. Perhaps they relished a little bit of playful revenge for having to ferry tourists around the hot jungle, with uncomfortable howdahs strapped on their backs.

ELEPHANT STAMPEDE: After swimming, it was back to business for our pachyderm friends. The guides strapped the howdahs back on and took us on one more ride for the day. Trena and I got our very own elephant. Unfortunately, this one wasn't one of the mild-mannered animals they had used for the swimming party. She was obviously at odds with her mahout, and he was just as frustrated with her. They weren't getting along at all, and I suspected most of it was his fault. He seemed unnecessarily impatient at times.

As we went deeper into the jungle, far away from the camp, we entered a dense forest environment. The whole time, Trena and I peered into the underbrush, searching for a glimpse of a wild rhinoceros, but we saw nothing, only some egrets roosting in the trees.

At one point, we came into a clearing, and our elephant began to pull out thick clumps of tall grass. The mahout wanted to continue the journey, but she was determined to stop and graze. The mahout's commands grew louder, and she ignored him, even when he thumped his knees behind her ears. He tried hitting her on the forehead, and she rumbled her discontent while we begged him to stop. The second time he smacked her, she got fed up. She reared up and trumpeted, and started thrashing back and forth. One more attempt at discipline and she just lost it. The next thing we knew, she was running madly through the jungle, with us bouncing crazily on her back.

You've probably heard the phrase "an elephant running amok?" Well, this was it. The mahout yelled at us to hang on, because he couldn't stop her in her fury. She blazed through the jungle at full gallop (yes, they can gallop!), and we were at serious risk of being injured by low-hanging tree branches. We weren't in danger of falling off because the howdah had ropes around the sides, but tree limbs were snapping our faces and threatening to decapitate us. We ducked and shoved branches out of the way as best we could.

And what were we doing while this was happening? Screaming? Crying? Nope. For some reason neither of us can explain, this risky situation struck us both as being hilarious. I don't think I've ever laughed harder in my entire life. Dangerous as it was, there was an element of comedy to it that had us both in stitches the whole way. Tears were streaming down our faces as we repeatedly cracked each other up. Hysterical laughter? Perhaps, but I still can't remember it without smiling.

And where, you may ask, did we wind up? Were we hopelessly lost in the jungle? No, our peevish pachyderm, having been denied her snack, went straight to home to dinner. She even graciously let us get off before heading for the main course.

(I do regret that I never did speak to anyone in charge about the mahout's behavior. I wasn't as assertive back then as I am today.)

TIGER! That evening, after socializing with fellow travelers and swilling Nepalese beers at the bar, I decided to call it quits for the night. Trena, on the other hand, wanted to party on. She had gotten to know one of the Nepalese guides, and he had promised to take her out into the jungle to watch the elephants sleeping. I did my motherly best to remind her that "jungle boy" was armed only with a bamboo stick to defend her against wild beasts (including tigers). My warnings went unheeded, of course. As they disappeared into the darkness, I chided myself for being paranoid as I returned to our bungalow and went to bed.

Several hours later, I got up to use the toilet. I was sitting in the bathroom when there was a sound outside the window that froze my blood. I heard a tiger "cough." It's not a roar, but a quiet sound they make when they're hunting. I had never heard that sound before, but I had read about it, and there was no doubt in my mind I had just heard the real thing.

It was close! So close that I soon began to realize he was right outside my concrete shack! I could hear him sniffing around. Then I thought, had he heard me? Was he *hunting me*? I sat frozen, barely breathing, hoping he would go away. The bathroom had only a few latticed holes in the concrete, not enough for him to see through, let alone break into, but the simple mosquito screen over it left no doubt he could at least smell me. The walls were secure enough; I supposed that even a determined full-grown tiger would not try to peel back the tin roof. I cannot describe what it was like to realize that I was potential prey for a predator like that. It was amazing to me that, despite the fact that I knew I was safe, my animal survival instincts automatically overruled my rational brain. Thank goodness for concrete bungalows! I can't imagine how I would have felt in a bamboo shack!

Eventually, he moved away and I returned to the bedroom. I wanted to wake Trena and tell her that there was a tiger right outside our hut. I then discovered, to my horror, her bed was empty; she was still out there with a hungry tiger on the loose!! My stomach hit the floor! Was I about to hear screams? It was nearly midnight! At any moment, she could come traipsing blithely down the path, unaware of the danger and I had no way of warning her!

Worse than that, I was, after all, the responsible party. What was I going to tell Trena's parents? *"Hello, Mr. and Mrs. Isley, I'm afraid to inform you that your daughter, while on a business trip with me, was attacked and eaten by a tiger? And I swear, it wasn't my fault!"* If anything ever happened to her, I would never, ever be able to forgive myself for my role in the tragedy. I began to look around the room for something, anything, I could use as a weapon. Failing that, I thought maybe I could distract the tiger. Perhaps a piece of clothing on a string with which to tease him, giving Trena a chance to run. Just like a great big kitty cat, right? I got out my nylon laundry line and was busy trying to construct the biggest cat toy in history when, suddenly, the door opened, and there she was! I was never so glad to see anybody in all my life!!

For about two seconds, I wanted to wrap my arms around my prodigal "daughter" and squeeze her in relief. That was when the rage set in.

By Diana McLeod

"What the (expletive) were you doing out in the (expletive) jungle all (expletive) night?!!! Don't you know there is a (expletive) tiger out there? Are you insane? You could have been killed!!"

"Don't be such a worry wart," Trena replied. "We were all sitting at the bar when we all heard him. The guides were quite excited! It was soo cool!"

"Well, this is the last time I leave you out in the jungle all by yourself at night! Seriously??"

"Honest to God, it was no big deal."

No big deal? It was a good thing we were leaving at noon the next day. If we had been planning another night in the jungle, I swear to God I would have chained her to the bed!

Suddenly, I felt a surge of gratitude to whatever or whoever runs the universe for never having blessed (cursed) me with children of my own. I would never have survived the anxieties of parenting.

WHEN RHINOS ATTACK: The next morning, we got up early. I had finally shaken off my tiger terrors, and I was eager to head out on an elephant again. After all, we had been in the park for three days and we still had not seen a rhinoceros in the wild, except along the road, which, honestly, does NOT count!

We were in a dense jungle when it finally happened. A full-grown male rhinoceros came bombing out of the underbrush, aggressively charging straight at our elephant! I had just enough time to hang on for dear life as the elephant trumpeted and reared up onto her hind legs, and I still managed to hit the "record" button on the video camera. He came galloping at us so fast! If we had been on foot, we never would have escaped being gored or trampled!

He stopped just short of our elephant's trunk. Her front feet kicked the air above his head, which made him stop to reconsider. His piggy, nearsighted eyes looked up in confusion, and then he backed off, loath to attack an elephant, but he couldn't just surrender without at least demonstrating his prowess. The rhino sidled up in front of a nearby tree and began to spray, marking his territory just like a cat! Gallons of urine shot out of his rear like a fire hose. Then he posed for pictures, just as proud as could be. Our elephant driver whistled frantically, letting the other mahouts know he had spotted a rhino. Two other groups of tourists were able to make the scene before he finally disappeared into the underbrush.

We returned to the camp in triumph. It was the perfect ending to our stay in Chitwan. As our bus headed down the "highway" back to Kathmandu, I thought our dangerous adventures were over. As it turned out, I was wrong, because the road was collapsing. One sandy

101

lane had already fallen into the icy river, two hundred feet below, and the second half of the road looked as though it might follow suit. Needless to say, our bus lumbered safely past the dangerous point, or I wouldn't be here to write this. And after our adventures in the jungle, the perils of the road didn't seem that dramatic.

recommended Google search: Chitwan Nepal Images

LIVING LARGE: GIANT MANTA RAYS and KOMODO DRAGONS

INDONESIA 2012. We were on Kanawa Island, a little speck of beach and reef off the coast of Flores. There was a dive "resort" there, with about thirty bamboo hut bungalows and a single restaurant. An ideal vacation getaway, only one or two notches above "Gilligan's Island" (just the way Dave and I like it). The best part was the professional dive shop run by two very competent Americans, Ed and Marie.

Dave wanted to go diving. I was a bit nervous about diving again given a few bad run-ins with frighteningly powerful currents in Thailand. Ed's calm demeanor soon convinced me to relax. We started with an easy practice dive to get back into the game. Once that was accomplished, it wasn't hard to persuade me to go out to Manta Point, where we would have a chance to see a giant Manta ray.

Our dive took place in Komodo National Park. By boat, it took about an hour to reach the dive site. Right off Komodo Island, there is a narrow "corridor" where plankton-laden currents sweep up from the Pacific Ocean, over a shallow shelf, and into the Indian Ocean. "Manta Point" is part of that oceanic jet stream. In some spots, the current is so fierce it creates massive whirlpools the locals call "the washing machines." These are very dangerous and intense; they can suck a diver straight down thirty meters or more and not even large dive boats are immune! Dave went near the "washing machines" the next day, and he told me the dive boat got stuck in one of the whirlpools. The twenty-four foot boat spun around like a top, and it was hard for the divers to get back on board! I was glad I wasn't there to see it —it would have freaked me out!

At Manta Point, the flow moved along at an impressive clip, fast enough to make me quite anxious. It felt as though we were flying through the water. Ed knew how I felt about currents, so he grabbed my hand and held on tightly for the rest of the dive. His experienced assistance allowed me to relax and enjoy my surroundings.

At first there wasn't much to see. The bottom was littered with broken and dead coral. Ed took out a long steel hook and buried it under a rock, and we clung together, hanging onto the rope, waiting. I didn't even see the first manta right away. When Ed made me turn around, I did a doubletake. The manta was so large my eyes hadn't believed it at first glance. It was HUGE! It's hard to gauge sizes underwater, but the dive masters assured us later we had seen eighteen to twenty-foot "wingspans" on these magnificent animals.

And then, more mantas appeared, all in a row, following each other like a flock of gigantic black and white birds. Most of them cruised straight along the bottom, wings lifting and falling as gracefully as dancers' arms in a ballet *pas de deux*. They moved with quiet dignity and calm. Others were having a bit of fun, rolling, one after the other, in lazy corkscrew loop-de-loops.

The presence of divers didn't bother the mantas at all. They came so near to us that, at times, we had to duck out of their way. I had one fly over my head at a distance of about one foot! He dropped down in front of me, and the tip of his tail was inches from my dive mask. When he cruised above me, he blotted out the sunlight from above. It reminded me of the iconic spaceship scene from the movie "Independence Day." It certainly felt like we were surrounded by alien beings. Luckily, in this case, they were harmless and benign.

The mantas were on a mission of their own: they were visiting the beauty parlor. Manta Point is a prime habitat for cleaner fish. The mantas allow these small fish to groom them by eating harmful parasites, cleaning their gills, and acting as tiny toothbrushes. It's a classic example of symbiosis between species. The cleaner fish have made manta grooming an important part of their diet. Both species have learned behavior that is beneficial to each other.

The dive turned out to be quite spectacular. We counted between forty and fifty giant mantas, almost a record sighting. Even the local dive masters were seriously impressed. What a lucky day!

MORE GIANTS—KOMODO DRAGONS: A few days later, we took a boat ride out to Rinca Island in the Komodo National Park. This time, our quarry was land-based. After paying the guide fee, we set off into the jungle with a vigilant park ranger, armed with a ten-foot forked pole. We were in search of giant Komodo dragons.

Komodo Dragons once inhabited many Indonesian islands, but today they are pretty much confined to the islands of Komodo and Rinca, where they are a protected species. It's probably a good thing they no longer roam the more populated islands because they're very dangerous.

It would have been startling to see one in the dense jungle underbrush. The problem is that people underestimate them. Here are some chilling dragon facts: They can grow up to ten feet long and weigh up to a hundred-and-fifty pounds, and they can run up to eleven miles an hour. A one-hundred-pound dragon is capable of devouring a ninety-pound pig in twenty minutes. They have serrated teeth like a shark, and bone-crushing jaws. And worst of all, if they bite you and you manage to escape, you haven't. Their saliva is full of a type of flesh-eating bacteria that will poison you within hours. The dragon will follow you until you drop, and devour you at its leisure. There is a well-documented case of a German tourist on Komodo island who was never seen again; only his camera was found. Villagers on these islands have to keep a close eye on their children!

We got to Rinca later in the day than we had wanted, so we were not lucky enough to see one in the jungle, but four semi-tame dragons were hanging out underneath the kitchen shack at the national park, hoping for handouts. They were all half asleep in the sand.

As we watched the dragon beach party, a large male dragon burst out of the trees, marching toward the kitchen. He headed straight for David, and our guide shouted to Dave to back away slowly. The dragon flicked his long tongue, using it to smell his prey. The guide edged closer, and readied the stick, just in case. When the dragon changed his mind and lay down lazily in the sand, everyone relaxed again.

We even got to see what passes for dragon intimacy. One male was attempting to mount one of the females. He tried hard, but she just didn't want to bother. It was just getting too hot in the noon sun for her to expend that much energy. Or maybe she decided she didn't need his services after all. Female dragons have evolved with the unique ability to impregnate themselves. They have all the DNA needed to make babies without doing things the old-fashioned way. Perhaps this is a response to the flesh-eating bacteria in his saliva. Or his bad breath.

recommended Google search: Komodo images

recommended Google search: Giant Manta images

By Diana McLeod

FISH SCHOOL

INDONESIA 2012. Each time I swam away from them, thousands of Yellowback Fuselier fish followed me. As I looked back, their eyes locked onto mine and they frantically chased after me. I felt like the Pied Piper of fish. As soon as they caught up, they reformed their circle beneath me, taking shelter directly under my body, just inches away. They swam in a squirming, synchronized ball, packed together as tightly as fast moving ten-inch-long fish could get.

The reason for this behavior was circling beneath them. Schools of two to three-foot long Trevally fish, each one intent on dining on the enormous bait ball, were hovering below, just waiting for the right moment to strike. These fierce predators were built for high speed, with powerful jaws that could swallow the smaller Fusilier fish whole. Their backs shone with rows of purple spots that glowed in the morning sunlight. They herded the smaller fish like wolf packs, closing in on their prey, mouths opening in anticipation of their next meal.

The Fusiliers huddled together for protection whenever the Trevally came near. The circling behavior of the small fish is a defense mechanism. It confuses the predators, making it more difficult for them to focus on a single individual. When the baitfish spotted me, they saw me as a human shield, since my big shadow discouraged the Trevally from lunging at them below.

It was unnerving to be snorkeling in the middle of bait ball with predators all around, but the Trevally were not biting, as long as I was there. No wonder I was the adopted mother of the fish school! Whenever I moved away, the feeding began. The Trevally pack herded them, circling around and around, going faster and faster, until they exploded up through the ranks of the Fusiliers like underwater ballistic missiles. The bait ball scattered into a series of smaller groups. A few of the unlucky ones didn't survive, but the score would have been far higher if they hadn't been so tightly packed together.

The most unusual thing about this fishball was that we didn't even have to get into the water to see them. This particular school of fish hung out every day, right at the end of the dock on the tiny resort island of Kanawa (off the larger island of Flores, near the Eastern edge of the Indonesian archipelago.) The fish are always in that area so that they can hide under the boats whenever they tie up there. They provide shade for the baitfish and a challenge for the Trevally.

If you ever want to adopt a whole school of fish...

PARANORMAL, SPOOKY ANY CREEPY

DEATH AND ANCESTOR WORSHIP:

STRANGE BURIAL PRACTICES IN TANA TORAJA, INDONESIA

The bones were sticking out of a decaying wooden coffin, almost as if they were leaking out of it like tears. A couple of skulls had already tumbled out, looking like they wanted to cry, alone and abandoned by their fellow eternal bunkmates. Shipwrecked on a lonely ledge, high up under the overhanging cavern ceiling, they were left high and dry, their only solace that they were out of the reach of would-be grave robbers looking for macabre tourist souvenirs.

HANGING COFFINS: Nobody knows when the custom of hanging coffins began on the island of Sulawesi, but many speculate that early settlers might have migrated there from ancient China where the suspension of coffins along cliff faces was once a common practice.

Today, the best place to see these coffins is in Tampang Allo. They're tucked into a secluded limestone cavern on the edge of the village. Most are hewn out of massive trees, intricately carved, and their decorated lids have the same boat-shaped "rooflines" seen on Torajan houses. One of the local guides told us these coffins that have been carbon dated, and some are over nine hundred years old, hewn out of virtually indestructible mountain hardwoods.

Entering the caverns is quite an experience. On this delightfully sunny morning, life is vibrant outside. Dragonflies and butterflies patrol the edges of the rice paddies. Purple morning glories and tropical irises create bold brushstrokes of vibrant color along the banks of the brook, especially when seen against the impossibly green backdrop of baby rice plants. Taking two steps over the tiny footbridge to the cave, I've crossed the Rubicon. The sun is gone, and the cold dampness of the underworld has swallowed me whole.

Inside the caverns, I am greeted by grinning death—a pile of skulls forms the welcoming committee. The atmosphere still seems to reek of mortal decay, even though this burial site probably hasn't been added to for at least fifty years. Above, just below the crushing weight of the cave ceiling, haggard groups of *Tau Tau* effigies of the dead stare longingly at the half-light streaming into the cave entrance, almost as if they know they could never pass into the bright sunshine ever again. High above the cavern floor, some of the suspended wooden coffins still hang in space, supported on long poles. They are like hardwood ships, bravely floating on against the tide of dripping dampness and cancerous wood rot. Part of me is fascinated, but the better part of me wants to leave quickly and breathe the sunlit air again. The encounter with death doesn't frighten me, but I've lost all desire to linger. I'm still alive, and it's time to go.

BOULDER BURIALS: As we leave the city of Rantapao behind, the road twists upwards through bamboo forests and rice fields. Banks of paddies cascade down the hillsides like sets of watery stairs, and each step holds its own unique reflection of the sky. From one viewpoint, high up on the mountain, they look like glittering pieces of shattered mirror. Here and there, round boulders interrupt the harmonious patterns of the paddies like poorly placed punctuation marks. The farmers have stoically worked their way around them, sometimes using them for edging.

Some of these gigantic rocks are "occupied." They have miniature doors in them, marking family burial sites. Square tombs are chiseled into each rock face, and the little chamber inside is hollowed out to house many family members, with the latest deceased person put in on top. Group burials are practical in this area since the rock is granite, and it takes a grave sculptor a year or two of chiseling solid rock in the tiny, cramped space to carve out a new tomb. Occasionally, photos or effigies of the deceased are left outside the entrance. One or two burial sites have lost their doors altogether, and you can glimpse piles of bones inside each stone crypt.

The best place to see a boulder burial is Lokkomata. The rounded stone itself is over three stories tall and at least a hundred feet long. It juts out of a hillside, right beside a small waterfall. This behemoth is virtually peppered with burial chambers on all sides. There must be at least fifty tombs inside this one rock. A condominium cemetery.

TAU TAU—EFFIGIES OF THE DEAD: The village of Lemo is the most impressive example of this bizarre custom. Beneath the village, there is a limestone cliff, and small tomb chambers are carved into it at various levels. However, the galleries of Tau Tau are the most dramatic and unusual aspect of the place. Long, indented "porches" have been hewn into the rock face, and wooden statues stand on them. These wooden effigies are reminders of village ancestors entombed in the cliffs. Their shell eyes stare out, unseeing, over the valley, blind spectators to the changes made by the living. The oldest ones have ragged, tattered clothing, and bits and pieces of their wooden bodies have fallen away. It's eerie to see their hands outstretched as if they're beseeching the living to remember them kindly.

The village of Londa has newer Tau Taus, which bear a very close resemblance to real people. They have personality, individual facial characteristics, and jewelry, hats, scarves, purses, canes, and other distinguishing features. Several statues even wear glasses. According to one source, the Tau Tau makers from Londa traveled to Bali to learn the art of realistic wood carving.

Footsteps of a Nomad

INTO THE DARKNESS: The most macabre encounter of all was in the caves at Londa. This village has a vertical cliff face with a long, multi-roomed natural cavern at its base. The interior is accessible with a hired local guide holding a large Coleman lantern. Only members of families with ancestors interred there are allowed to bring "guests" inside.

A few steps into the twisting passage and all traces of daylight faded away. Stacks of moldering modern coffins were all around us, piled in heaps and stuffed into every crevice. There were no fresh bodies, thank goodness, but there was still an odor of decay. Cans of opened soft drinks and cigarettes adorned some of the newer coffins, left for the dead to enjoy. Coca-Cola would be proud, I thought.

I was the last person in our group to exit the cave. Was it my imagination, or did the darkness behind me suddenly seem to swell with malice? Did I feel a chilling draft on my shoulders as if skeletal hands were reaching out for me? Surprisingly, no. The cave didn't feel haunted at all. The Torajans honor their dead so intensely there didn't seem to be any malevolent spirits lingering here—at least not while the sun was still shining outside.

BABY GRAVES. At first, this felt like the strangest burial tradition of all, but later, as I thought about it, I grew comfortable with the idea. The custom is this: if a baby dies in childbirth, or before the child gets its first teeth, it is interred inside a living tree. There is only one type of tree used for this, and it must be of a substantial size. A hole is dug into the tree, and the body placed inside. A patch, made from beeswax and coconut fibers, seals the spot, and the tree continues to grow.

We counted about ten graves in one baby tree. Is this macabre? Maybe, but if I were a grieving mother, I would prefer my child to become one with the living rainforest, rather than buried underground.

CIRCLES OF STANDING STONES: There are many villages and burial sites around Tana Toraja with circles of megalithic raised standing stones. These stone circles are amazingly reminiscent of Stonehenge and other Neolithic sites in Western Europe. (Fans of Atlantis and ancient aliens can let their imaginations run wild now.) Menhirs stand as a memorial to deceased ancestors. Even today, menhirs continue to be erected; four new ones stood in the field right behind our guesthouse.

INTERMENT of the deceased does not take place in Tana Toraja until the family has had plenty of time to prepare for the expensive funeral rituals. In the meantime, the body remains with the family, in the home. The corpse is immediately embalmed and left to mummify, and the person is referred to as "sick," not dead. The funeral and interment take place several years later, when the family has amassed enough money to pay for an extravagant send-off.

By Diana McLeod

A funeral is a grand event, and Torajans spend far more on funerals than other cultures spend on weddings. Dozens of animals are sacrificed, and the entire village is fed. Families will pay tens of thousands of dollars for specially bred albino water buffaloes with auspicious markings, only to sacrifice them at the ceremony, in what, to us, is a very gory ritual. All of the people who show up are given food and drink, and meat to take home afterwards. Upper caste funerals can take days, with both Christian and animist priests taking part.

'MA NENE'- THE BIZARRE CUSTOM OF "WALKING CORPSES": Three years after the remains are entombed, family members enter the crypt, remove all the bodies, clean them, and dress them in new sets of clothes. They take the corpses back to their home, in one of the strangest "family reunions" ever. Today, people even pose for "selfie" shots with their long-dead relatives. Their loved ones are re-interred after they've had a brief "holiday."

We did not witness this ritual ourselves, but National Geographic did a fascinating story about this aspect of Torajan culture in the April 2016 edition. Take a look for yourself! (WARNING: the images are disturbing).

All of these customs demonstrate the power of ancestor worship in this society. Even today, although most of the population is Christian, these bizarre rituals remain a vibrant part of the cycle of life and death. Torajan culture has not only survived into the twenty-first century, but some traditions seem stronger than they were than twenty years ago, when we first visited the region. Tana Torajan culture is surely one of the most unique on earth.

recommended Google search: Tana Toraja Images (some are very disturbing, but this search is well worth it!)

FULL MOON OVER TRANSYLVANIA:
IN SEARCH OF DRACULA

Transylvania Romania is the perfect setting for the Dracula story. It has ancient villages rife with superstition, Gothic churches and graveyards, dark forests, haunted castles and dangerous mountain passes. There is even a famous historical figure to base the story on: Vlad Tepes (Vlad the Impaler). They called him *"Dracul"*, which is the Romanian word for dragon. His brutal reign was legendary.

The little villages of Romania seem almost unchanged from medieval times. Wooden houses and sheep shacks cluster together on rutted paths. The carpentry is old-fashioned and homemade, with crooked rooflines, odd little dormer windows, and crude, hand-hewn clapboards. We saw several old-fashioned horse carts clattering along the dirt roads. The drivers wore that blank look people get when they've driven the same road, day after day, every day of their lives. Women sat in the back of the wagon, with the hay. They also wore that same stoic stare—the look that women get when they've known, since early childhood, which village boy they will inevitably marry.

Part of me wanted to get off the train and explore these villages. I've lived in enough small towns to know they can be microcosms of humanity, with their own communal triumphs and tragedies, scandals and jealousies, broken dreams and enduring hatreds. Little villages can be downright Shakespearean in their own way. I yearned to meet these people, and somehow convince them to talk to me. If only someone could get them to open up and reveal their ancient ways, their superstitions, and their family secrets! Surely there must be a mysterious world hidden behind the handmade lace curtains in the kitchen windows...

Even more sinister were the isolated farmsteads at the edge of forbidding forests. Here and there, we saw a single lonely cottage with weathered gingerbread trim in the center of a cleared hollow, within reach of the threatening trees. Shepherds in crude sheepskin coats herded their flocks in hardscrabble fields, while watching the forest carefully. The mountain forests of Romania are still very extensive, easily supporting populations of wolves, bears, and mountain lions. On winter nights, terrified families must hear dreadful howling in the mountains. I'm sure they lose some of their flocks to predators every year. Imagine what it must be like to peer out the windows at night and see pairs of glowing, yellow eyes! No wonder Romania generated so many tales of werewolves, dire wolves and vampires!

The larger towns felt friendlier to us. There is less suspicion of outsiders in a big town, and the neighborhoods are more welcoming. Still, the churches had that wonderfully mysterious Gothic character to them, and the churchyards harkened back to days of medieval fear and superstition about the dead. The gravestones, with their Eastern crosses, cast haunting shadows on the church wall. A new grave, in the corner of one cemetery, had just displaced an ancient one. Rotten pieces of an exhumed coffin lay carelessly strewn off to one side of the new grave. But where were the remains of its occupant? Would that spirit be restless now that it had been disturbed? Walking past the graveyard, by the light of the full moon, I remembered the stories of the legendary undead of Romania.

BRAN CASTLE: Bran Castle is one of the great spooky castles of all time. It should be, since it was once used as a temporary residence of Vlad Dracul the Impaler (the historical Dracula). He used Bran Castle as a center of operations when he commanded his armies to overrun the city of Brazov and the surrounding countryside. It was never his primary residence, (that castle is now in ruins), but there is little doubt that he stayed there, since Bran occupies a strategic pass. It was built in the 1300s, and Vlad's armies used the fortress during the following century.

We visited Bran on an appropriately gloomy, overcast day. The stern outline of the fortress loomed over the little town below. Outside, the castle walls ascend several stories before breaking into a series of towers and turrets. No two towers are alike. In the lower stories, the windows are just arrow slits. A single footpath leads up the hill to the main gate.

Inside that gate, there was an open courtyard and an old well, surrounded by several trees. Balconies look down from the floors above. We found a staircase, and began to explore the citadel. The rooms upstairs were built in an asymmetrical fashion, following the curves of the jumbled mass of towers. Nothing was square, or standard, so it was very easy to get lost inside. We kept turning around in long passages, and up or down narrow, claustrophobic staircases.

I was gratified to learn that the last occupant, Queen Maria of Romania, left the castle in a relatively pristine medieval state. She added a few touches of feminine decor, but the character of the old castle has remained happily unchanged. The furniture she left behind was simple and perfectly appropriate for an old castle: wonderful old Baroque four-poster beds in very dark polished wood, antique cabinets and armoires, carved wooden chairs, prie-dieus, bearskin rugs, and brass candlesticks. Queen Maria never ruined the place with modernization or inappropriate objects d'art. The more I saw, the more I was grateful to her for her good taste. Bran was a fine experience for a medievalist like me!

I learned more about Queen Maria. She apparently was a lovely person, who spent a great deal of her time helping her country's poor. She obviously adored the old castle and tried to preserve it for us to enjoy today. But what was it like for her to live here, wandering around the creaking hulk at night? Did she shiver when the wind howled down from the mountains, whistling and moaning among the old towers, disturbing her sleep? Do fourteenth-century spirits still wander the halls? The castle must be rife with ghosts, especially since a legendary master of torture and murder stayed here during one of his campaigns. I noticed that the tour did not include the lower levels of the castle. We did not see the dungeons. I know that Bran Castle had dungeons since it was used as a military fortress. Why were they closed to visitors? Is it because they are unsafe? Or is it because they are too disturbing for some people...

The adventurous part of me wanted to hide under the beds and stay behind after the museum closed in the evening. What an experience it would be to spend a night locked inside! Imagine waiting to see what might materialize by the light of the full moon! Truly, Transylvania really is the perfect setting for tales of terror and darkness.

recommended Google search: Transylvania Images

AN EERIE FORETELLING

I do not regard myself as a psychic, and I make no claims of any abilities in this area whatsoever. But, one time in my life, I experienced paranormal warnings so disquieting, that when my foretelling came true, I was stunned by the accuracy of my vision. My husband Dave also showed signs that he might have experienced some unconscious foreshadowing of what was to come. You be the judge:

We landed in Colombo, Sri Lanka, in March of 2003. The Sri Lankan capital was a colorful mix of old colonial buildings, modernity, and the typical haphazard construction visible everywhere on the Indian subcontinent. People were friendly and welcoming. Even in the city center, the smell of flowers and spices survived the barrage of exhaust fumes.

At the old British era railway station we bought tickets on the funky little train that runs down the coast. Sri Lankan passenger trains are very old and very crowded, but they are charming. I got a window seat in one of the old wooden coaches while Dave went to stand by the open vestibule door, to take train pictures.

The ride was absolutely lovely. Inside the train, I was welcomed by friendly smiles all around. A couple of people were able to converse with me in English. Unlike crowds in India, these folks gave me enough personal space. They didn't swarm around me and pelt me with questions. One generous family even shared their snacks with me. I passed around our postcards of Vermont (always a big hit) and we made friends. Their adorable little girl hung out the window, waving happily to people outside.

By Diana McLeod

The western side of Sri Lanka was spectacular. The train traveled right down the coastline, almost on the edge of the beach in some areas. You could see the pounding surf as it sparkled in the bright sunlight. At other times, we were in a lush, tropical jungle. I'd never seen so many species of wildflowers outside of a botanical garden. The natural beauty of Sri Lanka is legendary. I could easily understand why the British were so taken with the place, calling it "Serendipity -- an Eden on Earth."

There was no logical reason for my mood to shift, but it did. I grew especially uncomfortable as the train passed through shantytowns at the edge of the beaches. From the seaward side of the train, I could gaze directly into the backyards of little bamboo huts built right on the sand. Mothers were hanging up freshly washed laundry, while bare-bottomed toddlers played happily at their feet. Kids were playing soccer, cricket, or volleyball. Fishermen worked on their boats or mended nets.

I got a strong impending feeling of disaster looking at all these people. The hair on the back of my neck rose. When Dave came back to our seat and joined me, I told him, "I feel like I am looking at ghosts. These people are living too close to the sea. Something bad is going to happen. Maybe there will be a storm. I really feel as if I am seeing dead people." I remember complaining about my feelings to him at least twice. I've seen plenty of rickety shantytowns, built too close to the sea, in other parts of the world. I couldn't understand why these villages bothered me so much.

It got worse. I tried to enjoy my trip, but I couldn't shake the uneasiness. The whole thing made no sense. I turned my eyes away from the people outside, but that didn't help. I got the same feeling of dread from many of my fellow passengers and from the train itself. The Sri Lankans were all so nice, and so friendly, but that didn't make me feel any better. There was nothing wrong except in my own head, so I tried to shake it off. By the time we got to Galle, I decided I was being silly.

From Galle, we took a tuk-tuk (a three wheeled taxi) to the beach town of Unawatuna and began to look for accommodations. Dave visited lots of guesthouses and rejected each one. I was stuck in the back of the tuk-tuk, crammed in with the luggage, unable to move.

By this time, I was miserably uncomfortable, so I begged him to settle on something quickly. He rejected many hotels, despite my whining. He couldn't even say exactly what was wrong with them, but kept asking me to have the patience to look at one more. Finally, he found one he liked; it sat on a high ridge, facing away from the sea. (The "Rock House" turned out to be a terrific guesthouse, and well worth the wait.)

We spent a lovely three days at the beach at Unawatuna. We snorkeled and swam, rented a motorbike and drove down the coast to explore other beaches. I had a great time. The bad feelings never returned, and I quickly forgot about them.

On Dec 26th, 2004, slightly less than a year later, the great Tsunami smashed into the coast of Sri Lanka, devastating everything in its path. The hardest hit areas were south of Colombo, all the way to the southern tip of the island. Every little town and village along the seacoast were flattened. The shantytowns by the beach were the first to go. Most of the population drowned. Galle was overcome, as was Unawatuna. Later, I met an Australian who had gone there afterward to help with disaster relief. He said that all the beachfront properties in Unawatuna had been destroyed and that most of the villagers and tourists perished. Our guesthouse was one of the few that survived. The instant I saw the pictures on TV, my strange feelings flooded back to me, and I finally understood.

The little train was swept off the tracks and shoved deep into the jungle. It was called the "Death Train" because over a thousand people lost their lives on it that day. Many of them were regular commuters. When Dave saw pictures of smashed up passenger cars on CNN, he was pretty sure that the actual car we had ridden on was part of the debris. (Each car had a name painted on its side. Our car, he remembered, was ironically named Queen of the Sea.)

Coincidence? Exaggeration? I have tried to tell this as accurately as possible. You be the judge. But I will confess that if, before a flight, I ever get similar feelings about my fellow airline passengers, I am probably not getting on board.

GHOST TOWN: POMPEII ITALY

The dead were frozen in the poses in which they perished. A mother cradled her child in her final moments, shielding him in her arms. A man clutched at his throat, choking on burning ash as nearby, cringing bodies seemed to writhe in agony. You could see the suffering in every gesture; in every mouth opened in a silent scream.

They all perished during a volcanic eruption on the 24th of August in 79 A.D. At midday, the first dark ash clouds boiled out of nearby Mt Vesuvius, shooting kilometers high into the sky. By three p.m., pumice rained down on the city, forcing citizens to take shelter. Roofs collapsed under the weight of the accumulated ash, crushing many people to death, or burying them alive. Others tried to flee, but boiling clouds of searing hot ash either scorched them to death or suffocated them, encasing them in thick, choking, burning dust.

By Diana McLeod

The entire city was eventually buried under layers and layers of volcanic ejecta. There were no survivors in Pompeii. The only reason we know anything about the date and time of this eruption was because some people in the nearby city of Misenum (now Naples) survived. In fact, an eyewitness account still exists, because Pliny the Younger was staying in Misenum. He describes the terror as it overtook his family's neighborhood, miles away from the volcano. Here are just a few of his words:

> "On Mount Vesuvius, broad sheets of fire and leaping flames blazed at several points, their bright glare emphasized by the darkness of night....

> "...Ashes were already falling, not as yet very thickly. I looked around; a dense black cloud was coming up behind us, spreading over the earth like a flood... We had scarcely sat down to rest when darkness fell, not the dark of a moonless night, but as if the lamps had been put out in a closed room.

> "...You could hear the shrieks of women, the wailing of infants and the shouting of men... Many besought the aid of the Gods, but still more imagined that that there were no gods left, and that the universe was plunged into darkness for evermore..."

Pompeii was lost to the world for centuries and only recently unearthed. Today, it is a true "ghost town" because streets and buildings are preserved, just as the volcano left them, like a ghost town in the old West, abandoned in a hurry by its inhabitants. Its buildings, temples, shops, and homes are still there for all to see. But there is more. We can even see some of the inhabitants and witness their final moments for ourselves.

How is this possible? Because of an observant 19th century archaeologist. When digging in the ash, he came across pockets of air inside the ash, and he wondered what might have been inside those empty spaces at one time. He experimented with pouring wet plaster down inside the holes. What he came up with, when he dug out the plaster casts, was nothing short of extraordinary. There, brilliantly preserved, were the forms of the deceased. The bodies had burned away in the intense heat, but their three-dimensional outlines were indented into the compressed ash, making amazingly accurate and detailed "statues" of the dead. A few of the castings even revealed hairstyles, beards, and articles of clothing. There was even a dog among them. I couldn't help but wonder: if souls suffer a sudden and violent death, do they sometimes remain chained to the world of the living? If that is so, then how must they feel about being put on display in front of millions of tourists every day? It made me shudder, just thinking about it.

Footsteps of a Nomad

The volcano left us a remarkable snapshot of daily life in a Roman town. Today, you can walk down the streets of Pompeii and wander right into people's' houses, many of which survive with even their roofs intact. Paintings and mosaics, open gardens and architectural embellishments adorn many of the upscale Roman villas. Temples and civic buildings edge the main streets and avenues. The Roman Baths remain, with marble pools still ready for bathers. At two-thousand-year-old fast food restaurants, you can still line up at sales counters and imagine what dishes they were serving that day. One establishment even had a charming picture of the proprietor and his wife painted on the wall. A house had a "Beware of Dog" sign outside the front door. Little personal touches, like decorative niches and intimate family portraits still welcome the visitor to various homes.

The "Villa of Mysteries" is a rambling estate that survived with many of its roofs intact. Today, you can wander through room after room, marveling at the exquisite, priceless artwork on the walls. Thousands of people come each year to appreciate its architecture, the interior decor, and the estate gardens. It is so well preserved, you can close your eyes and expect to reopen them and find yourself in the middle of a Roman dinner party. I could easily arrange the furniture in my mind, just as it must have been in its heyday.

Most of the place didn't feel very haunted to me, but the presence of the plaster bodies made me wonder, so I decided to check out whether or not there have been reports of paranormal activity at Pompeii. I went on-line, searching the web rather thoroughly, and, curiously, there were few claims of incidents on the Internet—except at the arena. There, gladiators and slaves fought and killed each other as a spectator sport. Thousands of lives were lost for entertainment.

I remember that, while visiting that stadium, I experienced what many others have also written about. As I ducked into the shade of the stands, trying to escape the hot sun, I felt a dreadful chill   Nearby, there was a portal to the tunnels beneath the stadium's stone bleachers. Modern iron bars prevented anyone from entering. Streaming out of that passage came a dank, fetid breath of cold air. More than just wind, it made the hairs on my arms stand on end, and I felt the presence of death.

After I read and thought about it, it all made perfect sense, because it was into this tunnel the bodies of the deceased were dragged after each arena game. If there are ghosts in Pompeii, they are here. Although it is also said that ghostly screams can be heard echoing in many areas of the city at night, and many tourist pictures are rife with mysterious floating orbs....

recommended Google search: Pompeii Images

By Diana McLeod

A REAL TRADEWINDS GHOST STORY

There are many interesting old items that we sell at our store, but *phurbas* are the most unusual of them all. They are old mystical spirit daggers from Tibet and Nepal. I do not sell them lightly—not after one incident that occurred about ten years ago.

Tibetan *phurbas* are dagger-shaped objects made out of metal or wood. The metal ones were often the property of a monastery, used by the important lamas, while wooden ones belong to individual monks. They aren't real daggers; their use is strictly spiritual, shamanistic or occult. Three faces of the demon Mahakala, Guardian of the Wheel of Life and dispenser of justice, grace the top of most *phurba* handles. Entwined snakes, symbols of healing, crawl down the three-sided "blade." Metal *phurbas* often have points made from a meteorite. The chunks of iron from outer space are considered to have special powers.

Tibetan spirit daggers are shamanistic devices dating back into prehistory, long before Buddhism took root in the Himalayan regions of Asia, when ancient healers first employed them for simple transference magic. A shaman would stab the *phurba* into the ground. Illness would flow from a sick person through the *phurba* and into the ground, and healing energy would flow out of the earth to heal the sick person. *Phurbas* were used to summon demonic influences, or to drive demons away or capture them. The daggers were used to set the limits of magic circles and as receptacles in which to store all of one's negative emotions. During an obscure and bizarre ritual called *Chöd*, in which a monk or a nun would visit a graveyard at midnight, the *phurba* might be waved about to invite demons to partake of his or her flesh. This ritual was done to rid oneself of the last vestiges of ego.

The important thing to remember about *phurbas* is that they can retain something from their previous history, and they may still hold energies or emotional baggage from their former owners. Not all of those energies are benign.

Tibetan monks have come to visit us at *Tradewinds* to see what we have brought back from Nepal. Several times, they have brought serious students of Tibetan Buddhism with them. I remember one such visit very well. The high lama held the first *phurba* in his hands and closed his eyes. Then, he turned to one student, and said: "You need this in your practice." He grabbed the second one, handed it another student, and said: "You need this one." There was one *phurba* that he gave him pause. "Do not ever sell this item," he cautioned me. "It should be burned."

He never told me why, but I followed his advice.

ONE CUSTOMER'S ENCOUNTER WITH THE PARANORMAL: A shopper bought a *phurba* from me once, and said he was going to use it to enhance his dreams. I cautioned him that was not what they were supposed to be used for, but he said he was going to do it anyway. I sold him the *phurba,* and I didn't expect to see him again.

Two weeks later, he was back in the store and wanted to show me something. He claimed he put his *phurba* under his pillow when he went to bed. He dreamed about monks, heading up a steep Himalayan trail. The monks were bringing supplies, strapped on the backs of pack animals, up to a mountain monastery. They were probably Yaks or Dzo (a yak/cow hybrid). In his dream, he scurried after the monks, following them up the trail. The monk in front of him gave him disdainful looks. After more hostile eye contact, the monk said something to his pack animal, and the animal lashed out and kicked the dreamer, knocking him right off the cliff!

My friend claimed that he woke up on the floor of his room, some distance from his bed. After telling me the story, he pulled back his long hair. On the side of his neck was an ugly, painful-looking bruise about five inches long. It was curved just like an animal's hoof, and it was turning an impressive shade of purple. I saw it myself. I can't imagine how else it could have happened, or how he ever could have faked such a thing.

He and I discussed his experience at length, and we came to the conclusion that the dream contained a message. The line of monks going up the mountains represented the lineage of Buddhist teachings being passed down from generation to generation. Getting in the line was a privilege attained only after years of spiritual work and study. The reprimand was clear: he was not ready. My advice was for him to get in touch with a Tibetan Buddhist teacher who could educate him spiritually enough to be admitted into the lineage. The *phurba's* previous owner would not tolerate his presence until he was worthy. He should put it away until he was ready to try again. Until then, he would get kicked off the mountain.

My customer and I both agreed on this interpretation. Still, he was determined to put the dagger back under his pillow when he thought he was ready. He left, and I don't know what happened after that. Did he, or didn't he? He never came back to tell me.

Two weeks later, I was introduced to his wife. She explained that she had been present when he had his dream, and she'd had her own experience that fateful night. She told me she woke up around midnight and saw a black shadow figure standing at the foot of her bed. She thought it was an intruder and felt she needed to "get a gun, or call 911." Then the figure vanished, and her husband went flying across the room. She only then realized she'd had a paranormal experience. I felt that she was a highly credible person. She didn't ask for this to happen to her, it just happened. Her husband's experience could have been generated by "wishful thinking," but not hers, because she had no advance knowledge of what he'd done.

I confess that, although I've tried, I've never felt any residual energies in *phurbas.* I might have felt something "electrical" once at an antique shop in Bangkok, but it could have been my imagination...

By Diana McLeod

PART III

A FEW OF MY FAVORITE COUNTRIES

Dear Readers, I have not included stories from every country I've visited—far from it! I haven't included a single story from France, for example, although I've been there several times. This does not mean I don't appreciate France! The country is wonderful, but my stories from France just didn't make the cut. My apologies to France, Holland, Germany, Switzerland, Spain, Portugal, Czech Republic, Slovakia, Poland, Jordan, Israel, Qatar, Australia, New Zealand, Myanmar, Laos, Cambodia, South Korea, Singapore, the Philippines, and Canada. I'd love to return to each of these countries and do a sequel.

TALES OF INDIA

CULTURE SHOCK TO THE MAX

Dave and I first went to India in 1990. Before we left, we discussed our trip with Dave's older brother Mel, a very experienced traveler who had lived in India. He recommended we challenge ourselves with culture shock, just for the experience of it. In his opinion, there was nowhere on the planet quite as extreme as India, and he advised, for total immersion, that we plunge ourselves straight into the chaos of Old Delhi on our very first day. We took his advice and headed straight for Chandni Chowk, the famous bazaar surrounding the great mosque of Old Delhi, the Jama Masjid.

As we stepped out of the rickshaw, the slender minarets and the magnificent onion dome of the mosque loomed over me. The Jama Masjid was an ethereal vision in red sandstone and white marble, but utter chaos surrounded its tranquil beauty. The street I had stepped out onto was a mad swirl of auto and bicycle rickshaws, cars, trucks with blaring horns, and a nearly continuous stream of foot traffic. Muslim men in white caps and long robes jostled with boisterous Hindu office boys and roaming street vendors with baskets of food on their heads. Children ran in traffic, begging from me incessantly. Hustlers accosted me, talking a blue streak, offering to "guide" me

119

while shopping (so they could get commissions). "Madam, madam, you must come to my brother's shop! Madam, Madam...!" A bull (!) wandered aimlessly down the street, following right behind me. Luckily, I saw his horns coming out of the corner of my eye. Young boys shoved and elbowed, and one even gave me a rude pinch. I practically tripped over the first leper I saw in India. The disease had ravaged his body terribly. He was lying right on the busy sidewalk, begging for alms.

The barrage continued as we went deeper into the market. The colors of the merchandise were overwhelming. The Indians love sparkle and dazzle, so everything was made using the brightest, most vibrant colors, with as much glitter, sequins, gold and silver thread as they could squeeze onto the goods. The spicy smells from the curbside kitchens were intense, especially when mixed with charcoal smoke from the cooking fires and acrid exhaust from passing trucks. My ears were bombarded by hawkers, competing Bollywood songs blasting from music stalls selling bootleg tapes, and the blare of the loudspeakers from the mosque as the time grew close for afternoon prayers. When I heard a tambourine and singing in the gardens below the mosque, I followed the sound. A group of young transvestites was dancing for the crowd, swaying lewdly in bespangled saris.

Dave disappeared while chasing an interesting photo op, and I soon got lost in the bazaar. Around every bend were new products, new sights, new sounds, and new smells. The sari sellers tried to wrap saris around me. The incense sellers happily fanned clouds of thickly scented smoke into my face. I walked away, turned a corner or two, and suddenly wound up in the chicken market. I found myself between towering, stacked cages full of filthy, clucking chickens! The reek of poop and butchery was horrendous. When the chicken vendor greeted me, grinning, bloody hatchet in hand, I fled in horror. Luckily, I wound up discovering the bangle stalls. Indian women crowded around them arguing loudly with the vendors in Hindi, trying to knock them way down on their prices.

It took quite a while to escape from the market maze. I fought off two "guides," a fortune-teller, and a couple of would-be boyfriends, and made my way back, guided by the minarets of the mosque. There, to my eternal relief, I found Dave. He was snapping pictures as fast as he could.

That night, I couldn't sleep. My tired brain was disturbed by memories that just kept popping up out of nowhere. I couldn't shut them out. This continued for many nights until I finally realized what was happening. India had overwhelmed my senses so much that my mind was unable to process the images fast enough. They had gone subliminal! The flashbacks continued to disturb me for several weeks, until one day, I managed to get the hang of it. India had caught me up and swept me into the wild, unruly current of its unique stream of consciousness.

recommended Google search: Chandni Chowk Delhi images

By Diana McLeod

Our invitation to MY BIG FAT INDIAN WEDDING

On the second day of our first trip to India, we got lucky. We met a street hustler who insisted on taking us to his "brother's" store (so he could get commission on our purchases). Since we had not been in India long enough to know better, we tamely followed him to the shop. On the way, we passed a huge, colorful series of tents. It looked as though a circus was in town. We asked what the tents were for, and he offered to show us inside.

"These are wedding tents", he explained. "Each one can hold a different wedding reception. In fact, I happen to know the family whose son is getting married tonight. I myself will be a guest at this wedding.

He led us into the biggest tent. Inside, it was amazing. There was seating for at least a thousand people, maybe even more. Every chair was extravagantly carved and gilded, and the chairs sat on rows of at least fifty premium hand-knotted Kashmiri carpets. In the front of the hall, on a carpeted podium, were two gigantic thrones for the bride and the groom. These gleaming, silver monstrosities were over eight feet tall with gaudy, red velvet cushions.

The venue was a busy place. People were rushing everywhere, bringing in tables for the food and setting up the entertainment. The father of the bride and the father of the groom were shouting orders and supervising the chaos. When they saw us, they came over. Our friend introduced us, and they invited us to the wedding! We thanked them, but said we had nothing appropriate to wear. We would not be able to return to our hotel until after the wedding, and had only the clothes on our backs.

The proud fathers assured us that it didn't matter. We were foreigners, and it would be an honor to have us attend. Dave and I were skeptical about it being an honor to have two disreputable tourists in tee shirts at their fancy wedding. We assured them they needn't invite us just for the sake of politeness. No, they insisted, they really wanted us to come, tee shirts and all. Our "friend" promised to bring us back at the proper time, and then he hauled us off to our shopping destination. (Note: this wedding took place in 1990, when foreigners were more of a status symbol than they are now. But, even today, tourists may we still be honored in this fashion.)

The shop our friendly hustler took us to was quite ridiculous. It wasn't a tourist shop, but a store for the richest of Indian families. I looked at saris, thinking maybe I could afford one. The prices were astounding. Most were more than $2,000 U.S. dollars! Some had threads of real gold spun into the silk; others were encrusted with jewels or real pearls. We couldn't afford anything at that shop, but in the end, we did buy one rather overpriced silk painting.

121

When it was time, we returned to the wedding tent. Partygoers were streaming into the entrance. A special machine showered each group of guests with chrysanthemum petals. Crystal chandeliers glittered overhead. Inside, the tent looked like a palace. A luxury banquet was spread out in royal style. There were even ice sculptures, and gleaming, six-foot bronze statues of Hindu Gods, each one with six arms, holding platters of fine delicacies. Giant potted palms decorated with colored lights surrounded the food area.

There must have been a thousand wedding guests. The men were all dressed in perfectly tailored suits (India is famous for its tailors), and the women were splendid in magnificent saris, even fancier than the ones we saw at that overpriced shop! They all looked like Maharanis. Each lady was positively dripping with 24-carat gold and enough large, precious gemstones to make Tiffany's drool. It turned out that our host was an extremely wealthy man, owner of a large manufacturing concern. This was going to be a major society event.

Thoroughly ashamed of our attire, we wanted to hide in the back. It was not to be. As soon as the father of the bride saw us, he rushed over and escorted us to two reserved chairs in the very front row! We were mortified, but what could we do? Young men from both families came over to socialize with us. They immediately hauled us off to the bar, and gave us both eight-ounce glasses of pure Indian Scotch whiskey! We were very wary of drinking to excess, but there was no way to politely refuse. We dumped several drinks in the potted palms! (We felt badly for the plants, but better them than us!)

The buffet was amazing. The affair was catered by the Taj Mahal Hotel Group—one of the top five-star chains in India. We loved everything. It was one of the most sumptuous feasts we had ever experienced. The spices were so rich and aromatic! The dessert table was a feast in itself, with platters of milk sweets (similar to fudge) covered in real gold or silver foil. The foil is eaten, along with the sweets, giving wedding guests the luxurious experience of actually ingesting small quantities of precious metal.

The bride and groom sat on the two gilded thrones in the front. The bride was all but hidden under clouds of spangled red silk. What we could see of her was covered in cascades of gleaming gold jewelry. Gems adorned her hands, feet, toes, and forehead. Her nose was pierced with a huge golden hoop, held in place with delicate chains. Her necklaces were so heavy I felt badly for her. The groom wore a beautifully tailored suit with a flamboyant vest, jeweled rings, solid gold bracelets and a Maharajah's turban.

As the buffet wound down, the entertainment began. The families had hired a troupe of performers, including singers, dancers, and acrobats. There were over forty performers participating in a huge variety of routines. Classical Indian music and performance art mingled with the latest modern "Bollywood" movie songs and dance routines. Tumblers and jugglers tossed people and flaming batons through the air. The funniest act was an Indian "John Travolta," dressed in the famous white disco suit, dancing to a cheesy rendition of songs from "Grease." The entertainment was still going on when we left, several hours later.

The evening was delightful. I've always been grateful we were invited. What a wonderful experience! There were some awkward moments, though. My clothes haunted me the whole time. Also, it was my first experience with the peculiar segregation women endure in India. They either sat with their husbands, or huddled in large groups on one side of the room. There was almost no socializing between the sexes. The men ran everything. They talked with me, and made sure I spent time at the bar, but I was pretty sure I was the only woman publicly encouraged to have alcohol. I've since learned that Western women are looked at differently than their own women. It's almost as though we are not regarded as "real" women. We are hermaphrodite half-breeds, neither men nor women; almost a different species.

Women's issues were visible everywhere. The worst example was the bride. The poor girl was required to spend her entire wedding day staring at her hands, which were folded in her lap. She must do so to demonstrate that she will become a pliant and obedient wife. I watched her eyes flickering through her veil and her eyelashes as she attempted to catch furtive glimpses of the entertainment.

We were also uncomfortable when some family members, who were a bit drunk, began to heap abuse on our "friend." He was a member of one of the families, but he was apparently the "black sheep." He was a *lepca*, a social parasite who preys on tourists for commission on their purchases. The family was delighted we had come to the wedding, but, at the same time, some of them berated him for parading his "work" in front of the other family. They apologized to us for him. We protested that, without him, we would have missed this wonderful experience.

Our humiliated "friend" said goodnight and left. Somehow we managed to ditch our last drinks, thank both proud fathers, hail an auto rickshaw, and find our way back to our seedy hotel, where scenes from the wedding swirled in my head until I finally fell asleep.

recommended Google search: India Weddings Images

AN INCREDIBLE ACT OF FAITH:
THE KAILASA TEMPLE AT ELLORA, INDIA

Personally, I am seldom excited by travel stories that just describe a temple somewhere in Asia. They are boring if you haven't been there yourself. However, I must make an exception for this temple because of the incredible act of faith that created it.

Sometime after 700 A.D, a man who lived near what is now Aurangabad, India had an idea. He would design a temple. It would be an imposing edifice, dedicated to the Hindu god Shiva, the Destroyer and Regenerator of the universe. It would represent Mt Kailas, the semi-mythical Himalayan peak Shiva called his home. The plans for the temple were impressive. The man envisioned a palatial building one hundred feet tall, covering twice the area of the Greek Parthenon. It would have many levels, each covered in delicate sculptures and airy porticos. The top stories would be capped with elaborate towers, representing Himalayan peaks. Its magnificence would be unequaled in the ancient world.

But here's the punchline: the temple would not be constructed, but *excavated.* Workers were to dig into solid rock, and *chisel out the temple as a sculpture,* from top to bottom!! Not only were they going to carve out the temple, but to produce a sufficiently dramatic site, they also had to quarry out an enormous courtyard area surrounding the temple so it could be appreciated from all sides.

Think about carving a hole a hundred feet deep out of solid volcanic lava, without the use of any modern tools. The hole had to be big enough to fit a multi-story building and a surrounding courtyard. Hundreds, maybe thousands of workers would be on the site for years, breaking up the tough volcanic stone and removing it from the site. The workers would all need to be fed, and their families would need to be housed. Expert stonemasons and engineers would have to be brought in as supervisors. As the hole got deeper, it would become harder and harder to remove the debris. Huge cranes would have to be built. Two hundred thousand tons of rock would have to be safely lifted straight up out of the pit, loaded onto some form of transport, and hauled away from the immediate area. As for the temple itself, highly skilled stone carvers would have to do all of the work. One mistake, and the entire project would be ruined.

King Krishna I of the Rashtrakut dynasty contemplated the building plans before him. The expense would be enormous. The logistics would intimidate any builder. Even today, with modern technology and machinery, this would be a monumental project. There were serious risks. What if they worked for years, only to find a fissure or an air pocket in just the wrong spot? What if they encountered a cavern, or an underground river, or a layer of weaker material underneath the stronger volcanic stone? What about groundwater welling up and flooding the pit? What if they dug for years and years, only to face heartbreak at the very end? Any one of these possibilities would ruin the project.

The King and his builders also had to know the project would take centuries of labor. They must have realized the temple would not be completed during their lifetimes. In all likelihood, they would only live long enough to see the top story of the central tower! King Krishna would build his greatest temple knowing he would never be able to worship there. The temple's designer also knew he would never live to see the completion of his entire life's work. Kings love to design great monuments to demonstrate their personal glory. This King was building something beyond himself, something only future generations would see.

There were other dangers as well. What if a war started and all the slaves and workers had to be diverted to defense? What if some natural disaster swept over the kingdom, and the project had to be abandoned? What about the next generations? Would the King's successors continue the project after his death? Would their faith be as strong as his? Would they be willing to spend all their blood and treasure on that belief, knowing that they, too, would not live to see the temple finished? Or would the project someday lie half-finished and abandoned; a monumental waste of all his efforts?

Despite all the incredible risks, the King gave the orders to start work, and they began to carve their monumental sculpture out of solid rock. It eventually was completed, and it still stands today. They dug out 70,000 square feet of solid rock. The temple occupies an area of over 18,300 square feet. Covered with masterpieces of Hindu art carved from solid stone, it stands as a testimony to the power of faith. In this case, a faith that truly moved mountains!

Dave and I were fortunate enough to be able to visit Ellora in 1990. Even today, Kailasa is still a working temple, and Hindus worship there daily. I'll never forget the day we spent exploring this unique temple.

recommended Google search: Kailas Temple Ellora India Images

A DELIGHTFUL DINNER OVER A CAMEL DUNG FIRE

We met them in Jaisalmer, the golden city, a fabulous dreamscape straight out of the Arabian Nights! Deep in the desert of Rajasthan, India, Jaisalmer is an almost forgotten outpost that, long ago, was a famous caravan stop on the fabled Silk Road. You can still see it as it once was: sandcastle walls and curvaceous onion domes atop delicate, arched porticos, their spires reflected in the waters of the desert oasis. It's a labyrinth of incredibly ornate sandstone palaces and historic *haveli* houses owned by well-to-do merchant families, hiding their mysteries behind delicate stone screens, above narrow, exotic market streets. And it is the desert home of many lovely, friendly people.

We encountered two of those people while taking photos of the city palace and the castle grounds. Durga and his wife Paravati were desert musicians. (Yes, curiously, they were both named after female Hindu goddesses.) They dressed in the colorful outfits of the country folk in that area. She wore a full skirt with spangles and bits of mirror sewn onto it, and her limbs jingled with heavy anklets and glass bangles as she danced. He wore an embroidered vest over his shirt, long, baggy white trousers, and a bright red turban. Durga played the desert violin, an instrument fashioned from what looked like a half a gourd covered in goatskin. The neck of his fiddle was carved out of wood and it was played with a curved, horsehair bow.

Durga could play and sing very well, and he occasionally accompanied himself by making strange, percussive clicking noises with his mouth. Parvati sang and danced, her anklets jingling. They performed on the street near the museum, making a living from donated tourist dollars.

We enjoyed their music, so we began a halting conversation with them. Their English wasn't bad, which was remarkable, especially considering they probably never had the opportunity to study it in school. They were nomadic, tribal people; maybe they'd never even been to school. We talked about playing music, and violins, and we showed them pictures of the snow in Vermont, which they couldn't believe was real. They told us that the children of Jaisalmer had rarely seen rain.

It was an interesting conversation, and we enjoyed each others' company. Then, they invited us to dinner, which made us uneasy. There were two reasons to back out of a dinner invitation. One was that we might not be able to eat the food offered (tourists should never eat anything raw or washed in the local water if it hasn't been properly cooked). The second was because we knew firsthand how tough it is to make a living as street musicians. Feeding two foreigners dinner might be too much for them. I didn't want to be a burden.

As I recall, we begged off with a lame excuse. It was one of those awkward moments because we hated to refuse them, yet we were sure it would be for the best. I felt incredibly guilty about it, though. We pretended we had a prior engagement.

That afternoon, we decided to take a camel ride out to some monuments in the desert. These were a series of *chattris* (columned, open pavilions with elegant onion-domed rooftops), which were funerary cenotaphs dedicated to Jai Singh II (1688-1743). It was a romantic destination! The ride out and back took several hours, and the sun was just setting as we arrived back in town. The camel guides had us disembark just outside of the city, in a sandy area where many of the poor workers from the city lived. There were tents and huts set up nearby.

As the camels knelt to let us off, two of those people looked up with big grins on their faces. It was Durga and Parvati! "You came, after all!" they exclaimed. "Welcome! We will make you tea and Aloo Gobi (cauliflower and potato curry)."

Sure enough, we were right beside their tent. There was no getting around it; we were going to their "house" for dinner. Sometimes, when you travel, you just have to go with the flow. We accepted sheepishly and took a seat around the campfire. Parvati went to fetch some extra provisions and dried camel dung for the fire. Durga took out his fiddle and played while she cooked, and their young children shyly scoped us out.

Soon, the curry was cooking merrily on the fire, and chapati breads were heating on the warm rocks. Parvati smiled joyfully, and Durga was laughing and singing. At other nearby campfires, people were clapping along to his lilting melody. It was a magical moment. The vibrant orange sunset over the ancient walled city, the camels, the tents, the campfire, the cooking smells, the music... and then, the food! As I recall, Parvati made a delicious and aromatic curry, and it was a wonderful, magical dinner after all.

After dinner, things got awkward again. Parvati hugged me, and then she took off her heavy silver anklets and offered them to me as a gift! I told her that we had no money with us to pay for them. (We really didn't have any; we had left it all at the hotel as a precaution against robbers in the desert). She said she didn't want money. But, I protested, I had nothing to give her in return! All I had was the contents of my little daypack.

I could not accept her gift and walk away. These people had nothing but a pup tent to live in! Inside the tent, I saw nothing but sleeping blankets. They had no possessions but the clothes on their backs. And they had just fed us out of kindness and friendship. I decided I could part with my red plastic wristwatch. It wasn't worth much, but Parvati loved it, although she certainly had no use for it. I also gave her my umbrella (used for sun protection). This one had an automatic pop-up button. When I deployed it, Parvati burst into peals of lilting laughter. She grabbed it and ran to all the neighbors' tents, popping the umbrella for each group. I was glad to give up the umbrella; it would be a godsend for the family when the April hot season would send desert temperatures up over one hundred degrees for three months. And I found one more thing in the bottom of my pack: a precious packet of needles and thread, which I had put in my bag so I could mend something on the train. Parvati's eyes went wide when she saw the needles—this was a gift of great value to her.

As for me, I lugged those heavy metal anklets all over India. I had no use for them (far too jingly for me), but they were very, very special, nonetheless. I wouldn't part with them for the world. They reminded me of the childlike joy that seemed to radiate out of Parvati. I can just picture her now, sporting my red plastic wristwatch along with her tribal bangles as she sits regally beneath her new purple parasol.

recommended Google search: Jaisalmeer India Images

OM SHANTI: India's spirituality

India is chaos. Everything is confusing and overwhelming, from the crowded streets to the religious diversity. There are so many ethnic groups, so many unique regions, so many languages, and so many gods. The visitor is bombarded with sights, sounds, smells, and tastes. It is a land of extremes, like the vast gulf between the untouchables and the upper castes. In such a state of chaos, I wonder how it is that India engenders feelings of inner peace (*Om Shanti*). What is it about India, amid the suffering and the struggles of millions of people, that awakens latent spirituality? And, if India does do a better job of uplifting the human spirit, then what are we doing wrong here in the West? What can we learn from this apparent contradiction?

PRIMORDIAL RELIGION: Perhaps it is because of the extreme age of the Hindu religion. The roots of Hinduism are thought to have begun as early as 7000 BC, and Indus valley civilization reached its peak between 2800–2000 BC. The most ancient writings from this period have yet to be deciphered! The Upanishads, the ancient Sanskrit texts that first alluded to the concepts of karma and reincarnation, were written starting in 800 BC. Buddhism and Jainism branched off from Hinduism around 400 BC, adding new energy to India's spiritual fire.

The philosophy behind these religions blossomed at the very beginnings of human civilization, and its influence has been global. One controversial scholar has even argued that Christ may have visited India in his early adulthood, during the period of his life when the Bible does not account for his whereabouts. Some evidence suggests that Christ may have visited Orissa to learn yoga and meditation, and to listen to the teachers and philosophers there. If that is true, then India's influence is undeniably global. This theory is plausible. Christ would have been drawn to India because it was arguably the world's other most sophisticated religious center of the time.

128

By Diana McLeod

VARANASI: Even the most casual visitor to the city of Varanasi cannot avoid appreciating a dawn boat ride down the river. It is impossible not to feel empathy with the pilgrims who have come to this sacred place to celebrate the rising of the sun (Surya) and to thank the River Goddess Ganga for her life-giving water. Worshippers have come continuously for over three thousand years, possibly even longer. The timeless spirituality of their prayers is not lost on anyone.

And yet, the holy river is hopelessly polluted. Mobs swarm around the *ghats* (the massive lines of stairs leading down to the riverbank). Silence, even at dawn, is not an option. The continuous hum of the crowd is punctuated by blaring conch-shell temple trumpets, drums, temple bells, hawkers, traffic noise, and the raised voices of holy men preaching to groups of disciples. The disturbing stench of smoke from funeral pyres sometimes assaults the nostrils.

The first time we went to Varanasi, twenty years ago, I made my own pilgrimage to the water's edge. Dave had gone off by himself to take pictures, so I wandered down to the *ghats,* threading my way through the crowds. Walking down the stairs, I passed a group of lepers begging for alms. In those days, leprosy was still prevalent, and these poor souls had lost most of their hands and feet to the disease. Their noses and ears were rotting away, and their bodies were covered with hideous open sores. And yet, one of them smiled at me with the sweetest and most blissful smile imaginable! His eyes were filled with astonishing light. Was it actually joy? How can peace of mind exist side by side with a flesh-eating disease? How was it that I, the rich foreign tourist, was the one who walked away unsettled, wondering if *I* was the one who was looked at with compassion?

THE FLOATING OFFERING I MADE: I had brought a sentimental item with me all the way from America—a tiny doll's sandal. This toy was one of many gifts given to me when I was seven years old by an Indian lady, Miss Padma Shakya Narayan. I was fascinated by her, and she was kind enough to "adopt" me as her friend. She was my first introduction to a person from a culture outside of my own, and our friendship was exciting and intoxicating. Meeting her was an event of significance in my early life.

When we visited India for the first time, I decided to bring the little sandal to Varanasi. I bought a banana leaf "boat" with a candle and flowers in it, set the miniature shoe among the flowers, and lit the candle. My little raft floated serenely down the Ganges—my gift to the river. It joined hundreds of other candle rafts on their way into the river's embrace. Each one held a wish, a dream, or a prayer.

The next day, Dave and I returned to the ghats. We saw that a large crowd had formed on the riverbanks. A Hindu holy man was preaching, and the people were drawn to his words. I will never forget his face. He had a radiant look that caught our attention and gave us pause. Such dynamism and energy! It was almost as if he gave off an electric current. At the heart of that current was compassion as well as a supreme sense of humor. It was as if he had figured out the punch

129

line of the great cosmic joke, and he was trying to share it with us, but we were incapable of understanding.

Was he an enlightened being? Watching him, we both decided that it was possible. Dave and I were captivated by him for almost an hour, and we listened to his preaching, even though we couldn't understand a word of what he was saying. It didn't matter. Whatever he was teaching wasn't communicable with words anyway.

ELLORA: So many places in India have acquired their own unmistakable spiritual aura. Ellora is famous for a series of caves and rock temples carved into a series of stony bluffs. We visited them in 1990, and I will never forget that visit. There was an entire monastic "university" of tunnels and man-made caverns inside the cliffs. Between the fifth and seventh centuries A.D, these caves were humming with discourse, populated by some of the greatest religious minds of the time, and Buddhism bloomed and flowered.

One chapel stands out. It is a meditation hall, sometimes called the "Carpenters' Hall," because the carvers sculpted ceiling "beams" carved out of solid rock. In the front of the chapel stands an impressive stone Buddha image, about fifteen feet tall. This room has an almost palpable aura of sanctity about it. It is as if the ghosts of the past are still there, still worshiping and debating, and keeping the place holy.

We had taken a local bus to get to the caves. Our bus held forty tourists from many parts of India, our guide, and the two of us. We were lucky; groups from several diverse regions were on board, so the tour guide resorted to English as the most common language. (English is taught in public schools).

The Indian sightseers were a boisterous group, but when we got to this famous cave, they suddenly fell silent. None of these people were Buddhist. Nevertheless, when they entered the ancient sanctuary and gazed upon the compassionate face of the Buddha, they were obviously all moved, as were we. Minutes went by and still, there was silence. Afterward, I turned to the tour guide and asked him if this usually happens.

"Always,'" he replied, smiling. "Everybody feels something here. This place is still sacred to all."

SIKHISM: One of the world's newest religions, Sikhism was founded in India in the fifteenth century. Based on the teachings of its founding Guru, its core principles are faith, meditation, and charity for all. It teaches that no single religion has absolute answers or a monopoly on truth.

Dave and I were mightily impressed by a Sikh community we visited in Gwalior, India. We were drawn there by their elegant new temple, situated high on a hill overlooking the city. A devotee met us at the gates and proudly offered to show us the community. We toured the temple first, and found it to have the simplicity of a mosque, the beauty of a Hindu temple, and the calm, meditative atmosphere of a Buddhist shrine.

Next, we were shown the kitchens. Inside, volunteers were preparing food for more than a thousand people. Sikh temples feed anyone who is hungry three times a day, every day. Giant steaming cauldrons of rice and *dahl* lentils were cooking over wood fires. Over a hundred people were slapping *chapati* dough for bread. This temple feeds between one and two thousand of the city's poor. It is a huge undertaking.

Lastly, we were shown the guesthouse where anyone who needs shelter may stay with the community for as long as they like. The guesthouse included both private rooms and a communal sleeping area in the huge dining hall. We were invited to leave our hotel and come to stay for free for as long as we wished, and we were invited to stay for meals as well.

We declined the hospitality, but left a very generous donation for the temple. I could see exactly where the money was going, and it was all to the good.

THE TAJ MAHAL: The Taj is only a tomb, created out of a man's love for a woman, but its soaring white towers and marble dome stun visitors when they see it for the first time. It appears to float on the horizon like a mirage. People linger here, staring, mesmerized by the exquisite beauty of this monument to love. It was never meant to be a spiritual refuge—except for one man's broken-hearted spirit—but it has become swept up in the intense spirituality of India.

HOLY LAND? Perhaps it is the chaos, and not the "holiness," we Westerners actually respond to. The constant stream of images, colors, sounds, smells, contrasts and contradictions strain our minds, knocking us out of our usual thought patterns and habits. All the mental noise gets pushed aside. We are forced to live in the moment, forgetting the past and the future because we have to face the constantly changing "now." To be in India requires simplification. It also requires tolerance, calm, and Buddha-like patience. And sometimes, just when you least expect it, India provides the traveler with a truly "*Om Shanti*" moment.

recommended Google search: Varanasi India Images

CHAOS ON STEROIDS: DELHI, INDIA

DELHI 2016. How can I describe the chaos that is India? I'm staying in a little alley guesthouse in Pahar Ganj; a cheap but well-run little dive that only costs me $18 a night including breakfast. In the morning, I prepare myself for the onslaught of India and head off down the alley. Immediately, a motorbike almost runs me down, and a porter with an overloaded handcart squishes me up against the wall, right beside the fresh omelet street vendor. The omelet guy has cartons of unrefrigerated fresh eggs balanced precariously on the corner of his portable stove table. I wonder how often they wind up cracked on the pavement when a bicycle rickshaw driver catches them on his big wheels. As I wait, unable to proceed, the omelet seller offers me one of his omelets. I've already had breakfast, but I wouldn't dream of buying one from him anyway because the public male urinals are right down the alley, way too close for comfort. The stench nearly knocks you over until you learn to breathe through your mouth (a habit you learn quickly here). There are other powerful fragrances here as well. A few steps later, I am consciously savoring some of them: sandalwood incense, jasmine, curry spices, cardamom, and the aroma of fresh bread from the *tandoori* oven across the street.

I emerge onto the main bazaar street, and I walk past the Citibank ATM, which won't accept any of my debit cards, even though we called each company in advance and told them the specific dates when we would be in India. As I walk along, I get accosted. First of all, there are female beggars, each with an infant. (The unfortunate child is sometimes rented and may even be drugged). Some of these women attempt the "milk scam." They tell foreigners they don't want money, just please buy some milk for the baby. The formula is usually sold right back to the store from whence it came, and the money is spent on other things. The infant, of course, takes the breast, never the expensive bottle.

A young Eastern European woman approached me. She claimed her bag was stolen in the railway station, including her money and her passport, and she was desperate. She said she had only ten rupees in her pocket. My reaction was: "I never hand out money, but you must be hungry, let me buy you lunch."

"No, thank you," she said, "I just need money to pay off the guesthouse."

"Honey," I replied, "if what you said was true, you would take me up on my offer, and then you would eat like a starving person because you wouldn't know where your next meal was coming from."

Seeing her scam wasn't working on me, she took off in search of a new mark. She was probably a drug addict who supported her habit by scamming tourists. Some people go to India, get hooked, spend all their cash on drugs, and then they can't go home. They remain in India, victims of their own bad choices.

By Diana McLeod

While I am dodging the women, the men get started. These guys are the commission *lepcas*. They don't have shops of their own, so they spend all day trying to chat up tourists and talk them into going with them to specific (and usually horrifically expensive) souvenir shops, where their victims pay the inflated tourist price plus the "guide's" 40-50% commission. India's commission salesmen are slick. They have disarming smiles, a charming demeanor, are flirtatious and often quite good looking. They like to target older women like me (lucky me!) Fortunately for both me and them, I refuse to waste their time. I have my contacts, and the last thing I need is a commission guy following me around. I smile, flirt back, and say I'm too busy, sorry. They tell me to keep smiling, and I do. The energy on this street is infectious. I often find myself with a bemused smile on my face, laughing at all the chaos.

While all of this has been going on, I have been dodging traffic from all sides: bicycle rickshaws, motorized rickshaws, an oxcart, cars, a white horse decorated for an evening wedding procession, and a porter with a giant metal box on his head, which would have grazed my scalp if I had not noticed him coming up behind me. Luckily, I ducked. I also had to swerve to avoid big sheets of cardboard being thrown from a third story window. A motorbike nearly ran over my foot. A cow strolled down the street right behind me, horns inches away from my rear. All of this happened within one block. Is it any wonder I had to backtrack to find the shop I was going to in the first place?

The pedestrian traffic is just as difficult. I dodge businessmen, tall, turbaned, dagger-wearing Sikhs, ladies in spangled saris with children in tow, guys hovering around the street food vendors' carts, and hazards of all kinds. Bewildered tourists, overwhelmed by it all, simply stand and gawk in the middle of the road until a cacophony of horns forces them onwards.

I have yet to mention the distractions on either side of the street. The shop displays compete loudly for my attention. Glittering belly dancer outfits dazzle me, along with Aladdin-style curled sandals, brightly colored cotton clothing, spangled harem pants and beaded purses, bangles, sequined scarves, glittering belts, costume jewelry and embroidered *salwar kameez* (India style casual ladies' wear). It's all an eyeful. How can I remember where I'm going with this sensory barrage going on all around me?

As if this wasn't enough, there are other things I mustn't miss underfoot. Treacherous potholes, ankle-twisting obstructions, unnamable disgusting substances, piles of litter, and even the occasional fresh cow-pie are all landmines that must be avoided.

On top of all this, there is a theatrical performance. A group of young men, costumed as Hindu gods and goddesses, are prancing down the street to the insistent beat of a loud drummer. They dance in front of each shop, deliberately blocking customer access until the hapless shopkeeper ponies up with a "donation."

133

The drums and cymbals only add yet another layer to the constant noise of vehicles, street vendors hawking their wares, competing Bollywood pop songs emanating from various restaurants, and above all, the horns. Indians love their horns! Some drivers seem to keep one hand on the horn at all times. The truck horns are so loud they physically hurt my ears. The car horns have fewer decibels but can still be painful. The auto rickshaws have horns that sound like angry ducks. Bicyclists, who sometimes don't have a horn, have this habit of saying "ssh-ssh" to get you out of their way. It took me years to realize that this soft "ssh-ssh" sound was directed at me!

At night, you can add a forest of neon and colored blinking lights to the other distractions. I take my dinner at a restaurant called "The Exotic Rooftop Cafe." The waiter is flirty and sure we've met before. I don't believe his BS for one minute, but I think: *Diana, you're growing old, so enjoy the attention while it lasts.* The boys on the way back to the guesthouse flirt, too. When I have a sneezing fit due to the dust and the dirt, they laugh and call out, "One more, for good luck... "

recommended Google search: Pahar Ganj Delhi Images

THE PERFECT LOCATION FOR
AN INDIANA JONES MOVIE

If I were a Hollywood screenwriter for adventure movies, I would be incredibly inspired by everything in India. It is such an exotic land, full of romance, danger, and mystery. But one location has intrigued me for years.

We took a local bus tour out of the city of Aurangabad to see some UNESCO World Heritage sites, including the famous caves of Ellora. We also visited a historic fortress on that tour, and it was this that caught my imagination and sent it racing.

Daulatabad Fort was built by Mohammed Tughlaq in the 14th century. He was Sultan of Delhi at the time. History has judged him to have been somewhat mentally unbalanced. Surely the mind that thought up this fort might be considered a bit paranoid, to say the least!

As we approached the fort, we couldn't help but notice the primary defense strategy. The defenders had chosen a high hill to build on, which looked like one solid piece of rock. They cut away the sloping areas until they had created sheer cliffs, turning the hill into a giant cylinder. The walls were easily a hundred feet high, straight up, and cut without a foothold, crevasse or any natural means of access. At the top, the rock had been cut fairly flat. At one time, royal palaces were perched up there, along with plenty of room to shelter most of the royal court as well. Most of the ancient buildings were gone now, or in ruins, but a few remained intact. Around this giant plug of stone, two outer fortress walls encompassed five kilometers of land. They were very high and crenellated, with only a couple of elephant gates in each wall.

Let's pretend you are the medieval invader of this fort. You've got a large army, complete with battle elephants. First, you have to break through the two-foot thick elephant gate, which is bristling with spikes. Bowmen are raining arrows mercilessly down on you as you try to ram the gate. They are probably pouring boiling oil on you as well, but somehow, you manage to get through.

The defenders retreat to their next line of defense—the second wall atop which eight huge cannons are mounted, and aimed right at you! Now you are under heavy artillery fire as you fight your way across a large, open courtyard. Your army cannot get through the first barrier all at once because of the gates, so troops must follow slowly behind, which gives the defenders ample opportunity to reload.

Against all odds, you make it through the second set of gates. Now, you gaze down into a deep trench, which was once a moat. Little staircases descend into the trench and come back up the other side. They are so narrow, only a single person at a time can descend. Your elephants are now useless. The army is suddenly on foot and hopelessly spread out.

When Dave and I were at the fort, our guides claimed the Sultan kept enough water in the trench to have crocodiles living in it. They also claimed there was another pool of water on top of the hill, which could be released to flood the trench, making it impossible to cross without encountering hungry crocs.

Somehow, you manage to survive the flooding of the moat. You outwrestle the ferocious crocodiles. Now, you must fight your way back up the steps on the other side and through a thin doorway. There are slits above this entrance, through which boiling oil can be poured with deadly precision. Somehow, you get past the oil and you kill the warriors who are waiting for you on the other side of the wall. Next, you must head for the narrow opening that leads inside the mountain, and enter the "tunnel of death."

The most ingenious part of this fort is that, even here, inside the walls, the cliffs soar straight up into the sky. The only way to get to the top is from within. The tunnel is a narrow pathway, which is cut through solid rock, looping around inside the hill. You must proceed, single file, into the darkness, to face the terrors within.

Luckily, you are a smart invader, which means that you have brought torches. Unfortunately, the defenders have turned the tunnel so that the next level is directly over your head. Holes in the ceiling have been strategically placed so they can douse all of your torches with water. Thus, despite all your planning, you are stumbling around in pitch blackness.

As you feel your way forward, the tunnel rises steadily, then comes to a dip. You wonder why... You are now on a smooth flat floor, in a wider room, which runs for about twenty paces. There is a hiss in the darkness, and suddenly you know the chilling answer. The retreating defenders have dumped baskets full of deadly snakes into this basin. At any moment, you could step on one!

At last, with incredible luck, you ascend out of the snake pit. You feel your way forward, climbing rapidly now. And then, there is a tiny light at the end of the tunnel! You go faster. The faint beam of daylight is growing brighter than before.

Alas, now the fort's' defenders play the cruelest trick of all—the coup-de-grâce—literally. Each person coming through the tunnel is obliged to crawl out through a tiny hole on his (or her) hands and knees. Even the kings were forced to enter the citadel this way. (And today we complain about airport security.) At the end of the tiny crawlspace, each person must exit head-first. On either side of the door, two soldiers wield giant axes. Anyone who fails to identify themselves as a defender would immediately have their head cut off! There is even a trench thoughtfully cut in the floor of the courtyard so that heads would roll conveniently into the gutters.

One would think that, with all those security measures, the fort was impregnable to attack, but the stronghold actually did fall to invaders. They overcame the defenses in classic Indian style. They simply bribed all the guards and took the fort without any major casualties. It only goes to show that the cleverest defense mechanisms are always vulnerable to human treachery.

BLUE MAN

Dave and I were sunbathing on the beach at Kovalam when a man who sold clothing approached us. Dave took a liking to a pair of blue pants. He haggled with the guy, got what he considered to be a fair price, and bought them. He wore them for about two hours before the seam split completely up the back. And then he got his big surprise: his entire lower half was dyed bright blue! It was almost too bad his other half didn't get the same treatment because the local population would have mistaken him for the Hindu God Krishna! Poor Dave was blue for days, which was unfortunate at the beach!!!

By Diana McLeod

LIAR, LIAR PANTS ON FIRE: A SURVIVAL GUIDE TO INDIA

Before I launch into this story, I want to make one observation: People in India are some of the nicest, kindest, most personable people everywhere. Dave and I adore the Indians—they are sparky, fun loving and generous to a fault. Ninety-nine percent of Indian society does not deserve a bad reputation, and one should never conclude I think ill of them all because of the actions of a tiny few. But of course, in every society, there are always those who make a living off the tourists, and some are in the criminal class. In India, these folks all congregate where foreigners are apt to be. As the Indonesian proverb says: "Where there is sugar, there are ants." The first-time tourist will be targeted by them to the point they will probably become convinced the entire population consists of scammers, con artists and high-pressure salespeople, which is certainly not the case. And most of the scams are genteel, relatively speaking. They take a modest commission from you, which you won't even realize if the scam is done well. There is very little serious crime in India compared to many other countries, including our own. This is remarkable for a country with massive urban centers when so many are desperately poor.

If you are going to go to India, you'd better have an excuse ready. You'd better have an arsenal of excuses, one for every contingency. In fact, you'd better turn yourself into a big fat liar. Apply a protective layer of B.S. like sunblock, or carry it around with you like Mace. You're going to need it, the minute you step outside.

In our society, just saying "No, thank you," is enough. Not so in India. Dave tried that once. Actually, he said "no" at least fifty times, but the guy he was saying "no" to followed him for over five minutes, continuously pestering him. You need a special reason or excuse. You develop a series of "invisible friends." "I have an appointment." "I'm meeting my friend in fifteen minutes." "I'm going to the train station. I don't have time because I'm flying out this afternoon."

It's hard to walk down the street in a tourist area without being accosted by scammers and hustlers. They'll follow you around endlessly. If you don't have a good excuse ready, you'll never get rid of them. The classic *lepca* is desperate to get you to visit somebody's shop, where there is a "special sale today." That "special bargain" is a rip-off price for you and a commission for him. If you are not confident about where you are going, you will instantly acquire the unwanted services of a "guide" who will promise to take you where you want to go, but who is sure to take a detour... to the very shop you were trying to avoid in the first place. If you walk slowly or aimlessly, browsing the shop windows like the tourist you are, you're doomed. Then there are the money changers, the fortune-tellers, the fake "holy men"...

137

Try getting a taxi to visit a museum. Oh, you'll get a taxi without a problem. But drivers hate taking you to a museum because they'll have to drop you off and never get a chance at all those shopping commissions. As soon as they get you out of the neighborhood (and hopelessly lost), the B.S. will begin. "I don't know why you want to go there; it is closed for renovations. Oh yes, they had a terrible fire. It was in the papers. You didn't know?" "Oh, the museum is closed today." (Really? Whoever heard of a museum that closes on Sundays?) Or (our favorite), "The museum is closed because Rajiv Gandhi died," to which Dave responded by reminding our driver that Rajiv Gandhi had been dead for years.

Scams are everywhere, and the scam artists are very good at it. The worst part is, as I said before, that the Indian people are also the nicest, friendliest, most charming people in the world. Sometimes you do get invited to real family events and weddings. It's incredibly difficult for the tourist to figure out which invitations are sincere and which are scams. On our first trip to India, one guy took us out to a restaurant for lunch and then invited us to a special event followed by a family dinner. He said he would need some money to buy extra concert tickets for us, and he would pay us back the next day. Dave and I felt like we were on the spot. Our friend had already used up his cash to buy us lunch. If our "friend" were on the level, accusing him of scamming would have been unspeakably rude. The chances were equally good that he was sincere. Jet-lagged and caught off guard, we couldn't think of a gracious reason not to give him the ticket money. We had already told him we would accept his invitation. We were stuck, netted by a master scammer, a true artist. The small amount of money we lost that day was worth it, and it paid for a valuable lesson we would never forget. We vowed to develop a virtual Rolodex of excuses why we couldn't do this or that. Today, I would deflect this scam with ease: "Oh, we left our wallets in the hotel safe. Tell us where the ticket office is, and we'll go and pick up our own tickets."

I got better at it. I became quite a B.S. artist in my own right. One day, in Delhi, (shamelessly bragging here), I became so hot that my pants really should have been on fire.

My friend Ruth and I arrived in Delhi together. Ruth had a professional broadcast-quality video camera, and we had agreed to pay for her ticket from Kathmandu in return for her shooting a T.V. commercial for us. Her camera was large and weighed about ten kilos.

We arrived at the railway station and piled into a three-wheel taxi to go to our hotel. But instead, we got hijacked down a side alley. The taxi parked at a building marked "Tourist Information Center." I was familiar with this classic scam. Tourists are told this is a government service, provided to ensure their hotel is safe and accredited. The scammers pretend to call the hotel and then announce it is already fully booked. The tourist is taken to a different hotel. The scammers get a commission from the new lodgings, and the hapless tourist is none the wiser and usually winds up at a much less desirable location.

By Diana McLeod

I told Ruth to wait for me in the taxi with all of our stuff. I would take care of it. The scam played out just as I suspected. I didn't dare accuse them of scamming me—there were four large guys in there and I was alone. If I had accused them, there could have been violence. No, I had to counter-scam. As an idea came to me, I broke into a sudden grin. "So you are sure that my hotel is fully booked?" I asked.

"That is correct. I am so sorry, Madam."

"This is GREAT!" I crowed. "Do you know what this means? You see, I am friends with the son of the family that owns that hotel. The guy's name is Raju. He's filthy rich! He knows I'm coming today because I just talked to him yesterday. If the hotel is full, that means he'll pick us up and take us to the family compound. I'll stay there! It will be awesome! Servants everywhere, swimming pool, everything! Now you will tell the driver to take me to my hotel right now!"

They were stuck. The tourist information scammers had to go along with my counter-scam if they were going to maintain their "helpful" facade. Even the driver grinned when he was told to take us to our original hotel after all.

It didn't stop there. David had given me instructions to get us all train tickets to Jaipur, including one for him. His plane was delayed and he hadn't arrived yet. Ruth went with me to the train station. She was unwilling to leave her TV camera in the hotel room, so she lugged it with her.

When I got to the station, the officious little clerk insisted I present all three passports to get three train tickets. (This was because of the "foreigners" quota.) He was a pretty rude guy. I explained my husband had been delayed and I didn't have his passport. He didn't care. India is famous for this kind of bureaucratic nonsense. I knew Dave was expecting me to get the tickets arranged, and I didn't want to disappoint him. The station manager's office was right next door.

"I want to see the manager," I said.

The clerk smirked at me. "That won't do you any good," he sneered.

For some reason, his arrogance wound me up. "Oh yeah?" I sneered back. "Just watch me! I'm going to get those tickets."

He rolled his eyes and grinned. "I bet you won't."

I knew what he was thinking: I was going to go and make a scene, acting like the typical outraged foreigner. But that would have been the dumbest thing to do. Instead, I looked at Ruthie, who was still lugging around the heavy camera, and cooked up a whopper.

I went into the station manager's office looking fretful and ready to burst into tears at any moment. I started with a respectful "*Namaskar*," which is a special greeting reserved for high officials, Brahmin priests and V.I.P.'s.

I explained I was desperate to get three tickets on the Pink City Express, but that my husband's flight was delayed so I only had two passports. I explained my situation: that we were best friends with an Indian family (my friend Raju again), and that we'd come all the way from America just to attend the wedding. We had even hired an American professional videographer to make a video as a special wedding gift. (This incident took place in 1995, in the days before small DVD cameras and cell phones). Dave was going to be the still photographer. If we missed meeting the family at the train station, we would have no way of finding the family's home, and their only telephone was at Raju's business, which was closed for the wedding! Even if Ruth and I took the train by ourselves, my husband would miss the beginning of the wedding of his best friend, and he would have to struggle to find us in Jaipur. I had a photocopy of his passport. I hated to be a burden, but was there any way the station manager could bend the rules for me, just this once?

He took one look at our worried faces and another look at the huge camera Ruth was lugging and signed the waiver straight away. Indians are so sentimental about weddings!

I loved seeing that officious little clerk eat crow. And, while I still feel a little bit guilty about telling that nice man a whopper, my pants only felt slightly singed. It was the only way to get my tickets. India had taught me well.

India has improved since those days. There seems to be less hustle now than there used to be. And, while India is famous for tourist hustle, every country has its share of B.S. artists. We Americans aren't used to "in your face" pressure tactics being used on tourists—but if you think our country is superior, have you checked your email lately?

NEVER, NEVER DRIVE A BICYCLE RICKSHAW YOURSELF!

INDIA, 1995. For those of you who don't know, a bicycle rickshaw is a pedaled taxi. Its front looks like a typical bicycle, but the rear is a widened loveseat on wheels. It is made to hold two people (although I have seen them with six passengers and luggage!) Behind the passengers is a folding canopy, which pulls forward to shelter them from rain or hot sun. Bicycle rickshaws are very picturesque. They can also be quite dangerous in the wrong hands.

These contraptions can be hazardous in traffic. Most of them are old machines rented out to impoverished young men with no other way to make a living. At best, they have half the control of an old-fashioned English-style bicycle. At worst, they have dying brakes and such sloppy steering they seem to have minds of their own. Most of the guys who drive them do their own mechanical maintenance, which usually makes matters worse.

I've had a few very close calls on these little suicide machines. In Kathmandu, I remember taking a steep hill on two out of three wheels when my driver lost his brakes in the face of multi-lane oncoming traffic. Another time, my rickshaw almost ran into a six-foot deep, unmarked construction ditch. That was a close call! And we were involved in one serious accident, which occurred in Agra, India. Dave was driving...

It was a beautiful moonlight night. Our hotel was a little distance outside the city. The road took us past a military camp, which had training fields surrounded by barbed wire fences on both sides of the road. The road was empty of traffic, and our driver asked Dave if he would like to try driving. The idea sounded fun. Dave agreed, so he hopped into the front seat and the driver sat in the back with me.

The road ran on an elevated embankment about eight feet above the level of the fields. It was two lanes wide, flat and well paved. Neither Dave nor I thought we might be in any danger. We did not realize how difficult bicycle rickshaws are to steer.

Dave started off, trying to get the old rattletrap moving. He had some trouble building up momentum. As he got started, the handlebars turned slightly to the left. The machine responded by veering violently, taking him completely by surprise. I looked down at the eight-foot embankment, with a six-foot high barbed wire fence at the bottom, and my heart began to pound.

Dave also saw the danger. He gave the handlebars a turn in the other direction. Again, the rickshaw swerved wildly in response, and we headed for the other side of the road! The driver and I both yelled, and Dave did his best to react, but it was too late. We rolled straight down the embankment and crashed into the barbed wire at high speed.

The impact was more of a bounce than a crash because the barbed wire reacted like a vertical trampoline. Dave somehow managed to hold on to the handlebars, which saved him from being hurled face-first into the fence. The driver and I weren't as lucky. We both flew straight up in the air, tossed skywards like rice at a wedding. I landed on a sharp rock, right in the middle of my back. I still don't understand how my back survived without breaking. Somehow, I was unhurt. The driver had the worst of it. He was hopping around, holding one leg and screaming. I was sure his leg was broken, so we were dreadfully afraid for him.

There was no one around to help. At last, a motorcyclist approached us, and we flagged him down. We asked him to call the police so that we could get our driver to a hospital. His response stunned us.

"No!" he said. "Not the police! No ambulance! They will only cause more trouble. This is India, not America. They'll beat him, and arrest him, and they'll give you trouble also. Never mind about him! You are important people. He is not. He is nothing. He is not your concern. Just walk away and leave him. If you want to give him some rupees, give him some rupees. That is all."

The motorcyclist was a wealthy, high-caste Indian. He was wearing a dress suit with a tie, and he sported gold rings on his fingers. Our driver was from the very lowest castes in India. He was probably a *Dalit* (an untouchable).

We were horrified by the upper caste callousness. In the end, we did take his advice, but only after we realized that the "broken leg" was just a severely barked shin. As the pain dissipated, our driver was able to stand on it without limping. He would have a big bruise in the morning, but no serious harm was done. We also checked the bike over. It had a bent rim on the front tire, and a few other damages, but again, nothing serious.

In the end, we gave the driver enough rupees for several days of recovery, including enough to cover all repairs to the rickshaw and more. The motorcyclist thought we were crazy to do that much. He drove away, promising to send a second rickshaw for us. When the new rickshaw came, the driver promised to pick up the injured man on his return trip.

The whole experience gave us a revealing view of the Indian caste system, and a personal lesson: NEVER, NEVER DRIVE A BICYCLE RICKSHAW YOURSELF!!!

THE WEDDING CRASHERS

"Stop the car!"

Dave and I were in the back seat of our friend Sudarshan's SUV in Jaipur, India. Our host was chauffeuring us back to our hotel after a lovely dinner at his home in 2014. It was the busiest time of India's wedding season, and Dave was determined to photograph as many Indian nuptial celebrations as possible. He had just spotted a wedding palace beside the road, and the venue was all decked out for the huge party taking place inside. The reception even had two elephants greeting guests at the door. We had not been able to photograph elephants at a wedding yet. This was Dave's big chance. "Stop the car," he said, "We'll get off here."

Sudarshan couldn't believe we were serious. He finally pulled over. "How will you get back to your hotel?" he asked anxiously. "And how are you going to get into that wedding? Do you know these people?"

Dave laughed. "We'll get home on our own, by motor rickshaw, Sudarshan-Ji," he said. "As for the wedding, we'll just invite ourselves. Why not? We've already crashed two weddings thanks to you, and another one on our own. Thanks so much for the dinner and the ride! We'll see you at work tomorrow."

Dave leaped out, ran across the street, and started taking pictures of the elephants, while I followed with my video camera. The elephants were beautifully decorated with traditional colored chalk designs and bespangled cloth headpieces. The turbaned mahouts were happy to pose them for us as they greeted the guests.

It did not take long for us to get noticed. A young man emerged from the fancy tent, introduced himself to me, and asked us what we were doing there. I told him, quite frankly, we were doing a photo essay for our website in the U.S.

"Most Americans have no idea just how spectacular Indian weddings are," I explained. "We were driving by and saw the elephants. We haven't yet been to a reception that was fancy enough to have elephants. Your family must be quite important."

That was Step One. Step Two was to mention we were in the jewelry business. *Everybody* in Jaipur is in the gemstone and jewelry business. The young man I was talking to was also in the jewelry business. What a coincidence!

We were suddenly V.I.Ps. We were whisked into the silken tent, down the red carpet, under the glittering chandeliers, and out onto the wedding pavilion's lawn. It didn't matter we were not appropriately dressed for the occasion. We were wealthy foreign business prospects, immediately welcomed by the entire family.

We declined dinner, explaining we had just come from another party, but our host insisted we try a few dessert delicacies. He snapped his fingers, and a waiter veered in our direction, carrying a tray of iced dessert drinks served in crystal stemware. Mine was deliciously strawberry. Dave tried mango. Other waiters were ordered to tempt us with elegant pastries and Indian sweets wrapped in real silver foil. I had to try a few, even though I had already stuffed myself with a delicious dinner at Sudarshan's.

I met both sides of the family, while Dave quickly excused himself so that he could get better pictures. It was a very colorful scene! There was a broad expanse of lawn, with tables scattered here and there, packed with family and friends who were still finishing their dinners. There were other tents on the sidelines in which cooks and caterers were still preparing meals and drinks for latecomers.

The centerpiece of the wedding reception was a raised stage with an amazing backdrop behind it. This thirty foot tall (mostly white) stage "set" looked like an Ancient Greek theater wedded to a Mexican wedding cake. There were Greek columns (Ionic, Doric, and Corinthian), little porticos and niches with oversized fake Greek vases in them, and fake Greek marble statues everywhere. Carved Rococo flourishes (garlands, cupids, etc.) adorned the layers of architectural excessiveness like icing on the cake. (We had already been to two other events, and the façades on their stages had similar themes. The classical Greek motif was apparently all the rage in Jaipur that year, and all the wedding pavilions were going for the "Greek chic" look).

The stage in front of this overblown ornamentation is not where the actual marriage took place; that ceremony occurred much earlier. These lavish parties are the equivalent of our wedding receptions at home. The bride and groom were stuck on the dais, sitting in throne-like chairs, posing for endless photographs. Dave happily joined the swarm of photographers and was quickly invited right up onto the stage for close-ups. The family was very proud to have an American photographer interested in documenting their event. The fathers of both the bride and the groom made sure everyone noticed Dave's presence.

We were still in time to catch some of the entertainment. Indian weddings usually hire uniformed brass bands, and their primary role is to play for the groom's procession. On the way to the wedding, the groom parades down the street on an elaborately caparisoned white horse, accompanied by the musicians, his entire family and his friends. Sometimes the band is requested to play again at the reception later on in the evening.

In this case, the band was a surprise to us; a Scottish style bagpipe band, of all things! The Indian bagpipers were decked out in full Scottish regalia, kilts and all—a remarkable throwback to the days of the Raj when India was an English colony. Somebody's great-grandfather must have been a British loyalist. The pipes blared out a proper Highland marching song, and the drummers swung their sticks in Scottish style.

I looked around the crowd, easily noting the generation gap. Older people listened attentively to the band, but the younger generation paid it almost no mind. Their musical taste was all Bollywood and Indian hip-hop, these days.

Meanwhile, my young friend was delicately lobbying me to visit his jewelry showroom. I had been upfront with him since our first meeting, and I stuck to the facts. "I would love to visit your showroom," I told him, "but tomorrow is my last day in Jaipur. I have to be on the Ajmer Express train at 5 P.M., and we have to wrap up our business elsewhere first. I will only be able to come if I finish my other business much earlier than expected. But I have your card, and I will try to visit sometime in the future." It was all true. This was my last night in Jaipur.

After the entertainment, we said good night, thanking our hosts profusely for inviting us to their party. The elephants waved goodbye as we hopped in a motorized rickshaw to ride home to our hotel.

recommended Google search: Jaipur weddings Images

(NOTE: some of these images are promotional shots from wedding planning companies; most weddings are not as fancy as the ads).

By Diana McLeod

HUCKLEBERRY FINN IS ALIVE AND WELL—IN KERALA, INDIA

In Southern India, in the province of Kerala, there is a place of childhood dreams. In this land, it is always summer. There are endless canals, bayous, and larger lakes to explore, all full of fish, frogs and turtles. Boats and rafts are everywhere, and even young children can borrow them and paddle to their hearts' content. In the heat of the lazy afternoons, the kids dive in and swim among the pink water lilies and purple water hyacinth, splashing and playing water games. A piece of hemp rope, hanging from a tree branch, provides them with a Tarzan swing.

The land is fertile. Fresh fruit is always ripe for the picking. Banana trees and papayas grow along the riverbank. Coconut palms provide cool shade, sweet milk, and fresh coconut meat. When the children get tired of swimming, they pull out their fishing lines and wait for a bite. They can even dig for freshwater clams, which can be steamed over an open fire.

Overhead, the nodding palm trees arch gently over the canals. White egrets and brilliant blue kingfishers soar past on tropical breezes. Beyond the canal banks, beyond the thin strip of raised levee and the line of brightly painted thatched huts, one can see acres of emerald-green rice fields.

It all makes you want to go there, doesn't it? About thirty years ago, some enterprising locals had the idea to adapt traditional rice barges to accommodate tourists. The wide-bodied barges, with distinctive curled bow and stern decorations, were turned into whimsical houseboats. Arched structures of rattan mats, lashed with bamboo, covering the center of the boat, provide the living spaces. These days, the rattan rooms are artfully decorated with fanciful windows, latticework and verandahs. Some houseboats even have second-story balconies. The boats head out into the canals for romantic overnight trips. Most houseboats dock around the town of Allephuza (formerly Alleppey), Kerala.

We prearranged a houseboat rental on the Internet but worried we might not get the best experience since we couldn't view the boat in advance. Luckily, our barge was perfect for us! These boats are delightful! I can only describe them Tolkien-style: if Hobbits had boats, these would be their favorites. I was like a little kid, grinning from ear to ear as I explored our ride.

Everything on board was made of organic materials, mostly rattan and bamboo. There was only enough battery-powered electricity to power a couple of feeble lights and the fan above our bed. The boat had two bedrooms; one for the crew of four, and one for the two of us. Our bedroom had an eco-friendly toilet, sink, and even a shower. The kitchen was in the stern. In the bow, there was an open dining area, two comfortable chairs, facing forward, and even a lounging mattress with round pillows so we could enjoy the scenery from any angle. I felt like Queen Cleopatra on my barge.

We were also very pleased our crew did not use the motor unless we were in deep water. Most of the time, they poled the boat. Poling, of course, was deadly slow, but our purpose here was to stop being in a hurry, at least for a day or two. Except for one other day in Thailand, this was my first chance to slow down and stop working in several months! We moved with languid grace through the canals. The only sounds we heard were natural ones—the poles in the water, the footfalls of the captain's bare feet as he walked the pole down the deck, the wind in the palms overhead, and the calls of birds and frogs.

The water flowed past tiny villages built along the levees. The thatched huts and colorfully painted cottages were neat and tidy. Mothers did laundry in the canals, and little children splashed in the water. Men worked on their boats or lounged on their front porches. People didn't seem to mind our presence. They smiled and waved cheerfully, even though they must have to greet tourists many times a day.

Time moved so slowly that it was lunchtime before I knew it. (Does that make sense?) We casually tied up the boat by the side of the canal, and the cook served us a delicious vegetarian lunch. What an elegant dining experience! In the afternoon, we moved into some of the larger waterways. We crossed a broad lake and made a circle trip down a series of little canals. Some of them were tiny; we barely squeezed through, and we had one of the smallest houseboats we had seen.

School got out, and suddenly the levees were swarming with children. They ran or bicycled home, with two or three kids balancing on a single bike. In no time at all, the school uniforms were discarded, and they were all jumping into the canals to cool off. Little groups of kids dove in and splashed around our boat as it went by. The youngsters were all easy smiles and silly poses as soon as the cameras appeared.

How could the day go by so quickly? It did, and all too soon we were tied up for the night. We had a lovely dinner and watched the sunset fade. Peace and tranquility settled over the twilight scene like a benevolent mist. I felt divorced from all thought, existing only in the sensual experience of the moment.

Suddenly, an explosive series of sounds made me jump. It was loud, like gunfire. What the...? I ran up onto the bow to see what was going on. Fireworks! Someone in the area was celebrating a wedding! A wealthy local family had hired one of the largest houseboats for a marriage party. Anyway, we had a very nice view of the fireworks, and their glittering reflections dancing in the water. It was very romantic.

That night, we opened up the rattan windows of our little bedroom so we could look directly out onto the moonlit water. All was quiet, except for a few frogs. There didn't even seem to be any mosquitoes, but we kept the net down just in case. I don't remember what I dreamed that night, but I'm sure my dreams were happy ones.

recommended Google search: Kerala Canal Images

EGYPT

A FUNNY THING HAPPENED ON OUR WAY DOWN THE NILE...

Egypt! Fascinating, exotic and ancient, a land lucky enough to have the spectacular remains of one of the world's oldest and most famous civilizations as its heritage. We had traveled south, all the way down to Aswan, so that we could journey to Abu Simbel, the famous temple on the Southern border, built during the realm of Ramses II. It was now time to return to Cairo. The question was: how would we get there? I watched the traditional wooden sailboats (called feluccas) flitting around the Nile, and learned that some of them go on overnight cruises, most of the way back to the capitol. This was my idea of adventure travel! We signed up for a "cruise."

Our felucca was about twenty feet long, with a lateen rigged sail. It was primitive—no engine, no toilet, no cabin, and nothing in the way of amenities. The deck was flat, with thin, futon-like mattresses to sit on. Our luggage and that of our companions were all stashed below the deck. The felucca was piloted by our wiry little turbaned and mustachioed captain, Muhammed. His crewman was also the ship's cook. There were eight tourists on board including ourselves.

We sailed off down the Nile on a bright, beautiful, late morning. The Nile's slow current gave the felucca extra impetus as we cruised downriver. It was so pleasant to be under sail! The natural sounds of the boat and the water soon gave way to a lively conversation as we got to know our fellow adventurers.

After cruising for several hours, the boat stopped for lunch at a colorful camel market in a small town. At sunset, we tied up at a secluded spot along picturesque palm-lined riverbanks, and we all had hot stew cooked over a camp stove. Cold beer even miraculously appeared (for a price), and we talked for a long time with our new acquaintances. Later, bedrolls were brought out of the hold, and we tourists bedded down on the deck.

The next day, I got up the courage to ask if I could steer the boat. This took some nerve, as there were tourist cruise ships all over the river. They were huge, towering three to four stories high above us, and they went very fast. We had no engine, only our sail to keep us out of harm's way. Dodging the cruise ships was unnerving but I loved the challenge, and Muhammed kept a careful eye both on my steering and the river traffic.

The second night, we tied up at a sandbar island in the middle of the river, along with about six other feluccas, each with a load of tourists. After dinner, a huge party got underway on the beach. Because we were in the middle of the Nile and no authorities were around, things soon got pretty wild. The boatmen built a large bonfire on the beach. Loads of cold beer appeared like magic, and the college-age kids were all smoking marijuana. Somebody started to tap out rhythms on a drum, and everyone sang together. I remember harmonizing on a rousing chorus of "In the jungle, the mighty jungle, the lion sleeps tonight." The "a-wim-a-way" part got quite out of hand.

I was tired. The night before, I had not slept well. The desert got bitterly cold at night! Feeling the chill once again, I resolved to turn in early, but Dave wanted to keep partying, so I left and returned to our boat.

Curling up in my bedroll, I drifted off to sleep. After a while, Dave slipped in beside me. He got under the covers and snuggled in close to my back, wrapping one arm around me, which was very pleasant because I was shivering in the desert air. I snoozed for at least another hour or so. And that was when it happened. By the light of the moon, I saw Dave walking onto the boat. He got into his bedroll and went to sleep. I could see the outlines of his face in the darkness.

And that was when it hit me. *If Dave was over there, facing me, how could he be behind me at the same time?* Holy crap! I was snuggling with somebody else! I was floored. For a second, I just lay there. Then I sat up in a hurry, grabbed my pillow and prepared to attack.

It was Captain Muhammed! I smacked him with the pillow and kicked him out of my bed, which I did very quietly, not wanting to wake anyone else, especially my husband! Muhammed gave me a sheepish and somewhat toothless grin and crawled off to his own blankets. I couldn't believe Dave never noticed! He'd had to step around me on the deck. How did he fail to see that telltale white turban?

The next morning, we sailed for an hour or so until we saw the enormous pillars of Kom Ombo mirrored in the Nile waters. What a wonderful way to reach an ancient Egyptian temple—by felucca! The stone steps beside the Nile still served their original function, and we docked there, entering the temple grounds in the very footsteps of the Pharaohs, who would probably have come by ship. Our felucca wasn't exactly Cleopatra's royal barge, but still... We spent about an hour or so at Kom Ombo, marveling at its impressive architecture, and then we moved on.

Our final stop was the magnificent temple at Edfu. This time, we had to leave our boat behind to enter the town. The Temple of Horus was breathtaking, especially because actual rooms inside the massive edifice were perfectly preserved. The level of detail on the hand-sculpted, stone wall murals was exquisite. These were the inner sanctums of the temple, and we were seeing them just as the Pharaohs must have.

Outside, in the courtyard, giant statues of falcons representing the god Horus stood guard. One, sadly, was showing signs of significant wear from thousands of tourist selfie shots. Horus, the God of the Sky, Hunting, and Warfare, was depicted as a man with a falcon's head, or sometimes as a bird.

Afterward, we returned to the boat to pick up our gear. I took a moment to give Muhammad a stern lecture, trying to explain that his actions could have serious consequences in other peoples' relationships. He didn't care in the slightest. He just gave me a snaggle-toothed smile and a shrug. No doubt he couldn't wait to cozy up to his next batch of unwitting female tourists. As we left, I talked to the other girls on the cruise. Apparently, he had visited us all. Nobody was seriously molested, but we were all still quite offended.

I recommend this tour to anyone who is willing to rough it a bit. Just watch out for naughty captains!

recommended Google search: Kom Ombo Images

recommended Google search: Nile felucca Images

MEXICO

DO-SI-DO IN MEXICO

A wild night of dancing on a Mexican Ferry

Picture a passenger ship cruising the ocean on a moonlit night, with at least seventy people dancing on the back deck, having an impromptu fiesta ... and it was all because of my little violin. The year was 1985, but I remember this night as if it was yesterday. It was one of the most unexpected, incredible travel experiences we've ever had.

It all started when we had to take an overnight ferry from the Baja California peninsula to mainland Mexico. We were young, and travel funds were dear then, so we booked deck passage and expected we'd have to sleep right on the open deck that night.

The stern deck was a vast empty space with just a few picnic tables and benches to sit on. There were over two hundred other folks back there, huddled in family groups. Luckily for us all, the weather was perfect that night, the ocean was calm, and the full moon was extraordinarily bright.

Back in those days, I traveled with a child-sized violin. I tuned it up and started playing, and soon I had an audience of young children. Slowly, my audience grew as some of the adults came over to listen as well. Eventually, somebody asked me, in English, if I could play some music so everyone could dance. I looked around and realized they were all staring expectantly at me.

It couldn't possibly work! How could one tiny, squeaky little violin make enough noise for all those people to dance? And what kind of dancing could they possibly do? And then I had a crazy idea.

I asked if anyone in the crowd spoke English well, and an English teacher stepped forward. I told him only one type of music might work in this situation. It was music that they'd never heard before—folk music from the U.S. Given its complicated dance steps, it might be difficult, but if everyone was willing to learn, we would teach them how to do it. We would need some time to prepare, and then everyone would have to pay attention and listen very carefully. He translated everything for the crowd. To my delight, they all said yes.

We got straight to work. Dave and I had had considerable experience teaching square dancing on the Middlebury College campus. When I was in school there, they used to hire us to lead school dances, teaching the students each dance first. I knew all the fiddle tunes from the Champlain Valley Fiddlers' Club, of which I was a member, and Dave found it easy to learn the calls. Our job now was to explain each dance to our translator, and to translate all the square-dance calls into the Spanish language, which Dave would have to memorize.

It worked! We got all the dancers into squares, taught them everything, and then we were ready to start. The Mexicans were eager learners, and quicker than the college students had been at picking up the steps. Luckily, Dave has a powerful singing voice, so he was able to make himself heard without a mike. We started with the easy dances first, and we worked our way all the way up to a full-on Virginia Reel, which is a very complicated dance. After teaching six different dances, we repeated them all over again.

As the Mexicans gained confidence, they relaxed and swung their partners with ease. The back of the deck made an ideal dance floor as we steamed across the tropical sea in the moonlight. *"Duck for the Oyster, Dive for the Clam, Duck for the hole in the Old Tin Can!"* (No, it doesn't translate into Spanish exactly...)

When we finally finished, huge steaming plates of food from the ship's cafeteria arrived for us—gifts from our dancers. Cold beers

By Diana McLeod

magically appeared every time we finished one. Mexicans are very generous and hospitable people! And then, they decided to thank us by sharing their folk music with us. Somebody started to sing an old Mexican love song, and everybody else joined in. It was touching. We responded by trying to think of songs everyone might know. Beatles tunes worked very well. The Mexicans were familiar with the English words even though they did not always understand their meaning. And then came the most magical moment of the night—two hundred people singing "We all live in a Yellow Submarine!"

MOMENTS OF TERROR ON POPOCATÉPETL

Did you know that there is a 17,887-foot volcano within striking distance of Mexico City? And that it erupted in 2015? Today, the volcano Popocatépetl has a seven-mile restricted zone around it because of the danger it poses. City officials live in fear of a major eruption because tens of thousands reside within the immediate evacuation zone. But in the 1980s, when we were exploring Mexico for the first time, the volcano was more dormant, and the national parklands near the top were still open to the public. We didn't hike all the way to the crater's rim due to the altitude, our lack of specialized ice-climbing equipment and a decided lack of ambition. We only went up to 12,000 feet, to a broad ridge covered in thick, alpine grasses, which somehow managed to grow in the sandy, black ash dunes, and we camped out for the night in full view of the snow-capped peak above us.

It was a beautiful evening, sitting on top of the world, watching the fading sunset blush the clouds below us. Later, we kept watching as the stars wheeled slowly overhead, lighting up the snow of the summit above (even at twelve thousand feet, we were still looking up at the equivalent of Mt Washington). We bedded down in our little pup tent for the night, expecting to have to battle the cold and the thin air.

We did not expect to have to battle a bear! In the middle of the night, we heard a very large animal grunting and snuffling around our tent. It was too big and too loud to be a dog. We knew it must be a bear. But what kind of bear? I didn't think Grizzly habitat extended way down to the Sierra Madre in Mexico, but I wasn't sure. We never got a good look at it, whatever it was, but we finally managed to scare it off by banging our pots and pans and yelling loudly. It disappeared back down the ridge and into the forest below the tree line. Was it a bear? Or a *chupacabra*? (a mythical devil-beast) We'll never really know.

Our troubles weren't exactly over. We were eating breakfast the next morning, enjoying the bright sunshine and the splendid view, when mountain climbers hiked past our campsite, heading for the top. We wished them well, watching as they made their way up the base of the cinder cone. They got far enough away that we could just barely spot their brightly colored windbreakers against the black ash, when,

151

all of a sudden, the ground began to shake. Dave and I looked at each other in dismay. We both knew we were too close to survive an eruption. Popo had been dormant for over fifty years. Just our luck!

If it was going to be the end of the world, there was no point in running because we'd never run fast enough. Might as well just sit and enjoy the last big show of our lives...

But it wasn't an eruption. It was a landslide, a big one, and it dislodged one boulder the size of an apartment building, which came rolling down, perilously close to the climbers! It shook the whole mountain. Luckily, no one was crushed. We were very relieved to see all those red and blue jackets still painstakingly making their way up the trail after the juggernaut had passed. What a relief it was when all was quiet once again!

We were still in doubt as to whether or not we should have attempted the ascent when we met some climbers coming down. They were all U.S. Marines, stationed in Texas. They were in top physical condition, but they confessed the mountain had nearly bested them. They were deathly ill from altitude sickness and utterly spent. They said the last, steep climb to the crater's rim was hellish—that is, if hell freezes over. But the view from the top was apparently worth it all. I'm sure it must have been fantastic, but I thought the view from where I was sitting was pretty good, too. It was certainly good enough for me!

P.S.: As I edit this, I realize that the landslide was evidence of the coming eruption. The mountain was bulging with fresh magma, pushing out all those boulders.

recommended Google search: Popocatepetel Images

THAILAND

SEX AND THE CITY: Bangkok and the Wild, Wild East

Thailand has a certain reputation—and deserves it. Things go on there, out in the open, which conservative New Englanders are unprepared for. We have to steel ourselves for these unexpected encounters and laugh them off when they occur.

LOST IN TRANSLATION: Dave was once in a Bangkok bar by himself, and, of course, he was immediately accosted. The young lady flaunted her recent chest augmentation surgery and asked him if he was interested.

By Diana McLeod

He tried to discourage her. "No thanks," he said, trying to explain. "I'm married. Me, I'm a good boy."

She frowned, unable to process his meaning in English. Then she thought he was being very clear. "Oh!" she exclaimed, "you don't want girl! You want boy? OK! I get boy! I get boy!"

MISS TIFFANY'S is one of the most famous televised beauty pageants in the world. Its contestants are some of the most beautiful, voluptuous women you have ever seen in your life. But they are all men! *Katoi* transvestites are everywhere in Thailand, and we often encounter them. They have gained acceptance in Thai society, more than in America.

I've had several business relationships with gorgeous *katois* over the years. I used to buy handicrafts from one who was so lovely, she would turn every male head wherever "she" went. I am friends with young "lady" who has worked at one of our favorite silver shops for years. At first, I was confused as to what gender to call her, but was told she definitely prefers "she." She's a real sweetheart. I've also known a couple of others who were fabulously bitchy. One ran the front desk of my old hotel in Chiang Mai. Her pouty, rude petulance was part of the hotel's charm.

SAY IT WITH FLOWERS: Dave bought most of his cloth goods in Chiang Mai from two young women. They did him a favor by agreeing to sew labels onto some cotton bags he had purchased at a different shop, and they did the work for free, as a kindness to him. He wanted to thank them, so when he stopped in at a local convenience store, he bought them some roses. The girl selling the flowers asked him if the roses were for his girlfriend.

"No, not for girlfriend," he replied, "just for friend."

She misunderstood, frowned and smacked him with the flowers. "Boyfriend no good!" she scolded. "Boyfriend no good!"

I guess she was tired of competing with the gorgeous *katois* in town.

"THE ART OF THE DEAL": Professional "girlfriends" usually latch onto men as soon as they arrive on vacation. They hope for a couple of all-expense-paid week-long bookings, with extra cash and consumer goods thrown into the bargain. Here's a story about an especially enterprising young lady.

We were taking a ferryboat out to an island beach destination. I was on the lower deck, sitting with our luggage, while Dave went up to the upper deck to take pictures. A young "girlfriend" approached him. He listened to her sales pitch, and then pointed to me. "I'm here with my wife," he explained. "I don't need a girlfriend."

She didn't give up. Instead, she came down to chat with me. "I talk you husband," she said, in halting English. "He very nice. So I think: First wife headache, second wife OK. First wife want massage? Second wife OK! First wife no like laundry, second wife OK. OK?"

The massage-on-demand concept was tempting...

The sad part is that while some of these women are career working girls, others are simply dying to find the foreigner who will love them and take them home, away from Thailand. They want to believe in the Cinderella story. Once in a blue moon, it works out, but most of the time, the girl gets dumped at the end of the vacation. Hearts do get broken. It's hard to have a real relationship with such a large language barrier or age barrier.

BEACH OF THE CAVE OF THE SEA GODDESS

Where in the world is the best beach? You know: the perfect one, with the softest whitest sand, the brightest hue of turquoise in the sparkling waves, and the most dramatic and breathtaking scenery? I know of one, and it is in Thailand. Luckily, you can only reach this beach by longtail boat, so many tourists miss it entirely, which makes it even more perfect.

I start out by boat from the mainland at Ao Nang Beach, near Krabi, and I jump off at Railay Beach. There are bungalow hotels here, but Nature herself has thankfully limited construction. Bypassing the main beach, I cross over to the east side of the peninsula on foot. A quick walk up the east side brings me to a cliff face where rock-climbing classes take place every day. The trail turns right and curves along the edge of the escarpment. At times, it winds beneath the edge of overhanging caverns. The air becomes blessedly cool, and one must dodge stalactites hanging at head level. Sunshine pierces through holes on the cliffs and through the lush jungle greenery draping the cavern's edge, pooling light on the cave floor. It feels like a quiet chapel. In fact, it is: locals have built tiny Buddhist shrines inside rocky niches.

The trail meanders beside the cliff, soon reaching my favorite beach. The view is spectacular. To my left is a massive cavern, overhanging a quiet lagoon. The sea cave reaches way out over the ocean. Giant fifty-foot stalactites hang overhead (if you dare to swim beneath them). To my right is a beautiful tree-lined beach and another dramatic cave-riddled escarpment. Across the little bay, yet another fantastic limestone island rears several hundred feet up into the sky.

What makes this beach unique is *Tham Phra Nang*, a small cave shrine dedicated to the princess-goddess of the Sea. She is an ancient goddess, from the area's pagan past, but she still commands respect. Her spirit houses are garlanded with fresh flowers, and even the hotels send employees to bring her daily offerings.

Both Muslim and Buddhist fishing people still come here, despite the fact that worshiping pagan goddesses is a mortal sin in their religion. The sea is too dangerous for them to ignore, especially after the devastation caused here by the great tsunami. (Inexplicably, the cave shrine did not get destroyed, even though most of the bungalow hotels on the same side of the beach were severely damaged.) The cave chapel is made even more colorful by the giant wooden phallic carvings people leave here. Apparently, the Sea Goddess is a Goddess of Fertility, as well as of the ocean harvest.

There are only a few buildings out here, and they all belong to the luxury resort called Rayavee. But that does not mean real Thai food isn't available. Longtail boats pull up onto the sand and turn into floating restaurants, with open-air stoves on board. I can get a delicious homemade lunch of *pad thai* for just a few baht, without missing out on any sunbathing time.

At about four p.m., it's time for the monkey show. Troops of wild monkeys leap down from the cliffs above, performing death-defying acrobatic stunts no human could ever hope to emulate. These monkey families have learned how to exploit the tourists to their best advantage. They are perfectly happy to pose for photos, as long as they get fed (a lot) for this service. They swarm down into one large tree right beside the beach, and they amuse everyone so much they need not forage again for the rest of the day. The few who are not satiated cannot resist stealing corn from the corn-on-the-cob lady. This poor woman often loses a third of her corn to the monkeys, a fact she seems thoroughly resigned to.

At last, it is time for me to go. The sunset deepens into twilight tones, and I need to catch a boat before they leave for the day. Farewell, Sea Goddess!

P.S. I wrote this story in about 2007. We returned to this area in 2013, and it has changed considerably. The hotels have expanded, prices are up, and there are many more boats and tourists than before. The noise of the motors and the pollution of the boat engines are a serious problem now. And Krabi has been overrun by Russian tourists, many of whom can afford foreign travel because they are involved in the Russian underworld. Nevertheless, I still recommend this beach. The beauty of the landscape is unchanging, although it is sadly not the peaceful paradise it once was. Best to come here first thing in the morning for a tranquil experience.

recommended Google search: Railay Thailand Images

LIVE FROM BANGKOK: KHAO SAN ROAD

I must prod my jetlagged body to stay awake. (I have traveled twelve time zones, and I am now exactly on the other side of the world.) The hotel bed looks tempting, but I must resist sleep so I can re-set my internal clock. A stimulating environment is what I need. I take a deep breath and leave the serenity of my hotel behind.

I slip down a little back alley. This secret shortcut takes me directly to the heart of Khao San Road. I pass noodle vendors, several tourist laundries, and four super cheap back-alley guesthouses with massage parlors attached. Idle workers call out to me, "Hey, Miss, you want massage?" I suspect that, here in the back alley, they are half-hearted about getting female clients. They make their best money with the men. Or, maybe I misjudge these girls. Most of these places, I'm sure, are perfectly respectable family businesses. But which is which? Are the older women their mothers, or their madams? It's impossible to know for sure. But it doesn't matter and I don't dwell on it. They all flash me friendly smiles.

The alley is home to a tattoo parlor/whiskey bar and a little leather shop. Somebody is playing a didgeridoo. I can hear the whining voices of Chinese soap opera characters blaring from a TV somewhere. Two Australians are haggling with an old lady over her laundry prices. There is a large pile of garbage in one corner of the alley. I steer clear, wary of rats. Two student travelers who've just arrived in town are also taking the shortcut, sweating profusely under the weight of their giant backpacks.

At the end of the lane, I steel myself as I prepare for sensory overload. Khao San Road is the heart of the backpacker/student tourist district of Bangkok. Khao San is only about three blocks long, but it is a famous mecca for young, bargain-hunting tourists from around the world. Cheap guesthouses, bars, travel agencies, street-side restaurants, email centers, tattoo parlors, souvenir shops, and tailor shops all compete for elbow room along this little stretch of Banglampoo. It also houses the wholesale silver shops where I do my work. Garish neon lights crowd out the sky, and street vendors plaster the sidewalks with colorful goods, all competing for the tourists' attention.

Bootleg CD sellers blare competing music selections—"Hotel California" and Hip Hop, full blast with the bass turned way up. The neon amphitheater of Khao San reverberates and pulsates with sound. Lately, this area has become something of a street circus as well. Performers gather crowds, making the tarmac even harder to negotiate. Hip-hop b-boys and garage bands compete with schoolchildren doing traditional Thai dance. In the early evening, the street practically seethes with people. Khao San is at its peak—plugged in, blaring, and moving at fast-forward speed. Am I ready for this in my jetlagged state?

By Diana McLeod

I pick one of the street-side beer-bar/restaurants and take a seat beside the sidewalk. The jet stream of humanity flows around me and I feel like a rock in the middle of a fast moving river. Khao San offers some of the most entertaining people-watching anywhere: beach goddesses with bronzed skin and dreadlocks, Japanese punks with red dyed spikes in their hair, Australian boys with no shirts and nipple rings swilling quarts of beer right on the street, the odd straight, middle-aged and completely bewildered and overwhelmed couple from Iowa, little local beggar boys holding signs reading they are deaf, which gets them tips from the tourists until someone calls out to them and debunks their scam, little girls who sell roses, hostesses in spiked boots and micro minis who pass out coupons for the big disco, young Thai couples who come here on dates because the tourist district is so interesting, Thai *katoi* ladyboys in drag, who cruise the street hoping to pick up foreign men, Euro babes in skimpy outfits with perfect bodies and blasé expressions carefully implanted on their faces, eternal hippies carrying African drums and wearing their uniforms of tattered, tie-dyed beachwear, the grouchy old lady from the guesthouse up the street, who scolds everyone for not taking their shoes off at the door, the squid cart vendor with a cartload of nearly transparent dried squids hanging from clothespins, the guy who sells nothing but little mirrored disco balls, the seventy-year-old hammock seller, who has been selling his wares as long as I can remember...

The faces blur into the noise, lights, music and beer. The restaurants morph into keg bars as the bar scene blossoms. The VW bus-bar arrives on the street, parks, and opens for business, with the top peeled off. Bartenders pop up through the cut-off car roof, mixing blender drinks at warp speed to satisfy the crowds. Even the local gas station closes for the night and transforms into a bar; the bartenders setting up shop among the gas pumps. Working girls arrive for the evening shift at Suzie Q's nightclub. With every hour, the volume rises along with the humidity. Couples meet, pair off, and disappear into the steamy night.

I come to this place every year when I arrive in Asia from New York. Khao San is my first stop. I spend at least five days here, buying silver. It can be a lonely, loud, obnoxious environment for a solo traveler. Then why, after all these years, does this sordid late-night snapshot of humanity still fascinate me? I guess it is because it is a living photo gallery, and no two images will ever be exactly alike.

If you ever go to Bangkok, you will be offered luxury accommodations at the large downtown hotels. If you want predictable, five-star pampering, by all means go there. But if you want a walk on the wild side, I recommend you bunk in Banglampoo.

recommended Google search: Khao San Road Thailand Images

KID AND TOY SEAFOOD

To set up this story, I must briefly introduce you to the Bangkok gem show. The Bangkok Gem show is a world-class jewelry event, held in a massive convention center. Tens of millions of dollars worth of gems and jewelry are on display and for sale in the vast halls. There are so many gems my eyes inevitably become strained from the glitter!

Most of the international buyers never leave the artificial environment of the show. They fly into the city and are immediately whisked away by limousine to five-star hotels. They shuttle back and forth from their hotels to the convention center on fancy air-conditioned buses, and they never step outside to venture into Bangkok. Most of them order breakfast from room service, an American-style fast-food lunch from the convention center, and dinner from the bland international menu at their hotel complex. I sometimes feel a bit sorry for them because they think they have experienced another country, but, in truth, they haven't.

As for me, I stay in the funky backpacker-tourist ghetto of the city. My room is a fraction of the cost of a five-star. I have to take a cab up to the convention center. On the return trip, I usually sign up for one of the free shuttle buses and get dropped off at the Oriental or the Shangri-La, from which I can take a local river-taxi ride back to the Banglampoo district.

The return shuttle bus rides are often a lot of fun, because they are full of international jewelry buyers and sellers. On one bus ride, I met two women from Texas who were buyers for MMA International. MMA is a large American catalog company for sterling jewelry. I get their catalogs, and I've bought silver chains from them on occasion.

Neither Marsha nor Anne-Marie had been to Bangkok before, and although they seemed very conservative, they both looked as though they might be persuaded to step "outside the box." Since we were enjoying each other's company, I took a chance. I invited them to join me for dinner. I told them that, if they dared, I would show them an excellent authentic local dining experience.

They were nervous, but they agreed to go. We hopped into a cab and took off into the Bangkok night. I told our driver to head for one of the main streets of Chinatown. The truth was, I only had a vague idea of where I was going. But I knew if I couldn't find exactly the place I was looking for, there would be plenty of others nearby.

By Diana McLeod

My guests sat in the back and glanced uneasily at each other from time to time. We were deep in Chinatown now. Neon signs competed for air space above the crowded street. I directed our driver to take us into the heart of the restaurant district, where the evening coolness had brought out hordes of hungry diners.

Recognizing the street corner, I told our driver to stop. Sure enough, there it was, in all its glory! I pointed, grinning. "That's it! My favorite—Kid and Toy Seafood."

Marsha and Anne-Marie looked at me in horror. "But it's just tables set up on the sidewalk! Metal tables with little plastic stools! Aren't we going to eat in one of the real restaurants?"

My companions watched the action as the "maitre d'" hustled hordes of patrons to tables where eager customers were getting fed with astounding speed. They also saw the banks of fresh fish spread out on shaved ice, and the line of grills sizzling with fat filets.

I grinned. "In the fancy restaurants, the fish might not be as fresh. Those places are rarely full of patrons. Out here, the fish comes straight from the coast each day, arriving just in time for dinner. Besides, it is about six times cheaper, and I've never seen faster service or better cooking. You can pre-select a fish if you want. You haven't eaten in Bangkok until you've had street food, and you just haven't had seafood until you've had Kid and Toy!"

The "maitre d'" didn't give Marsha and Anne-Marie time to say no. He hustled right over and exuded charm. They found his smile irresistible. We followed him to a table we shared with a Chinese couple. The table was steel, with no tablecloth (very practical). The beer arrived almost instantaneously. We ordered my favorites—grilled whole red snapper in sweet, spicy chili sauce, and grilled tiger prawns. Tiger prawns are like miniature lobsters, and they are fantastic.

It could have gone either way. This place was far funkier than anything these two women had ever seen before. Many Americans would have blanched. To their credit, my companions dug in and loved it. They even tried the hot sauce on the snapper and found that they could handle it. I introduced them to "morning glories," a variety of Thai greens similar to spinach. By the end of the meal, they were completely taken in by the Kid and Toy experience.

The wait staff added their usual wry charm to the occasion. Our server, who was Cambodian, joked and jived with us like a waitress in a Brooklyn diner. Patrons also came over to chat, delighted to see American business travelers eating there. We laughed and fooled around with everyone, and I know that Marsha and Anne-Marie loved the experience as much as the food.

The best part of travel are those moments when you connect with local people; when you become a part of the scene instead of looking at it from afar. I am sure when Marsha and Anne-Marie got home, this was the adventure they talked about the most...

159

PERU

THE CORN FESTIVAL IN CABANACONDE PERU

When we planned the trip to Peru, we picked out our primary destinations and then decided to add one more. After consulting some guidebooks, Dave chose the famous Colca Canyon. This canyon is one of the largest in the world. The plateau's fearsome edge plunges almost straight down 3,400 meters (11,000 feet)! Giant Andean Condors with six-foot wingspans can still be spotted circling above the abyss. It sounded like a fascinating area to explore.

From the city of Arequipa, we took a long bus ride to Chivay, which is at one end of the magnificent canyon. The trip took us up on the high *Altiplano* and over a 16,000-foot pass. (OK, 15,911 feet, which is close enough!) The *Altiplano* is an incredibly bleak windswept desert, with almost no human presence at all. The few tiny stone hut villages were desolate-looking places. Shepherds tended flocks of sheep or alpacas, despite the frigid winds.

Herds of wild vicuñas scampered around near the road, foraging among the winter grasses. Peru has three species of camelids: llamas, alpacas, and vicuñas. Of the three, only vicuñas are completely undomesticated. They are small, with reddish hair, and they look almost like deer, except for their camel noses. A few years ago, they were brought almost to the brink of extinction by hunters seeking their fur, which is supposed to be among of the world's finest. The Peruvian government has since outlawed hunting and has designated the land around the road as a national park. The vicuña population has recovered nicely. In a couple of hours, we saw several significant herds.

In the city of Chivay, we got our first close-up look at alpacas. These placid animals are domesticated and covered with such thick wool they remind me of cartoon creatures from a Dr. Seuss children's story. Their faces are quite comical—they look as if they are puckering up to kiss somebody. Three ladies with two white alpacas were getting on the bus at Chivay. The baggage handler simply picked up the alpacas, folded their legs under them, and unceremoniously stuck them into the luggage area under the bus. The two animals knelt calmly in the dark, along with peoples' suitcases, for the entire bus ride. I was able to get a videotape of the three ladies posed with their animals. The women were all done up in regional dress, with colorful puffy skirts and embroidered hats. The alpacas had brightly colored wool pompoms decorating their ears. The ladies were all chewing coca leaves. When I took their pictures, both the animals and their owners were placidly chewing their cuds. People do resemble their pets....

At Chivay, we boarded a local bus for the three-hour ride along the canyon's rim. Dave and I were unable to get seats together, so I sat with a young man from one of the villages along the way. His Spanish wasn't easy to understand, but we did manage to have a pleasant conversation. He said we were lucky to be going to Cabanaconde because it was the opening day of a fiesta celebrating the planting of maize. He was a charmingly earnest fellow, a subsistence farmer with a young family to support. His hands were rough from years of labor. When the bus stopped at his village, he shook my hand and said goodbye; then he kissed me on the cheek. I was very surprised by that!

The road to Cabanaconde was dramatic, winding along the knife-edge of the gorge. The river at the bottom gave the canyon country some verdant greenery and real trees, which was a welcome change from the grim Altiplano. As we went along, the canyon got bigger and deeper, until it was impossible to see the river. The bus drove through several long tunnels, stopping at intriguing local villages.

The further we went, the deeper the canyon got. About thirty minutes outside of Cabanaconde, we passed El Cruz del Condor, a famous overlook where giant Peruvian Condors are apt to be seen circling overhead, riding the winds. Twenty minutes later, we got our first glimpse of Cabanaconde, the village perched right at the canyon's edge. The chasm looked like it went down forever, and the rugged mountains on the opposite side of the canyon seemed so far away, they were fading into the afternoon haze.

All around the village, well-engineered stone terracing sculpted the hillsides. The terraces were built in pre-Inca times, but are still used today. Unfortunately, they were not yet planted. We had arrived in late September, which is early spring in South America. Hacked-off stems from last year's corn still stubbled the barren fields. Plowing had yet to begin.

Looking at the grim concrete and tin-roofed shantytown with its crumbling central park and its rundown church, it was hard to imagine anything exciting ever happened here. The streets were nearly deserted, although it was only about 6 PM. A couple of general stores lined the main street, but they had no customers. We hoped the scenery would entertain us because the town certainly wouldn't.

Wrong! The population was gathering in the street behind our hotel for the annual corn festival. Townsfolk were dressed in their festival finest, with garlands of flowers, fruits, and vegetables around their necks or over their shoulders. People were drinking *pisco*, a local brandy. A brass band began to play, and circles of dancers quickly formed. The ladies twirled in their big skirts, and the men clapped, stomped and swung their partners to the lively rhythm.

One man assumed a unique role in the festival. He wore a comical, long-nosed mask, and he was dancing in a clownish, rude way. I guess he was supposed to represent some local Kokopelli-like fertility god. He was hilarious. He kept dancing up to people and trying to embarrass them. As soon as he saw us, he came up to me and waggled his bum suggestively right in my face. Everyone looked up to see how I would react. I pretended to be shocked, overacting like crazy, which got the crowd howling with laughter. Next, he sidled up to Dave and did the same thing. My husband is not a shy person. He got right into the spirit of the thing and outdid the fellow at his own game. Dave was holding his camera, with a long telephoto lens on it. He positioned the camera right behind the rudely waggling bum and made a rather crude gesture with it! I wondered if he had gone too far, but the villagers all screamed with delight, including the ladies. We were welcomed into the party since we were obviously not averse to a little bawdy fun.

The procession was soon on the move. Young men began the parade, carrying heavy plows down the street, followed by a brass band and dancers, with the rest of the village following. They made their way down into the *zocalo*, where they celebrated for quite a long time; then the townsfolk headed down the side streets until they had done the tour of the village. After that, they went back up to our hotel and started all over again, with another round of *pisco* brandy. It was going to be a long night!

CABANACONDE PERU: A MOST UNLIKELY PARTY TOWN

THE SEVENTH BEST BAR IN THE WORLD: How do I know that Cabanaconde Peru has the seventh best bar "in out-of-the-way places around the world"? I rely on the travel experts. This impressive rating comes directly from the most respected travelers I know of: the Lonely Planet guidebook people. Dave and I trust their judgment, but this was something we just had to see for ourselves.

Cabanaconde Peru does rate as an "out of the way" place. It's a very basic little village, and most of the buildings are humble shacks. There are almost no vehicles, so the streets often seem deserted. People there are simple subsistence farmers, descendants of pre-Incan tribes. It was hard to believe there would be any nightlife whatsoever in the humble little place. But Cabanaconde boasts one of the most spectacular views of the Colca Canyon, which is one of the world's deepest. The town thus attracts tourists, mostly backpackers, looking for a rugged mountain holiday. Would there be enough of them around? Was the Pachamama Ital Bar going to live up to its world-class reputation?

It did. The minute we walked into the little hole-in-the-wall bar, we felt its good energy. The owner, Luiz Julio Orlando (Peruvian) and his girlfriend Lief (from Belgium), both spoke excellent English. They had the fantastic knack of making each newcomer feel like an old friend, and they did that with everybody. The funky little bar and restaurant/hostel was packed with both people and enthusiasm. And what a great mix of interesting people! Backpackers from all over the world got introduced to Peace Corps volunteers, and tourists chatted companionably with locals. At one point, the music got cranked up, and the place broke into spontaneous salsa dancing.

We had to try the *pisco*. Luiz makes a mean whiskey sour using the local stuff. I guess you would have to classify *pisco* as a type of brandy. Dave soon switched back to his usual favorites, but I thought, *When in Rome...* I then tried some hot, spiced *pisco* to take the chill off. The drink warmed me deliciously, inside and out.

MOUNTAIN BIKES: We had to pull ourselves away from the bar that first night in Cabanaconde because we were going to hike down the canyon in the morning. We returned the next evening after the big trek, and had another *pisco* party. The third day, we arranged with Luiz to rent some mountain bikes, to take them up the mountain road to El Cruz del Condor. We grabbed lunch and hopped in an old pickup truck with the bikes. Luiz sent along a local guy to be our guide. The driver dropped off the three of us with our bikes at the scenic turnoff.

El Cruz del Condor has the most famous view of the gorge. An imposing Christian cross dominates the site. It's not the deepest point of the canyon, but it is a straight drop down to the Colca river churning 1,200 meters (3,900 feet) below. Impressive rapids give the river its voice, and the roar echoes around the canyon walls. A waterfall spurts out of the mountain on the other side, pouring like a gigantic fire hose into the whitewater cauldron below.

CONDORS: Overhead, condors ride the updrafts.. The giant condor is considered the world's largest bird, with a wingspan of up to 3 meters (nine feet). We had already seen several, circling at a distance, but we wanted to see them up close. The very best time to see them is early in the morning, yet the area is often so crowded with tour buses and vendors, we felt our experience would be ruined, so we tried for an afternoon sighting.

We did see condors. In fact, we saw lots of them, but sadly, not a single one came near enough for a decent close-up picture. We also spotted a coyote and an adorable pair of picas (furry little mammals like rabbits, but with long, bushy tails). They were so confident of their camouflage we were able to walk right up to them. We wouldn't have seen them at all, except for the sharp eyes of our bike guide.

The road back to Cabanaconde was almost all downhill. We were able to just sit on the bikes and zoom like the wind! With the golden pre-sunset glow suffusing the evening light around the canyon, it was very memorable. The sun was just setting as we turned into the village. Soon we were safely back at Pachamama's bar, ordering the first round of hot piscos.

recommended Google search: Cruz del Condor Peru

"POSTCARDS FROM THE EDGE;" COLCA CANYON PERU

When I say "the edge," I'm not kidding. My mule had the terrible habit of walking right along the outer edge of the two-foot wide trail. She loved to dawdle along the steepest places, while I made an effort to savor the spectacular view without looking straight down. At one point, her foot slipped, sending a shower of small rocks over two thousand feet below. Her body lurched towards the abyss, and my heart pounded as she struggled to regain her footing...

We were hiking out of the small village of Cabanaconde, Peru. The trail dropped over the edge, zigzagged down the rock wall and into the gorge, which, at its deepest point, is twice as deep as the Grand Canyon and breathtakingly steep. A roaring river gouged it ever deeper at the bottom. Our plan that day was to hike all the way down into the abyss and to ride mules back up if we could. Even with mules, it would be a grueling day for two out-of-shape, middle-aged gringos who live at sea level! We would descend 1300 meters (4225 feet), and we would have to come back up the same way. Besides the distance down, there was the altitude problem. Cabanaconde itself is at 3290 meters high (10,700 feet), so we would be trekking at high elevation.

It started with a gentle walk through terraced cornfields. These old stone enclosures are pre-Incan yet still in use today. Just as I was starting to get used to the easy slope, we came to the abrupt edge of the canyon's rim. It was almost literally straight down. The trail snaked along an uncomfortably narrow path with a drop-dead cliff at the end of each hairpin turn. I was thankful I had brought my big hiking boots. *How many tourists have slipped off the edge in sneakers?* I wondered....

The scenery in the canyon was fantastic. The mountains were dramatically rugged, and the colors of the exposed rock on the other side were varied and beautiful. As we descended, we saw dramatic basaltic lava formations. Gnarly cactuses lined the edge of the trail, and little birds flitted between them, somehow dodging their spines.

It was brutally hot, dry and dusty. Our legs were getting tired, and we still couldn't even see the bottom yet! I soon began to wonder if we might have bitten off more than we could chew. Luckily, to my endless relief, we encountered a man with three mules. He was heading down for the day, hoping to rent transport to tourists for the trip back up. We got an initial price quote for return mule fare. It was not unreasonable, so we told Juan we would probably rent two of his mules.

About halfway down, we could see the bottom. The desert canyon wall ended abruptly in a beautiful green garden called the Oasis. Palm trees and other lush tropical jungle plants sprang up out of nowhere, nourished by the presence of water. The Colca River was just below, churning through the narrow gully at the very bottom of the canyon. The local people had expanded the greenery by diverting water from the river upstream and making it flow onto the green lawns and into several glittering blue swimming pools. From where I was standing, the oasis rippled in the waves of dry heat coming off the hot rocky trail like a desert mirage. I couldn't wait to get there!

An hour later, the heat was so intense we were almost stumbling down, and the tantalizing swimming pools seemed no closer! The line between the oasis and the desert was so clear it was as though somebody had put up a fence to separate the two ecosystems. It was heaven and hell—and we were still in hell. I began to worry about getting heat stroke. (I'd had it before, in India, which put me at high risk of getting it again). Dave began to push me to keep going. It was well after two in the afternoon, and we had to get back up the mountain before dark.

The last part of the downhill trek was horrible. My mouth was so dry I couldn't swallow, and my legs were trembling. There was no relief from the cruel, desiccating sunlight. It took everything in me to struggle towards the blessed shade of the first trees.

Fifteen minutes under the cool jungle canopy with a bottle of water, and I was a new person. Dave ordered some food, and we went for a swim in the lovely little pool. My body temperature dropped dramatically, and I no longer felt ill. The Oasis was like heaven on earth. I wished we didn't have to leave. My eyes drank in the rich greenery, the gorgeous flowers, and the swaying palms, and I stayed in the pool until I was actually cold. The little guesthouse at the oasis was tempting, but we didn't have anything with us, not even a toothbrush, so we prepared to return.

The journey back up was much better. We walked back to the corral, where Juan was waiting. The mules were placid, well-trained animals. Mine was the leader. She would go far ahead of the others, leaving her owner completely out of sight. Then she would pick out a rest spot—which seemed to be inevitably right on the edge, with a terrifying drop-off—and wait for the other mules to catch up.

The view from mule-back was spectacular when I dared to look. The canyon was so profoundly deep my mind struggled to comprehend its true dimensions. I spotted the black shape of a condor, wheeling majestically over the canyon's rim. The huge bird was at least half a mile away, yet I could still see its massive wings. A blessed afternoon breeze alleviated the heat.

Less than halfway up, we encountered other tourists on foot. They were French. She was considerably older than I was, and she was nearing collapse. They had come down, just as we had, and then started back up on foot. Foolishly, they had packed only one liter of water between them for the uphill climb, and it was already long gone. They had drastically underestimated the deadly combination of desert heat, exertion, and high altitude. We gave them our water, and they were grateful. The husband grudgingly hired Juan's last mule for his suffering wife and sent her along with us. Even so, she swayed in the saddle, and we worried that she might pass out and fall off the cliff. She made it to the top, which she would never have managed on foot!

Luckily for her, Juan and his mules saved her from disaster on the mountain.

The final walk through the terraced fields at the top was a delight. Afternoon sun burnished the mountainsides with soft, slanting light. The French lady headed straight for her hotel, but we lingered among the fields to take pictures, using the weathered steppingstones of the ancient Conde people to climb from one terrace to another. Thorn bushes were just beginning to bloom, and they attracted a pair of hummingbirds. The sun quickly dipped behind the mountain's purple haze, leaving us just enough twilight to walk back to the little village before dark.

Our new friend Luiz greeted us with a big smile at Pachamama's bar, just in time for happy hour.

recommended Google search: Colca Canyon Peru Images

LAND OF THE INCA: THE LEGEND OF THE ICE PRINCESS

She was very young, only twelve to fourteen, when they brought her to the mountain about five hundred years ago. The little girl walked a great distance, trekking for weeks through frigid Peruvian high-altitude deserts and over tortuous mountain passes. Priests brought her on her last journey. She was well fed and well cared for, and dressed in the finest woolen garments and jewelry. They left her with exquisite little dolls, statues, and pottery. Was she dragged to her death, or did she come voluntarily? Did she know what was about to happen to her?

Archaeologists think she knew. She was handpicked to be the perfect virgin sacrifice to the Apus, the ancient gods of the mountains. Imagine the bravery and courage of the young girl, walking willingly to her death! Imagine her struggle, climbing into the glaciers, gasping in the brutally thin mountain air as each agonizing footstep brought her closer and closer to her demise! What could her thoughts have been? How does the human soul prepare for such terrifying moments?

At last, they reached the top. While the young girl sat huddled in the icy wind, the priests gave her a very intoxicating drink of spiced liquor. They built a fire and performed rituals of purification. She was struck in the back of her head with a sharp stone. The priests arranged

166

her little corpse in a fetal position, placed ceremonial offerings around her, and abandoned her to the mercy of the mountain.

The mountain's cruelty was actually kind to the little girl. She was covered by snow and ice, which kept her in a remarkably good state of preservation. Over time, she was lost: a gift to the glaciers. Even the gods she honored were forgotten. When the Spanish overran Peru, they forcibly converted the entire population to Catholicism. She was the mountain's secret, and she remained there, frozen in time.

Eventually, the mountain gave up its secret. In 1995 an expedition climbed Mount Ampato, (20,700 feet). The eruption of a nearby volcano had melted a lot of the glacier near the summit, exposing a large section of the mountainside. The team, led by archaeologist Johan Reinhard, was doing high-altitude excavations around the world. As they crested the summit, they spotted a curious bundle that had rolled down from the mountaintop and onto one side of the crater. Investigating, they discovered the bundle was, in fact, the well-preserved body of the little girl. It had come loose during the ice melt following the eruption, and the corpse had rolled downhill about twenty meters. The archaeologists followed the path of the body back up to the actual burial site and found a treasure trove of sacrificial offerings strewn along the way.

Team members carefully carried their precious find down the mountain. She was well cared for and immediately transferred to a specially designed refrigeration facility. The well-preserved mummy has generated worldwide press. They even named her: "Juanita, the Ice Princess."

Dave and I had the opportunity to visit her this year, on our trip to Arequipa Peru, where a museum was erected in her honor. Exhibits introduce the public to her story, beginning with a film about the discovery, and the history of her life and death. A series of rooms display the ceremonial artifacts left around her body. Some of them were exquisitely beautiful, especially the little figurines and dolls. At the end of the tour, we were able to walk around the icy glass coffin where she rests.

From the side, she is eerily beautiful. She has a proud profile, with high cheekbones and shining black hair. Her delicate eyelashes are closed as if in sleep, and her well-preserved hands are folded daintily in her lap. It is hard to believe, looking at her from this angle, that she was brutally murdered.

One wonders how she would react if she knew her final resting place would not be on the mountainside after all. Would she be glad to be rescued from the lonely ice, or would she be angry to be on display? And would she believe we modern humans are toying with the wrath of the mountain gods?

PLAYING DRESS-UP ON THE UROS "ISLANDS" OF LAKE TITICACA

It was so embarrassing! Humiliating! But our charming hostess insisted! There was no way to avoid having Señora Cristina and her daughter outfit us in full traditional Peruvian dress. They tied an enormously bulky felt skirt around my waist; bright pink, it stuck out in pleated layers of thick material. I looked like a puffy ballerina who had unfortunately gained a hundred pounds. Next, they cinched me with a wide black belt and put a gaudy green bolero vest over my shoulders. Cristina's daughter plunked me down onto a footstool, and plaited my hair into two big pigtails, weaving garish pieces of colored yarn right into the braiding. After that, they tied a series of bright pink and blue pompoms onto the end of each braid. I looked like some kind of disco Pocahontas with a grotesquely large ass. Finally, they stuck the world's' stupidest hat on my head and stood back to admire their handiwork.

Dave was next. He was more modestly attired, with a traditional woven alpaca poncho and a Peruvian alpaca hat with silly little pompoms on the side ties. He looked like a shepherd who had lost his flock, along with his I.Q.

There was nothing to do but wear my heavy skirt and silly pompoms with as much dignity as I could muster. Cristina and her family were trying to introduce us to an authentic Uros experience. She had other victims as well, who were also duly attired. Two other couples were there to share our night on the "island."

The Uros "Islands" are not islands at all. They are floating rafts of reeds, anchored to large stones on the lakebed below. The islanders build and maintain their floating real estate, continuously cutting fresh hay to stack on top of rotting, waterlogged areas. Reed shacks house families on these strange spongy islands. Every aspect of the Uros culture is reliant on the reed plant, from their "land" to their homes to their reed boats. Walking around on their rafts is an odd experience. Most of the time they feel solid, but now and then you feel the floor tilt, and you must adjust your balance. When the wind picks up, waves on the lake get high enough to ripple the platform, and the entire thing moves, including the bed in your reed hut.

These reed islands float on Lake Titicaca, the highest navigable freshwater lake in the world. At 12,500 feet above sea level, the air offers little oxygen for lowlanders like us. This vast lake (over 190 miles long and 80 miles wide at its widest points) forms part of the border between Peru and Bolivia. Some of its islands are so isolated they are little microcosms of cultural differences, with distinctive costumes and language variations.

On Cristina's "island" there was electricity—all solar power, which lasted well into the night. There were also chemical toilets, so we weren't polluting the lake. Cooking was done over an open fire, which was interesting since the entire island was flammable.

By Diana McLeod

There was not much to do, but that suited us just fine. We went to find a sunny spot to lie down and bask in the afternoon sun. We found a pile of freshly cut reeds and nestled there. The reeds were comfortable and dry, and they smelled good. We got out our books and read for a while, and then napped. It was like sleeping on a warm, sunny haystack. Very pleasant!

After our nap, we walked around the island to take pictures. Colorful clay cooking pots were decoratively placed on the pathway to Cristina's kitchen. Dave was taking pictures when he discovered that one of them was full of kittens! We grabbed a reed and began to play with the tiny little fluffballs. Soon, all four of them were out of the pot, ripping and racing all over the place, trying to catch the rustling reeds. One of the tourists nicknamed them "Los Gatollinos."

In the late afternoon, one of the men took us fishing on the lake. We all climbed onto his small reed boat, and he paddled the length of the islands. The boat was of ancient design; it looked like it belonged on the Nile in Moses' time. It was quite windy, and I was suddenly glad I was wearing all those extra layers of silly garments. The fisherman propelled the boat with a single oar, sculling just like the old-timers do in Maine (it is a dying art in our country, but I was taught how to scull as a child). The reed boat was so buoyant it barely dipped below the water's surface, making it easy to move. The fisherman chose a likely spot and set his net among the reeds. He told us he would return the next day to pick it up, and hopefully get a couple of trout. (Trout is not native to the lake, but it was very successfully introduced, to the detriment of at least one native species.)

Speaking of trout, guess what was on the dinner menu... When we got back from the fishing expedition, Cristina was already beginning to prepare the evening meal. We all went to the dining room in anticipation. She and her daughter sang as they cooked and we took pictures as they labored over the wood fire. Their broad smiles seemed to be permanently implanted on their faces.

Dinner was very tasty! We ate trout, potatoes, quinoa, and vegetables, with homemade flan custard for dessert. Everybody went back for seconds. The wind was rising, and the reed huts were not exactly well insulated. We would all need those calories for the cold night ahead.

But Cristina had other ideas. Her family cleared away the table and brought in a boom box. They were determined to teach us the local dances. How hokey could this get?

Very, but we danced anyway. The cheerful Peruvian music was lively and easy to tap one's feet to, although dancing at high elevation was challenging. Peruvian ladies are supposed to keep their thick skirts twirling at all times; this took a lot of energy! The men had it easier since they got to dance in place whenever they spun the girls around. My partner was Cristina's husband, and he kept me spinning until I was gasping for air, but the exertion also felt good. In fact, we all got quite a powerful exercise high, thanks to the altitude.

After the dancing, we traded songs, although we struggled to come up with sing-along songs everyone knew. Sadly, Americans don't sing anymore; we don't know songs as a group, which is regrettable. Christina and her family knew many songs! They also knew songs foreigners had taught them. They even sang us a song in one unidentifiable foreign language, which turned out to be Japanese! The world is indeed shrinking.

In the morning, everybody was up early and eager for breakfast. Cristina made us another delicious meal, while "Los Gatollinos" terrorized the dining room, much to everyone's delight. It is hard to drink tea with a kitten hanging off one's arm! After breakfast, I was finally able to shed those horrible clothes! My scalp was sore from the weight of all the pompoms!

Cristina was a wonderful hostess. She hugged us and kissed us goodbye when the boat came to pick us up, making us feel as though we had truly been honored guests on her most unusual island.

P.S. About the clothes: Where did these outlandish feminine styles come from? They came from the Spanish. They are copies of sixteenth-century European dress. The skirts, the belts, and the boleros were introduced by Spanish ladies, and the conquistadores pushed European attire onto the locals, even in remote parts of Peru. On several of the real islands of Lake Titicaca, women even continue to wear the lacy black Spanish mantilla over the head. We also saw embroidered white blouses worn under the boleros, which were no doubt copied from antique Spanish styles. The only uniquely native Peruvian element of the ladies' dress was the use of the colorful woolen pompoms.

recommended Google search: Uros Islands Peru Images

By Diana McLeod

SACRED VALLEY: INCAN AND CHRISTIAN CROSSCURRENTS IN CUZCO

The old city center of Cuzco far surpassed my expectations. Nowhere else in Peru does the colonial style flourish as it does in Cuzco. Tourist wealth helps a great deal, keeping the historic city protected from unfortunate modernization. Magnificent cathedrals and historic colonnades surround each of the three central squares. Gardens in the *zócalo* parks grace the city with bright flowers, greenery, and shade, right in the heart of the old town. Behind it all, mountains ring the neighborhoods. It is an ideal place to stay while visiting nearby archeological ruins.

The stamp of the conqueror is everywhere in Cuzco. The Spanish did all they could to destroy the symbolic heart of the Incan empire, and they replaced it with European symbols of power. They tore down the palace of the Incan king, leaving nothing but the foundation stones. They stripped all the gold and jewels from the Temple of the Sun, leaving only a few bare walls. Then, they surrounded the ruins with a high-walled Catholic monastery, keeping the local population permanently shut out of their own most sacred space. The locals were forced to work for the Spanish, using the stones from their own ravaged monuments to build cathedrals for the foreign god.

The Spanish marched into a strong indigenous culture and pillaged it so thoroughly that there is pitifully little left for those of us visiting the city today. For the Peruvian people, especially for those who yearn to know more of the Incan civilization, it must be a terribly sad experience to learn their country's history.

The tale of conquest is a remarkable story when you realize that the Incan empire was at the height of its power when the Spanish came. The Inca were the late bloomers of the indigenous civilizations, organizing at about 1100 AD. At the time of the conquest, the Inca controlled territory all the way from Colombia to Chile—over half the length of the entire continent of South America!

When the Spanish arrived in the sixteenth century, they had a famous meeting with the Incan emperor Atahualpa. The Spanish arrogantly announced they were claiming the entire Inca empire for the King of Spain. Atahualpa was, needless to say, quite taken aback, and asked by what authority the Spanish could make such an outrageous claim. According to legend, the Spanish interpreter handed him a Bible, claiming it contained the word of God. Atahualpa held it to his ear and listened. "It does not speak to me," he said, tossing the Bible aside. The outraged Spanish used this act to rationalize the atrocities later committed against the unfortunate Incan king, including his murder.

Today, Cuzco is famous for the blending of the two unique cultures. Here are some little snapshots of Cuzco attractions we enjoyed.

THE CATHEDRAL was large and imposing, in pure opulent Spanish style, with a heavy emphasis on suffering. Even the angels look as though they have indigestion. Our favorite detail: a painting of the Last Supper. On the table, right in front of Jesus, is a Peruvian delicacy—a whole roasted guinea pig! And the shrine dedicated to earthquake relief isn't too surprising in this volatile area.

THE MARKET: A lively traditional marketplace, with something for everyone, tourists and locals alike. We bought lots of hand-knitted alpaca wool clothing for friends and family. After shopping, we went to the food court, bought fruit smoothies, and got to know some friendly local folks.

CUISINE: Peru is home to an exciting form of nouvelle cuisine. Chefs are combining the old and the new, creating savory new dishes which are very intriguing. We had several gourmet dinners at trendsetting new restaurants. Surprisingly sophisticated and delicious! And while you're in Cuzco, don't forget to try the purple corn juice! This drink sounds disgusting, but it is uniquely special!

BURIED TREASURE UNDER THE SUN TEMPLE RUINS: The remaining ruins and surrounding walls of the old Incan Sun Temple of Qoricancha contain some of the most impressive stonework we've ever seen. A Spanish monastery was built right around the ancient temple, and today, it's still run by Dominican friars, even though it's now a museum and a World Heritage site. In the 1990s, because of persistent rumors of Inca tunnels and hidden gold beneath the temple, ground-penetrating radar was brought into the Church of Santo Domingo, which was also built on the site. An open cavity, directly beneath the Church altar, about 30 feet down, was discovered. This operation was initiated by the Abbot, who supposedly was given a piece of Inca gold by a digger who claimed to have discovered secret passageways. According to one man who claims to have seen the Abbot's gold himself, the Abbot is keeping it hidden safely away, and he will not reveal proof of the treasure until his death or retirement in order to avoid embarrassing the Catholic Church during his tenure. Of course, the Church will never approve excavation, so the mystery continues...

recommended Google search: Cuzco Peru Images

By Diana McLeod

NEPAL

TIDINGS OF JOY

March 1990 was a terrible time of strife in Nepal. People demanded democracy, but the King and his corrupt family refused to give up power. Violent clashes between police and civilians rocked the streets of Kathmandu, and the situation was building to a head. The population had no weapons to fight with, only the strength of their own convictions.

Protesters gathered in the capital, vowing to storm the Royal Palace and scale its thirty-foot fences. The military announced that anyone attacking the compound would be killed by the army, who were pledged to defend the Royal family. Undeterred, two-hundred-thousand unarmed men, women, and even children prepared to march straight into the guns.

Horrified by the coming bloodbath, Dave and I fled Kathmandu two days before the threatened massacre. Together with our chosen trekking companion, Jody, we went to Pokhara, the starting point for the Annapurna trek. If we'd had any medical training, we would have volunteered to stay to tend the wounded, but our presence wouldn't have helped the protesters. Feeling like helpless bystanders, we headed for the mountains.

In Pokhara, the situation was equally tense. Insurgents had been rounded up and jailed, or worse. At our guesthouse, the manager was frantic with worry about his brother, who had gone "missing" for months. We talked all evening, anxious about the looming disaster in Kathmandu.

Late that night, only hours before the deadline, the King decided to back down. He agreed to the formation of a democratically elected Parliament and the writing of a Nepalese Constitution. Nobody truly knows what happened to change the King's mind. Did his conscience prod him towards justice? Or did his army commanders simply refuse to execute his orders? Did they lose heart when confronted by the prospect of butchering innocent civilians?

Whatever happened, it worked. The population went wild with joy at the news. There was rejoicing in the streets like never before. In Pokhara, the police, many of whom were rooting for the protesters anyway, opened up the jails and freed all the political prisoners. We witnessed the ecstatic reunion of our new friend and his brother early that morning.

By eight a.m. celebrations in the streets of Pokhara were whipping up into a frenzy. The town was jammed with singing, dancing people, all wearing red pigment on their faces. (Red is the festival color in Nepal.) We inched our way through the throngs while shaking hands and hugging total strangers. At one point, Dave joined a spontaneous dance party. Soon, we were decorated with red ourselves, and there were huge grins on our scarlet-painted faces. It was such a relief and joy to know that violence had been averted and thousands of sincere, honest, hardworking Nepalese were not going to get mowed down just for asking for a few basic human rights.

Eventually, we found our transport up to the trailhead. It was a jeep, which, at that time, was the only motorized public "bus" available. I was "lucky" enough to be offered the front passenger's seat. (I felt privileged until I discovered the broken spring, which constantly threatened to impale my tender flesh.) Poor Jody fared far worse. She had to climb through the window into the squirming pig-pile of humanity in the back seat. There were about eight or nine women and children squished in back there! Dave had the most challenging ride. The Jeep was equipped with makeshift metal handholds and footholds all the way around. All of the men rode clinging to the outside of the vehicle. There were even people draped over part of the hood.

The jeep carried twenty-one people and their luggage for two hours, straight up the streambed of a mountain creek. It was one rough ride! The guys got pretty wet whenever a wheel sank into loose stones and sand. At times, we were surrounded by gushing whitewater up to the tops of the wheel wells.

At last we reached the trailhead. Everyone unloaded and we began our hike up into the hills. The mountain trail was highly scenic, climbing through pristine countryside dotted with tiny little villages and terraced rice paddies. Stone and wood farmhouses were built much like they must have been a thousand years ago, with few signs of modernization.

When we got to the settlement where we intended to spend the night, locals stopped and asked us about the red paint on our faces. To our surprise, we soon realized they hadn't heard the monumental news. They had no idea what was happening in their own capital city!

Luckily, our companion, Jody, spoke excellent Nepalese. We called the villagers together, and she told them the dramatic story of what had happened. It was amazing! In a land where there were no wheeled vehicles past the river (because of the impossible terrain), nobody had yet told these people that their country was going to be a brand new democracy.

It happened the same way in the next village and the next. We were the bringers of good tidings wherever we went. From town to town, Jody spread the news, explaining to the people what a Constitution was, and what a Parliament was, and what it would mean to their country. What a magical experience this was on our first trip to Nepal!

recommended Google search: Birethanti Nepal Images

recommended Google search: Pokhara Nepal Images

By Diana McLeod

"THE GODS MUST BE CRAZY"

KATHMANDU, NEPAL 1994. Krishna P had a shipping company in Kathmandu, which we hired for our air cargo. Krishna was an unusual person. He had lived in New York for years, and America had left its mark on him. He wore a sleek leather jacket, expensive designer sunglasses, and he drove a sexy new car. Krishna loved to wine-and-dine clients since, to him, that activity was the most important aspect of what he did. His English was nearly perfect, and his New York big-city attitude almost made us feel like country bumpkins.

One day, he invited us to his house for dinner. Since Krishna was a young bachelor, he still shared a comfortable urban family apartment with his mother and a bunch of younger siblings. The women greeted us warmly and then fled to the kitchen. In classic Nepalese fashion, the ladies of the house came out only to serve us. They never eat with the honored (male) guests. If I had been Nepalese, I'd have joined the women in the kitchen, but, being a foreigner, I inevitably found myself in some sort of twilight zone between the sexes. The ladies regarded me sympathetically as neither a man nor a true woman, but some kind of trans-gender anomaly—a female in pants.

It was wonderful to spend time in a real Newari home. (The Newars are the aboriginal Kathmandu Valley ethnic group.) We talked for a while, ate some dinner, and then Krishna offered to show us a movie on VCR. He had a bootleg tape of a recent cult classic. It was (of all things!) the film *The Gods Must Be Crazy.*

If you have seen this movie, you will know that seeing it for the first time in a Hindu home in Kathmandu was one of the weirder cross-cultural experiences of my life. If you haven't seen it, try to look it up. It's about an African tribesman whose life is completely turned around by a coke bottle thoughtlessly tossed down from a passing airplane. His naive perspective on modern life is priceless. The whole movie is about the clash of human cultures.

That evening, as Krishna drove us home to our hotel, modernity continued to contrast with traditional Newari life. We drove past antique temples. In one shrine a nighttime ceremony was underway; people were showering statues of Ganesh, the elephant-headed god, with chrysanthemum petals. The prayers were temporarily interrupted by a jet plane, which roared directly overhead near the airport. We passed an ancient stone water fountain. People were offering prayers to Hitimanga, the Water God, as they collected water from stone spouts carved in his image. Nearby was an email center, which, even at this late hour, was crowded. There were several Buddhist monks huddled around one of the computers, enjoying a hot new video game. We passed a new shopping center with western style boutiques. Lepers were begging outside. They had built a little campfire, and were huddling around it for warmth. We rode in the comfort of Krishna's modern car, but we passed porters carrying heavy loads with nothing but a cloth sling suspended from their foreheads.

ULTIMATE CULTURE CLASH: Later that week, Krishna invited us to the Dakshinkali temple to witness one of the strangest rituals in Nepalese Hinduism. Every Friday, people gather at this ancient temple on the outskirts of Kathmandu, for a ritual that most cultures of the world would find utterly barbaric. Animals are sacrificed to the Hindu Goddess(es) Durga/Kali. (Durga and Kali are two incarnations of the same female diety, so they sometimes are thought of as one) Hindus hope that the sacrifices will bring the blessing of the Goddess. Usually, families come here when a momentous event in their family history is about to occur, such as a wedding, or the opening of a new business.

The temple and the ritual are ancient. The practice probably pre-dates the arrival of Hinduism here, and the association with the Hindu goddess came much later. We know some temples in this valley are over 2,000 years old, and this is probably one of them. Every Friday, families bring chickens or goats to be sacrificed here. If the family is affluent enough, and the occasion warrants it, they offer up a water buffalo. After the ritual sacrifice, the family is allowed to keep the meat. Special priests perform the rituals, and they work all day long at their gruesome task.

I was a bit queasy about this, but I knew it was a "must-see." I had grown up next door to a farm, so I was accustomed to the occasional slaughtering of animals. That day, Dave was sick. He had come down with a moderate case of tourist stomach, so he wanted to stay at the hotel. I chose to go anyway. In the conservative society of Nepal, it was not proper for Krishna to go on a road trip with another man's wife, so he invited his mother along as a chaperone. They picked me up at the hotel, and the three of us went off to see the temple.

We got there rather late. There were apparently not that many sacrifices that day, so the slaughter was already almost over. I witnessed the demise of one last goat, and that was it. I'm glad I missed most of it. The priests' robes were quite red, and the gutters were full of blood. The stone temple itself was not particularly memorable. The focus was on the slaughter.

But all this, although it was shocking enough, is not the real point of my story. The moment of ultimate culture clash came when we walked up a little footpath that led from the main temple and onto the forested hill behind it. A shrine was perched on a bluff overlooking the main temple. It was a beautiful spot. The shrine was a little open pagoda, with a classic Newari roofline. Inside was a single standing stone, a simple rock, garlanded with flowers and daubed with honorary red paint.

Krishna and I watched from the railing as his mother entered the pagoda. She had brought flower garlands and red pigment. She bowed low before the stone, uttering ritual prayers. Krishna explained that this pagoda was a shrine dedicated to the Goddess Durga/Kali's mother. Obviously this was the woman's place, just as the sacrificial temple below was really a place for the men.

I turned to Krishna with sudden curiosity. He had lived in New York City for a long time. He was sophisticated enough to appreciate movies like *The Gods Must Be Crazy*. He was a creature of two different worlds. What was his real perspective on the ancient culture that was his birthright? I asked him what he thought of his family's Newari religion.

He snorted. "What do *I* think?" he replied cynically, "I think, look, there's Mama, praying to a rock again!"

I was stunned. In one generation of globalization....

THE DAY I WENT POSTAL IN KATHMANDU

Guess how old I am? Hint: we started our business before email. Even before the fax machine. If we wanted to communicate with our customers, we had to do it by snail-mail. So, we decided, in the early days of Tradewinds, to try a bulk mailing in the form of postcards from Kathmandu. The idea worked very effectively; customers were delighted to get postcards from such an exotic location. But the project turned out to be more of an adventure than I thought.

For a year, we collected names and mailing addresses until we had about nine hundred people on the list. We printed out our message, the names, and the addresses onto computer labels, which I carried overseas. I bought some colorful postcards in Nepal and hired the boys at my hotel to apply all the stickers. But when I got to the city post office, they didn't have nine hundred stamps. I had to go up to the head office of the Postmaster General of the whole country to get them, right out of his office locker. Back downstairs, I paid for them at the stamp counter. The man who counted the piles of rupees was lightning fast. He had two thumbs on each hand, and he had learned how to use them amazingly well.

Back at the hotel, the boys were once again hired to apply all of the stamps. After that, I needed to take them to a small post office to get them franked. In an impoverished country like Nepal, the stamps were valuable. They were well worth steaming off my postcards to resell them, so I was determined to get the franking done while I was present.

177

I went to the little post office in Basantapur and told them I had postcards to mail.

As soon as the guys saw my huge stack of nine hundred postcards, they refused. "Sorry, Madam, we are closed," one said emphatically, slamming his window shut.

I put my hand through the grille to stop him. "No, no, your hours are posted on the wall," I pointed out.

He looked chagrined. Then he said, "We cannot do this now, because who will stand at the window and help the customers? You have to leave these here, and we'll do them later, when we have time."

"I'll stand at the window and wait on the customers while you frank my stamps," I volunteered. "If I need your help, I'll ask for it."

I smiled sweetly and stepped inside before he could say no. He shrugged and showed me the cash drawer, the stamps, and a few other things I needed to know. The guys franked my stamps while I waited on some very confused local folk. They couldn't believe a white woman was working behind the counter!

In the end, it was a lot of fun. I had a great time being the Basantapur Postmistress for several hours. After the work was done, the guys invited me for *chai* tea and cookies, and I brought out my collection of Vermont postcards to entertain them. They loved the foliage shots and the maple sugaring photos, but the biggest hit was my moose picture.

It's much more rewarding and efficient to email everyone, but I do miss the days of those old postcards.

GETTING NAWANGED

In the early years of Tradewinds, we imported wool products from Nepal: hand-knitted sweaters, socks, hats, and gloves. These were produced by a small family business, owned by a charming Tibetan lady named Tsepak. Every year, we would sit in her little shop and drink tea together while placing orders for her products. Tsepak was a delightful person with a ready smile and the calm demeanor of a serious practicing Buddhist.

One year, when Dave and I visited Kathmandu, we met some folks from Colorado, and when we went to visit Tsepak, they tagged along. Despite the fact that there were four of us, she graciously invited us all to her house for dinner. It was during Losar, which is the Tibetan New Year celebration, and it was a festive time. We were delighted to accept.

The folks from Colorado were thrilled by her invitation. As recent converts to the teachings of Tibetan Buddhism, they were very excited to meet a real Tibetan, and they bowed and scraped and were a bit over-the-top with their starry-eyed admiration. I could tell that Tsepak was a bit amused by them. She was a very humble lady, and she harbored no illusions of personal grandeur.

We had never been to Tsepak's house before, and we went on foot, following her directions. Our friends couldn't wait to get there. Dave and I were nervous about them; they were acting like a couple of groupies at a rock concert. We were glad they were appreciative of the invitation, but we hoped they didn't create undue awkwardness when they met Tsepak's family.

We turned the last corner and found, to our amazement, we were at the "Free Tibet" embassy! The Dalai Lama has set up a series of consulates in many countries to foster the cause of Tibetan refugees around the world. We doublechecked our directions. This was the right address.

It turned out that Tsepak's husband, Nawang, was the Dalai Lama's second consul in Nepal. She had never told us, but this invitation was more of an honor than we first thought! Our friends were giddy with excitement. We were led down to a private apartment in the back where Nawang and Tsepak lived. It was a very modest, cozy home. There was no pretense whatsoever, and the only fancy possessions they had were Buddha images and paintings in their family shrine.

Nawang was a funny guy. He and Tsepak were a great couple. He reminded us of a mischievous leprechaun, and he and Dave hit it off right away. Nawang invited us to be seated and called for food. The embassy staff prepared the dinner, which was classic Tibetan fare. We had *momos* (dumplings) and *Thukpa* (thick chicken soup), rice and other dishes I have since forgotten, but they were all good.

After the meal, Nawang immediately hauled out the booze. He announced solemnly that, because it was Losar (Tibetan New Year), the host must serve each guest eight drinks for good luck during the coming year. We had to drink in order to celebrate. He said all this with a big twinkle in his eye, and Dave and I immediately suspected this "tradition" was total B.S., made up on the spot. Nawang was out to get us drunk—especially Dave!

Nawang started pouring Dave and himself huge glasses of straight whiskey! He gave the rest of us tiny little drinks. He and Dave were soon inebriated. Meanwhile, our new-age friends from Colorado were still treating our hosts as if they were sainted incarnations of the Buddha. Tsepak finally turned to me and whispered, "Your friends are acting very strangely. Don't they realize that we use the toilet just like everybody else?"

Dave tried to beg off the booze, but Nawang would have none of it. He kept insisting the guest must have eight drinks for good luck. Dave was sure that Nawang was making this rule up, but he bravely met the challenge head on.

The last drink was the kicker. They did it on purpose, I'm sure. They brought out *chang*. This was not the barley brew I'd had before. This was the real Tibetan stuff: alcohol made from warm, fermented milk. This drink consisted of milk/yogurt so old and curdled it had become seriously alcoholic. Little chunks of gelatinous white goo floated ominously in the fetid mixture. I never found out what kind of milk it was, but it was probably either yak's milk or mare's milk. It stank to high heaven. It was their national drink... and the guests must drink eight drinks....

We each bravely downed our cups of *chang*, while trying to smile and lie about how good it tasted, which wasn't easy, because it went down like snail slime. Luckily, we'd all had our eight drinks by this point, so we were able to refuse refills.

It was time to go. We had done our duty as guests, and everyone said good night. Our friends from Colorado, who still insisted on seeing this dinner as a great spiritual encounter rather than the drunken bash it really was, bowed solemnly on their way out the door. Dave was in no condition to find his own way home, so I led the way back to the tourist district. I had to admire the fact that he was still on his feet at all, after all that 'Tibetan "hospitality."

It was a bit of a rough night for some of us. From then on, we've often referred to getting drunk as "getting Nawanged."

P.S. On a more somber note: The Chinese have established their own Tibetan embassy in Kathmandu. Several years after this evening had taken place, Chinese pressure forced the closure of the Free Tibet embassy in Nepal.

A STROLL DOWN MY STREET IN NEPAL

KATHMANDU, ABOUT 2002. Every year, in Nepal, my days are always too short. I'm there to work, so I don't have free time to explore the city anymore. In fact, when I do get to go outdoors, I usually wind up walking up and down only one street, the one that runs between two silver shops and my hotel. Luckily for me, it's a fascinating stroll. I could take this street a thousand times and not get bored. There is always something new to discover. Come and walk with me. I'll give you the tour.

The road starts on the edge of the tourist district, crowded with tempting markets that sell clothing and other souvenirs: purses, pashmina shawls, silver jewelry, Buddhist paintings, statues, and beads. One shop in particular always attracts my attention. The goods are rare: antiques and unique pieces created by master artisans. A gem-encrusted chest, inlaid with precious turquoise, dominates the window, flanked by ornate silver plaques and Tibetan-style prayer boxes. The quality of the workmanship is breathtaking. So are the prices.

Waving to my friend Ram in one of the silver shops, I leave the tourist district behind. The road takes a jog around a modest Buddhist stupa, and suddenly we are in the cloth district of the city. These stores are full of spectacular silks and satins, most of which are used for religious purposes. Tibetan monks shop here for brocaded decorations for their monasteries and temples. Some merchants specialize in maroon and orange material for monks' robes. Others sell nothing but Buddhist prayer flags. Further along, gossamer silks and cotton fabrics are available for ladies' clothing. Spectacular wedding saris from India dazzle the eye. Many have spangled embroideries hand sewn all around the hems.

If you are distracted by the colorful fabrics, you might just miss one of Kathmandu's oldest and strangest shrines. It doesn't look like anything important, just an old board nailed to the wall, covered with pieces of metal in an odd bulging shape. But the metal bits are crusty old coins, and they have been nailed to the wall, and to each other, by the hundreds. In the very center of this mess is a hole. If you peer into the hole, you can catch a glimpse of a timeworn image. It's impossible to figure out what it is simply by looking at it. But if you ask anyone local, they will tell you that this is the shrine to the Toothache God.

This old altar gets lots of attention. Pedestrians pause and reach into the opening to touch the deity reverently. Some stop long enough to mutter a brief prayer, and they offer the image rice and decorate it with red powder. Nobody nails coins to it anymore because the Nepalese currency is all paper bills now. The old coins no longer have value. (The government has very recently begun re-issuing a few new coins, but the new ones don't have holes in them).

Sadly, the old Toothache God does not always grant wishes to its worshipers. Dentist shops have moved in nearby, deliberately clustering around the old shrine. They present themselves as the modern alternative, but most of them look like an American dental office from the 1800s. There is little or no sterilization or anesthesia, and scary-looking implements are used to pull teeth. The signs on these shops amuse me. Most have a giant tooth hanging above the door, or a wide, toothy smile. Others simply have a dusty display window featuring lots of used false teeth. A monk emerges from one dentist shop. He leans in front of the rearview mirror on a parked motorbike and frowns as he inspects his sore mouth.

Bhedasingh Chowk is a major intersection. Its main temple is still in use, and it has a classic pagoda roof and lovely brasswork. The nearby temples are now defunct pyramids, with large flights of stairs up to modest stone temples on top, locked and chained. The steps of these temples are home to a ready workforce. Wiry little men squat here and wait for porter jobs. These porters are the delivery trucks of Kathmandu. They still get plenty of work, even in this modern age, due to the weak economy and the tiny, medieval street system. Most of them are shorter than I am, and they are as skinny as starving birds, yet they have the stamina of mountain goats. These porters are from the Himalayas, born and bred at a high altitude, which strengthens their heart and lung capacity. I have seen them walking with full-sized refrigerators on their backs, or carrying massive couches, desks and other large furniture. They lift amazingly bulky, heavy items with a simple tumpline strap around their foreheads.

Behind the temples is a small pottery market. Terracotta pots and planters, statuettes and incense burners are displayed on rickety wooden shelves in front of each shop—great subjects for photography in the morning sun, especially if you get the shopkeepers to pose with their merchandise.

Back on the main street, I find myself in the gold district. These shops are not for foreigners, but mainly for young brides-to-be. Custom dictates that families of females must give an enormous dowry to the groom's family for the wedding. The brides' parents ensure that their daughters can maintain control of some financial security by purchasing heavy, 24-karat gold jewelry, which the woman often manages to keep for herself. The gold shops have the most exquisite necklaces in them! They are far too ornate to sell in the West, but I admire the delicate filigree work every time I go past!

I try not to forget to look at architectural details. Many of the old buildings have fallen, but a few still stand. Medieval Kathmandu can still be glimpsed today. Ancient old brick edifices with four-foot doorways and mysterious inner courtyards rub elbows with their modern neighbors. Here and there, the delicate latticework of antique balconies and ornate wooden windows still exist. (If you ever go to Kathmandu, don't forget to glance up from time to time. The most beautiful examples of traditional architecture are up above!) Many little shrines are built right into the sides of these old houses. There is a lovely niche dedicated to Kali, complete with a spirit bell, right on this street. Pedestrians ring the bell and touch a hand to the goddess as they hustle past.

It is easy to miss the little shrine if one is studying the traffic flow. This street is wider than most, but it is barely wide enough for two vehicles at the same time. Opposing cars pass with inches to spare on each side. Sometimes, everything comes to a halt, including pedestrians. (In most of the old town, sidewalks do not exist). Walkers are often forced to take refuge in the shops on either side. Right now, a modern SUV is ruining everyone else's commutes. Car horns behind me are honking impatiently, and bicycle rickshaws have come to a halt. The bicycle rickshaw-wallah behind me is not looking very happy. He's got one wheel in a pothole, two overweight ladies in his rickshaw, and no momentum to get himself started again. He is as small as an American twelve-year-old. How is he going to manage? He is getting out to push. Luckily, two male pedestrians lend him a hand. Kathmandu is a kindly city.

Pausing for a brief moment, I study the crowd around me. Two elderly women have just come from the market, carrying their parcels casually on their heads. One is wearing a beautiful red sari, and the other is draped in peacock blue. They look like queens with their gold jewelry and their embroidered silks, but the effect is utterly ruined by the tacky purple and pink plastic flip-flops on their feet. (Horrible cheap neoprene Chinese imports...)

Two porters, fresh out of the mountains, gaze up at the wonders of "modern" Kathmandu as much as they can, even though they're nearly bent double under the loads they carry. It seems a terrible shame to make these fellows wait while rich people in fancy cars block the whole road. Beside the porters, a Buddhist monk waits with infinite patience. His prayer beads click as he mutters mantras under his breath. Several kids are spending their time staring at me, wondering what the crazy foreign lady is doing, scribbling on a notebook in the middle of the street.

A Hindu holy man with a painted face, dreadlocks, and a saffron-colored robe scurries towards me, preparing to bestow a blessing (for money). Unfortunately for him, I know this guy. Dave and I call him one of the "Baaksheesh Babas." (*Baaksheesh* is the word for bribery). They dress like Hindu holy men, but these guys just hang around the Durbar Square district, taking money from the tourists. They pose for pictures, give blessings, and charge the tourists an absurd amount of money for this "service." The holy man extends his hand to smear his painted "blessing" on my forehead. I waggle my finger at him and mutter "Buddhist." This is the best way to discourage Hindu hustlers.

At last the traffic problem is resolved. The crowd surges ahead in the direction of Indra Chowk; a classic five-cornered intersection with some remarkable historic buildings. Dominating the square is a magnificent temple to the Hindu God AkashBairab, the God of the Sky. (Bhairab is a ferocious incarnation of the God Shiva, the destroyer and regenerator) It gets even more complicated when you realize that different forms of Bhairab may be pre-Hindu local gods that became incarnations of Shiva when the Kathmandu Valley converted to Hinduism in the distant past. Or the Hindus could have co-opted the pre-Buddhist protector deity, Mahakala, and made him a form of Shiva. (Any experts out there think they know the answer? If so, we'd love to know).

This busy temple is a wonder of medieval Nepalese architecture. I remember how it looked before the UNESCO people returned it to its original look with a massive restoration grant. The poor old Malla Dynasty structure used to be incredibly ugly because somebody back in the 1940s decided to cover its lovely brick front with a checkerboard of black, white and green tiles. It looked like a kitchen floor! Now it looks perfect. The roofline is straight, and the restoration was beautifully done. At least one old gem will last a while longer. The magnificent bronze lions and the brass finials gleam with pride. I wish I were allowed inside, but I am not Hindu. (This story was written pre-earthquake. This temple survived, thanks to the restoration.)

On another side of the square, there are other temples, built on large stone platforms. No longer used for worship, these shrines have been taken over by the scarf and shawl sellers of Kathmandu. For years, we have bought scarves here, made out of warm, nubby, multicolored, handwoven wool. The temple platforms are draped with hundreds of colorful scarves and shawls every day. Local people use these shawls instead of jackets. Traditionally, they are worn by both men and women, loosely draped over the shoulders whenever it gets chilly. These temples and the shawl sellers are shown in the movie spoof *The Golden Child* starring Eddie Murphy. And I believe one of the guys who used to sell me scarves can be glimpsed in that film.

On another side of the square, a little alley houses the Kathmandu bead market, next to the main market street of the Asan Tole district. Brass shops spill their gleaming wares out onto the cobblestones, and sari shops hang fluttering curtains of colorful fabric out their windows. It is tempting to go that way, but I must turn in a westerly direction and head down the final stretch.

The last part of the street begins with a wonderful little shrine to Ganesh, the elephant-headed God of Good Luck, in the open square beside the AkashBhairab temple. It is tiny; only about 4 feet tall. Some of its lovely brasswork has been rubbed smooth in places by human hands, but there is still enough detail left to appreciate the skill of the artisans that crafted it.

This avenue has become a favorite market for ladies. Almost every shop here looks like a pharmacy, but none of them carry aspirin. (I've checked). They are focused exclusively on beauty products. The upscale customers can buy glamorous Western cosmetics, perfumes, shampoos, soaps, and creams. (Or, more likely, Chinese knockoffs.) Prices are very dear for the Nepalese budget. In the back of the shop, in plain packages, are locally produced versions of the same items. Prices are cheap, and the results are probably similar. There is no government supervision. What horrible ingredients are women putting on their faces here? The Gods only know.

At last, the street empties out into the plaza that borders the old Hanuman Dhoka palace complex. This area is a Malla Dynasty wonder. At one time, this was the Royal Palace. Fabulous pagoda towers reach for the sky, decorated with elegantly stacked curving rooflines and brass finials. The palace is now a museum for tourists.

Raju's shop is nearby, and it is time for me to go to work. But I've seen a tiny slice of Kathmandu, and I must be content with that.

(AUTHOR'S NOTE: Since the earthquake in 2015, the museum has closed. We hope it is being renovated. The towers on the West side of the palace survived the quake, and can still be enjoyed, along with many other temple monuments. There is still plenty to see, in spite of some horrendous losses. Most of the features described in this story still exist, two years after the quake.)

recommended Google search: Kathmandu Images

By Diana McLeod

ELIMINATING ALL WORLDLY DESIRE
(THE HARD WAY...)

SHIVA RATRI FESTIVAL, KATHMANDU, NEPAL 2006: The Hindu holy man untied his loincloth and slowly lowered it down, revealing his bum as he danced to the beat of the drums and cymbals. His butt was bumping and grinding like a Bangkok bar girl's. He showed off his buttocks, and then his legs, as the crowd clapped, cheered and whistled in encouragement. Slowly, the cloth slid aside until he was entirely naked. By this time, the crowd of curious bystanders had grown until we were all packed together like riders on the Hong Kong subway.

The "holy man" circled his loincloth over his head and tossed it into the audience like a stripper. The noise was deafening as he turned around, blowing kisses, with a lascivious grin on his face. As he danced forward, thrusting his hips lewdly, he grabbed his limp male member and spun it around like an old-fashioned fan dancer twirling her tassels. He grabbed it with his fingers and stretched it out as far as it would go, then he waggled his eyebrows at the mob and, like a true showman, waited for laughter and applause. He got plenty!

The lead *Sadhu* was surrounded by a group of about ten others, and they were all colorful characters. Most were wearing simple loincloths, some were in robes, some were smeared in ashes, and all were sporting long, dramatic dreadlocks. There were musicians, playing drums and cymbals, to accompany their star performer. Others rolled huge "cigars" of marijuana. Cannabis is a sacred mind-expanding sacrament for Hindu holy men, and they are allowed to have it in both India and Nepal, even though it is illegal for everybody else. However, since cannabis was the favorite weed of Shiva, the Hindu God of Destruction and Regeneration, and, since Shiva Ratri was Shiva's birthday, and especially since we were on sacred ground, the "sacrament" was legal for everyone, on that day only.

The music stopped suddenly and the crowd hushed. The striptease-Sadhu appeared to go into a trance, as his fellow priests performed blessings on him and anointed him with oil. One priest massaged his shoulders, as another brought the biggest, fattest pot "cigar" to his mouth and set it aflame. The holy man began to inhale with full, yogic breathing, sucking in vast quantities of smoke and forcing clouds of it out of his nostrils like a fire breathing dragon. The other *Sadhus* also lit joints, got high, and passed them out to the crowd. We were at Pashupatinath, the most sacred Hindu temple in Nepal, but the temple grounds soon began to smell and feel like a rock concert.

And then, just as the noise level began to rise again, they brought out the instruments that brought the crowd to awed silence. First, a hammer wrapped in leather. Next, a piece of log with a flattened top and bottom, just tall enough to reach the *Sadhu's* crotch. The holy man, in a trance, set his penis on the log and took the hammer in his hand. He raised it above his head as one of his helpers brought him another huge joint. He took the time to inhale some more "anesthetic," steeled himself, and then he let the hammer fall.

Three times, the hammer came forcefully down on his poor, mortified flesh. Three times, the men in the crowd winced and gasped, some visibly shaken. Faces were pale. At first, I was sure there was some trick to it; there must be some way of secretly protecting himself from real damage, but my theory was disproven by what came next...

One of the assistants brought out the next apparatus. It consisted of a flat board, with straps around it on both ends. On this board, there was a stack of six bricks. The assistant went around to the crowd, allowing people to examine the bricks and feel their weight for themselves. Then he brought the board back to the star of the show. The head *Sadhu* wrapped the straps tightly around his penis. Another joint was inhaled, and his eyeballs rolled back as he went into a deeper trance. He not only lifted the bricks off the ground, but he managed to keep them aloft for longer than any of us would have thought possible. When he finally brought them back down, he brought himself out of his stupor, untied himself and did a little victory dance for his audience.

It had been both a sensational show and a stunning demonstration of the power of yogic meditation and mind control over pain. The crowd went wild. The other *Sadhus* jumped into the throng, collecting as many donations as they could, as fast as they could. Everyone gave generously, especially the men.

Some readers may be put off by the concept of this show and the subsequent passing of the hat, but it is important to understand that these Shiva devotees take a vow of absolute poverty, and they survive on donations alone. This group was not local. They had traveled many miles on foot, probably all the way from India, to come to this important pilgrimage site on this special day. The *Sadhus* were collecting money for provisions on the long journey home.

recommended Google search: Sadhus Images

By Diana McLeod

OF MONASTERIES AND MODERNITY

KATHMANDU, NEPAL, ABOUT 1997. At Tradewinds, we sell Tibetan *Ghao* prayer boxes. They are small silver boxes, worn on chains or beaded necklaces. Tibetans typically put written mantras, incense and other precious things inside and take them to their Lama to be blessed. I decided it was time to learn how to prepare *Ghao* boxes properly. Since I had no idea how this should be done, I sought professional help.

I went out to Boudhanath, the great Stupa standing at the heart of the Tibetan Buddhist community of Kathmandu, and walked around it, wondering which nearby monastery to approach. In the end, I asked a couple of young teenage monks for advice. They were hanging around one of the local "convenience stores," drinking Coca-Cola, with their maroon robes and their rosaries, their Nikes and their Walkmans. I recall one was listening to "AC-DC" on his headphones. These guys were just temporary monks, living at the monastery and receiving a Buddhist education.

They took me back to their monastery and introduced me to one of the older lamas who spoke English well. I told him my intentions, and asked if the lamas could write some prayers for me. He frowned, shook his head disapprovingly and disappeared, returning with a single piece of paper with tiny little mantras printed on it, and a little packet full of saffron.

I looked at the paper in dismay. "But I have fifty *Ghao* boxes," I said. "There aren't enough prayers."

He looked at me quizzically. "Madam," he replied as if he were patiently addressing a stupid child, "why don't you just photocopy these?"

"Photocopies are acceptable?"

"Of course! We do it all the time. Where do you think these came from?"

"I see. And in the future?"

"When you return, bring this paper and get it blessed when we bless the *Ghao* boxes. The blessing will be passed on to all future photocopies. The prayers you use must always be washed in water steeped with saffron to purify them. Then they should be dried, rolled up, tied with the Buddha's colors, and placed inside each box, with a little piece of monastic incense. After that, the people can put anything special inside, like a picture, or even ashes, into their box."

I thanked him profusely and made an appointment, one week later, to meet with the High Lama who was the Abbot of the monastery. Then I went to find a holy photocopier and some maroon and yellow embroidery thread.

All that week, I rolled prayers every evening, working by candlelight because Nepal was experiencing power shortages. It was a calming, pleasing task. A few days later, Dave joined me in Nepal, and we went back to the monastery together.

When we got there, we found the lama I had already met, and he instructed us on how to greet the Abbot, and how to present him with a *Kata* ceremonial scarf (with a donation to the monastery folded inside). I inquired about the Abbots' religious status, asking, "Is he a very important Lama?"

The monk straightened his shoulders and looked down his nose at me. "Madam," he said huffily, "he is a most important Lama. He has a Mercedes."

He gestured and, sure enough, there was the very important automobile, parked outside. After this made an impression on us, he went on to explain that the Abbot was, in fact, a *Tulku*, a reincarnated Buddhist saint, and he was known as Chöling Rimpoche.

We put the prayer paper, the *Ghaos,* and my packet of incense on a silver tray and went to see the Abbot. He didn't seem very holy to me, just chubby, grumpy and unenthusiastic. The Abbot's receiving room was gorgeous, with elaborately painted wall murals, fine Buddhist statuary, and thick Tibetan carpets. The ceremony was over in a couple of minutes, and my *Ghaos* were blessed. Dave took a couple of pictures.

Years later, we finally lost the original paper, but I still have its "children." I hope the "transference magic" of the photocopier will carry the spirit of the original blessing to wherever my *Ghao* boxes go.

I have since learned that devout Tibetans often make use of technology to pack their ritual objects. Microfilm became very popular because Tibetans believe every time a prayer moves, it gets sent to the heavens. Each spin of a prayer wheel is far more effective if it has thousands of teeny tiny prayers in it. I bet you anything, there are now prayer wheels out there, stuffed with flash drives....

recommended Google search: Boudhanath Kathmandu Images

(most pictures are of the stupa itself)

By Diana McLeod

LIGHTS OUT IN KATHMANDU

It is late in the evening in Kathmandu, and I am heading back to my hotel, enjoying the walk. The little street is quiet at this hour. Shops are closed for the day, and there are few pedestrians. I like twilight time because my white skin doesn't show as much, and I can blend in with the locals in the shadows. I feel like less of an intruder in this culture, and more like I belong here.

This neighborhood is one that I know well, and it has grown on me. The corner pharmacy is squeezed into a two-hundred-year-old building with five-foot ceilings and funky wooden doors. Inside, I spot my druggist. I remember when he started selling prescriptions in his early teens. He has cured my ailments for years. The barber, who always sets up outdoors under the big tree, is busy with a late customer. I wonder how he can see well enough in the gathering gloom to cut straight. At the corner, the ever-present group of bicycle rickshaws is ready to hire out. The drivers call out softly to me, "Rickshaw, madam? Very cheap!"

Suddenly, the power cuts out and the street plunges into darkness. I'm surprised—I thought we had another hour before they cut the juice. Nepal has been plagued by drought, so the big dam lacks the water needed to provide sufficient power for the growing city. Rolling blackouts are the order of the day. My life is timed around power cuts. I can't work when the power goes out, so I have learned to plan my meals around them. In the evening, whenever I need to work, I go to a restaurant fancy enough to have a generator and work while I eat.

In another city, this much darkness would be frightening. In Kathmandu, it's not. Despite the city's real poverty, there is almost no street crime. People here believe in Karmic retribution for sins. Anyone who steals will be reborn into a life that is even *more* full of suffering! The only way to escape this fate is to stoically bear whatever trials the Gods hand you in this life, and hope for the best in the next one.

On the street, people are gingerly picking their way along, trying to avoid each other. Pedestrians are just black outlines. Huge potholes and construction ditches on one side of the street suddenly become very dangerous. A bicycle rickshaw weaves past me in the dark, just missing me. How can he possibly see where he is going?

In the buildings along the road, candles and oil lamps are being lit everywhere. Downtown, in the tourist shops, they are lighting Coleman lanterns and revving up gas generators. In this neighborhood, it's candles only, because they are cheaper. The glow of candlelight gradually transforms the darkened street. Suddenly Kathmandu looks as it must have five hundred, or even a thousand years ago. The ancient little shops, the pedestrian shoppers, the utter quiet of an alley with no motorized traffic, the Hindu shrine on the corner where some evening worshipers are quietly chanting their prayers, all are primeval and pristine. The candlelight instantly transports me backward in time to another, simpler world.

189

Footsteps of a Nomad

The locals curse their impoverished country with its pathetically small power grid. How can they climb onto the twenty-first-century bandwagon of globalization when their country hasn't even achieved the basic modernization of electricity on demand? I must confess, I, too, am frustrated when I can't get online at the local Internet center, which uses a crude system of car batteries linked together for power. But how can I express to the local people how precious these moments are, here on the streets, in the glow of simple candles? How can I describe to them how beautiful it is here by candlelight, when their eyes are strained each day? They curse the dark and look forward to being just like us. They are unfamiliar with the impersonal, unnatural coldness of the modern Western city, with its 24-hour, pulsing, electronic heart of neon, fluorescent tubes, steel, glass, and concrete. Having never experienced it, they crave it, like a child who has been denied sweets. It is an ironic thing. I resolve to enjoy the moment and savor it for them.

It is very dark in the alley to my guesthouse. The staff has placed candles along the main stairwell, which is charming as well as practical. I climb the several flights to my room and almost enter, but something tells me to keep going. I have chosen a new guesthouse, and this one has a rooftop garden. I have never been up there before. On an impulse, I resolve to explore. I want to see the city by candlelight! The whole power grid is dark, but the moon is rising. It should be perfect!

I am excited now as I race up the last three flights. Out of breath, I emerge onto the rooftop garden. There is no artificial light up here, and I can barely see the potted plants on the balcony's ledge. I get out my trusty flashlight, (NEVER leave home without one in this town!) and climb the stairs to the next level. Up here, solar collectors gleam in the starlight. Laundry clotheslines share the space with prayer flags. (This hotel is run by devout Buddhists) There is one more circular staircase winding up to the final, tiny enclosed balcony, which offers a vista in all directions. The views from here are well worth sharing!

To the east, the moon is rising, and the clouds have parted to reveal the stars. I can see into the windows of the next building, two stories below. A young lady brings a candle to her window, drips wax and secures it onto the concrete sill. Her face is gently framed by the soft silk of her *dupatta*. She pauses for a moment, looking out into the darkness. With the candlelight warming her face, she reminds me of a Renaissance portrait of the Madonna.

To the south, I can see the heart of the city. The lights are out, all the way to Durbar Square with only candles and starlight providing illumination. Enchanted, I am struck by the softness of the rooftops under the stars, without the ugly orange glare of sodium streetlights to ruin the natural lighting.

In the west, the Himalayan foothills surround the city. One of these is crowned by the ancient temple of Swayambhunath. The power is on in that section of town, so the towers of the temple and the dome of the Stupa stand out as if blessed by the Gods. The painted eyes of the

Buddha, which stare out in all directions, seem to be looking directly at me. I cannot really make them out from this distance, but I know they are there, so I feel pierced by their gaze.

Now the dogs of Kathmandu begin their nightly chorus. Barking starts in one section of town and gradually moves to another. A second canine group takes up the complaint and answers with a series of howls. For a minute, all is quiet, then one new dog begins, and the chorus starts again. The dogs have their own power grids and "rolling bark-outs" that move back and forth around the city. I wonder if this is aggression, or are they talking to each other? Are they competing, or forming pack alliances? Do they remember their wolfish roots on some level? Dave and I always used to joke that the city was misnamed. It should be "Dog-mandu."

And in the north — the best view of all — I catch a rare glimpse of the real Himalayan peaks. It is not easy to see them from the city. Kathmandu's air pollution is better than it used to be, but smog and mountain mists usually obscure the view. Tonight, I am lucky! Behind the foothills, the snowy peaks of the Langtang range glisten in the moonlight. The only reason I can see them so well is that the power has been cut.

Lights out!

P.S. In 2017, Nepal finally got a new energy minister. He has done a tremendous job, cleaning up corruption and improving the power situation. The last time we were there, he was being hailed as a hero by the people of Kathmandu.

TURKEY

WE ACTUALLY LIVED IN A CAVE

CAPPADOCIA, TURKEY. Imagine a rock valley, with little farms and apricot orchards nestled between colorful, sweeping cliffs. All over this valley, hundreds of strange,conical stone shapes stick straight out of the sand. Some rise fifty to seventy feet tall. Many of them have doors, windows, and balconies. These bizarre pillars have cave homes carved out inside them. Some are abandoned to erosion, but others are still inhabited! At the top of the valley, a giant outcropping of rock is virtually honeycombed with tunnels and dwellings, which, at one time, held at least seven levels of inhabitants. The world's first high-rise apartment buildings! Now imagine a whole series of little valleys, each with unique geological wonders, housing more of these crazy dwellings.

If you are now picturing something that looks like it was drawn by Dr. Seuss, you are getting the idea of just how bizarre the Cappadocian landscape truly is.

It was so easy, a caveman could do it. And they did, starting thousands of years ago. Actually, this story began long before that, when volcanoes erupted in central Turkey, in the area that would come to be known as Cappadocia. For months, they spewed out a particular form of ash and lava geologists call tuff. This soft, flaky ash blanketed the entire region. In some places, it was hundreds of feet thick. Sometimes, it fell in layers of color, making striations of yellow, orange, beige, or peach, all swirling together like multi-flavored sherbet. Over the centuries, the tuff hardened. Both man and nature have carved out spectacular formations in this rock. The result is an area of the world that is truly magical and unique.

The most peculiar feature of this rock is its softness. A single person, working with simple tools, can carve out a square meter per day. A small living space could be excavated in a month. Cave rooms are cool in summer yet easily heated in winter. Prehistoric people found them to be safe, well insulated, and virtually maintenance free. Additions were easy; an ambitious cave dweller could just dig deeper, dig further back, or carve out stairs and go up a level. You could design the living space with built-in shelving, sleeping lofts, and storage bins. Interior work could be done in bad weather when it was impossible to work outside.

The geology of the region makes these homes truly unique. Many of them are dug into strange conical rock formations the Turks call "fairy chimneys." The rock is so soft it dissolves easily. Many areas have completely eroded away, leaving behind strange looking towers, which usually have darker, stronger rock on their tops. The tougher layer acts as an umbrella, protecting the softer rock below. Some of these formations are extraordinary. They often look distinctly phallic. One area is aptly named "Love Valley."

These hidden valleys even housed underground churches! One wave of inhabitants, who lived here during the Middle Ages, was devoutly Christian, and they created over three thousand underground churches. We only had time to explore a few, but these ranged from tiny chapels to magnificent arched and columned cathedrals. One even had a second level for balcony seating! Many had brilliantly painted interiors.

CAVE HOTELS: The town of Goreme still has many inhabited cave dwellings. Our hotel was one of Goreme's famous cave hotels. Our room was built utilizing one of the ancient cave dwellings, modernized for our comfort, featuring a hardwood floor, a full modern bathroom with hot water, and central heating. It was cozy and comfortable, although we used the shower sparingly to keep dampness from accumulating. The front of the cave was walled off with cement blocks, with a curved "hobbit-hole" window, curtains, and a wooden door. The

By Diana McLeod

walls held arched shelves, used by people who lived here long ago, and indentations that probably once held torches or oil lamps.

The hotel's reception area was in another cave, with a ladder up to a second-story loft. If you went further in, you would reach the high-speed Internet cave, lined with carpets and Turkish style low divans with cushions. A desk held a new computer system with a large flat-screen monitor and Internet access, which was free for guests to use. I loved emailing home ("Dear Mom and Dad, I'm emailing you from a cave..."). Another door opened into the dining room/backgammon cave, with tables set up for breakfast.

BETTER HOMES AND CAVERNS: We were also fortunate enough to be invited into a local cave home. This one was inside a hollowed-out fairy chimney, with a nice patio porch complete with colorful potted geraniums. Our hostess invited us into her kitchen. (She was hoping that we would purchase some of her homemade glass jewelry). The kitchen was well laid out and nicely decorated, with a gas stove, plumbing, and electricity. Except for the unusual walls and ceiling, it looked quite clean and functional, although the appliances looked like they had been purchased back in the 1960s.

We did not get to see the upstairs, but there must have been several bedrooms and a bath. One side of the house had a lovely second-floor porch and balcony, while the other had small windows. There was even a third level, but I suspect it was used only to roost pigeons. And, of course, it wouldn't have been a proper modern Turkish house without the large satellite TV dish on one side!

recommended Google search: Cappadocia Turkey Images

recommended Google search: Cappadocia Cave Church Images

PALACE INTRIGUE:
THE FABLED TOPKAPI PALACE OF ISTANBUL

The Turkish Sultans built their palace on a bluff overlooking the Golden Horn district of Istanbul. Today, the Topkapi Palace is one of the largest preserved royal residences in the world. Dave and I took the tour, and we were impressed. The famous harem alone has over 300 rooms and open courtyards. The harem and the sultans' quarters are elaborately decorated with high-quality tile work, pillows, divans, chandeliers, and stained glass windows. The palace's open pavilions and magnificent reception halls are surrounded by beautifully tended gardens, with marble balconies overlooking the sprawling city below. In its day, it was a world unto itself, with its own stables, infirmary, markets, even a private zoo. Here are some glimpses of life in that world.

193

SULTANS AND THEIR HAREMS: The sultans of Turkey kept hundreds of women locked away in the gilded cage of the Topkapi harem. The culture was based on slavery, and females of that era were essentially slaves. Beautiful women were sought out from around the world for the personal amusement of the ruling sultan. Many women were presented to the sultan as gifts from foreign potentates. Black African eunuch slaves kept the women in a guarded area of the palace where no other man could ever see them. Wives and concubines were taught that their only chance for elevation within this closed society was to please the sultan and especially to have children by him. Only favorites would attain positions of power. There was a luxurious marble swimming pool off to one side of the harem, where the sultan could sit and watch his beauties bathe. From there, he could select his choice for the night. The Queen Mother was privy to everything that went on in the harem. She would know if the chosen one failed to please her son, and she would make that woman's life miserable from then on. Woe to the woman who was blamed for a poor performance because the sultan had imbibed too much wine or opium, or because he was suffering from a headache, or even a bad mood!

THE WORLD OF THE PALACE KITCHENS: We did not fully grasp the scope of palace life until we saw the kitchens. The kitchens of Topkapi were enormous facilities for an army of slaves and chefs, and it was their job to prepare food for the royal court every day. (On an average day, they fed over 4,000 people, but this number would swell during festivals and feast days.) Huge rooms held massive ovens, open fire pits, and gigantic cauldrons. The roofs of these warehouse-sized kitchens bristled with chimneys. The serving dishes and silverwware alone occupied several large cavernous halls.

The head chef must have wielded great power, but he must also have lived in a virtual pressure-cooker of stress every day. He continually had to increase his repertoire of new delicacies for the Sultan and his entourage. He had to command an army of slaves, and he had to train them to perform challenging tasks, teaching them how to shop for specialized ingredients in the marketplaces, how to bake delicate pastries and how to cook meats and all the other dishes properly. He had to produce gigantic banquets on time, three times a day, and he had to present them with elaborate artistry. If the Sultan chipped a tooth on a stone in a poorly washed salad, or if a dish failed to please, or if the dinner was late for any reason, it was the head chef's fault. Excellence would be taken for granted, but a poor performance could cost him his job, or even his head.

THE JEWELS OF THE ROYAL TREASURY: The Ottoman Empire was fabulously wealthy in its day, thanks to its strategic position in the world. Istanbul was a hub of commerce between Europe and Asia. Goods came overland from Africa, Asia, and the Middle East, and European goods flowed in the other direction. Eventually, the Turks stole the secrets of silk making from the Chinese, and Turkey became a major silk producer.

By Diana McLeod

The Empire grew rich and powerful from intercontinental trade. Sultans began to amass a vast hoard of gold and other treasures, and they were well known for ostentatious jewelry. Many of them wore rings and bracelets, long strands of heavy pearls, and fabulous turban pins encrusted with spectacular gems. The most famous of these is the Spoonmaker's Diamond: an 86-carat pear-shaped beauty. Legend has it a spoon maker found the stone in the trash in Istanbul while he was casting about for metal with which to make spoons.

Dave and I gawked at the fabulous collection of treasures. The sultans were apparently very fond of emeralds, and they had the largest collection of raw emerald crystals we had ever seen. Three of these were large enough to make up the entire hilt of the legendary Topkapi dagger, a ceremonial knife with a solid gold scabbard encrusted with large diamonds. We saw one raw emerald crystal large enough to fill my hand. The sultans drank from gold and gemstone tea and coffee cups and smoked from golden hookah water pipes. One pair of solid gold candlesticks were taller than I am, and they weighed 48 kilos each. I tried to count the numbers of 2- to 3-carat diamonds decorating the sides of them, but I didn't have that much time... They must have had over 300 stones per side!

One of my favorite pieces was a gift presented to one of the sultans. I believe it came from the Moghul princes of India. It was a large pearl that had formed into an unusual shape—it looked like the torso of a man. A goldsmith had crafted this gem into a figurine of a sultan, sitting on his golden throne. It was a marvelous little gemstone-covered miniature.

(Note to readers: this next paragraph was written in 2008. Alas, political developments in Turkey have not panned out as I had hoped back then.)

When we left the palace, it was a jolt to return to modern Istanbul, but we also felt relief. Turkey has come a long way since the days of the sultans. It has the most secular society of any of the Muslim countries. So far, the government has managed to keep Islamic fundamentalism out of the law books. Women and minorities today have more rights (on paper) than in many other countries of that region. This is an issue being fought over, right now, in Turkey, and it has made headlines internationally this year. As the world holds its breath and wonders what the Turks will do, I hope Turkey continues on the secular path, and does not go backward, towards Islamic Sharia government. The world needs more democracy and fewer sultans!

recommended Google search: TopKapi Palace Images

recommended Google search: treasures of Topkapi Images

ISTANBUL ON A MAGIC CARPET

Istanbul! You need only say the name and dramatic images come to mind. When I think of Istanbul, I think of sultans and their harems, bustling markets full of exotic goods, caravans and ships, and the luxurious Turkish carpets that are famed the world over. I picture an amazing city drenched in history, religion, and romance. Istanbul is all of those things, and more.

THE SIGHTS: This city has many attractions that are not to be missed. The most famous of these are the Blue Mosque and the Hagia Sophia. Both are architectural masterpieces. The Hagia Sophia was built by the Roman Emperor Constantine as a Christian church. The famous domed structure was one of the wonders of the ancient world, and it was the seat of Eastern Orthodox Christianity for centuries. It still can awe visitors today. The Blue Mosque, with its elegant minarets and cool, blue tiled interior is an oasis of calm and worship in the bustling city.

To appreciate Istanbul's beauty, you need to see it by boat. Luckily, there are many little ferries whose paths crisscross the Bosphorus, and somehow, they manage to keep on schedule without colliding with the gigantic international cargo vessels that crowd the busy harbor. Dave and I rode the ferries just for fun. The outlines of the city from the water are gorgeous because the city fathers have wisely managed to avoid allowing high-rise buildings in the old part of town. The gentle domes of the mosques and their ethereal minarets still dominate the skyline. The famous Topkapi palace towers are visible on one prominent bluff. On the other side, the graceful span of the Bosphorus Bridge links two parts of the city. To the south, a medieval watchtower still stands guard over some of the newer neighborhoods. It is a splendid view!

TURKISH HOSPITALITY: For a big city, Istanbul is a pretty friendly place. The Turks are outgoing people who do not seem to mind the hordes of foreigners in their midst. People were very gracious about having their pictures taken, and they were wonderfully helpful with directions. Many times, they escorted us to where we were going! People went out of their way to be cordial and to give us little extras. They were always ready with a smile and a joke. We soon got to know business owners on the street where our hotel was, and we felt very much at home there.

We visited a fancy hotel in order to take pictures of the Blue Mosque from their rooftop restaurant. It should have been obvious to the maitre d' that we were probably not going to spend money—we were just there for the photo op. Not only did he tolerate us setting up tripods around his seated guests, but he was even kind enough to suggest we go up on his roof, which a *National Geographic* photographer had done the previous year. He even sent one of his waiters downstairs to fetch Dave a ladder! (In the end, his kindness paid off after all. We did eat dinner there, and we sent him lovely photos. It was also a good thing that Dave didn't fall off the ladder. By the time he got his twilight shots, he'd already had a beer or two!)

TALES OF CARPET SELLERS: Istanbul has hundreds of fabulous carpet shops. Since the average tourist has little or no idea what qualities to look for in a good carpet, rug sellers in Istanbul have to sell carpets with charm, along with a healthy dollop of B.S.! They've been practicing their techniques on tourists for thousands of years. There's quite a variety of approaches. They will use flattery shamelessly, kissing ladies' hands and making flirty comments. One "Carpet Cassanova" told me how green my eyes were, and that nobody in Istanbul has such a color in their eyes. (Not true! *Everybody* in Istanbul has that color of eyes! Well, almost everybody.) Some lies are meant to impress you. One guy proudly showed off a miniature carpet that was being woven in his shop. These little masterpieces are usually framed and put on walls. The tiny carpet was very impressive, but the guy completely exaggerated the technique, claiming the carpet was designed with over two million knots per square inch! Dave decided it must have been knotted by specially-trained spiders.

My favorite carpet shop encounter went like this: As we walked down the main street in the heart of the tourist district, every carpet seller tried to engage us in conversation as we passed by. I knew if I responded at all, I might get sucked into useless conversations and sales hustle, but I just could not bring myself to be so rude as to ignore them entirely. So the conversation usually went as follows:

"Where are you from?"

"Vermont." (I continue walking).

"I know that place!"

"No, you don't."

It usually ended right there. But one fellow kept shouting at me.

"I really do know that place!" he yelled.

"No, you don't," I replied firmly. (I was now at least twenty feet away, with my back to the man.)

"Yes, I do!"

He paused. "Brattleboro!" he cried triumphantly.

I stopped in my tracks.

"Newfane!" he cried. "Wilmington!"

I turned. Either he had a confederate in the store, who had quickly Googled Vermont on a laptop, or he actually knew something about our home state. Reasoning that nobody could search the Internet that fast, we turned back and met the shopkeeper.

He was a genuinely nice guy, who, it turned out, had done a series of home carpet shows in southern Vermont in 2007. In the wintertime, when tourist business was quiet in Istanbul, he sent a container full of carpets over to the U.S., and he trucked them to people's homes by invitation. This gentleman struck both of us as a sincere fellow whose prices were (probably??) fair. We liked him, and we became friends.

In fact, he was well received in Southern Vermont, and he was planning to return the following winter with more carpets. It's apparently possible to get a magic carpet from Istanbul without even leaving home.

recommended Google search: Istanbul Images

AUSTRIA

BEWARE! THE HILLS REALLY *ARE* ALIVE... WITH THE SOUND OF MUSIC, IN AUSTRIA

Those darned song lyrics from that iconic movie kept popping into my head all day long. I couldn't help it! The splendid Alpine views made me want to run through meadows with outstretched arms, singing at the top of my lungs. Picturesque churches, nestled in village dreamscapes beneath snowy peaks, brought back images of kindly old nuns singing "How do you solve a problem like Maria?" I loved Austria, but the movie flashbacks were a few of my least "favorite things."

The trouble was—it was all true! I had come to Austria fully expecting the days of Heidi to be long gone. Of course, most of the traditional chalets would be largely replaced by modern housing. Surely the magical Austria of my imagination could not possibly exist in real life?

I was wrong. Oh yes, the villages had gas stations, and convenience stores, and occasional industry, but picture-postcard romance still thrived in the small towns. Chalets and farmsteads were exquisitely decorated with gingerbread woodwork on windows and balconies. Flowers gushed like waterfalls from window boxes. New homes were, for the most part, built just like the old ones, so they blended right in. Immaculate gardens and yards were tended with great pride. Every community seemed to have a series of bike paths or little walking trails running right through each town.

Manicured meadows surrounded mountain hamlets, and idyllic, family-run dairy farms dotted each valley. Gazing up at the majestic Alps, while walking through flower-filled fields and listening to the gentle jangle of cowbells, felt like a sentimental pastoral dream.

Amusingly, our perceptions were clouded by another set of memories. Dave brought it up while we were driving. He said, "I keep looking at all these chalets, and I think they are the same tacky fake ones I grew up with. I have to remind myself that, no, these are the real deal."

He was right. We both grew up in the era when the "Swiss Chalet" style came into fashion in the Northeastern U.S. It was all the fault of that same darned movie!!! Everybody went crazy for fake chalets, especially in ski country. Dave's family skied all the time, and his parents and all their friends always stayed in chalet-style places when he was a kid. Hotels in ski towns took on names like "The Matterhorn," "Edelweiss" and "Sitzmark." It got to be too much! Luckily, I was not as exposed to American ski culture as Dave was, so I didn't have to fight quite as hard to blot out those unfortunate comparisons.

Both of us fell in love with the little mountain hamlets. For once, humans had contributed to the scenery, rather than being a blight on the landscape. We need to do more of this in our country! We forget, in our quest for value in construction, that aesthetics do matter. Ugly utilitarian cities and cookie-cutter suburbs can be a terrible drag on the human soul.

Vermont, luckily, is one place where we can still find a bit of the village aesthetic. After all, it is important to remember the end of the movie. Maria Von Trapp (the real one) escaped Nazi Europe during the war. She and her family fled to America, where she searched for a location that reminded her of her native Austria. The family settled in Stowe, Vermont, where they lived when they were not touring as the Trapp Family Choir. In the 1960s, the family opened The Trapp Family Lodge. Maria lived in Stowe until her death in 1987.

For that ultimate compliment to Vermont, I will forgive her for all those pesky songs playing endlessly in my head.

recommended Google search: Austria Images

CORKSCREW TUNNELS AND HAIRPIN TURNS:
On the road through the Austrian Alps

Never let a man drive a Mercedes Benz. Once he does, he will be spoiled for life. He will never be truly content to drive the old clunker in the driveway again.

We rented the fateful vehicle in Innsbruck, Austria. Dave had devised an ambitious plan to tour a highly scenic and challenging Alpine road. It was going to be a long day. We had to traverse a substantial distance through rugged terrain, going way down near the border with Italy, and back up north again. In the morning, we left Innsbruck for Lienz, and then we returned through a high mountain pass in the Hohe Tauern National Park.

In the car, I got out the map and studied it, which turned out to be amusing because village names were very entertaining. Here are just some of the towns we passed through on this trip: Schlitters, Fügen, Zell-am-Ziller, Finkenburg, Oberfelben, Heiligenblut, Wörgl, Rattenberg, Brixlegg, Vomp, Vomperberg, Unterschick, Pill, and Wattens. We attempted to pronounce them with our dreadful Austrian accents.

There was a super-long tunnel on the road to Lienz for which we had to pay an equally impressive toll. When we finally popped out on the other side, the mountain view had changed. We were now looking at the range that divides Austria and Italy. Even the towns were different; more Italian, and less Tyrolean.

At Lienz, we turned northwards again. The road went up steadily, through mountain gorges and incredibly scenic valleys. When Dave stopped in one isolated little village to take a picture of the local church, there was not a soul was in sight—the town looked utterly deserted. Then, we heard music coming over a P.A. system, so we decided to investigate.

The entire community had gathered in the village square for a harvest festival. To our amazement and delight, most of the villagers were wearing real Trachten (traditional Tyrolean clothing.) The men wore lederhosen and jaunty alpine hats, and the ladies were beautifully decked out in full skirts with bodices, frilly blouses and actual lace stockings, most of which were probably hand-tatted. The women held bouquets of flowers, and their hats were wide, broad-brimmed affairs with ribbons streaming down their backs. Since this was a community festival for the locals and not a put-on affair for tour groups, the folks were proud and delighted to have their pictures taken. We were almost the only tourists there!

Everybody was busy swilling beer, socializing at picnic tables, and watching the local dance troupe performing on stage, accompanied by a small band. There seemed to be two types of dancing: polka dancing, with men and women dancing together, and dances for an all-male group. They performed a highly energetic dance, with lots of foot slapping and stomping.

To everyone's' amusement, a little boy climbed right up onto the stage and joined the men's dance, next to his dad. The tiny toddler imitated his father quite well. He was more or less able to follow the complicated dance movements. We whipped out our video cameras and started shooting. I really should have submitted the footage to "Austria's Funniest Home Videos," if there is such a thing. The small child, wearing his tiny lederhosen and imitating his dad, was hilarious, and the crowd was soon cheering him on while laughing uproariously at his antics.

After the dancing, the crowd gathered near the street for the fancy tractor contest. All the farmers had driven their tractors to town, proudly festooned with flowers, pumpkins, ribbons, scarecrow figures, and other harvest-themed decorations. One tractor, which looked like it was going to win, pulled a decorated hay wagon full of small, blond children and an adorable baby goat.

We wanted to stay longer, have a beer, and get to know the people, who were all very nice, but we had no time. We shot some more pictures on the way out of the festival, including one of the town constable. He had worn his pistol belt right over his lederhosen. When Dave aimed a camera at him, he jokingly tried to pose with the gun. He went to pull out the weapon, forgetting he had stuck one of the ladies' bouquets in the holster, and ended up aiming flowers rather than the pistol. Everyone had a good laugh.

Back at the car, we calculated our distances and decided that we had better hustle back to Innsbruck. The festival and the traffic had added at least an hour and a half to our trip time. Austrian roads are confusing and not well marked, and we did not want to get lost at night. Dave decided he needed to step up his driving speed. We gunned it out of town, knowing the cop was busy partying, and we hit the road in earnest.

The road climbed steadily, up into a fabulously green alpine valley. Ahead of us were jagged, white-capped mountains. We rounded a corner, and discovered another toll booth! This road trip was going to cost us another $50! (Austria is lovely, but, for us Americans, it is NOT CHEAP!)

The toll also turned out to be the entrance fee to the Hohe Tauern National Park. I soon begrudgingly forgave the Austrians their fees when I saw the insane amount of construction and maintenance this crazy mountain pass required. On the map, the road looked like a piece of string dropped haphazardly on the floor. In reality, it was a dizzying, winding, rollercoaster ride, with hairpin turns, sheer cliffs, show sheds, and tunnels. One corkscrew tunnel allowed the road to circle right over itself.

We reached the glacier overlook from which we could gaze down on a permanent ice glacier. Above us rose the Grossglockner, Austria's highest peak. An early storm had blanketed the mountain with fresh new snow, and it stood out magnificently against the bright blue sky in the sunshine.

As we left the parking lot, we got stuck behind some slowpokes, but Dave decided to pass, even though we were heading for a sharp curve with a sheer 1,500-foot drop off. I put my hands up in alarm, but Dave was confident. "Piece of cake," he grinned. "This car was made for this kind of thing." Sure enough, it was a feasible pass, and he was able to make the turn easily.

The vista of the majestic peaks grew more impressive as we climbed higher. I gazed at the mountains, with the inevitable song lyrics from *The Sound of Music* running through my head. Dave, however, was humming a different tune. I heard *"Dum, da-da-da-DUM dum dum dum"* and I knew I was in for a wild ride. Yes, it was the James Bond theme song. There was some bonding going on, between the man and his car.

Dave is an excellent driver. A long time ago, we lived on a dangerous mountain road in Vermont, with some very tight fall-away curves. Dave had to drive it all the time, and he got used to it. The switchbacks on this mountain were far tighter, but they were better engineered, and the car was fantastic. For him, the excuse of lateness was just what the doctor ordered. He was having fun. We roared over the snowy pass and down the other side, leaving even the local Austrian drivers in our dust. Dave was putting all that German engineering to the test. I was hanging on for dear life.

The scenery, when I could take the time to look at it, was beautiful. Multiple waterfalls cascaded off the northern flanks of the Grossglockner, arcing into the deep gorge below. The descending sun backlit the craggy mountains against the brilliant sky, giving a golden warmth to the grassy highland pastures on the eastern side of the road.

It was both a disappointment and relief when we got back to a real highway again and made our way back to Innsbruck. And, when Dave contemplated the staggering bill from the rental agency, not to mention the cost of diesel in Europe, it wasn't too heartbreaking for him to return the Mercedes to its rightful owners.

recommended Google search: Austria Harvest festival images

By Diana McLeod

INDONESIA
DANCING MONKEYS BY THE LIGHT OF THE MOON

THE CAK RINA is a mystical, magical dance that only takes place on the night of the full moon. It is performed by fifty to eighty male dancers, from young boys to older men.

The scene itself is dramatic. We are seated outdoors, in a garden, in front of a soaring, twenty-foot tall stone temple portal, behind the raised flagstone courtyard that forms the stage. The ornately carved doorway is covered in tiny oil lamps, giving it a pleasing, candlelit ambiance. The flames give the portal an otherworldly appearance, turning it into a gateway to the Balinese spirit realms. The skies above are cloudy at first, but, toward the end of the performance, the full moon breaks through the mists above the palms. The stage is set, so let the dance begin:

It starts in silence as bare-chested men enter in groups, wearing only elaborate loincloths. Many of them carry torches. Circling forward, they sit in a series of concentric circles, swaying. Vocalizations begin. It isn't singing per se, but a combination of chanted words, percussive "Kecak" monkey sounds and deeper, gong-like tones. Each group of chanters has its own rhythm and style, and the various groups together are musically choreographed into a human orchestra. The vocal "drumbeats" rise and fall in an energizing way, syncopated and persuasive.

As the dance progresses, it becomes more and more frenetic. Arms reach for the sky and dancers stand up and leap about. The chattering "Kecak" monkey calls come faster and faster as various groups' rhythms cascade back and forth. The youngest boys have one of the most difficult sequences since their verbalizations are performed in direct counterpoint to all of the others.

The power of this performance is irresistible. Our bodies were soon swaying to the sounds of the half-human, half-simian "drummers."

At the end of the first dance, the groups become fragmented as the men slowly abandon their humanity and become transformed into Hanuman's Monkey Army. (Hanuman is the Hindu Monkey God; he and his monkey army are part of the epic classical Hindu story of the Ramayana.)

THE COMBAT BETWEEN SUBALI AND SUGRIWA: The Monkey King Subali was battling a demon inside a cavern. When his brother Sugriwa arrived, he saw blood flowing out of the cave. Assuming his brother was dead, he sealed up to the entrance of the cave, thinking it would make a proper tomb. When the Monkey King Subali came to his senses, he found himself trapped. Despite being grievously wounded,

203

he managed to shove a few stones aside and escape. He returned to his kingdom, only to find that his brother had taken the throne. His brother tried to explain, but the king felt betrayed and wouldn't listen. His anger knew no bounds, and the two brothers went to war against each other, with huge monkey armies. The Monkey King was tragically killed.

The second dance reenacts this tale. The two protagonists—the two brothers—emerge, one after the other, from the troupe of monkeys. Both are powerful dancers. One is a large, muscular man with long, flowing, bushy hair, which adds significantly to his character. He needs no distinctive costume; he is already perfect for the part. The other is an expert dancer, able to perform the most expressive and intricate hand gestures. He has been trained since childhood, or he would never be able to make his fingers and toes bend backward the way they do.

When the two brothers go to battle, the spectacle of warfare is played out by fire. Dancers set coconuts alight and hurl them across the stage like firebombs, knocking flaming bits off the torches and showering sparks and hot coals around the dancers' bare feet. As the smoke thickens, the Monkey King dies, and his body is carried away by the two mourning monkey armies.

The dance is a thrilling experience, and a chance to gain some insight into the spirit and mysticism of the Balinese people.

Recommended youtube video search: Kacak monkey dance

IS BALI STILL PARADISE?

It all depends on how you look at it. The trouble is, Bali has a heaven-on-earth reputation to live up to. The name "Bali" evokes perfect beaches, waterfalls, and a series of impossible clichés.

The truth is, Bali is getting too built up. The airport has been expanded, and roads get crammed with traffic. Old villages have spread together, joined by construction projects that have taken up every square inch of the land along most highways. Southern towns are jammed with hotels, resorts, shopping complexes, supermarket chains, restaurants and convenience stores, along with thousands of tourist handicraft shops. You can drive halfway across the lower half of the island on the main roads and never see a rice paddy unless you look very carefully.

Western culture has moved in. McDonald's, Kentucky Fried and Starbucks. Polo, Prada, and Pandora on Monkey Forest Road in Ubud. The cell phone and the selfie. Busloads of Chinese tourists. Many people book into self-contained resort complexes and never catch a glimpse of the real Bali at all.

By Diana McLeod

But do not despair! If you are there to experience the beauty and magic of Balinese culture, you will find it a million details, and in the thousands of temples and traditional homes away from the main roads. I did not have to look far at all, because I found it at the place where we were staying, in Ubud.

The path to our villa passes by a private family shrine for the gods and spirits, with pagodas and mini-temples beautifully carved out of wood or stone. My favorite is the empty throne. This honorary chair is for the ancestral, primeval god-energy worshiped long before the arrival of the Hindu gods in the fourteenth century. The name of this spirit is Sangyang Widhi Wasa; unseeable, unknowable and incomprehensible, a force beyond all human understanding. What an astonishingly sophisticated notion for such an ancient culture! It is surprising that these people, who have developed such a fantastic and imaginative pantheon of gods, demons, and high and low spirits, have always given the highest honor to a sacred presence that cannot even be described.

The little pathway winds past several rice paddies on the way to our villa. Rice is in various stages of growth; green and gorgeous. Cows graze in the neighbor's yard, and swallows and dragonflies swoop overhead. Flowers grow everywhere. At the very end of the path is the secluded paradise of the guesthouse pool. Surrounded by trees and flowering plants, and with a natural stream flowing right behind it, it easily takes the place of the fantasy waterfall at the beginning of this story.

Each day, the Ibu (mother of the family) dresses in her formal temple clothes and visits each villa and both shrines of the guesthouse, putting out offerings. The bamboo offering baskets are quite elaborate, representing several hours of work. Each holds a colorful collection of flowers and plants, artfully arranged. At our bungalow, we usually discover three offerings: one outside the garden gate, another inside, on the path to our door, and one on the empty throne shrine attached to the building. I feel at ease knowing we are under the protection of the vast, unknowable, mystical force that created the universe.

A curious bundle is tied to one of the decorative, upturned corner roofing tiles on our bungalow. I've spotted bundles on other bungalows as well. These are magical packets of protection for each house. Somebody prepared each packet, consisting of tiny bamboo umbrellas, curious weavings on sticks (which reminded me of American Indian "gods' eyes"), and little pouches full of herbs and magic potions dangling on strings. I'm confident somebody had had these blessed by the local Balian (traditional healer/wise man/shaman/magician). Or, maybe, the Balian had created the mysterious little bundles personally. In any case, I felt well protected and blessed by the Balian's magic.

Animal life adds to the charm. We are regularly visited by birds; graceful egrets, cute fantails, doves, and an adorable pair of sparrow-like birds who come down for regular birdbaths at the edge of the pool. We watch long-tailed mammals (mongoose? squirrels?) doing acrobatic leaps between the palm trees. Less charming are the fruit bats, which cling to our porch rafters at night. They hang upside down, munching on fruit, and they drop seeds and uneaten bits all over the porch floor. We never see them, only the mess they leave behind.

One morning, a large male monkey climbed onto our garden gate and eyed us while we were eating breakfast on our porch. Monkeys are well known for aggressive food stealing. He could have effortlessly jumped up onto the balcony, but he turned away and left. Perhaps the magic protection charms kept him at bay? Who knows...

In the evening, we are serenaded with live traditional dance music, wafting over from the Arma's cultural museum and performance center. Gamelan gongs and drums are most enjoyable to listen to, especially when accompanied by birds and the chorus of rice paddy frogs and geckos.

So is Bali still paradise? If by "paradise" you mean a five-star tourist luxury resort, you can find these easily in Bali. But if you want a cultural or traditional experience, you can encounter that, too. Just get off the main road and escape to quiet villages where traditions run strong. Every tourist should visit temples and attend some local cultural events. If you stay in a traditional guesthouse, with a real Balinese family running it, instead of a corporation, you may still find the quintessential Bali.

Bali has been inundated by Westernization, but it has not been overwhelmed. Bali is still Bali. If you don't believe me, take a walk in Ubud, and try to enter any of the Western stores that have invaded the streets like fast-growing weeds. If you want to step inside the Ralph Lauren "Polo" outlet, or Citibank, or Starbucks, you will still have to carefully step around the offerings left outside their doors by the sincere Balinese who work inside. Bali still wins. It hasn't lost its heart.

There is no "paradise" on Earth. Paradise is what you make it. Bali just gives you gentle reminders, all the time, that you can find it there ... if you look for it.

recommended Google search: Bali Temple Images

TRADING TABOOS IN A STONE-AGE VILLAGE

"Stop! You can't go up there!" The young woman approached me, a basket of vegetables in her arms.

"No? Why not?"

"It is forbidden."

I stopped climbing the steps to the raised grassy meadow standing right in the middle of the circle of huts. I had paid the admission price to see the village, so I couldn't understand why I couldn't visit the line of stubby standing stones and the larger megalithic stone structure at one end of the field. Suddenly I felt discriminated against, as if I was considered unclean or something.

She read my face and understood. "It is forbidden for everyone," she laughed. "We also cannot go there, except once a year, at festival time. It is the sacred place."

I felt better, although I couldn't imagine why a village would have a taboo sacred spot in such an inconvenient location, right in the center of the circle of huts.

"You cannot go there, but you can come to visit my house," she smiled.

I grinned back. "I would love to! Your English is fabulous, by the way."

She was delighted with the compliment. Like most of the people on the Indonesian island of Flores, her people had been converted to Catholicism by eighteenth century Dutch Catholic missionaries. Luckily, the Dutch had learned from the cruel excesses of forced conversions in the New World, and they approached local cultures with more sensitivity than the Spaniards had. As a result, Catholicism and traditional animism still exist side by side in these communities, more or less in harmony with each other. This young woman was able to keep her village's traditional beliefs, festivals, and sacred spaces, while assimilating the Catholic religion at the same time, along with its Western-style educational system.

A few minutes later, I was inside the traditional house. It was charming! There was an open fire near the door, vented through a hole in the ceiling, and an older woman was grilling small fish for lunch. The family was gathering for the midday meal. The women were all wearing their traditional hand-woven ikat sarongs, but the men were in Western dress. Toddlers and young children approached me with shy smiles.

The house was kept in the traditional primitive style. It was beautifully made, with bamboo flooring and an overarching thatched roof. Everything was clean and tidy. The center of the home was open, with a high ceiling. Comfortable little sleeping niches, curtained off for privacy, were in the back. Ladders led to a second level, with more sleeping and storage areas.

Two central posts formed the doorway to the rear sleeping lofts. Near them were two small primitive statues. My young friend explained that when you are a guest entering a traditional home in this area, you must pay your respects to them since they represent the ancestors of the family. Spirits of the ancestors still supposedly reside inside the wooden effigies.

"And how do I pay my respects to your ancestors?" I asked.

"You spit on them. Go on; you must spit."

I had real trouble with this. The two little statues were hand-carved and they rested in places of honor, guarding the house. I suspected my friend's words were mostly well-rehearsed speeches. Her English was probably nowhere near as good as it sounded. If I told her that spitting on someone (or something) was the ultimate sign of disrespect in my culture, I'm sure she wouldn't have understood.

Everyone was waiting expectantly. I had been annoyed by local taboos, but now I could not bring myself to override my own! I did my best to spit at the statues with the minimum amount of moisture leaving my mouth.

The family was very unimpressed. They gave each other a look as if to say, *These pathetic foreigners, they don't even know how to spit!* They would have been happier (and more honored) if I had left huge gobs of saliva running down their ancestors' faces!

I thanked the family profusely and left the house, musing about taboos and how ingrained they are in every culture.

BENA: Several days later, we went to Bena, which is considered the best-preserved historic village on the island of Flores. It deserved its reputation! Bena sat perched on a spur of a conical volcano. The view at the end of the village was spectacular. A sheer cliff fell away into a jungle-filled chasm, sloping down to the distant sea. On one side, the volcano loomed, so perfectly shaped it almost looks like a painted backdrop on an adventure movie set.

The village itself was a horseshoe-shaped group of traditional thatched-roofed houses. In its center were ceremonial terraces with amazing megalithic stone structures. Standing stones supported massive horizontal slabs. Each clan in the village had a stone altar, used for sacrificing water buffalo to honor the animistic gods as well as the spirits of their ancestors. Other stone structures probably marked ancient gravesites. All are places for humans to connect with the divine.

Other ritual structures were abundant in the town's center. The Ngada people have a pair of yin/yang male/female dual gender gods who balance the Universe. Both the male and the female have symbolic structures built for their worship. The male structure resembles a thatched umbrella (like those you might see at a beach resort). The female structure is a miniature hut, with just enough room for one or two women to huddle inside. When I saw the huts, I imagined young women being taken here by their mothers or grandmothers, to be taught the mysteries surrounding sex and childbirth. Special rituals for fertility must be performed here. I don't know if this is true, but it feels right to me.

Village life seems remarkably unchanged. Women work, weaving the elaborate fabric for the long, traditional ikat dresses they wear. Colors are applied to the threads and woven directly into the warp and weft, so the weaving is challenging. Intricate patterns must be followed precisely, down to the smallest details. I can't imagine how they work in such poor light! There is no electricity here. I don't even see any kerosene lamps in the huts. (Or maybe they have nice new Coleman lanterns and flashlights they hide during the day while the tourists are in town). Bena does collect admission fees because certain old styles (like thatching) are more expensive than tin roofing, and the villagers get paid not to modernize.

One man returns with fish caught in a nearby stream, while another works to sharpen his machete. He is sitting on his porch, beside a rack of water buffalo skulls. These are trophies of animal sacrifices his household has made to animist gods over the years.

There are signs of modernity if you know where to look for them, starting with the large parking lot at the edge of town. A cell phone emerges from someone's pocket. The school has a modern swing set on the playground. Near one of the megalithic, stone altars are new gravesites marked with ornate Catholic crosses. And my favorite sign of modernity: a young man is visiting his village friend. He wears body piercings and earplugs, and his hair is sculpted into a dyed blue Mohawk. "His tribal look" has come full circle; his piercings probably look quite similar to jewelry his ancestors might have worn.

I wish my visit could have been longer. I wish I had time to make friends and share a meal around a traditional fireside. I can only imagine the stories that have been passed down from generation to generation in the traditional thatched houses of Bena.

recommended Google search: Bena Flores Indonesia Images

MONSTERS ON PARADE: HOW THE BALINESE CELEBRATE THE NEW YEAR

It is strictly forbidden to leave the hotel compound today. On the day of *Nyepi*, on the island of Bali, nobody is allowed outdoors because it's not safe. Our hotel owner would be severely punished if his guests got outside. In fact, the entire island is shut down. Even the busy international airport is closed. Government employees, including police and ambulance services, are cowering in their homes. Bustling city streets are deserted, and it's all because of the demons.

Today, on the first day of the Balinese New Year, the demonic forces of the Balinese underworld roam free. The Balinese take their demons very seriously, and locals must tiptoe quietly around their houses for the day. We foreigners regard this inconvenience as a great excuse for a house party. We've stocked up on all the essentials, and we are planning a rum-soaked bash this afternoon, together with our fellow guesthouse residents.

OGOH-OGOH: Last night, everyone gathered in the streets to watch a fabulous procession of bizarre statues of demons and demonesses being carried through the streets of Ubud. These "parade floats" were incredibly imaginative, elaborate effigies of various evil characters. Some stood up to twenty feet tall, and they were mounted on racks of bamboo, held up by groups of men or boys. They are called *Ogoh-Ogoh*. Various institutions and villages build them, competing for prizes. The elaborate sculptures take weeks to design and create. Many were so tall that overhead electrical wires had to be carefully lifted out of the way as they passed.

I saw pig-faced demons and monkey demons, Rangda hag-witches with grotesque bodies and pointed, sagging breasts, and fearsome warriors brandishing weapons. A fifty-foot long dragon had moving wings and glowing green eyes. My favorite was a sorceress-princess, wearing a period costume straight out of a Chinese soap opera. Her long, bony fingers seemed to cast evil curses over the crowd as she passed. Wild boar's tusks protruded from her red lips. The *Ogoh-Ogoh* all had vicious, clawed fingernails and toenails. Most had fangs of some sort. Many were coated with fur or thick hair. All of these characteristics were intended to demonstrate the animalistic nature of demons.

One of my favorite parts of the ceremony was the music. Balinese music is frenetic and thrilling. Thunderous gongs provide a throbbing beat, with clashing cymbals intentionally making enough noise to discourage actual demons and keep them out of town during the parade. The dramatic music energized the surging crowds. I found myself jumping to the beat and unconsciously clapping my hands. It was fun to let myself go, and become just another wide-eyed child, enthralled by everything.

Today, I sip my rum and wonder: should I be afraid of the demons after all? Are we Westerners too insensitive to the mystical realm? Do we ignore it at our peril? Or should I just enjoy the party?

recommended Google search: Bali Ogoh Ogoh Images

By Diana McLeod

JAPAN

A PRECIOUS HOUR IN A JAPANESE ZEN GARDEN

KYOTO, 2011. A Japanese garden is a thing of beauty. The Japanese have a special reverence for nature, and they express it eloquently in timeless garden landscapes. Every aspect of nature is artfully explored, from trees to flowering plants; from ponds to tiny waterfalls. Most temples have elaborate gardens built onto their grounds, and the gardens themselves are used as outdoor chapels for meditation and contemplation.

The Zen garden is particularly special, because many Zen masters use gardens as a metaphor for the soul's journey towards enlightenment. The garden becomes a teaching, communicating the master's messages. Even though he may have lived several hundred years ago, he can still talk to us through the careful placement of the ponds, and the paths through the bamboo groves, while he invites us to discover for ourselves the significance of the upraised boulders and artful groupings of stones. Sometimes, the master speaks using the language of fields of raked gravel. The stark patterns of ridged stone are a metaphor for the Great Void, the emptiness that occurs when all worldly preoccupations suddenly become unimportant. This is the time when the soul lets go, abandoning the ego. As the individual jumps off that mental cliff, enlightenment takes root, like the plum tree, just beyond the gravel's edge. After the harsh gravel lawns, the beauty of living nature becomes even more intense.

The first two Zen gardens we saw in Kyoto were my favorites of all. At Konshi-In temple, Dave and I entered an intimate world, called "Crane and Turtle Garden," created by Koburi Enshu in 1632. The temple has faithfully preserved this national treasure, although nature herself has creatively altered the landscape somewhat in the past few centuries. Tenju-An temple began with an austere white gravel expanse that gave way to natural-looking ponds and flowing water. This garden was blessedly empty of other visitors (Dave and I visited it early on a Sunday morning, so we had the place to ourselves.) We sat in quiet contemplation for a few minutes. Then we both felt suddenly afire with artistic inspiration. Dave's beloved camera took over. He shot several hundred photos, trying to capture the essence of the place. His ultimate picture of reflections in the pond, with two Koi fish in a perfect circle, was an exquisite expression of the harmony we both found in the garden.

As for me, I had only a tiny notebook and a pen, which was lucky because poetry just flowed out of me. I wrote eleven poems in one hour, using the Japanese *haiku* style. I didn't restrict myself to exact syllable rules; instead, I just let them form in their own way. In fact, I honestly haven't edited them. These are first drafts, written in pen.

211

Footsteps of a Nomad

The first, sixth and last ones just happened to come out in precise haiku form, all by themselves, without trying to count syllables. (The last one, I confess, was written at another Zen garden with a larger bamboo grove). Eleven poems in one hour! And I hadn't written poetry in years! Please enjoy the Zen garden experience with me.

Secret forest path
Hidden by the bamboo trees,
Where will you take me?

Pink blossoms kiss the moss-covered forest floor
"Spring snowfall."

Turtle basking, smiling, on a rock
He is my Zen Master today.

Stepping stones across the pool
A metaphor for going nowhere.

Above the Zen garden
The passing of a jet
Breaks my sound barrier.

Japanese maples unfurl,
First leaves of early spring,
Tiny hints of autumn colors
Promised in each bud.

I could spend all day
Beside this old waterfall
The bamboo grove is hushed.

By Diana McLeod

Stone gate, stone bridge and pines,
Harmony of still waters, clouds and willows
Man's idea, then nature, overtaking all.

In the immaculate Zen garden,
One rebellious dandelion.

Why did that wily old Zen Master
choose to plant his rock
In this particular corner of the forest?

Carp rising to the surface
Like errant thoughts
Quiet the mind
Beside the still waters.

Within the bamboo grove,
Sliced sunlight rests on fallen trees,
Joss sticks cast by giants.

recommended Google search: Zen gardens Japan Images

PISS ALLEY: TOKYO, JAPAN

TOKYO 2011. Traveling with Dave is a unique experience because my husband is a fabulous tour guide. I prefer it when he does all the travel planning because I go with few expectations. Everything becomes a surprise.

When we arrived in Tokyo, all worn out from a long overnight flight from Delhi, I expected a typical Tokyo dinner. Instead, Dave chose to skip the usual tourist restaurants with the fake traditional styling. He had studied this area of the city, and knew just where to go for a real experience. He hustled us back to the train station and under the elevated tracks.

Beside the tracks, he looked to his left and spotted a tiny little alley, sandwiched in between the tracks and the main road, famously known as "Piss Alley." (Named for Japanese businessmen who didn't quite make it home after drinking there with their friends). The entire alley was full of traditional, diner-style restaurants. They still had funky old wooden storefronts and classic red lanterns outside. Most had only ten or twelve stools or benches, and thin wooden countertops wrapped around a central cooking area, with the whole kitchen open to view.

The one we selected had room for twelve diners, all served by one solitary chef. The man apologized, because there was no English menu, and he only knew a few words. But Dave and I have done this before— it's half the fun—we use the "point and eat" method. Most of it was easy since all the ingredients were in plain view. Yakitori servings (kabob sticks) were on display. We ordered chicken, scallops, and beef with scallions. The chef slathered them with mouth-watering sauces and grilled them up. Then we pointed at a green leafy vegetable, lightly cooked in a savory sauce, along with an order of sauteed garlic cloves. It was fun to watch as our seatmates got their food. There were pearl oysters, octopus, squid and clams, and a few other mystery foods we couldn't quite identify.

Our fellow diners were laughing, joking, and knocking back drinks and beers. One pair of young businessmen wore classic suits and ties, but they also had punk haircuts, and they were starting to cut loose. Everybody was relaxing after a hard day's work. Several female executives were in the latest business-chic designer clothes, somewhat inappropriate for a little greasy spoon diner, but they were enjoying the intimacy and the charm of Piss Alley after a formal workday. One guy spoke English well enough to help us with additional menu options.

We returned to Piss Alley when we went back to Tokyo at the end of our trip. This time, we got to know three of our fellow diners. I asked the man next to me if his fish dinner was good, and he answered me in excellent English. We soon got to talking, and we wound up buying rounds of drinks for each other and having a great conversation, camaraderie, and fun. We shared some of our favorite international toasts and learned a few Japanese ones in return. The restaurant owner finally politely shooed us all out when it was clear we were finished eating. (When your restaurant only has twelve seats, you have to make the most of them).

This charming glimpse of old Tokyo has only been saved from the wrecking ball because it is too close to the elevated train tracks, but I'm sure its days are numbered. Ultramodern skyscrapers are pressing in all around it. Sooner or later, some architect will solve the problem of what to do with Piss Alley, and the little diners will be gone. But, until then, if you ever go to Japan, try to stop at this tiny sliver of old Tokyo. You'll feel a little bit more at home in these intimate places, and you can hoist some beers with the locals. Where else, in such a bustling and impersonal city, could you pull that off?

recommended Google search: Piss Alley Tokyo Images

SIX FEROCIOUS LIONS: THE SPRING SANNO FESTIVAL IN TAKAYAMA JAPAN

Six ferocious lions chased me down the street, their jaws snapping loudly and violently. The local population ran away from them, screaming and hiding in mock terror. I ducked into somebody's garage and stuck my video camera cautiously out the door. The lions surrounded the building and ran into the shop next door, terrorizing the shopkeeper. One came charging into the garage after me, threatening the camera with his big teeth. Back outside, they danced a fierce lion dance, bobbing, weaving and stomping their feet, accompanied by loud drums and gongs. Their dance ended with a coordinated rhythmic snapping of jaws, then they moved down the road to attack the next shop.

Actually, the lions go from door to door, chasing away evil *Kami* spirits (like me) and giving each homeowner luck and prosperity for the coming rice planting season. Their costumes are a curious mixture of dragon and lion, with dragon scales painted on their fabric backs and carved wooden lion faces.

It was the Spring Festival in Takayama, Japan. Takayama has two festivals each year, one for the coming of spring, and one for the autumn harvest, and these have been a tradition for centuries. Most of the men of the city are active participants. They all get into costume and parade down the main streets of the city. Groups of them push extraordinary multi-story wheeled parade floats through the streets. Many of these are antiques and are now considered national art treasures.

215

These tall wagons are the most unique element of this festival. Each one proudly represents a district of the city, and each district is constantly in competition with the others to build and maintain the most magnificent float in the parade. They are very tall, elaborate chariots, covered with fabulous paintings, silk curtains, carvings, and ornamental woodwork, most of which is lacquered or gilded. One massive parade float held giant drums, gongs and a small orchestra of other traditional instruments and players.

The tops or sides of some of the floats have small curtained pavilions. We later learned that some of these are stages and backdrops for *Karakuri* puppet shows. Small groups of puppeteers climb up inside the floats, and manipulate very realistic mechanical puppets made of wood and cloth. Unfortunately, we arrived at the festival rather late, so we only got to see the very end of one of the puppet shows. In ancient times, the lifelike wooden figurines must have seemed nothing short of miraculous, especially to the children. In this day of television animation, the old puppets were picturesque but somewhat stilted and slow moving. Still, I admired the skill and creativity of the puppet makers, especially when one puppet's wooden hand picked up a fan and flipped it open. I am still trying to figure out how that was done!

The processions continued all afternoon. They represented all aspects of medieval Japanese society. There were the lords of the land: the *Daimyos*. The local *Daimyo* rode in a magnificent rickshaw chariot, surrounded by a retinue of armed guards. His robes were of the finest silk, and his swords hung proudly by his side, as the most significant emblems of his rank. Standard-bearers preceded him, announcing his presence. Servants followed him, shading him from the sun. *Samurai* warriors strutted all around him, wearing their armor and holding burnished shields. Most of their belts held genuine *katana* swords. I was sure I was seeing most of the finest preserved family heirlooms still in the town. Many of these blades were borrowed from sacred ancestral shrines, and brought out only a couple of times a year, just for these festivals.

Below the *samurai* were the *ronin* (paid soldiers) and peasant farmers, who acted as bearers for the floats, or as bearers for the *daimyos'* rickshaws or for the other wagons and rolling carts which carried drums and gongs. Others supported the chariot of the head priest of the temple. Behind him came a very special golden palanquin shouldered by priests. I later found out this contained the *kami* (spirit being) of the Shinto temple. Once a year, the *kami* leaves the temple and parades around the town. Local Buddhist priests also joined the procession.

Beyond this, there were groups of musicians of all stripes, both young and old. Schoolchildren carried banners, struck gongs and sang songs. Old men, dressed in peasant straw hats, played flutes and drums. Each group of parade participants walked with great civic pride in their heritage.

By Diana McLeod

As they passed by, I realized no women were participating. Only schoolgirls were welcomed to march in the parade if they were young enough to fit in with the boys. I found it sad, since in early Japanese history, women were taken more seriously than they have been in more recent times. From the 11th century up until the 16th century, women enjoyed many equal rights and privileges, including the right to inherit land equally with their brothers. Women of the *samurai* class were considered warriors just like the men. They were given swords and *naginata* spears, and they were taught how to use them. They were expected to fight and die for their *daimyo* in a pinch. It was only later, in the 17th century, that they lost most of those rights, and they were seen as pawns in the games of power between families.

My thoughts on women's rights were interrupted by the reappearance of the six ferocious lions, as they chased everybody down the street one last time.

recommended Google search: Takayama Japan Festival Images

CAMBODIA

THE GREATEST JUNGLE RUINS EVER DISCOVERED

Imagine a French explorer, hacking his way through the Cambodian jungles at the end of the nineteenth century. Following rumors of the ruins of a lost civilization, he has wandered deep into the snake-infested forest. Suddenly, through the trees, a waterway appears. This is no natural river, but a huge, rectangular manmade moat, with a dramatic causeway traversing its center, leading to a mysterious island. On the far side of the bridge, three massive stone towers flanked by mysterious porticos are reflected in the water. Imagine the awestruck visitor, walking along that grand promenade, marveling at the fancifully carved stone serpents that form its balustrades, astounded by the marvelous ruins he had just discovered. Surely he is trembling with excitement, and wondering what treasures he might find inside.

Our foreign visitor approaches the monument eagerly. And then, after climbing the steep steps and walking through the shadowed passageway to the other side, there comes another shock of discovery. Peering through the dense jungle beyond, he learns that these towers are themselves only the gateway to the temple grounds. The gigantic spires of the inner sanctuary are far off in the distance, soaring over two hundred feet in the air, surrounded by magnificent arched galleries, thousands of feet long, full of exquisite carvings and bas-relief murals.

217

Surprisingly, this temple was not entirely abandoned. A few Buddhist monks had taken up residence in the inner sanctum, but most of the place was left to the jungle and the bats. The French explorer must have been stunned by the scale and sophistication of the ancient builders. When he brought back word of what he had seen, Angkor Wat became an international *cause-célèbre* in Europe. It was soon known as "One of the Seven Wonders of the Ancient World," as it deserved to be.

Even today, Angkor Wat still holds the record of "largest religious structure ever built" (over four hundred acres—bigger than the Vatican). Inscriptions tell its story. King Suryavarman II of the Khmer Empire ordered its construction early in the Twelfth Century. It took 300,000 laborers and 6,000 elephants. Millions of tons of stone were quarried more than forty kilometers away and rafted down a series of canals. The creation of the vast moat alone was a work of engineering genius.

As I stood on that same causeway almost a thousand years later, I tried to picture what it must have been like during the Khmer Empire. This temple was built to impress, and the sheer spectacle of the Royal Court's procession to the glorious new temple must have been jaw dropping. Too bad we'll never know. If only there had been an eyewitness...

But there was an eyewitness! In 1296, a Chinese diplomat named Zhao Daguan arrived at the Khmer court. He penned this description:

> *"When the King goes out, troops are at the head of his escort; then come flags, banners, and music. Palace women, numbering from three to five hundred, with flowers in their hair, hold candles in their hands and form a troupe. Even in broad daylight, the candles are lighted. Then come other palace women, bearing royal paraphernalia made of gold and silver. Then come the palace women carrying lances and shields, with the King's private guard. Carts, drawn by goats and horses, all in gold, come next. Ministers and princes are mounted on elephants, and, in front of them, one can see from afar, their innumerable red umbrellas. After them come the wives and concubines of the king, in palanquins, in carriages, on horseback, and on elephants. They have more than one hundred parasols, flecked with gold. Behind them comes the Sovereign, standing on an elephant, holding his sacred sword in his hand. The elephant's tusks are encased in gold."* *

Today, with millions of visitors each year, the temple itself is practically overrun. We waited in line for about a half hour for access to the upper central tower temple. Later in the afternoon, we managed to catch some peaceful moments at the site by trying the same trick we discovered on our first visit, twenty years before. Near closing time, we headed for the unpopulated east side to catch the dramatic silhouette of the towers against the orange sunset sky. There were only about five people back there! At closing time, guards gently herded us around to the side of the building, and we were able to enjoy the temple, glowing in the golden light of sunset, after the last of the tourists had left the main building. As we savored a few quiet moments, several monks slipped discreetly out of the side gate, their orange robes bright slashes of color against the shadowy stone steps.

Here's another stunning fact: Angkor Wat is only one of a thousand ruined temples in the jungles near Siem Reap. Many of them are remarkable and would have become world famous if it weren't for the spectacular quality of Angkor Wat. Here are descriptions of just two more:

STONE FACES IN THE JUNGLE: The Bayon

A magnificent stone bridge welcomed us onto the grounds of Angkor Thom, the ancient royal city of the Khmer kings. On the span of the causeway, over fifty larger-than-life-sized statues wrestled with the body of a giant seven-headed serpent, illustrating the Hindu myth of creation. To our left, the figures represented powerful gods. Balancing them, on the other side, were fifty demons. Together they pulled the snake's body to churn the vast ocean of milk, creating the universe.

At the end of the bridge stood the world-famous arched gateway with its smiling stone faces. Passing under that portal felt like entering a lost world. Beyond, at the end of a long boulevard, the towering hulk of the Bayon gradually emerged from the forest.

The gigantic stone heads of the Bayon have captured the imagination of the entire world, enthralling everyone from artists and poets to tee-shirt makers. The temple has an air of quintessential mystery that makes it irresistible and unforgettable. It is an artistic achievement for the ages.

Originally, it was designed as a multi-story pyramid, with fifty-four ascending towers, holding a total of two hundred and sixteen giant stone faces, gazing out in all directions. Today, all but two of the perimeter towers have fallen, but the central section has survived, including the grand pathway around the third story. There, high above ground level, we could wander amid the sculptures, appreciating the enigmatic Mona Lisa smiles of the ancient images at close range.

The faces are supposed to represent the gentle features of the Bodhisattva Avalokiteshvara, the Buddhist deity of compassion and mercy, but his Royal Highness King Jayavarman VII, who ordered the temple's construction, managed to immortalize his own features in the process. Few today know his name or his history, but almost everyone in the world is familiar with the famous likenesses, if only in the movies.

TA PROEM

The fifteen-foot high wall was overtaken by an enormous tree that had grown right on top of it. Gnarled roots crawled down both sides, squeezing the stones like giant knees, reaching down to grip the earth with clawed toes as the tree finally encountered the soil it sought. Inside the wall, another gigantic tree grasped the ruined temple's doorway in a twisted, snaking embrace. Beyond it, a darkened passageway beckoned, and beyond that, two additional overgrown courtyards, each with carved doorways, led to more mysterious rooms, long hallways, and open terraces full of collapsed masonry.

The builders of these temples never reached the level of sophistication needed to build large, domed halls of stone, so, instead, they built towers, with small interiors, all connected by long corridors. Each tower held a religious symbol or statue at its center. At the temple's heart stood the largest tower and most significant shrine. This temple was Hindu, so most of the altars still held lingam and yoni carvings, (The Hindu symbol for the joining of the male half and the female half of the universe) although some of the Hindu sculptures had been set aside to make way for more recent Buddhist offerings.

The archeologists who cleared the vegetation out of these ruins made a conscious decision, many years ago, to leave some of the encroaching trees intact, so that, today, this temple still retains its romantic flavor. Unfortunately, the number of visitors has increased so much in recent years that the temple no longer has that "lost city in the jungle" vibe, unless you make a point of staying until closing time. It wasn't quite the same as it was twenty years earlier when we shared the ruins with a couple of other foreign travelers and a few local Buddhist monks. (Dave and I still remember their shy smiles and naughty giggles when they asked us if we knew what a "lingam" was. (It is a phallic symbol—the one on the Hindu shrines.)

recommended google search: Angkor Wat Images

recommended google search: Bayon Cambodia Images

recommended google search: Ta Proem Cambodia Images

* Quotation is from Andrew Forbes; David Henley; Colin Hinshelwood (2012) Angkor: Eighth Wonder of the World   Cognoscenti Books, p.108 ASINB0085RYW0O.

By Diana McLeod

CHINA

CHINESE REGGAE

Rule #1: When you are traveling and somebody local invites you out, take advantage of the opportunity whenever you can. (This rule clashes completely with Rule #2.)

Rule #2: NEVER let Australians run your social life because you will undoubtedly regret it in the morning.

Let me rephrase that. ALWAYS let Australians run your social life despite the fact that you will regret it in the morning. After all, there is no such thing as a quality vacation without a little adventurous self-abuse, is there?

We met Peter at Sam's Guest House in Chengdu, a city in Sichuan Province, in Southwest China. He was an English teacher who had been working in a small town near Chengdu for several years, so his Chinese was pretty proficient. When he invited us to hear him play guitar at a local watering hole, we readily agreed. He was going to meet a few friends there, all fellow expats from a variety of countries. Most of them were the only English speakers in their neighborhoods, so this evening would be a rare chance for them to get together and hobnob in their own language.

We all bundled into a cab, and Peter did a great job of directing the driver in Chinese. We wound up at the Shamrock Pub, a fairly authentic Irish pub located on a well-to-do Chengdu boulevard. It was so out of place! It looked like it had dropped out of the sky, having been carried all the way from Ireland on a twister straight out of an Oz movie. Inside, it was pure Ireland, but with a very international crowd, and an even more international menu. I ordered Mexican food, Peter ordered New Zealand steak, and we all drank Chinese beer except for one Guinness drinker. We ate dinner with two Aussies, one Brazilian and his Chinese girlfriend, one French speaker, and three Dutch from The Hague. The conversation was all over the map, and very lively.

Peter tuned up his guitar and took the stage, entertaining an increasingly drunken audience. As the dinner patrons finished up and the bar crowd began to pour in, the audience gradually became more and more Chinese. Peter entertained them with a series of Australian and Irish folk songs.

The Chinese patrons were the young, affluent children of the new upper classes—the ambitious new socialites of Chengdu. They had smartphones, trendy clothes, and the ambition to quest outside their own rather monolithic cultural dictates. They came to the pub for an "exotic" foreign experience. I soon decided that the highpoint of the Shamrock Pub experience was watching the Chinese trying to become a wee bit Irish.

Footsteps of a Nomad

After his last performance, Peter decided to move on. We bundled into another taxi and went in search of a near-mythical watering hole someone had told him about. Apparently, there was a genuine reggae hangout in the city, and Peter was determined to find it. We wound up at a fancy new shopping mall, the upper floors of which held a series of chic theme bars and restaurants.

We wandered past an Italian wine bar with fake prosciuttos hanging from the ceiling and an all-Euro menu with prices to match. Next was a rave bar. Peeking in the windows, we could barely make out the crowd of shadowy figures gyrating to pumping hip-hop. Laser lights pulsed and spun all over the floor. Did they have the drugs to make the experience truly Western? Who knows? A rock climbing bar had a fake rock "cliff" off to one side. The combination of rock climbing and alcohol seemed rather dicey to me despite the safety lines. They still are a bit backward in China when it comes to liability insurance.

Upstairs, Peter followed his nose to the Hemp Bar. This place was remarkable, given that only a generation ago, everyone in China had been required to wear blue "Mao Suits." Freaky reggae-inspired psychedelic murals radiated from the bar's walls to ceilings. The bartender wore tie-dye, and Bob Marley blasted from every speaker. Funky old overstuffed furniture gave the place a "San Francisco in 1968" feel. Two of the guys playing pool had punk haircuts, one with a blonde dye job, and the other had purple hair and even some body jewelry.

You may wonder why this is such a big deal. It's important because China has never tolerated a counterculture before. These kids had grandparents shoved in re-education camps for non-conformity. Now, suddenly, the outside world is flooding in, and the legions of China's young elite are experimenting with everything. The Chinese government may try to keep a lid on it, but in the end, they really won't be able to. The Internet, Facebook and music websites are popping the cork off the bottle and letting the genie out. It's not just about haircuts and tie-dye. Who knows what will happen when a fifth of the world's population learns to experiment with freedom of expression? Change is coming to China, and it is coming incredibly fast. Let us hope that globalization can come gently, because, if it doesn't, the world is in for a bumpy ride.

Rule #3 (and this one is strictly for my benefit): When you are out hoisting a few drinks with good friends, try not to get too philosophical. Just enjoy the party.

Written in 2008

By Diana McLeod

THE DAY WE BECAME CHINESE TV STARS

Dave is a train aficionado, and he will go to great lengths to see working steam engines around the world.

He persuaded me to visit one railway in Shibanxi, China, where picturesque narrow gauge steam trains are the only way in and out of a mountainous coal mining area.

We took a room in the local guesthouse/restaurant/pharmacy and general store and spent several days photographing the agricultural village with its surrounding terraced farms and its daily local mixed passenger and freight trains.

On our final day there, we were amused to see pigs loaded into the baggage car on their way to market. They squealed dreadfully as a group of men struggled to force them up into the car.

While reboarding after a long station stop, we were surprised to find a TV crew among the local farmers. They had come from Beijing to photograph the train, with two broadcast-quality cameras, movie-making equipment, and a staff of about fifteen. The director introduced himself to us and asked if we would be willing to act in one of the scenes. He was from CCTV (the Chinese National Television network.) I told him we would do our best. They were shooting a film about China's past, and the antique steam locomotive was a perfect prop. An actor, dressed in Imperial costume, was playing the part of a nineteenth century Mandarin government official.

The director wanted us to act the part of American railway consultants who were trying to persuade the Imperial government to modernize. We were supposed to walk beside the Mandarin, talking rapidly about railway improvements, in English, while the official walked away from us, refusing to listen.

The director thought the scene would play better with real foreigners in it, rather than other Chinese actors. The only problem was our attire (which, after three days of grubby living and dirty steam trains, was not at all acceptable). The director actually asked Dave if he would be willing to return to his hotel room to get his business suit! Dave and I burst out laughing and explained that he didn't travel with one. Dave wound up wearing the director's black leather jacket. Luckily, I had black pants with a black vest-like sweater, so I didn't look too bad for a quick shot. I slicked my hair straight back and hid my ponytail under my jacket. But neither of us could fix the fact that we were wearing modern sneakers, or that a woman would never have been involved in railway construction in the nineteenth century.

We did three takes of the scene, which the two cameramen shot from slightly different angles. The director worked in English for our benefit, yelling "action" and "cut" in classic Hollywood style. Our co-actor was decked out in a magnificent silk brocade robe. He wore an antique Mandarin hat with a peacock feather and a wig with a fake pigtail of hair down his back.

After the shoot, everyone shook hands. The director promised we would get pictures of the finished scene by email. He took our business card, winked at us, and said, "Keep in touch, OK?" making his best attempt at fake sincerity. We knew we would never hear from him again, of course. The scene probably wound up on the cutting room floor. But maybe we have been on Chinese TV and seen by a fifth of the world's population. We will never know....

recommended google search: Shibanxi Railway images

BHUTAN

LAND OF THE THUNDER DRAGON

A LANDING WORTHY OF A THUNDER DRAGON: The view was breathtaking from the plane. We were beside the tallest and most famous peak in the world—Mount Everest. Blessed with perfect weather, we could see the Nepalese side of the mountain in all its glory. Great plumes of snow were blowing off the back of the rock face. For a few minutes longer, the Himalayas stretched beneath us, and then clouds obscured them.

Our engines cut back abruptly as the plane began its descent. The Australian pilot (who, I found out later, had been flying with Druk Air for years) explained, over the P.A. system, that the plane was going to follow a river valley into Paro, the only airport in Bhutan. When the plane broke through the clouds, I saw it myself: we were descending between two mountain peaks, into a narrow gorge. The plane twisted and turned, steeply banking as it followed sharp bends in the river!

Soon, mountainsides were on both sides of the plane! Imagine flying on an Airbus jet, looking out the windows, and seeing a terraced pasture full of goats to your left, and another field, with farmers plowing it, to your right. So close! And we were still swerving and banking hard to thread our silver needle through the narrowing gap! Not only that, we were plummeting downward with greater airspeed than usual, due to the high altitude of the tiny airport we were heading for. (7,300 feet above sea level). Dave and I looked at each other in amazement. This was the craziest airport approach we had ever seen attempted by a commercial jet.

But our "stunt pilot" landed us safely. Druk Air apparently does this several times a day, every day, and is the only airline allowed landing rights at Paro. Not only does the pilot have to find his way between two 14,000 foot peaks and through the narrow valley, but he has to do it using only visual means, according to the Druk Air website. Autopilot is not an option. (Remember the clouds when we began our descent? Our Australian pilot must be an adrenaline junkie.) And landing in foul weather must be a real heart-pounder. What a job! But Druk Air hasn't had an accident yet....

Once on the ground, we passed through the immigration formalities and anxiously went in search of our guide. I should explain that entrance to Bhutan is severely restricted by law. The most important rule is that each tourist is required to spend a certain amount of money every day. Part of this is government tax, and part of it is designed to stimulate the local economy. For us, these requirements make this place about as expensive as Switzerland. The government also forces tourists to go on a "group tour" and to hire a tour company, transportation, and a guide. These policies constrict tourism so much that only those who are fully committed to the preservation of Bhutanese culture will visit.

Dave and I have always abhorred group tours. We also dislike hiring professional guides. But friends of ours had been to Bhutan the previous year, and they had found a lama (a Buddhist priest), Ngodrup, who had been to the U.S before. He was running a little tour company on the side. We emailed him and asked if he could take us on. Ngodrup replied, informing us that he only guided one or two groups a year, and hired tour guides took the rest. He also told us that a "group of two" was acceptable. I had high hopes of having a lama as our guide because I wanted to pepper him with questions about Buddhist practices, so I asked Dave to email back and plead with Ngodrup to take us himself. He responded he was going on a meditation retreat in India, and he couldn't promise he would get back in time for our arrival. He assured us not to worry; someone would meet us at the airport.

We were so happy when we saw a lone figure in Buddhist robes waiting at the airport entrance! It was indeed Lama Ngodrup Dorji, back from India, just in time. I liked him right away. He spoke with a soft voice and a lilting accent. His face was animated and kind, but with a puckish half-smile that revealed a lively sense of humor. Little did we realize, at the time, we had hired a real prankster as our companion.

Before we left for the trip, I worried Ngodrup might be a quiet, shy man who would be totally overwhelmed by being stuck in a car with Dave for a week and a half. Not so! Ngodrup was as big a talker as Dave! Not only that, he had lived in the States for several years, so his English was fantastic. He even shared Dave's passion for American and world politics. The two of them were soon debating and discussing with gusto. This was going to be a fun trip.

On the way to Thimphu, the capital city of Bhutan, we started to learn a little more about our host. Ngodrup was a married lama. He did not live within the monastic community, nor was he celibate. He had two young sons, and a seemingly happy marriage. This is fairly common for some Buddhist sects. (Many Buddhist saints have been known to take on consorts or wives.)

Ngodrup and his wife spent several years in western Massachusetts. He worked as a teacher at a school for special children with severe autism, personality disorders, and other problems while his wife attended Mount Holyoke College. That's why his English was so perfect. It was so refreshing to speak English without simplifying our vocabulary. Ngodrup even understood our sarcasm and our jokes, and zinged us right back with his own.

In Thimphu, Ngodrup took us for our first Bhutanese lunch. WOW! What a meal! There were about ten main dishes, all beautifully prepared. The only thing we didn't like was the local butter tea. They had one dish called "chili cheese" which was very spicy but delicious. It was vegetables, cooked, in a very thick, melted cheese sauce, with lots of hot chilies stuck in to spice it up. While we were in Bhutan, I used the chili cheese as a condiment, slathering it onto some of the other blander dishes. Dave and Ngodrup ate it all by itself. They were both "Thunder Dragons" after eating all those hot chilis!

After lunch, we walked around Thimphu. Most of this city was relatively new, and it was already falling victim to modernism. We saw a few of the depressingly faceless concrete block buildings that are everywhere in Asia. Luckily, all of the old buildings and half of the new ones still sported touches of the distinctive local architecture. Even the brand-new Toyota dealership was covered in traditional carvings and wall paintings.

Although some people were in Western, Indian or Nepalese dress, most still wore classical Bhutanese traditional formal attire. (National dress is required in government offices, banks, and schools). Men wore knee-length long coats, belted high at the waist, and knee socks. Women wore long, sarong-like dresses, held up by elaborate brooches, over blouses, with silk brocade jackets.

In order to really understand this little country, it helps to know its philosophy. Bhutan has been ruled by a series of amazingly enlightened monarchs. In 1953, King Dingme Dorji Wangchuck established the country's first legislature. Since then, his son, Jingme Singye Wangchuck, in a stunning move, transferred most of the power of the absolute monarchy to the legislature. He even granted them the ability to impeach a king. (In all of world history, only a handful of examples exist of rulers voluntarily handing absolute power back to the people. It is such a rare thing! Doesn't it give you hope for humanity that it can happen at all?)

Jigme Singye also introduced the concept of "Gross National Happiness" in Bhutan. Today, there is a Government "Gross National Happiness Commission" with as much political power as any of the other government ministries. What is "Gross National Happiness?" Quite simply, it is development with values. All development in Bhutan must be approved and signed off on by this minister before a change is permitted. If the proposals in question do harm to traditional values, they are not allowed. Traditional values, quality of life and national happiness in Bhutan are protected in the same way our government is supposed to protect an endangered species.

Is Bhutan really Shangri-la? No. There are a few issues, as there always are with humanity. National pride is exceedingly strong, which is good, but national pride can also have a downside. As Bhutan works to retain its own culture, it necessarily rejects other influences. This has sadly resulted in accusations that Bhutan carried out "ethnic cleansing" of Nepalese and Indian Hindu families living within its borders. Some Bhutanese who are ethnic Nepalis have fled the country. Families of Bhutanese refugees now live in our town of Burlington, Vermont. Apparently there is a limit to gross national happiness.

Despite that one sour note, Bhutan promised to be very special. I still couldn't wait to experience this little gem of a country. Ngodrup left us at our hotel and drove off to spend one more night with his family before our big adventure the next day.

OVER THE DOCHULA PASS AND ON TO TRONGSA: The next morning, our hotel presented us with a breakfast big enough to feed at least six people. Ngodrup picked us up in a Land Rover. When we got out of Thimphu, we started up a steep ridge. The pagoda-style roof of a *dzong* (a medieval fortress) soared above the tree line. As we crossed the river, I spotted a water-driven roadside prayer wheel. This charming device ensures that Buddhist prayers are offered to the heavens, twenty-four hours a day, seven days a week. They can be powered by even the smallest of trickling roadside brooks. The road followed the side of the ridge, winding and weaving along the contours of the hills.

Bhutanese roads are incredibly tortuous. Even the main highways are barely two lanes wide, with no shoulders and only a few guardrails. The whole country clings to vertical drop-offs, so most of the time, a driving miscalculation would prove fatal. There is virtually no flat land, except in a few river valleys. Hairpin turns are everywhere. It is not possible to drive faster than twenty miles an hour, but even at that slow speed, constant dangers on the road exist, especially in the form of farm animals, which are allowed to wander wherever they like. Ngodrup was a fantastic driver; neither overly timid nor too aggressive. He was very creative at passing other vehicles, especially big trucks, without making me gasp in terror. But driving long distances on narrow roads must have been exhausting for him.

An hour later, we were still going up, driving through genuine virgin forest in the middle of a large national park, heading for the Dochu Pass (10,233 feet above sea level). As we hit the cloud line, well below the pass, jagged streamers of mist swirled like dragons' breath, catching on the trees. Huge pines huddled in groups, their drooping arms clothed in shawls of gauzy green moss, with their heads bowed together as if in conversation. In an hour of driving, we had only seen one solitary hut. Otherwise, the forest was pure and untouched.

At last, we reached the pass. One of Bhutan's queens had commissioned the building of a shrine and a temple at the top. One hundred and eight chortens (small bell-like structures) commemorated fallen soldiers in a Bhutanese victory over the Assamese. They were arranged in the form of a mandala (a Buddhist circle). Above the road, the cloud forest was virtually overwhelmed by prayer flags. As we walked around the shrine, Ngodrup wandered up into the woods. His maroon and yellow Buddhist robes were a large focus of color among the tangles of bright fabric squares. As he got further up the hill, drifting mist softened the color palette and airbrushed the clarity of my photos, creating a whole new impressionist version of the scene.

Our vehicle's brakes were sorely tested on the way down. After another hour of hairpin turns we saw the village of Thinly Gang, perched on a narrow ridge. Rice terraces cascaded down the hillsides, sculpting the contours of the land like curving green stairs. Farmhouses clung to the slopes. In the center of "town" a few very funky general stores constituted the only commerce we'd seen in several hours.

The traditional homesteads enchanted me. I have never seen mountain people take so much time and effort decorating their homes. Not only were they fancifully painted, but even the wooden beams were cut to stick out at various lengths, all around the top of the first story of each house, creating patterns and layers. The ends were often carved or shaped, and they all had colorful motifs. On the front of each house, families often painted two round images of a variety of subject matter, mostly animals: tigers, dragons, phoenixes, snow leopards, or monkeys. Occasionally there were Buddhist themes.

Then, I stared in shock at a different style of painting. A couple of buildings were prominently decorated with very large depictions of penises! They were very graphic, fully erect, and painted in lurid pink or red. Some of them were even wreathed in flames. Ngodrup told us they advertised the homeowner's masculinity and fertility, and were intended to bring the family security, good luck, and many children. I was amused. I couldn't help thinking, the bigger the painting, the smaller the... But that was none of my business. Still, I wondered what the village ladies would have to say about some of their men and their ambitious paintings.

The harmonious nature of the community tugged at me. Farmsteads were just beginning to come alive with the first signs of spring, with apple trees, cherry trees, and plums in full bloom. I suddenly yearned to live there, to move into one of the little farmhouses and experience the simple pastoral lifestyle. I wanted to touch the earth and farm again as I had once briefly done; to witness the slow changing of the seasons and the growing of the rice crop; and to relish the rare excitement of market and festival days. It made me wonder: what do Americans miss out on, by going too far and too quickly? We crave constant change and stimulation, and we've lost the ability to have a simple life.

By Diana McLeod

Back in the car, we headed down the ridge, crossing the river at Wangdu. The open air market at the top of the bluff looked like a photo-op goldmine. Ngodrup promised we would spend time there on our return trip.

The road continued up the river valley for a while, passing a series of prosperous villages. Then it threaded through a tighter gorge, climbing higher until it was several hundred feet above the river. As we made one hairpin turn, we caught our first glimpse of Trongsa Dzong. The medieval castle's stone knuckles clung to the edge of a spectacular cliff. The pagoda-roofed complex was dramatically imposing, with whitewashed walls more than five stories high. Golden rooftops caught the light and glowed, adding to the magical quality of the ancient palace.

The fabulous old fortress was right across the river from us, but we weren't there yet. The Bhutanese road turned away, up the river valley, following the contours of the land until the river was small enough to cross. A million twists and turns later, we were on the other side, making our way back to where we had just been. It reminded me of trekking in Nepal where we would often get a clear morning view of our next destination, right across the valley. The villages looked deceptively close to each other! But to reach them, we would have to descend 1,500 feet, cross the river, and then climb back up another 1,500 feet, which would take the better part of a day.

We spent the night at Yankhil Resort, a tourist hotel outside of town, where the well-trained staff pampered us almost to excess. The sumptuous modern rooms all provided great views of the *dzong* and the town. We had a luxurious bathroom, a private deck, and an electric heater. Still, I hoped our status as foreign tourists would not always keep us so isolated from local people and typical living conditions. I was to get my wish during the next week...

recommended Google search: Bhutan Images

(includes penis paintings)

BHUTAN AND THE ART OF ARCHERY

as the diary continues...

The next morning, Dave and I walked into the town of Trongsa. When he decided to take a shortcut across a field beside the *dzong*, I thought we should stick to the sidewalk, which veered off to the left of an earthen wall, but Dave insisted on cutting across the lawn. He has never been one to "stay on the path." As we walked in front of the mound, I heard shouting. We were standing right in front of a small circular object with a painted bullseye in the center. There were vicious looking holes in it!

I spun around. The archers were standing about 30 yards away! We had stumbled right into the middle of their practice range, directly between the archers and the target! Gazing beyond the colored rings, I saw powerful arrows stuck deep into the earthen wall right behind us. Any one of them could have killed us!

Luckily for everybody, the Bhutanese archers had already spotted us, and they were patiently waiting for us to get our big, ignorant, tourist butts out of their way. Sheepishly, we scurried off the archery course and turned around to watch from a safe distance.

Archery is the national sport of Bhutan. Young boys receive their first bows and arrows when they are still toddlers. Men practice, hone their skills, and enter fierce competitions between villages. Festivals are built around these events, and the entire population turns out to watch, dance and urge their heroes on. When archery is practiced, it is customary to wear formal Bhutanese national costume, so these archers were decked out in traditional dress, with knee-length shirt-coats over long stockings. The bows they carried were another story. They were using modern, high-tech fiberglass and carbide steel weapons, propelling their arrows with deadly force.

Unfortunately for us, the practice was ending for the day. The next time we encountered archery practice, the fun was just beginning. (I'm skipping ahead chronologically here.) We were in the town of Jakar, on a Saturday morning. Saturday is the day off for Bhutanese workers, so the young men of the town were gathering for a day of recreation. Instead of toting golf bags, these guys were all sporting quivers and formal dress clothes. The practice range was in a field on the edge of town. When we saw the crowd gathered there, we stopped to watch the fun.

A target stood at each end of the field. The archers gathered at one end, and each archer got two shots. After everyone had shot their arrows, the group moved to the other end of the shooting range where they retrieved their arrows and shot in the other direction. These guys used local bamboo bows, which made them much more photogenic than the archers in Trongsa. Even the simple traditional bows still shot arrows so fast that my eyes could not follow them in flight.

By Diana McLeod

I dislike sports. I really do. But archery in Bhutan was very entertaining because it was about each individual and his arrows, as well as the team. We sat and watched these archers practice for several hours, and I loved every minute of it! Every guy had a distinctive style, and each shot was a performance. The nocking of the arrow was a ballet gesture, executed with almost feminine grace. The archer then paused to aim, and it was time to observe his face. The intensity of concentration was remarkable! The archer's world was reduced to that one act, without future or past, and without any sense of separation. He became the arrow and the target.

As the arrow loosed, the archer came to life again. If the shot were good, he would literally chase his arrow down the field, willing it to fly true. Each archer had his very own battle cries or shouts. These theatrical performances usually ended with an emphatic lunging step, some arm waving, and more shouting. If his aim were off, the archer would not bother, or he would stop running and walk away, shaking his head and grimacing. After an exceptional shot, they would all jump around triumphantly, yelling war whoops. The enthusiasm was infectious. Each winning shot energized the whole team.

Arrows rarely hit the target. They were shooting from about eighty feet away, trying to hit a mark only about sixteen inches across. When a shot did hit the target, the whole group would join the archer in a celebration dance and victory song. Team members also tied a yellow cloth around his belt for the rest of the day, marking his achievement for all to see.

They also took note of poor performances. If an archer were not up to his usual standards, his compatriots would tie a hand-carved wooden phallic symbol around his waist. The implication was clear: since his mojo wasn't working, they would lend him a wooden one. It must be traumatic for some of these guys to have their masculinity mocked so publicly! (I would hate to be born a Bhutanese male with poor eyesight or bad eye-hand coordination!)

Although this was only a practice match, a little refreshment stand was set up under a tree. Beer and *Ara* (homemade Bhutanese liquor) were available for those who wished to start drinking—at ten o'clock in the morning! I wondered how much the archers themselves would consume over the course of the day.

I also wondered about stray shots. People were sitting within about eight feet of the target. One spectator was standing right beside it! (He did jump out of the way once or twice). A little hospital sat on the edge of town. I would wager one leading cause of traumatic injury in Bhutan is due to stray arrows, especially since every bare-bottomed male toddler in Bhutan is running around with his own child-sized archery set. These must be quite a hazard in the hands of a three-year-old, but they will ensure the future popularity of Bhutanese archery for many years to come.

THE TRONGSA DZONG: In the morning, we set out to visit some of the historic buildings of Trongsa. The famous *dzong* was nearly as imposing from the inside as it was from across the river; a sprawling multi-level fortress with ethereal golden rooftops and vivid Bhutanese architectural detail. What a magnificent medieval castle!

Trongsa Dzong got its start from religious visions. In 1543, an ancestor of the current Kings of Bhutan was meditating in the nearby village, and saw lights hovering above the spur of rock. He discovered a spring there, making it possible to support a community right on the cliff's edge. A temple was built, expanding into the walled complex that we see today. It has recently undergone a complete restoration.

Inside, the dzong holds a large monastery, a series of temples, and all of the district's government offices. At one time, it was the rulers' residence, but the Royal Family have now moved into more modern housing. It was charming to see government offices in such a historic setting. In Bhutan, there is no such thing as faceless big government. In a country of only about 700,000 people, everybody knows everybody else. If you have business with a minister, you simply go to see him.

Continuing our tour, we visited the Watchtower, which sits on a hill overlooking the town. This medieval fortress has now been turned into a world-class museum. The most important object on display is the actual crown of the Bhutanese kings. The elaborately embroidered cloth headdress has a three-dimensional head of a raven sewn in silk on top of it. As we slowly climbed up to the fortress's upper levels, we saw collections of textiles and royal garments, religious art and artifacts, ancient weapons, and other historic items.

We slogged our way up to the roof (despite having some trouble with the thin air.) At the very top, we visited the little glassed-in meditation room called the Warrior's Temple, which was used by the kings in the old days. A hermit lama now lives there. Ngodrup paid his respects to the lama as we toured his beautiful little shrine. Outside, we admired the bird's-eye view of the dzong from above. The vista, with the gleaming castle in the foreground, and the gorge, the river valley, and the mountains beyond became a vivid snapshot of Bhutan in my memory, which will stay with me for life.

By now, Ngodrup was hungry. (Ngodrup was always hungry. I had no idea what he did with the gigantic breakfast the resort staff fed us, but it was apparently already gone.) He wanted to try a new place to eat, and he was curious about the "Oyster house" he had seen in town.

I was curious, myself. I couldn't imagine finding a genuine oyster at the Oyster House. The coastline is 300 miles away, and it is in Bangladesh. I would never eat an oyster from those waters, which are probably some of the most polluted on earth! I suspected some British tourist gave the restaurant its name, thinking it would sound upscale and thus appeal to foreigners. The Bhutanese probably have no idea what an oyster is.

Ngodrup ordered a full-on traditional lunch; luckily that did not include any shellfish! There were plenty of tiny dried river fish, which Dave and Ngodrup crunched happily. I tried the rice and veggies, the chili-cheese, the buffalo stew, fried chicken and chapatis (flat bread). It was all good, although it was, as always in Bhutan, too much food!

After lunch, we got back in the car to go over the next pass and up the river valley to the town of Jakar. We zigzagged crazily out of Trongsa, winding back and forth in an attempt to gain altitude. At last, we were over the top, and the road descended into a large, seemingly untouched virgin forest. To our delight, it looked as though the rhododendron trees were about to bloom. On our return trip, they would add a whole new dimension of beauty and color to the landscape.

As we were driving, we experienced just how small Bhutan is. Over and over again, the same thing happened. We would pass a vehicle coming the other way. Both cars would brake and back up. Windows would roll down, and Ngodrup would lean out and chat with whoever was in the other car. We met his old friends, his relatives, and friends of his relatives' friends. I think Ngodrup knew almost everybody in Bhutan, including the King. Despite the socializing, traffic was rare. We would sometimes go half an hour without seeing another car, even though we were on "the main highway" for northern Bhutan. I was glad we had a sturdy vehicle with decent tires.

Our destination, Jakar, a large town on the fork of a river, boasted a downtown area with a couple of restaurants, a "mall" and even an internet café. A large *dzong* perched on one side of the surrounding hills. Our hotel was up on another high hill, with a commanding view of the town and the *dzong*. The old wooden hotel was considerably more rustic than our previous place, and our room had a tiny little woodstove! We found that delightful. Dave and I once heated our house with wood, long ago, and we sometimes miss it. Dave immediately set to building us a fire, but we discovered there was no kindling. We inquired, and our host told us to use the local pinecones. The pine pitch simply explodes into hot flames.

Our hotel owner confessed that his business was not going well. His dining room was capable of seating fifty people, but we were the only guests. (It was the very start of the tourist season. We were there for early spring, before things bloomed.) The Bhutanese have been on a bit of a hotel building boom lately, and Jakar had too many new hotel choices for the numbers of visitors they were likely to get in the future.

We found our hotel quaintly appealing, and I liked the wood heat. We did smoke the place up a bit until we got the damper setting just right. The next day, I asked the hotel owner about stove safety. He confessed he had suffered losses caused by Japanese tourists. Because of the language barrier, he had trouble teaching them how to use the stoves properly. One Japanese lady set her laundry on fire, and another burned half of the hotel down, so it had to be rebuilt. I was suddenly relieved we were the only guests!

(Writer's's Note: At this point, I will quit writing in precise diary form, so that I can tell the next two Bhutan stories properly)

recommended Youtube search: The archers of Bhutan

recommended Google search: Trongsa Dzong Images

THE PRANKSTER LAMA

Driving with Ngodrup was fun. As soon as we hopped in his car, a lively conversation started up right away. Ngodrup was always in fine form, pointing out places of interest, cracking jokes, and telling stories. Conversationally, Dave and Ngodup were like two peas in a pod. They both loved to debate and discuss, to tell tales, and to fool around. They fed each other gag lines and playful insults like a couple of old vaudeville comedians. They debated political issues from the American Teaparty movement to Bhutanese politics. David told Ngodrup about his travel adventures, and Ngodrup entertained us with Bhutanese legends of dragon eggs, Buddhist saints, buried treasure, protector demons, wicked witches and mad yogis.

By the fourth day of our trip, Ngodrup and Dave were cementing their friendship, which meant that Dave was becoming perfect cannon fodder for Ngodrup's pranks. We spent the morning attending a puja (monastic ceremony) at an old temple. Then we drove to a monastery at a sacred pilgrimage site. The religious complex there was built directly over a cave (a small indentation in the cliff face) where Padma Sambava (the founder of Vajrayana Buddhism) supposedly meditated. Ngodrup took us inside, and we toured the sacred interior while he performed a series of prostrations. There was a hushed and deeply religious atmosphere inside the old shrine, which left us utterly unprepared for any sudden irreverence.

As soon as we emerged from the building, Ngodrup placed his hand on the cliff wall, not ten feet from the holy site. He looked at Dave with a very solemn look on his face. "To finish your visit to this pilgrimage site, you must atone for past sins," Ngodrup said. "It is customary to bang your head against this rock three times."

Dave looked dubiously at the rock.

"Bang your head three times," Ngodrup insisted. Then he looked at me, raised one eyebrow, and winked. "Hard!" he commanded.

It almost worked. After all, we'd seen many places in Asia where pilgrims perform strange rituals.

By Diana McLeod

For a second, Dave almost fell for it, but Ngodrup and I were already cracking up. When Dave realized he was being pranked, his mouth just fell open. The three of us laughed so hard we had to sit down and wipe away tears.

Later that day, at yet another temple, we walked the inner *kora* (a *kora* is a circular pathway inside the temple that goes from shrine to shrine and is used for walking meditation. *Koras* can also circle around outside a temple complex as well). When we came to a stone bench with a pile of linked chains on it, Ngodrup explained this was a steel "cloak." Pilgrims would bear it as a heavy burden while walking the *kora*, to atone for sins. Ngodrup picked it up and put it on his back to demonstrate. Then he handed it to Dave.

Dave was very dubious about this, but neither of us could see any other possible explanation for the strange item. "How many times do I have to do the *kora*?" Dave asked.

"Three times," Ngodrup replied.

"Why is it always three times?" Dave muttered.

Ngodrup smiled innocently.

This time, Dave believed him, but he performed the *kora* at a jog. The weighty metal links clanked and clattered, making Dave look like a deranged bat as he ran through the darkened temple corridors.

Ngodrup thought this was hilarious. He was clutching his stomach and howling with laughter as he watched Dave run.

Dave finally finished the third lap, jingled over to us and shrugged off the cloak. "You're pranking me again, aren't you?" he asked.

Ngodrup was giggling too hard to reply. We still don't know whether or not he was telling us the truth....

THE MASK: Ngodrup is the head lama at two temples in his ancestral village of Shinkar, a tiny, remote settlement of about two hundred people. When we toured the temples, Ngodrup took us into his mask room, where the masks worn by the lamas during festival days are kept. The masks were depictions of fearsome wrathful deities, animal spirits, black magicians, and other characters in Buddhist stories.

Downstairs, in the main temple room, there were two sealed chambers that we were not allowed to enter. These belonged to the wrathful deities of the Shingkar valley. Ngodrup explained to us (in all seriousness) that there were three wrathful spirits in Shingkar, and it was his duty to pay homage to them and keep them happy so no calamity would befall his little town. He even pointed out where each of the wrathful spirits lived, high up on the surrounding hillsides. A series of masks hung above the doors of the sealed chambers in his temple. Most of the masks were quite typical, but one open-mouthed, monkey-faced mask seemed really unusual. There are simian characters in

Buddhism, but I didn't recognize this one, so I asked Ngodrup about it.

"It's a *Yeti*," he explained.

"No, *really*? But there are no high Himalayas around here! Aren't Yetis supposed to be only in the high altitude regions of Tibet?" I asked skeptically.

"Why can't they be here? There could be Yetis here!" Ngodrup's innocent demeanor was beginning to crumble. Lying did not come that easily to him, and he was unable to hide a hint of a smile.

"OK, what is it really?"

He made me wait for the answer, continuing to protest he had been telling the truth the first time. Finally, he grinned sheepishly, knowing we were not buying it.

"It's a Halloween gorilla mask," he confessed, between giggles. "It's latex. I bought it in California."

"But what's it doing here in the temple?"

"Why not? It's guarding the wrathful deity room. I thought they would approve."

I guess it was appropriate. Ngodrup seriously believed in the wrathful deities, and Bhutanese people approach their local wrathful deities much like trick-or-treaters. You must give them treats or they start to play tricks on you. Or much worse. But the Halloween mask was certainly the weirdest item I have *ever* seen in a traditional Buddhist temple!

"I EAT, I SLEEP, AND I SHIT." This is the charming answer I got when I asked Ngodrup to describe his religious practice. It's a standard answer many serious practitioners of Buddhism might give to people who are casually seeking their wisdom. It is a crude answer, but it's also a serious one. It is a reminder that inner peace does not exist outside of basic living. Buddhism teaches that enlightenment is found in the most mundane of tasks, and in the most humble of activities. Looking for enlightenment outside of daily life will get you nowhere. This is why Zen monks chide their anxious disciples to go home and do the dishes.

Ngodrup is married, with two children, and he is running a tour company. He is practicing his Buddhism in the most difficult of circumstances—without detaching himself from the world. It is said to be easier to quiet the mind and let things go during a retreat into monastic life. It is harder when you have worldly attachments, financial obligations, and family ties distracting you. Ordinary life—with a liberated, enlightened mind—should be natural for all humans, but most people can't find that harmony. Still, despite his complicated modern existence, Ngodrup has begun to tap into a profound spiritual well of inner peace and joy. You can see it plainly on his face. And, of course, his actual practice involves getting up at some unholy hour of the early morning and meditating for several hours before beginning his day.

I wanted to discuss this further with Ngodrup, but I knew he was going to continue dishing out more of the same. The trouble is, there are no magic formulas to convey; there is no "answer" to the question about the meaning of life. That's why the smart-aleck reply is so common. You apparently either get it, or you don't.

When Buddha wanted to teach his disciples about enlightenment, none of his words succeeded in enlightening them. Words get in the way, because they compartmentalize something that can't be realized intellectually. Finally, he called his disciples together and passed them each a flower. As one disciple accepted the flower, he also grasped the Buddha's message, and he attained enlightenment on the spot. The rest did not.

So what actually happened? What was conveyed? I don't know. I have more dishes piling up in my kitchen sink. I guess I'd better go and do them...

"*TOO* BAD." This was Ngodrup's answer to all complaining and whining. He simply made fun of the whiner, whether it was Dave or me. Once again, he was reminding us to let go. All self-pity comes from attachment: attachment to ego, attachment to plans (there was lots of whining about poor weather and poor visibility on the trip), and even attachment to physical comfort. We received no sympathy for any of our attachments. Ngodrup had no mercy. Fussing of any kind was met with his relentlessly smiling "*TOO* BAD" brick wall of an answer. He didn't let us get away with anything. Talk about tough love!

LET'S DO LUNCH

Here are three unusual experiences we had in Bhutan. Each one happens to involve lunch.

DRUK STAR LUNCH: On Sunday in Jakar, Ngodrup's usual favorite eatery was closed, so we had to search for a new luncheon restaurant. We found an old inn that was open for business. Ngodrup ordered too much food (as usual). He talked with the innkeeper and discovered she was a cousin whom he had never met before. (Ngodrup has family everywhere in Bhutan!)

While they were chatting, some high school kids came in and sat down in front of the TV in the corner. Many seats were soon occupied. Some of the kids ordered soft drinks or tea. We wondered what program they were there to see. It turned out to be, "Druk Star." In English, the name meant "Dragon Star." It was, of course, the Bhutanese version of "American Idol."

We lingered over lunch to observe this cross-cultural experience. How would the Bhutanese government manage the sudden deluge of cultural pollution? After all, the Bhutanese have gone to great lengths to keep their society unique and pure, to maintain "Gross National Happiness."

I thought the producers of "Druk Star" handled it very well. Each contestant was judged on their ability to perform Bhutanese traditional music as well as Western songs. They had to wear Bhutanese formal garb for the Bhutanese performances. Most of the contestants also played the *dramyin*, which is a type of stringed lute common to the area. In between songs, the moderator talked a lot. It was apparent he was reminding the teenagers they were responsible for maintaining their cultural identity while absorbing music from the West. The Bhutanese are well aware that traditions in neighboring countries are being cast aside by the younger generations. So far, the outlook looks favorable in this country. The kids watching "Druk Star" were captivated by all of the performances.

After listening to the show for a while, I felt the Bhutanese should continue to enjoy local music. They don't do so well with ours. Thanks to Eastern influences, their voices have that dreadful, piercing, Chinese-style, nasal twang which is hard on Westerners' ears. But cultural prejudice goes both ways. I'm sure most Bhutanese get their first taste of American pop or rap music and wonder why on earth the rest of the world loves it so much.

FARMHOUSE LUNCH: The road from Jakar to Shinkar was arduous, traversing some very high mountain passes in remote areas with only a few yak herders' huts. There were few villages and none with anything remotely like a restaurant. At about lunchtime, we arrived in the beautiful mountain village of Ura. Ngodrup was planning to eat lunch at the only real "restaurant" there, but he was dismayed to discover the establishment was already full! The Bhutanese Minister of Health and his entourage were crowded into the tiny little building, having a meeting with locals.

We decided to drive down into the town and take a look around. The village, nestled in a magnificent valley, was pristinely lovely. Except for the electric poles, it could have been a scene from hundreds of years ago. Everything was perfectly traditional. The houses were all built in the local style, with brightly painted accents. The farms were prosperous, with well-tended gardens and healthy herds. Once again, I felt the strong appeal of the simple life. I wanted to move in, plant potatoes and watch the springtime turn the landscape green.

Ngodrup had other things on his mind. He refused to let a closed restaurant deter him from his lunch. He was a man with a bottomless appetite! While we were busy taking pictures, Ngodrup was arranging things. This mountain village was isolated, but, thanks to a serious investment on the part of the forward-thinking government, it was miraculously still within range of a communications tower. And Ngodrup's was not the only phone in town! He walked us over to one house, and to our surprise, he wandered right into the yard and up the stairs. An elderly lady and her daughter greeted us inside. The second floor of the house held a single large room with a woodstove in the middle, and a traditional clay cooking hearth which was also connected to the stovepipe.

On a crackling fire, several dishes were being heated for us. Our hostess served us rice, lentils and "chili cheese," followed by a drink of homemade *ara*. *Ara*, (called *arak* in some countries) is the Bhutanese version of distilled rice or potato wine, and it delivers a potent kick! (You know you've truly visited a country when you are invited to try the local homemade moonshine). I noticed that grandmother also poured herself a very healthy mugful.

Ngodrup conversed with the ladies in Bhutanese. They had known each other a long time. Then he told us a little bit about the family. "This lady's son got scholarships to study abroad," he said. "He eventually went to Oxford, in England."

It took me a minute to imagine a young man going all the way from this remote village to Oxford!

Then Ngodrup told me this tiny village had produced not one, but two Oxford scholars!

The farmhouse looked entirely traditional at first. There was no real furniture to speak of, only some plain wooden stools around the fire. Bedrolls were piled in a heap on one side of the room. Kitchen shelves held staples, spices, and dishes. Pots and pans hung from hooks on the walls. There was no running water in the kitchen. But when the kids came home from school, I saw a DVD player, hidden in a cupboard. The kids started going through their music collection and popped in a CD. The music was local.

The real surprise was the bathroom. When I asked if I could use the facilities, I honestly expected a simple outhouse. But when I went downstairs and opened the door, I was impressed. The traditional farmhouse had a thoroughly modern bathroom, with a flush toilet, a full tiled bath, an electric water heater, a brand new washing machine, and even a dryer! Apparently, the Oxford scholar was sending home extra cash, and the ladies knew just where they wanted to spend it.

When we left, we thanked our hostesses with bows, smiles, and "*Kha din Che*," which is Bhutanese for "thank you." I'm sure Ngodrup slipped them a little cash, which they will probably spend on expensive, imported laundry detergent.

LUNCH WITH THE KHENPO: Towards the end of the trip, we visited the Phobijika Valley, home to a government-protected winter sanctuary for endangered black-necked cranes. These birds have been revered by Buddhists for centuries, and legend holds that previous incarnations of the Dalai Lama rode from monastery to monastery carried on the backs of these magnificent birds. The town is also home to a famous monastery, the Gangten Gompa.

On the way, Ngodrup pointed out a restaurant. He was already thinking ahead to lunch, even though it was well before noon. Dave and I were still digesting the mountainous breakfast the hotel had stuffed us with, so we turned it down. (I swear, the tourist meals they fed us were the size of a small Himalayan peak–so big they were downright embarrassing).

Ngodrup looked profoundly disappointed when we weren't ready to eat lunch yet because restaurants are few and far between in that area. Indeed, we soon turned off the main "highway" and took a dirt road that climbed high up a mountain pass, driving through a pristine virgin forest, with no sign of human habitation. It was a lovely day, and the rhododendrons were just beginning to bloom. Dave stopped to take pictures several times. While we were admiring the view, Ngodrup was on his beloved cell phone. He returned, triumphant—he had just arranged lunch.

When we got to the town of Gangteng, we turned off the main road and headed up a winding driveway, as guests of the Gangteng Buddhist Institute. The *khenpo* (head teacher) of the Institute was a longtime friend of Ngodrup's. Our guide had turned on the charm and sweet-talked his old friend into giving us a luncheon invitation.

The school and monastery were home to around two hundred monks. The *khenpo* was a kindly looking man in his early sixties, with a serene smile and a touch of Ngodrup's puckish sense of humor. A monk ushered us into a comfortable reception room with Western style seating. Young monks flitted in and out, bringing us tea and snacks, while the kitchens prepared the main course.

Dave and I listened while Ngodrup and the *khenpo* caught up. Apparently, they had known each other for years and had even been schoolmates together. The conversation soon turned to America and American politics.

The *khenpo* was particularly interested in race relations in America. He, like everybody around the world that year, had been following the election of President Obama. The fact that the U.S. had just elected an African-American President struck him as remarkable. You could tell he had been brought up in a very closed society himself, and he was curious about his own reactions to people of other races (including Dave and me, of course!). Maybe he had encountered some strong local feelings towards white people, especially in such a major tourist town. (We must all seem dreadfully spiritually inferior to the Bhutanese. We rush into a temple, take our snapshots, and move on).

He knew a lot about the recent presidential election, but he didn't know much about the history of race relations in America. At his request, we talked to him about slavery and segregation, and he listened intently.

We all wondered whether or not the U.S. was ready to be a colorblind society. Dave and I told him that we were amazed at how far

By Diana McLeod

America had come since our childhood, but we wondered if angry Obama-haters could force the nation to backtrack because of ongoing bigotry. We also worried for our President's safety in a society obsessed with gun ownership.

It was a fascinating conversation. The *khenpo's* questions were probing and insightful. His English wasn't as well-honed as Ngodrup's, but it was pretty darned impressive. He had obviously given the issue lots of thought.

While all this was going on, the food arrived. The monastery served us very generously—there was more food than we could ever eat (even Ngodrup)! It was a tasty feast.

What a marvelous lunch! It was such a privilege to meet such a high-ranking Bhutanese lama and share an exchange of ideas and cultural insight with him. Telling the *khenpo* the story of Martin Luther King and the "I have a dream" speech was particularly inspirational to me. Once again, we thanked our lucky stars for a guide like Ngodrup, who was able to bring us into contact with local people, and into situations most tourists never get to experience. Later that day, we saw the magnificently restored Gangten Gompa, which was impressive, but my favorite memory of that day was of lunch with the *khenpo*.

Recommended Google search: Gangteng Buddhist Institute (and Gangteng Monastery) Images

Recommended Google search: Bhutan Farm Images

241

TIBET

TRAIN TO THE ROOF OF THE WORLD

When we heard about the completion of the railway to Tibet in 2006, we immediately planned to ride it. Dave loves trains, and the combination of trains and Tibet was too good to pass up. He began the arduous process of trying to figure out the train schedules, the permit and visa process, and the intricacies of trying to arrange travel across restricted zones in China. We got help from the Chengdu C.I.T.S office staff, who cut through the red tape for us.

We boarded the train in Chengdu. The railway station was a vast seething ocean of humanity, flowing past the flotsam and jetsam of vendors, squatting families, and luggage. After we got on board, Dave disembarked and wandered off in search of snacks, leaving me wondering if I was going to arrive in Tibet all by myself. (He likes to do this to me: he wanders off the train and he doesn't re-board until the last possible second—and he usually has both tickets in his pocket. I don't see him again until the train is already picking up speed.)

The train to Tibet is specially designed for the high altitude trip. Its modern interior is comfortable, especially in soft sleeper class, where the compartments are roomiest. Fortunately we got suitable compartment mates, neither of whom was a smoker. The guy in the upper berth dropped off his luggage and disappeared; he must have had friends in another compartment. A pleasant middle-aged lady from Chengdu took the other lower berth. We tried to communicate, but it was difficult. I introduced us by country, then by name. I pointed to Dave and said "*Janada*" (Dave was born Canadian). I then introduced myself as a "*Megwo*" (their name for Americans). I don't know how Americans became known as "*Megwo*," but that is what a fifth of the world's population calls us.

Our companion settled into her bunk and proceeded to watch TV for the next two days. Each berth had a fancy flat screen TV, and (thank God), a headset. She spent most of her time watching a modern day Chinese soap opera series. They ran back-to-back episodes of one popular drama. It had the same repeating plot line: aggrieved or outraged women who interacted with cruelly insensitive men. The only variation—sometimes the women would get angry with each other. There was lots of drama: crying, screaming and arguing. I was so thankful for those headphones!

Dave and I wandered down to the dining car to see what was for dinner. There was no English menu, which was surprising since this was supposedly a tourist train. We stared at other peoples' meals, and soon picked out a dish or two that looked good. We were planning to point to the food and order beer in Chinese (bijou). However, we quickly realized we were being ignored by the wait staff. They took everyone else's orders but left us alone. Dave went over to the kitchen window and tried to order, but the cooks just waved him away. Only one girl on the train crew could speak English, and she wasn't there at the moment. Nobody else wanted to tackle the language barrier, so we were forced to wait, at every mealtime, until she showed up. The Chinese saw no rudeness in this, but despite our efforts to be friendly, no one wanted to help us. I do not think they meant to discriminate against us, but it was very inconvenient. The girl who spoke English had to push a food cart up and down the length of the train, so she seldom came into the dining car. I wonder what would have happened to us if she hadn't been on board! Would they have fed us at all? Ordering was an adventure, but when we finally got served, the food was well prepared and delicious. Dave and I love eating in dining cars. There is nothing like dining on a moving train, savoring the meal and watching the countryside roll past.

The first day of the train ride, we checked out the landscapes around Lanzhou. Rocky hills dusted with snow surrounded dry, empty valleys. The occasional farming villages had built hundreds, maybe thousands, of plastic-covered greenhouses, with rolled up mats or quilts on top, to protect crops against cold nights. Houses were often built right into the sides of the hills. Apparently, cave dwellings are commonplace in this part of China. We called them "Chinese hobbit holes."

We soon found some companions on the train. Rupert was Malaysian. He was dating an English girl named Verity, and they shared a compartment with a young lawyer from Hong Kong named Mark. They were a lively bunch, and we had several good conversations and meals together. Rupert was excited to see yaks for the first time. He kept snapping photo after photo from the train windows. I kept thinking his yaks would only show up as little black dots on his film because they were too far off in the distance.

At the end of the day, the train crew gave every passenger an oxygen tube. The train was going over a high pass, 16,528 feet above sea level, and many of the passengers would experience symptoms of altitude sickness. Altitude sickness can be fatal. One passenger—an elderly gentleman—had already died of altitude sickness on this train the year before. The pass the train would ascend was higher than almost any mountain in North America except McKinley and maybe one or two others. Before buying train tickets, each one of us had to sign a health form, stating our doctors had given permission for us to take the train and we were taking it at our own risk.

The oxygen tubes could be plugged into ports located all over the train. Even the toilets had them. Our companion from Chengdu had hers plugged in for the rest of the ride. We wanted to acclimatize, so we didn't use ours. I felt the air thinning as we went over the big pass, and my heart and lungs pumped harder and faster. I compensated by using a yogic breathing technique instead of the pressurized oxygen. The yoga worked pretty well. Neither Dave nor I had any ill effects except a bit of lightheadedness. He is an accomplished deepwater snorkeler, and his lungs are powerful. Our friends were not so lucky. They had nausea and severe headaches, which eventually passed as we descended into the Lhasa valley.

That morning, while Dave was out, our compartment companion leaned over and offered me a breakfast treat from her bag. She had brought along a large plastic bag full of cold, congealed, barbecued chicken feet, claws and all. YUM!

I smiled and said thanks, but tried to explain *"Megwo,* no." She was amused. I offered her my Chinese Spring Onion Biscuits instead, which she politely turned down, and countered with some ugly oranges. I accepted one with delight. Although these Chinese oranges have wrinkled, shriveled skins, inside, they are delicious. Out of politeness, I tried to offer her everything else I had, but she was happy with her chicken feet. She sat there, still watching soap opera episodes, and proceeded to eat the entire bagful of feet, all by herself. I ate my orange, looked out of the window, and tried not to notice the chicken toes sticking out of her mouth.

We spent the second day traversing the Tibetan Plateau. When Americans think of Tibet, they envision snowy Himalayan peaks. There are plenty of those, but the vast bulk of Tibet is a high, dry plateau. Most of the land is only suitable for grazing. The plateau is huge. We went mile after mile without seeing a village or any sign of humans, other than herds of yaks, sheep, and goats. The few villages we did see were small and impoverished. Given the harshness of the terrain, it was a wonder there were any homesteads at all. The houses were hidden within high-walled enclosures, which served to keep wind, snow, and wolves out at night. Prayer flags up on the rooftops provided the only color. Tibet is a brutally forbidding country, especially in the winter. It is no wonder its people have always put so much of their energy into religious practice.

The miles clicked by pleasantly as we began the steep descent into the Lhasa valley. Between meals we played backgammon in the dining hall, and Dave won much more often than he deserved. Our compartment companion finally switched TV programs and started watching a different Chinese soap opera set in Imperial times. The heroines were still miserable, but at least they had great clothes and outrageous jewelry. Rupert and Mark came to join us at lunchtime, and we saw snowy peaks and a series of lakes out the window. The waters were brilliant turquoise in color. Migrating Siberian geese were enjoying the areas of open water.

The train was a wonderful way to enter Tibet and the experience gave us a real sense of the immensity of the country. It was a great ride, and I recommend it. Just remember to learn some breathing techniques before you go!

recommended Google search: Tibet Plateau Images

By Diana McLeod

THE MAGIC OF THE BUTTER LAMPS

The week before we went to Tibet, my friend Dolma approached me with a special request. She gave me some money and asked me if I would use it to pay for the lighting of butter lamps at the Jokhang temple.

Dolma was born in Tibet. When the Chinese occupied her country, her family chose to leave. They fled to the West, along with many of Tibet's top religious leaders. Dolma was too young to remember the terrible climb over the mountain passes; she just remembers growing up in India. Her family came to Burlington years ago, when the US government allowed a large number of displaced Tibetan families to immigrate to America. She has never seen her native land.

Although I agreed, I was not exactly sure how I would accomplish the task for Dolma. When we got to Lhasa, and I approached the Jokhang temple for the first time, I began to feel a bit intimidated. The Jokhang is the holiest and most famous monastery in all of Tibet (outside of the Potala, which is now an empty museum). It is a magnificent place, with many shrines and a large community of monks.

I asked the women at our hotel to write me a note in Tibetan. It read: "Tibetan Buddhist refugees in America have given me money to light butter lamps in the temple. Please help me to do this properly." I shoved this note in my pocket and kept it safe.

Armed with the note, we went inside the Jokhang. We toured the temple, and we were amazed at the beauty of the shrines. The Jokhang's most sacred chapel was dedicated to Maitreya, the Buddha of the future. This holy of holies can be seen only through a heavy chain-link fence. Tourists are forbidden entry.

Inside the shrine, the monks were reverently changing the brocade clothes of the Buddha. Layers of fabulous silk robes were replaced by new ones. The dressing of the statue was a matter of great ceremony.

The statue itself was magnificent. It was at least fifteen feet tall and covered in gold leaf. The face and the eyes were full of compassion and wisdom. Their timeless gaze pierced through our modern insensitivity and brought us closer to an understanding of Tibet's special style of Buddhism. The Buddha was crowned with a spectacular golden headdress, spangled with jewels, and on his chest were layers of finely worked solid gold breastplates, also crowded with precious gems and pearls. Gazing at him, I understood why this national art treasure needed an iron gate!

We approached the fence and gave the monks our note and some money. To our surprise and delight, they opened the gate so we could pass inside the shrine. What an incredible honor! This was the holiest shrine in the whole country, a chapel that represented the Buddha of the World's Future. We were even given permission to take pictures as the butter lamps were lit. Taking photographs is normally strictly forbidden because it is considered sacrilegious, but since we were going to take the pictures back to share with Dolma and the American Tibetan community, the monks allowed us to record these precious minutes.

The monks took a thermos of liquid butter and refilled the large chalices in front of the statue. One of them then replaced and lit the wicks. The glow of the butter lamps spread throughout the room, illuminating the serene face of the Buddha. It was a moment of great peace and oneness. We gave the monks our heartfelt thanks for allowing us to share in this sacred ceremony.

I left the chapel with feelings of overwhelming reverence and gratitude. My only concern was that I still had not used all of Dolma's money, and I wasn't sure what to do with the rest of it. We took a flight of stairs up to the top levels of the Jokhang. From above, the view was magnificent. The golden pagoda style rooftops gleamed whenever the sun pierced the patchy clouds. All around the valley, snow capped mountains loomed. The city of Lhasa snuggled into the bowl of the valley, along with the meandering river. The Potala castle, the ancient seat of the Dalai Lamas, seemed to float above its hillside in the far distance, looking like a page out of a fairytale. All around the city, little tree branches appeared on rooftops, sporting streamers of colorful prayer flags. The saddest sights around the town were the construction cranes. The Chinese are building several new Chinese-style districts in Lhasa, with ten-story modern buildings—a blight on the landscape in this ancient community.

I considered putting the money into a contribution box, but I didn't know how much money would go to the monastery, and how much would be stolen by the government. I also knew that some of the "monks" were hired by the police to keep an eye on the real monks so there wouldn't be any uprisings. Who could I trust? I carefully studied faces whenever elder monks walked past me, looking for someone with an inner light which would shine through in an unguarded moment. I was waiting for a sign.

I searched a long time before I saw the man I wanted to meet. His wrinkled face was bright with the inner amusement that comes from practicing joy and compassion every day. I knew he was for real. I approached and gave him my crumpled note written in Tibetan.

His face lit up even more as he grasped the significance of my letter. Tibetan people in America were making a donation to his temple, and they were asking for prayers to be said, and butter lamps to be lit. He was old enough to remember the terrible exodus over the mountains, and I'm sure he had lost many friends to cruel mountain passes and foreign lands. My new friend took the money and nodded to reassure me that my friends would get their wish. He handed me back the note and turned to go. Then he turned back to me and held out his hand, asking for the paper again. I knew he was eager to show the note to other monks. I could see the sudden inspiration in his eyes.

Another monk translated for him: he was going to arrange a prayer session dedicated to Dolma and to all Tibetan people living outside their native land. The entire Jokhang monastic community would be lighting butter lamps for Dolma.

I now could enjoy the rest of the lovely afternoon, knowing I had succeeded beyond all my expectations.

recommended Google search: Jokhang Lhasa Images

TIBET: OVERLAND TO EVEREST BASECAMP

Overland to Everest! Across the mountain passes of Tibet! It makes one think of trains of yaks, porters and primitive tents set up in the snow. These days, the journey is still spectacular, but it is considerably less rugged than you might think.

Mt. Everest is the tallest mountain in the world, and its glamour is almost magnetic for thrill seekers. The peak is right on the Nepalese-Tibetan border. It's possible to climb the mountain from either side, so there are two basecamps. One is on the Nepalese side, and the other is the Tibetan approach. These legendary places hold a special allure because you are as close as an average person can get to the mountain, and to the exceptional people who climb it.

Like most tourists in Tibet, we wanted to go there and visit the Tibetan basecamp for ourselves, while enjoying famous landmarks and towns along the way. The journey we were planning was eight days long. The Chinese government regards the area as a sensitive zone, so special permits are required for all tourists. The government also frowns on the use of public transportation by foreigners, so we were required to hire a company to provide us with a Land Rover, a driver, and a guide. We needed to find fellow travelers to share our journey since it was very expensive.

We were lucky to meet good friends straight away. Seth and Jody were both tough and outdoorsy (necessary, because conditions outside Lhasa were promising to be quite primitive, and because we didn't want to worry about altitude sickness), and they were also very interested in Tibetan culture and art. They were engaging dinner companions, and were not averse to Lhasa beer and cutthroat card games after dinner.

The four of us had to select a tour company. We went all over Lhasa, interviewing them, and the one we all had the best gut feeling about was Snowlands. They were competent and friendly, and the staff was 100% Tibetan. We were on the verge of agreeing to go with them, although we still had not inspected their vehicle. (If you ever hire a car in a foreign country, DO NOT sign up until you have seen your ride. Take a good look under the hood, check the seats for comfort, and, above all, kick the tires. Bad tires on mountain roads with no guardrails can kill you.)

Snowlands proudly presented its vehicle. It was the newest one we'd seen and it looked well maintained. However, all four of the tires were at death's door, and so was the spare. We promptly balked and negotiations went into overtime. When they realized the tires were going to be a huge issue, they finally agreed to get us new tires. We were delighted. We met our driver Purbu, and our guide Kunchok, both of whom were very likable. Purbu also had an impressive collection of well-edited music tapes, which made our journey very pleasant. His taste was eclectic and excellent. He played mixes of local Tibetan rock, most of which was quite enjoyable, Asian rock fusion, Bollywood hits from India and Western classics like Dire Straits. (You have no idea how important this is until you have made a long trip with a local company. Check your tunes as carefully as you would check your tires!)

Before leaving town, we all went shopping at a large Chinese supermarket to buy food for the journey. Dave and I got cheese and crackers, dried fruit, fresh fruit, tinned fish, biscuits and whatever else we could scavenge. There were many groceries in the supermarket we had never seen before. It was quite a challenge to keep Dave from buying mystery items, just for fun. The local people seemed highly amused by our curiosity.

THE JOURNEY TO SAMYE: The Land Rover came to pick us up at our hotel, and we stuffed our luggage and our bags of food in the back. It was pleasant to leave the urban environment of Lhasa and drive down the river valley. The cherry trees were just beginning to bloom, and there were loads of migrating ducks around the river.

The trip to the river ferry took several hours. We drove along a vast, sandy floodplain, following the river as it made meandering tracks through the shifting sandbars. The monastery lay on the other side of the river, and there was no bridge to get to it. (The Chinese had not deemed the monastery important to them, so no road had been built). The only way across was by local ferry—a broad, flat-bottomed open scow. A crowd of villagers was waiting to cross. Most of the people had been to markets, and they were loaded down with provisions for their homes across the river. Dave and I sat on our packs, next to an older lady who was happily chewing on a piece of aged yak cheese. That cheese must have been as hard as a rock because it was still in her mouth an hour later when we landed! Dave was offered a piece, and he tried it, but it was so nasty he had to toss it in the river when she wasn't looking.

The little boat successfully wove its way upstream through the maze of sand bars, and delivered us to the far shore. Here, the river basin was made up of sinuous dunes of golden sand. Gusty winds roared down the valley, lifting yellow clouds of tiny granules into the air, driving the sand into steep banks, hundreds of feet up into the craggy foothills. Yellow dust devils rose high into the sky. One could almost snowboard on the sandy slopes! The river itself couldn't compete with the flowing rivers of sand.

A dilapidated old bus took passengers and pilgrims from the ferry to the village of Samye, where a small collection of homesteads did their best to keep the advancing dunes at bay. Tibetan houses are usually built as compounds, with strong, high walls all the way around them. High ramparts and tree plantings kept out the worst of the roaming sands.

The same was true for the monastery. Thick walls ran around its perimeter. Inside, the multi-leveled golden pagoda rooftops of the central meditation hall shimmered brilliantly against the sunny blue sky. The rest of the monastery buildings huddled around the sanctuary as if they could glean warmth from its golden glow. Off to one side stood a little monastery guesthouse and restaurant.

The interior of Samye did not quite live up to promise of its golden spires, for years of neglect and abuse have left it in sad shape. The Chinese did quite a lot of damage to its beautiful murals during the early years of their rule. There were few pilgrims and little money flowing in, which meant that the halls were quite dark. Many were devoid of butter lamps, so it was hard to see the few treasures that remain. But some restoration work was underway, and we hope dollars from tourism will help to restore this national treasure.

The real magic of Samye is its history. Samye was the very first Mahayana Buddhist monastery in Tibet, founded over twelve hundred years ago. Padma Sambava himself presided over prayers here (after he fought a demon army and won victory.) In 790, disputes broke out between scholars of Buddhism, and this led to the famous Great Debate, right here at Samye, during which Padma Sambava established the principle of the Bodhisattva in Tibetan Buddhism. (A bodhisattva is an enlightened person who forgoes Nirvana and remains bound to the cycle of birth and rebirth in order to help others). At Samye, the concept of Mahayana Buddhism was born. It is energizing just to stand in a place where religious intensity once crackled like lightning through the halls.

That energy remains, and it was revealed to us later that day. We were walking past a secluded courtyard when the sleepy monastery came to life. The monks had just begun their afternoon debate. This custom dates back to the days of the Great Debate, and it has not lost any of its passion. The discourse usually takes place outdoors, in a sunny courtyard. Monks get into groups, with several monks sitting, facing one who is standing, and they wrangle over very complex religious issues. The discussion gets so animated that voices are raised and there is lots of wild gesturing, although most challengers have grins on their faces at the same time. When the standing monks feel they have made a particularly good point, they "bust a move." They leap forward, wheeling one arm overhead, and bring their hands together in a loud slap. It looks like a karate chop, and it is very startling. We all thought the debating time was the highpoint of the monks' day.

Footsteps of a Nomad

Our room in the monastery guesthouse was funky but serviceable. There was no running water. Toilets were simple outhouses, with drainage down the backside of the building, and they were built off to one side of a large, flat, open roof. The "facilities" proved to be excellent motivation for midnight stargazing. We all resigned ourselves to a night without a shower and wandered down to the restaurant.

The crowd at the outdoor restaurant tables was colorful. There were monks, families of pilgrims, local villagers playing Mahjong, and one sheep that wandered right up to our table and begged for scraps. The four of us were joined by Purbu and Kunchok. We talked about the journey to come, and about the various stops along the way. When we said goodnight and went upstairs to the balcony outside our room, moonlight glinted brilliantly off the golden rooftops of the temple as the stars of the Milky Way wheeled above. It was magnificent.

recommended Google search: Samye Tibet Images

recommended youtube video: Buddhist Philosophical debate in 2016

OVER THE PASS TO GYANTSE: We left Samye as early as we lazy Western tourists could, and took the ferry back across the river where Purbu was waiting with the Land Rover. It was a beautiful morning and Purbu had the tunes cranked on the car stereo. All of us were soon humming along to a lively Tibetan folk-rock mix.

There were two ways to get to Gyantse. One way was the safe, modern highway. The other led up a crazy mountain pass. Purbu had spent some time chatting with the folks at the ferry landing and assured us the pass was open to traffic. Our guides warned us that road was rough and treacherous, and would take a long time to drive, but they also recommended it highly. Of course, we also wanted to try it. After all, we were in a Land Rover with four brand new tires!

When we started up, the road ascended steadily for two hours, zigzagging back and forth up the mountainside. I have never seen so many hairpin curves in my life! The valley below became lost in the distant haze. There was little vegetation, only clumps of pallid, wispy grass. Finally, when we crested the top, we found a spectacular alpine valley with a brilliant turquoise-colored lake on the other side. Snowy peaks gleamed in the far distance. It was a glorious sight.

Dave immediately took off to get better photo locations. He wandered down a goat path. We watched him go for about a quarter of a mile until he disappeared behind the side of the hill. For about a half an hour, we didn't mind, since we were all enjoying the spot, although we did have to fend off a few hustlers who tried to sell us trinkets. After that, everyone became impatient to get moving again. I felt I should set off to look for Dave; and if I didn't go quickly, we would waste extra time.

By Diana McLeod

We were at 15,580 feet. Could I actually jog at that altitude? I'm not in the best of shape, even at sea level. Would I suddenly collapse with altitude sickness? (Altitude sickness can come on suddenly, and it can be dangerous, even fatal. Many people get altitude sickness in Lhasa, which is under 13,000 feet.) When it became obvious Dave was not returning on his own, I set off after him, wondering if I was making a grave mistake. Luckily for me, there was a slight downhill slant to the trail, and I had been practicing yogic breathing. Our guide watched me go and decided to follow me. His plan was to guide us down over the cliffs to the lakeshore. He told our driver to begin the long journey of switchbacks down; the Land Rover would meet us at the bottom.

I was able to keep up a very brisk pace, I'm proud to say. I could have gone even faster, but safety concerns on the rocky trail kept me to a slow jog. Kunchok, with his long legs, easily caught up to me. We found Dave, and continued along the goat path for a while. Then Kunchok guided us as we bushwhacked our way down the rocky outcropping, and it got pretty steep, which was a bit frightening since we were all scrambling on very loose scree. I was relieved when we safely reached reached the road again.

The car picked us up and we soon reached the lake. Its lovely turquoise waters were a cool respite from the rocky, barren terrain, but the water level was very low. Our guide told us, bitterly, the Chinese were draining the sacred lake for hydropower. People in a nearby town said the Chinese had promised the Tibetans they would replenish the lake "later," but the Tibetans did not believe it. I felt sorry for the farmers of that valley, and for the flocks of wild birds congregating at the lake as a stopover on their migration routes. It was yet another ominous sign of a dim future for the natural wonders of Tibet.

After the lake, we began to climb again. We followed a river uphill towards its source, passing through deep canyons on our long bumpy journey to Karo La Pass (4960 meters, 16,120 feet). Most of the road was under construction. At times, there wasn't a road at all, just a series of jeep trails in the rocky sand. Clouds of dust stung our eyes whenever we opened the windows.

At the top, we were in the midst of snowy peaks. Magnificent glaciers halted within a few hundred feet of us! There was a little *chorten* (Buddhist shrine) by the side of the road. Faded prayer flags radiated from its top like the spokes on the Buddhist wheel of life.

Dirty little children came running out of a nearby hut to greet (harass) me. They were well trained to beg persistently for money and candy. They had appraised our little group with young but seasoned professional eyes, and decided I was the most likely target. They stuck to me like glue, clinging to my body and pulling on my clothing, making it hard for me to enjoy the scenery. I put up with their attentions so the photographers of the group could film in peace. (The kids didn't get a thing from me—I don't believe in encouraging this behavior. Luckily, I didn't catch anything from them either!)

On the other side of the pass, the road was rugged and partially unfinished. Dust clouds from the raw roadbed soon turned our lovely Land Rover into a filthy brown mess. The "road" wound down through deep gorges with jagged cliffs. The rocky outcroppings were eye-catching due to endless variations of color and striation in the exposed rocks. The Chinese were busy here; road crews were working on the right-of-way, and a massive dam had already been built for hydropower. Nearby, a yak caravan wound its way along a trail in one of the gorges. The contrast between the new road and the traditional method of transportation was startling. The trip was a bit bone-jarring, but it was exhilarating, and the mountain scenery was well worth the dusty, bumpy climb over the pass.

After an incredibly long, scenic downhill journey, we finally reached a mountain valley near Gyantse. Gyantse was built on a level floodplain, with plenty of irrigation for agriculture. On one side of the city was a craggy escarpment of rock. A wicked-looking medieval *dzong* (fortress) crouched on the top of the cliffs; an apparently unassailable aerie built by medieval Tibetan kings. Its fierce towers and battlements gleamed white-gold in the rays of the setting sun.

When we reached our hotel, it proved to be a relatively modern (if somewhat sterile) Chinese-style hotel. It had excellent showers! The rooftop provided us with panoramic views of the fortress and the hills around the city.

While we were at our lodgings, another dust-covered Land Rover arrived; it was obvious it had also taken the road over the pass. Four or five people emerged. One woman, a middle-aged American, was loudly complaining about everything. The journey was horrible; there was nothing worth seeing; she had spent hours being jostled around on that dirty, dusty road for no reason; she hated the hotel; on, and on, and on. She actually said, "Today was pure hell!"

Nothing was good enough for her, and I felt great pity for her companions and her guides. They were going to have to put up with her for days. Mentally, I thanked my friends, Jody and Seth, who were enthusiastic, tolerant and fun. We had chosen our fellow travelers wisely. Of course, they had to put up with us (I'm sure Dave and I were more than a little annoying at times!). But this woman really took the cake! Why in the world had she chosen Tibet, if she desired comfort and luxury? What in the world was she expecting? From all the way up on the rooftop, I could hear her shrill voice, echoing around the courtyard, whining about everything. It just goes to show how much the perspective you bring with you colors your consciousness. It can influence you so much that the same exact experiences shared by two different people can be utterly different. That woman was a great life lesson for the rest of us!

Later, we had dinner at a Chinese restaurant. The food was good, and we shared beers with Jody, Seth, Kunchok, and Purbu. Dave and I were highly amused by the Chinese family at a nearby table. They were very loud and very animated. The poor waitress was kept constantly running for more food and beer. The Chinese custom is to share all of the dishes around the table. Everyone has their own bowl, which they use for rice and servings of other dishes. The little bowls have no room for bones or discarded food, which end up on the table or all over the floor. Many Chinese restaurants put plastic or newspapers over the surfaces, so they are easily cleaned. This restaurant had not done so, so the staff had one heck of a pile of chicken bones, spare ribs, beer bottles and spills of all kinds to clean up after the family left. They left behind a scene of carnage that it extended everywhere in a two-foot radius on, around *and* under that table. A pack of hyenas would not have left a worse mess!

THE KUMBUM: We awoke the next morning in the Tibetan city of Gyantse. Our companions, Jody and Seth, met us for breakfast, and then we went to visit the Pelkor Chode monastery. My strongest memories of Gyantse are of the Kumbum, the most famous of the monastery's many temples. Built in 1427, the Kumbum is one of the few intact stupa temples left in Tibet. This type of stupa is set up like a three-dimensional, cone-shaped mandala. It is seven levels high. The bottom level is the largest, and each subsequent level gradually becomes smaller until the top is reached. A series of golden parasols crown the apex. The eyes of the Buddha are painted just below the very top, and they look out serenely over each of the four directions.

From the outside, the Kumbum reminds me of a giant wedding cake. From the inside, it turns into a fantastic teaching device. The pilgrim enters the main gate of the Kumbum, and follows balconies on each level, in a clockwise direction. There are many little doors, and one feels compelled to enter each one. They lead to small chapels, each dedicated to various characters of Tibetan Buddhism, including Buddhas, bodhisattvas, and protector deities—demonic figures who converted to Buddhism and have assumed magical protector roles. Characters include Mahakala, the Guardian of the Wheel of Life, who is the Eater of Time, and Yamantaka, Conqueror of Death. They are usually represented as wrathful, fearsome monsters, who carry bloody swords and skull cups, and walk in the midst of flames.

Each of the seventy-seven chapels inside the Kumbum houses a large statue of the deity who is the main focus of that particular chapel. Each statue is surrounded by fabulous murals, which were lovingly hand painted on the walls by generations of monks. The murals tell the stories of Buddhism. There are thousands of these murals, and most of them are very, very old. Regrettably, most of the statues are newer. Many needed to be replaced following defacement of the temple during the early years of Chinese occupation.

Seth, Jody and I went through the Kumbum together while Dave wandered off to shoot photos. I was delighted by my friends' interest and enthusiasm for the artwork. For me, the Kumbum was a fabulous study in the evolution of Tibetan iconography. My knowledge of the subject was (and still is) still skin deep, but I can at least recognize most of the main characters, and I can spot stylistic differences from place to place in Nepal and Tibet. Jody and Seth shared my excitement as I showed them various pagan and pre-Buddhist characters and devices that had been "co-opted" into the Buddhist religion. We also discovered Newari influences that had to have come from the Kathmandu valley in Nepal. (During its history, this area had Nepalese rulers at various times.). I also pointed out legends from the life of the Buddha depicted on the walls.

Ironically, our hired Tibetan guide was not allowed inside many of the temples on the trip, so we had to rely on our own patchy knowledge. (Note to travelers: before you take your trip, spend some time reading books on Tibetan art. You will need to bring some information with you if you want to understand the complex iconography.)

The three of us had a great time inside the temple. We couldn't resist going into every shrine. Our experience was enhanced by the presence of a large group of pilgrims who had come from the Kham district of Eastern Tibet. They had all saved up enough to pay the steep Chinese admission price, and they each had enough money to leave one donation (of less than a penny) in each of the seventy-seven shrines. The women all had very long hair that had been carefully braided into dozens of tiny braids. They held the braids back with silver barrettes studded with turquoise stones. A couple of them wore elaborate headdresses, with turquoise, coral or amber beads. For them, this pilgrimage to the Kumbum was probably the trip of a lifetime.

Every level in the Kumbum had a staircase going up to the next floor. These staircases turned into ladders as we got closer to the top. Unfortunately, the ultimate level was locked. I guess only monks are privileged enough to see that shrine.

recommended Google search: Kumbum Gyantse Tibet

SHIGATSE: In the afternoon, we took the highway to Shigatse. The Chinese have built a fine modern road linking the two cities. The only problem with the new highway is that it intentionally bypasses traditional villages, so the tourist misses seeing the way people really live. New roadside "villages" have sprung up, many featuring traditional Tibetan style architecture, but they are nothing like authentic places. (Note to travelers: on one day of your journey, get off the highway. Make an unscheduled stop in a town where tourists don't typically go. It will be a highlight of your trip.)

When we reached Shigatse, we visited the Tashilumpho monastery. Tashilumpho is the seat of the Panchen Lamas. It was a very large, very well preserved monastery, but many of the meditation halls were closed when we got there, so it was not the most memorable monastic experience.

By Diana McLeod

Our search for email was more intriguing. Shigatse was our last "civilized" stop before the Everest region, so we had to find an email center. Our guide helped us locate one, inside a department store. We climbed the broken escalators to the third floor, and found one of the biggest Internet cafes I have ever seen. There must have been at least two hundred computers in there, arrayed in row upon row in several large rooms. Most of them were in use, even though it was mid-afternoon on a lovely day. I finished my email before Dave did, so I wandered around the floor, trying to get a handle on what Tibetan and Chinese teenagers were viewing on the Internet. Most of the usage was, of course, video games. The girls were all playing the latest interactive music and dance game. The boys were into the shoot-em-up video games, with army, karate and ninja themes. Only about a third of the young users were surfing the Internet, and most of them were emailing or into chat rooms. A few were searching online, exploring. It is my hope those young minds will educate themselves a bit, under cover of all the videogames, and reach out to the outside world. (We were able to get CNN and the BBC news in Tibet, although, of course, they were heavily censored.)

Our hotel in Shigatse was excellent. In the morning, we left our rooms almost regretfully, knowing how much we would miss the luxurious hot showers and warm beds during the next few days.

The day's journey began along the Friendship Highway (the road that links Tibet with Nepal). This well-constructed modern thoroughfare has "improved" Tibet enormously, but it has also diminished traditional culture a great deal. The Chinese are trying to re-direct economic activity around this highway, and they are constructing little "Tibetan" settlements along its flanks, complete with flashy gas stations and convenience stores.

Our guides said Tibetans were being offered subsidies to construct new Tibetan-style housing here, far away from their traditional villages. (The Chinese were probably doing this in order to show tourists and journalists prosperous Tibetan villages along the route the Olympic torch would take in 2008. (Our trip took place in 2007).

SAKYA: At midday, we took a side trip down a secondary road to visit the monastery of Sakya, which survived destruction during the Chinese takeover because it was built like a fortress. Thick mud-brick walls thirty feet high surrounded the entire complex with walkways all around. Guard towers capped each of the four corners.

The most memorable features of Sakya were not the main halls and chapels, but the demon rooms. Our guide asked one of the monks to open up the passage to a little-known room upstairs at the back of the monastery. Inside a locked cell was the statue of a hideous demonic figure. It had sharp, red, six-inch claws, vicious fangs, and ferocious eyes. According to our guide, the statue houses an actual demon, imprisoned for centuries by the monastery's monks. According to legend, the demon once escaped. He turned himself into a magical object so beautiful and wonderful that anyone who possessed it would

255

fall under its spell, and be destroyed by the desire for it. In the end, demon-hunting monks from the monastery sought it out and managed to recapture it. They took the demon back into custody, and have held this demon inside this statue ever since. Prayers, mantras, and bars on the door keep the treacherous creature locked in the room, and monks maintain a constant vigil over him. The whole story reminded me of an old "Twilight Zone" episode, in which some Christian monks have the Devil locked up in their monastery. I found the story of this demon so fascinating that I used the concept in a novel I wrote in 2012.

Unfortunately, the second demon room was locked when we got there. It is a protector chapel in which statues and masks of protector deities reside. Tibetans believe the masks house the powers of these demonic protectors, so they cannot be looked upon by ordinary people unless there are hundreds of monks present to magically hold back their powers. Therefore, the faces of most of these protector statues and masks are kept covered, and they are only unveiled at special ceremonies. Monks who wear the masks may become temporarily possessed by a demon, and they may temporarily wield some of the demon's tremendous magical abilities.

I would have liked seeing that chapel, but we were only able to view the door to it. Even standing in front of that door was an eerie experience because the monks have hung the desiccated bodies of slain wolves in the rafters above the entrance to the chapel. The mummified corpses are almost perfectly preserved, and the wolves look ready to attack unwary visitors. Apparently, there are other dead wolves inside, guarding the statues and masks.

I left, wondering if I was lucky the door was locked, after all. Wolves in the darkness make my hair stand on end. In my childhood, snarling wolves were the greatest recurring theme of my nightmares. If there is such a thing as reincarnation, then I am sure that wolves ended one of my past lives....

While we were at Sakya, we met a group of fifty pilgrims who had chartered a bus to come to this sacred place. They were sitting in a circle in the sunny courtyard, eating a picnic lunch they brought with them. They were a happy, animated group, all wearing their best clothes for the pilgrimage—in short: a photographer's dream. Dave immediately zeroed in and began snapping pictures. He has developed a people-friendly style that puts his subjects at their ease. When he gets them laughing and joking with him, they relax and genuinely smile while having their pictures taken.

The group was highly amused by Dave, especially when he flipped the video screen around so that they could see themselves on video for the first time in their lives. They offered him some yak butter tea. Dave was unable to accept their gift, and he was now in the awkward position of having to explain why, without the language skills to do so. The problem was, we didn't know if the tea had been made with boiled water; if it hadn't been, it could make him quite sick. (Besides, Dave and I both detest yak butter tea. It is the most god-awful "tea" we have ever tasted!) Lack of language has never stopped Dave from communicating. He pantomimed that he didn't want any. He pantomimed drinking, followed by a hand gesture from his rear end, and a horrible noise imitating the sound of terrible gas—or worse.

His audience burst into gales and shrieks of laughter. They were soon laughing so hard that tears were in more than a few eyes. I was laughing right along with them. It was hilarious. The image of a wealthy foreigner in intestinal distress was so surprising to them, and so admittedly human, it shattered all barriers between us.

recommended Google search: Sakya Tibet Images

SHEGAR: Our next destination was the town of Shegar. This little hamlet sits at the entrance to the Everest National Park. Here, the Friendship Highway turns aside and heads for the Nepal border. At Shegar, we got our first real taste of old-fashioned Tibetan-style living.

Our little guesthouse was designed and built for the simple mountain life. Our room was colorfully decorated in Tibetan style, with brightly painted borders on the walls that imitated the bright silk brocades in the temples. Hand-painted murals of Tibetan lucky symbols gave the place a very cheery, personalized look. Before I left the room, I carefully laid out the items I would need that night, so I wouldn't have to stumble around in the cold while searching for things in the dark. In the unheated Tibetan winter, I wore fleece booties, long underwear and a fleece headband to bed, as well as most of my clothes.

The beds had plenty of thickly stuffed quilts to keep us warm in the night. The "toilets" were at the end of the hall. They were two small rooms with planked floors. In the center of the room was a wooden cover; you lifted it with a stick, revealing a hole in the floor with footpads on either side. The ground was at least ten feet below, so these outhouses were completely clean and stink-free. The only problem with them was the frigid mountain wind which blew in, the instant the cover was open, and from a most unfortunate direction!

At the end of the hall, a set of very uneven homemade stairs led down to the inn's common room. This part of the guesthouse was heated. The warmth hit us like a trip to the tropics. It was one of the most cheery, homey places I had ever seen. A large kitchen sat at the back, cranking out food for an assortment of locals, guides, drivers, and foreign guests. In the center of the room, a very well designed wood stove cranked out a good deal of heat. The firebox was unusually long, providing as much radiant heat as possible. There was room on top for many teakettles, and the kitchen staff kept rotating them as needed. The entire dining hall had been painted in the Tibetan style, with colorful murals, decorated wood trim and painted tea tables. Benches were covered with squares of thick Tibetan wool carpet. So comfy! It was a perfect place for socializing while sitting by the fire, curling up in a quiet corner with a book, or for card games.

Purbu and Kunchok were already there, hanging out with friends from other tourist travel companies in Lhasa. Local guys joined their group. Their long hair was tied up in a flourish of red wool and yak-bone beads. Jody and Seth soon turned up. They were traveling on more of a budget than we were, so they had chosen a dorm room on the bottom floor. We all found ourselves a cozy table and ordered some Lhasa beer.

The menu was pretty basic but one item was in abundance—yak meat. You could have yak with rice, or yak with Chapatis, or yak noodle soup, or yak steak. All the breakfast items listed yak meat as the main ingredient as well. So many choices! It was a vegetarian's worst nightmare! There was one vegetable on the menu, which turned out to be nondescript cooked greens. Dave and I ordered the greens often so that we would get some balance in our meals. Luckily, yak is pretty good, tough but flavorful, with a more interesting taste than American beef.

We ordered yak dinners, cooked to order, and got on with the important business of playing cards. We played two games: hearts, which was our favorite, and a game with a very naughty title that Seth taught us. Dave lost at that game so consistently and so badly he became half-convinced Seth was making up the rules as he went along.

Everyone hung out in the common room until bedtime. There were a couple of other groups there, so the laughter and the conversation lasted late into the evening. Nobody wanted to go to their cold beds until they needed to. We were quite excited, because the next day, we would finally reach Everest Basecamp!

In the morning, the common room was already busy when we got there. The breakfast menu was depressingly yak-oriented. I settled for noodle soup with yak. Dave had yak with *chapati bread*. There were no eggs (too high altitude), and there was no bread for toast. Luckily, we had plenty of Indonesian coffee with us, lovingly carried from home, so we were able to make our own coffee. (If you are a coffee lover in Asia, you really should bring ground coffee with you to avoid Nescafe hell.)

THE ROAD TO EVEREST was a simple dirt track winding up and down in a spectacularly long series of switchbacks. The countryside consisted mainly of broad, grass-covered foothills often punctuated by upheavals of rock. The earth looked traumatized. Everywhere, you could see clear evidence of the forces that built the Himalayas. These mountains are the world's newest and they are still being created—a consequence of the spectacular collision of two of the Earth's tectonic plates. The plate of India is slowly crashing into the plate of Asia, and the Everest region is ground zero. These mountains are growing at the rate of several centimeters per year. All throughout this area, huge chunks of brightly striped sedimentary rock have been broken apart and crunched upwards at crazy angles, as if the Tibetan Demon-

Goddess of the Earth, Mother Tumna, actually exists, is imprisoned directly beneath us, and is trying to force her way out.

The jeep track went up and down, passing along a river valley for a while. We encountered one little village on a glacial floodplain and stopped to take photos. Young men were out plowing the fields. They all worked together, and so did their animals. There was one team of yaks, two teams of horses, and one team of donkeys, each with its own furrow to plow. Each team was decorated with colorful red and white headdresses made from dyed yak wool. Brass bells jingled at their necks. Goats, sheep and chickens wandered behind the teams, looking for tidbits the plows might unearth. When the drivers turned their teams in tandem, it looked like choreographed yak ballet. We captured great video sequences with the snow-covered Himalayas in the background. Afterward, we rewound the tape and invited the farmers to take a look. They loved looking at themselves on the small screen, and were as excited and giggly as little kids.

From the river valley, we started up again, heading for Pang-La Pass. Soon, we were marveling at another bizarre feature of unusual geology in the Everest region: "stone rivers." Thousands of years of snow and ice have created cascades of black stone pebbles. The loose black shale layers, unleashed from torn sedimentary rocks, have eroded very quickly, by geological standards, and they have broken into loose scree. The scree fields move. They actually flow, in shimmering streams, down the mountainsides, forming "deltas" at the bottom where the "river" widens as it reaches level ground. At the base of these "rivers," the stones are rounded and tumbled, just like river stones. Somebody should set up time-lapse photography here, so the movement can be captured on film! There were places where these "rivers" met the road, requiring maintenance vehicles to plow the road clear on a regular basis. At times, the invading wall of scree was ten feet high on the uphill side of the road.

The road careened back and forth up innumerable switchbacks as it climbed up the pass. Our driver and guide reverently uttered a Tibetan prayer several times as we crested the ridge. We were now at 5,120 meters (16,640 feet) on a series of rocky, windswept foothills. In the distance, at last, was the view we had all come to see. The "Roof of the World" lay stretched out before us. We could see Makulu, Lhotse, Gyachang, Cho Oyo, and, the queen of all, Chomolangma, (Goddess Mother of the Universe), whose Western name is Everest. We were lucky—the day was crystal clear, and all of the famous peaks were perfectly visible. We spent quite a while up there, marveling at the immensity of the vista. (Note to travelers: This really is the finest view you will see of the massif. Don't shortchange yourself in your rush to reach the basecamp. It is also well worth trekking up the scree hill to the left of the road to get the full view of the range south of Everest.)

The road descended on an even crazier series of switchbacks, deep into the valley. One good-sized, traditional Tibetan town was off to our left and looked intriguing. We really should have insisted on going there, but the desire to reach our destination was too strong, so we kept going. The road got rougher and rougher. At one point, the Chinese had even blasted a crude tunnel right through solid rock. I wondered frequently what the old trail must have been like before the road was completed.

Climbing again, we followed the river of glacial runoff coming from Everest. The ruins of an ancient fortress perched on jagged cliffs above us. Most of the land was deserted and barren. Jagged, crumbling foothills hemmed in the road and river on both sides. After a long, butt-bumping drive, we finally saw the little Chorten that marked Rongphu Monastery. Rongphu is only a couple of klicks away from the basecamp itself. It is an easy walk, for those who are acclimatized, with a rise of only 200 meters. The new Chinese road goes all the way to the basecamp now. The original trail is, for the most part, completely obliterated.

RONGPHU: Tourists can opt to stay at Rongphu guesthouse, a traditional Tibetan inn right at Rongphu monastery, or they can stay in the tourist "tent city" set up at the edge of the actual basecamp. This tent town is exclusively for tourists. (Real climbing expeditions have their own tent area, which is past the "DO NOT ENTER WITHOUT AN EXPEDITION PERMIT - $200 FINE" sign. (Expeditions do not generally mingle with mere tourists). Of our choices, we liked the monastery guesthouse the best. The view of Everest, while further away, was much more suitable for photos. The little monastery added much ambience (and some much needed scale) to our pictures.

Jody and Seth opted to stay in the tent city, so we took the car to the basecamp to drop them off and to take some pictures. Dave and I climbed a little hillock for the best view, and Everest reared up before us in all her glory. We were very lucky: the whole mountain was visible on that day. I think the view from the Tibetan side is more dramatic because the mountain's pointed peak is very distinct. I have not personally been to the Nepalese side, but the view I've seen from aircraft looks like a long ridge. After gawking at the mountain for a while, we left Jody and Seth for the night, agreeing to reconnect at Rongphu again around noon for the trip back to Shegar.

Back at Rongphu, we settled into our room before it became dark. Rongphu guesthouse had a somewhat charming common room, but the rest of it had seen better days. Dave and I liked having a private room, but the one we got was pretty filthy. They do not wash the "hotel laundry" very frequently up here! I could understand why, since there was no place to dry things without freezing them. Everyone slept with all their clothes and long underwear on anyway. I also wrapped my pillow in my windbreaker, as a precaution against local "wildlife" left behind by unwashed humans.

I also would be remiss if I failed to mention the "facilities." There was a ladies' room, but it was just that: a room! It had a dirt floor, which had been used and used until there was almost nowhere left to step. It was a real horror show! Unfortunately, before dark, outdoors was not a real option either because there was no cover.

By Diana McLeod

That evening, we got great pictures of Everest in the soft light of sunset. The little monastery chorten completed the photographs, adding a spiritual note. A group of yaks wandered lazily around the monastery grounds, and it was a pleasant, traditional scene. When we got back to the common room, we huddled around the woodstove with other tourists, and shared a couple of beers, dinner, and some lively international discussions.

Before bed, I went out in the moonlight. The yaks were all placidly standing in their pasture on one side of the building. I wished to avoid the "ladies' room," so I made my way right into the middle of the herd for privacy. The stars were blazing overhead, and everything was quiet except for the little stream that ran below the guesthouse. I could see the mother mountain, ghostly against the night sky; beautiful but deadly. How many haunted souls have been lost up there? How many spirits are condemned to try and try again, endlessly retracing their struggles up her cruel flanks every night? The mountain is impervious to it all.

recommended Google search: Pang La Pass Images

EVEREST BASECAMP: The next morning, we discovered a fascinating souvenir on the floor of our room. It was a seven-inch fossil ammonite (a chambered nautilus seashell turned to stone), and it was millions of years old. A tourist had probably found it while walking past road construction on the way to the Basecamp. It is hard to believe, but the Himalayas are remnants of an ancient seabed. Ocean sediment has been shoved up by the collision of two of the earth's tectonic plates, and this now forms the highest mountains on earth. You can find evidence of primordial plants and animals all over these peaks, even at extreme altitudes! The slow-motion collision that formed these mountains continues to this day. Everest rises approximately two inches every year. The area is prone to earthquakes when pressure builds up.

We had breakfast (if you can call noodle soup with yak meat "breakfast") in the guesthouse common room, and then we hiked along the road up to the actual Basecamp area (or as close as we could get to it). The Basecamp itself is at 5,200 meters above sea level (over 16,000 feet), so walking any distance is a challenge. It wasn't too difficult with a small daypack, but we really could feel the altitude.

Dave used the walk to get good photo angles. He even rock-hopped into the middle of the stream and sprawled on an ice-covered boulder to get a good picture of the mountain and the river together. I searched for more fossils, but didn't find any.

The tent city at the edge of Basecamp was still being constructed for the upcoming summer tourist season. Tibetans were busy setting tent poles and lines for large, Mongolian-style yurt dwellings, which would soon be packed with sightseers as the tourist season moved into

261

the busy months. It made me thankful we had come to Everest when we did—at the start of April— which I felt was perfect timing. We did miss the summer season when Tibet turns green, but we enjoyed the clearest weather, with no haze, and we missed the gigantic hordes of tourists. I bet the camp becomes quite a zoo during peak times, especially now that the road goes all the way to it. I also bet it becomes much more difficult to get clear views of the mountains when the weather warms up. I was glad to not be sharing our experience with hundreds of other tourists.

A series of expedition tents were set up, closer to the mountain, and strictly off limits to us. Only one group was there then—a Chinese expedition, part of Beijing's incredibly ambitious plan to carry the Olympic torch up to the peak of Everest before the 2008 games.

Jody and Seth met us on the way back to Rongphu. They had thoroughly enjoyed themselves in tent city the previous night. When we got back to Rongphu, we spent a few minutes taking pictures before we packed up the Land Rover. I was triumphant when I managed to get the "perfect" picture of Tibet—a monk, a yak, the monastery chorten, prayer flags, and Everest, all in one shot!

RETURN TO LHASA: Everyone said goodbye to the "Mother Goddess Mountain," and we headed back the way we came. Purbu and Kunchok (our driver and our guide) were glad to be returning home. On the way, we stopped for a few minutes when we reached Pang-La pass, for one long last look at the largest mountains in the world. By now, we were all familiar with the Tibetan custom of chanting a prayer as the Rover crested the top of the pass. We all said it in unison: "Shay-shay-shay-shay." I should have thought to ask what it means. Was it a Tibetan syllable? Or was it "thank you" in Chinese?

That night, we settled back into the comfortable guesthouse at Shegar and enjoyed one last evening of Jody and Seth's good company. We all ordered beer and dinner, and played one last card game. The guesthouse common room was warm and welcoming, and it was very pleasant.

The next morning, we left Jody and Seth by the roadside where they would try to hitch a ride to the Nepalese border. There was no traffic whatsoever. I hoped they didn't have to wait there all day. They looked a bit forlorn beside the empty highway. However, I was sure that any vehicle with room in it would stop for them, for a price. We wondered what kind of a ride they would get. (An hour later, we saw a local bus, bound for Tingri. It probably picked them up).

The final two days of the trip were pleasant, but there was less to remark on because we were backtracking on the main highway the whole way. That night, we returned to our excellent, warm hotel in Shigatse, and luxuriated in our modern bathroom. The hot water was divine. (The only water we had had in the mountains was a thermos full of hot drinking water to carry to our rooms; there had been no running water in any of the guesthouses).

It was also a relief to return to a place where one could get real vegetables. We had greatly missed them while in the mountains. At the little restaurant next to the hotel, we were greeted warmly by the young couple who had served us before, and they cooked us a savory dinner. On our way out, I noticed something astonishing. A tourist had left a bumper sticker on the restaurant wall. It read: MAD RIVER GLEN - SKI IT IF YOU CAN! A little reminder of Vermont, in Shigatse, Tibet! It's a very small world, these days.

Our last day's journey took us back along the Friendship Highway to Gyantse and then to Lhasa. The road wound down a river valley with picturesque gorges and footbridges. We saw people fishing from tubby round boats made from stretched yak hides. As we got into the lower altitudes, we noticed the first signs of spring in the valleys. The land was awakening, and buds on the poplars by the rivers were greening. Plum trees were in bloom, decorating little farmsteads with white or pink blossoms. Farmers everywhere were out plowing or planting. It was sad to be leaving Tibet just as the countryside warmed.

In a way, I regretted having come to Tibet so early in the season. I would have loved to have seen real spring, or early summer. On the other hand, we would have seen it through a haze of tourists. As it was, we were able to enjoy the peace of the monasteries almost on our own. We saw Everest without the mob. The mountains were clear because it was still technically winter, and moist air from the ocean had not yet begun to move north to ruin the view. Balancing out all of those things, I think we picked just the right time to travel there.

Returning to the our hotel in Lhasa, we found another reason to be content with the timing of our trip. While we were away, they had gone from off-season rates to high-season rates. What a huge difference! We could no longer afford our old room. After haggling hard, they finally agreed to let us stay for our last couple of days at the old rate. We also saw steep rate hikes at the travel agencies in Lhasa as well. I thought our Land Rover trip had been very expensive, but it would have been much more costly, maybe even financially out of reach, in the summertime.

Our last dinner in Tibet was at an Indian–Nepalese restaurant near the Jokhang. There, we met some Nepalese expedition climbers who were on their way to Everest. I wished them good luck, and I hope that the Goddess Mother Mountain smiles upon their ascent.

recommended Google search: Everest Basecamp Tibet Images

ETHIOPIA

ADDIS ABABA: RISING STAR OF ETHIOPIA

2013. The capital of Ethiopia is booming and its people are smiling. There is still dire poverty here, but the war with Eritrea is long over and the country is forging ahead. People are working hard, making real efforts to improve their lives. Despite rampant unemployment, I saw few people lounging on the streets. Everybody seemed to have something to do or somewhere to go. Change is happening fast, and for the better. It's exciting to see an African country on the move.

We'd been traveling for over thirty-five hours without a break, all the way from Bangkok to India, through Saudi Arabia to Ethiopia. Our hotel's van picked us up at the airport when we finally arrived at seven a.m. The driver was amiable, giving us the first of thousands of welcoming Ethiopian smiles.

After sleeping away most of the day at our hotel compound (guarded, with a sea of tin-roofed shacks directly outside the back window), we wandered into town. Our hotel, while nice, was not in the best of neighborhoods. Strolling down the main street, we saw the simple beginnings of local commerce: cell phone shops, general stores and mechanical workshops for vehicle repair. The restaurants were the grimmest we'd ever seen. Addis Ababa is known for its raw meat restaurants. Yes, raw meat. Restaurants have a butcher shop right inside the dining room, with shanks of fresh meat dangling from hooks. Customers select beef or goat, and they hack off raw pieces and serve it, barely warmed, with lime or something on it. I didn't want to look too closely. The smell of the restaurants was quite enough. They made me terrified of eating in this country.

People were delighted to see foreigners walking around their city. We soon attracted quite a following. Curious onlookers came up to us with big grins on their faces, asking us where we were from, how did we like Ethiopia, was it our first time in their country, what did we do for work and more. Everybody mentioned President Obama with pride, and they were obviously thrilled that America had just re-elected its first black president. You could tell how much Obama's win gave them hope for their own future. Many of them knew quite a bit about American politics. Their command of English was very impressive.

The locals loved shaking hands, doing the high-five, the fist bump or the African shoulder-to-shoulder handshake. Dave is especially good at talking and joking with everybody, so he got along very well. But there was also a darker side to all the friendliness: we were on our guard for pickpockets. Addis is famous for sneak-thieves. Everyone we met warned us about them. I wore my daypack with everything important wrapped up under a jacket, and only toilet paper in the

264

vulnerable back pocket (although even toilet paper can be precious there). All of our valuables were stashed in our secret pockets hidden under our clothes, along with our passports. This is how you should travel in African cities. Anything else would be crazy. Dave had the equivalent of $10 in his pants pocket, with his hand on it at all times.

Walking past a huge construction site, we learned they are building a modern rapid-transit train/subway system in Addis Ababa. The government is amazingly ambitious, working on roads, bridges and general modernization. America should be doing half as much infrastructure investment per capita as Ethiopia is! (China is helping— many of the construction companies working on big projects are Chinese owned.)

The first step in planning our trip around the country was to arrange transport. The Itegue Taitu Hotel (a rambling old African classic built in 1907) held both the "first class" bus ticket office and a recommended travel agency. The only northern bus out of town left at a very unappealing 5 a.m. Local transport looked extremely difficult, with brutally long bus rides (many rides were 12 hours without stopping except for a brief lunch, and 5 a.m. departures were the norm because the operators were not permitted to run after dark.) We stopped in at the private tour company, but the people at Red Jackal Tours seemed indifferent and disorganized. We weren't impressed, so we decided to continue shopping around.

The hotel's garden restaurant looked like a good spot for a drink. To our delight, we discovered Ambo, the local bottled soda water, which became our daytime drink of choice. With fresh lime, Ambo was very refreshing, safe, and sugar-free. While at the restaurant, we met two very intelligent (and very handsome) young male college students, and we struck up a conversation. They were studying English, French and tourism development at Addis Ababa University, and they were working hard. With students like these, Ethiopia should forge ahead in the future.

The next day, we walked downtown to another tour agency recommended by our guidebook. Abeba Tours Ethiopia was friendly and well organized. The price of the tour was astonishingly high for a developing country. Costs included a Land Rover (in good condition with two spare tires), an English speaking driver who was also a reasonably experienced mechanic, all gas, hotels in the "midrange," our breakfast, and all local guide and entrance fees to attractions and national parks. We would have to pay for our lunches, dinners, and, that most indispensable of commodities, our beer. At the time, the prices seemed excessive, but the alternatives were equally daunting. I thought about local buses and the stress of haggling over every little thing, worrying about getting overcharged (or worse) at every turn, trying to find hotels by ourselves with an already out-of-date guidebook, and the fear of missing half of the attractions due to lack of local transport. All of these things made us decide to go with the all-inclusive option. It turned out to be the best decision we could have made. It also turned out that the company was giving us about the best value they could manage for our money. When we saw how much cash they had to shell out for local guides and entrance fees, we understood why the overall daily budget was so high. The cost of vehicles was unbelievable. The government charges a 250% import tax for all vehicles! Our Land Rover cost the company over $100,000 U.S. dollars. The miles and miles of rough dirt roads and dust must do terrible things to a vehicle. All this we discovered later. But we liked the businesslike nature of the company, and we got an overall good feeling from the people who worked there. I also was shuddering from the idea of trying to find restaurants on our own, after having seen some of the local offerings. So we took the plunge, and spent the next couple of hours borrowing one of the company's cars and driving around Addis, looking for a bank that could change enough money to pay most of the tour bill in cash up front. It took some doing, but we finally got a large cash advance on one credit card. (Budget travelers: Ethiopia may not be the best country for you to start out in—unless you are ready for some very challenging travel).

That evening, we treated ourselves to an Italian restaurant, because our diet would soon be all Ethiopian (whatever that meant). On the way home, we met a friendly fellow who claimed to be a DJ in a local bar. We were walking together, having a pleasant conversation, when a deranged individual started screaming at us. He followed us, swearing and yelling that "we white people would perish on judgment day in the fires of Hell," etc., etc. Our DJ friend stuck right with us and made sure we got back to our hotel safely, despite the threat this potentially violent person posed. That's what Ethiopians are like. They are very generous, lovely people. His kindness set the tone for the whole trip.

Eventually, we decided to take two exciting road trips, one to the historic north, and one to the tribal south.

By Diana McLeod

NORTHERN ETHIOPIA OVERLAND:
an extended travel diary

DAY ONE: ADDIS ABABA TO BAHIR DAR

Our driver Sisay (pronounced see-sigh) picked us up the next morning at our hotel. At first, he seemed shy and taciturn. It took a few minutes to warm him up and get him talking. But once he relaxed with us, we knew we would become good friends. Sisay means "lucky" in the Ethiopian language, and apparently, he was lucky. Newly married after years of bachelorhood, he proudly showed us pictures of his wife. Wow! If the photo didn't lie, and if she had been taller, she could have made a superb living in Europe as a high fashion model.

The road north to Bahir Dar gave us our first glimpses of Ethiopian scenery. The rolling highlands were dotted with little villages, towns, and subsistence farms. The first thing that struck me was the extreme tidiness. All the shacks and huts were neat and clean! Dirt yards were freshly swept. Fences and yards were carefully weeded, trimmed and maintained with pride. Every owner obviously did their very best with the little they had to keep their property as attractive as possible. There was no garbage or mess anywhere. No trash of any kind was visible beside the main road. I've never seen a country with such an obsession for cleanliness, not even Bhutan. An Ethiopian farmwife would be appalled by my poorly groomed gardens at home! Of course, the lack of garbage is, to some extent, easily explained. When you live in a thatched hut, even a torn, tossed aside plastic bag can be a treasure during the rainy season since it can be used to plug leaks.

We commented on the numerous groves of eucalyptus trees, which helped to green up the countryside, but Sisay shook his head and told us they were a bad thing. Someone had introduced them to Ethiopia, and now they were overtaking local forests. Eucalyptus trees consume much more water than the indigenous trees, so they were adding to water problems around the country.

As we approached one town, we saw hundreds of people walking barefoot along the road. Many of them were driving livestock. Apparently, it was market day, and these farmers had hiked for miles, leaving home well before dawn. They carried no water, despite the dry heat and the dust. Most of them had probably never ridden inside a vehicle in their lives.

When we stopped the car for a photo, and the inevitable kids swarmed the car, we gave them our empty water bottles—treasures they eagerly took home to Mama. The plastic bottles would either be sold at market or used to store water, oil, local beer or *arraki* (the local liquor). A tossed aside water bottle wouldn't last a second by the roadside in this country.

Footsteps of a Nomad

Along the road, we saw an almost Biblical sight: the threshing of the wheat crop using cattle. The farmer's cattle are driven around in circles, crushing the grain with their hooves, while the farmer tosses the chaff into the air. It's a primitive, centuries-old technique, used ever since the domestication of cattle. It was almost hypnotic to watch.

Different towns sold specialized products by the side of the road. We passed one town selling *arraki*. The next village had bamboo mats for sale. Another had baskets, and another grew *qat* (an addictive plant with properties similar to cocaine).

As we began the climb further up into the Highlands, I could feel the altitude tugging on my lungs, and I practiced yogic breathing when it bothered me. Strange rock chimneys stuck straight up out of the sedimentary rock; evidence of ancient volcanic upwellings of lava. Ethiopia is on the edge of the African rift, where the tectonic plates are thin and spreading. We yearned to go to the volcanic region of Ethiopia, to see the world's only continuously active lava lake, but the Danakil Depression was just too hot at that time of year (over 120 degrees in the daytime). I could never have completed the arduous climb to the crater.

At one point, we came to a sudden overlook that instantly reminded me of the Grand Canyon. This was the famous Blue Nile Gorge. It extends nearly four hundred kilometers, with depths of up to fifteen hundred meters. We drove down one rugged escarpment, on lots of hairpin turns, and back up the other side. The canyon lands looked just like those like the U.S., but the baboons scampering over the rocks were purely African. Terraced villages with traditional round huts huddled close to the available water.

On the way back up, the road ended in a gigantic construction project. For the next few hours, the road was rough dirt. Bulldozers and backhoes were everywhere. At one point, we encountered a giant steam shovel that had fallen over sideways. We were lucky it didn't entirely block the road, which could have ruined our whole trip. We would have had to turn back! We were on the only real road that passed through these mountains. In Ethiopia, there is usually no such thing as an alternate route.

That evening we arrived at the lake town of Bahir Dar. The area is a rapidly developing tourist destination, not only for foreigners but also for well-to-do Ethiopians from the capital. People come for boat trips on the lake, and to dine at fancy restaurants down near the water. It's also a local honeymoon spot. After booking into a nice hotel, we strolled back to the lakeside to order some dinner, and were quickly befriended (accosted) by the first of many young "students' desperately seeking contributions for his "education." He told us his parents had cut him off, and then he asked us to buy him a new computer!

Our young friend wasn't shy about asking for money, and it was likely his whole "student" rap was entirely a scam. (Why, if he was broke, was he drinking expensive beer in a fancy restaurant?) We didn't succumb to the sad story.

Speaking of beer, we discovered, to our delight, that Ethiopia has quite an excellent beer. Saint George beer holds a credible place on the world stage of beers. It also has a great label, depicting St George slaying the dragon. It turns out that the Orthodox Christians have quite a thing for old St George. Many of the most famous churches in the country are dedicated to him. Dinner, on the other hand, was less than perfect. We ordered lamb "*Tibes*,"(which was plain stewed meat) (probably old goat, not lamb), and rice with vegetables (which meant rice with boiled cabbage and French fries). We worried—were we going to have to eat meat, bread and French fries for the whole trip? At least this meat was cooked...

DAY TWO: BAHIR DAR AND LAKE TANA

The Summerland Hotel provided a decent breakfast, plus the BBC and WIFI (the Holy Grail of travelers). Hopping in the car, we took off for a morning sightseeing trip. Our first stop was a scenic area—the city dump. Say *WHAT*??? But Sisay was right to drive us there because the nearby trees were impressively thick with flocks of African vultures, nicely posed for their morning photo op. Tall Maribou storks also patrolled the nearby fields.

Next we went to the Blue Nile Falls. The rough dirt road took us to the park near the falls where we picked up a local guide. The Ethiopian government requires all tourists to hire a local guide from the registered guide association whenever they visit any cultural or natural place of interest. (In a way, this is not a bad thing, because the official guides have the authority to chase away hundreds of would-be "unofficial" ones). Sisay had a huge folder full of money locked in his glove compartment, which he used to pay all the park and guide fees. When I saw how much money he had to spend just for this one waterfall, I began to understand why the tour package was so costly.

Our local guide led us along a trail up the hillsides near the falls. The waterfall was lovely and wide, although ever since they built a dam upriver, the water levels are much reduced in the dry season. Chomping on sugar cane and listening to exotic birds squabbling in the trees, we enjoyed the stroll until we got to the end. Dave reached into his pocket for a tip for the guide, and the man saw that Dave didn't have any 100 *birr* notes (the local currency). Our guide sneered, "Even if you gave me everything in your pocket I wouldn't take it because it wouldn't be good enough." We were quite shocked. We were going to give him about two or three dollars for less than an hour of his time walking with us (for which he had already been well paid). Since he rudely turned it down, we gave him nothing, and our relationship immediately turned to ice. Our driver, Sisay, was also shocked by this rudeness when we told him what had happened. He did inform us that the guides usually expect tips of between 50 to 100 Bir most of the time; fifty if it was a short trip, and one hundred for several hours. The tip we had offered, while on the modest side, should have been acceptable. (One hundred Bir is five bucks, in a country with an average yearly income of $400 per family.) These guide jobs must be jealously coveted! No wonder everyone was trying to practice their English with us! Our guide had already gotten several hundred *birr* from our driver. I suspect that most foreigners are not experienced at judging a proper tip, so they overtip like crazy on their first day, making this guy ridiculously spoiled.

We went back to town where Sisay offered to return us to our hotel for a Western lunch, but we wanted to learn about local food. So we followed him to a charming outdoor cafe, and we decided to share a double portion of traditional Ethiopian fasting food with him. Sisay is an Orthodox Christian, and he takes his faith very seriously. We were in Ethiopia just in time for the beginning of Lent, and all Orthodox Christians were required to restrict their diets to fasting food and fish until Easter. Lucky for us!! Fasting food was pure vegetarian, and we could finally get some healthy vegetables into our diet. The dishes were prepared on round tin dishes the size of a large pizza platter. A slab of *injera* was placed over the entire bottom of the pan and curled up at the edges. The staple diet of most of Ethiopia, *injera* is a spongy, thin brown sourdough bread. You break off pieces of it to scoop up the rest of the food. It was a challenge for me to eat with my right hand only (the left is considered unclean). Individual servings of cooked vegetables and grains were dolloped in a circle, around a central serving of "chipotle" chickpea paste with chilis and spices in the center. There were lentils, squash, eggplant, cooked spinach, and raw salad, which we, unfortunately, could not eat (food safety issues). After only meat, potatoes and bread for two days, we decided we would order fasting food at least once a day. And the *injera* bread is supposedly loaded with iron and calcium. The three of us had a very delightful and tasty lunch.

After lunch, Sisay took us to the boat launch for the trip across Lake Tana. Hopping into a small powerboat with a new local guide (Tomas) and a driver, we motored across part of the lake, disturbing the pelicans paddling near some papyrus plants. Lake Tana is so large that we couldn't see all the way to the far end. We passed several intriguing island monasteries, but since they didn't allow female visitors, we bypassed them. Instead, we stopped at a large peninsula. The forested shores had gentle trails leading up to two classic old-style Ethiopian Orthodox Christian monasteries: Azuwa Maryam and Ura Kidane Mehret. These thirteenth-century monasteries had churches built like oversized huts; circular, with thatched roofs, and large enough to hold an entire congregation. The peak of each roof was capped with ornate Ethiopian crosses; the top and the sides of these crosses were tipped with seven white ostrich eggs representing the seven Sacraments. Ostrich eggs, which are incredibly durable, also represent the strength and the longevity of the Church. (We even saw them, many years later, in Orthodox churches in Greece).

Inside Azuwa Maryam the walls were covered in artwork. Bible stories were introduced to generations of illiterate people in a series of simple paintings. Most were easy to recognize: Mary and the Angel, Mary with the baby Jesus (with an Ethiopian Wise Man bringing frankincense to his birth), Jesus suffering, the crucifixion, the martyrdom of the Apostles, the Last Judgment. In the paintings, the "holy" Christian saints were shown with two eyes, while "sinful" people were depicted in profile. There was even a picture condemning cannibalism as a mortal sin. Some paintings were surrounded by blue and white decorations, which, our guide explained, were inspired by sixteenth-century Chinese pottery designs. Lastly, he pointed out the angels painted around each of the doorways. Tomas wryly explained they were, "looking out in all directions, just like security cameras."

As we approached the second church, we encountered a service in progress. Inside, in a circular outer room, frail old priests in brocaded robes were chanting, singing and reading from ancient texts. The white-garbed congregation stood and listened, occasionally responding with softly spoken chants and prayers. Most of the people were leaning on long canes—prayer staves—which have religious significance in the Orthodox Church. The service felt freshly innocent and unspoiled by pomp and circumstance, although there was far too much emphasis on death and martyrdom in the religion for my taste.

In the central part of the church, one area was curtained off, out of public view. Thomas informed us this area was known as the "Holy of Holies," forbidden to all but priests. He said each Ethiopian church holds a copy of the Ark of the Covenant. Supposedly the real Ark of the Covenant is kept in a special shrine at the main cathedral in Axum, Ethiopia, where one dedicated priest guards it day and night. But I've also heard a contradictory story: when the Ark supposedly first came to Ethiopia, the priests had hundreds of copies made and distributed to all the major churches. Nobody truly knows where the original is hidden, except for the one priest who guards the True Ark. (Sounds to me like the making of yet another Indiana Jones movie.) On the other hand, it gives each Ethiopian church a sense of sanctity. Could this one be *the one*? Could the most sacred reliquary of all time rest behind these velvet curtains? My imagination went on fantasy Ark quests.

Afterward, several priests showed us their religious "museum," which contained vellum hand-calligraphed illuminated Bibles allegedly dating back to the fifteenth century. It was hard for me to see these fragile treasures propped up on their moldering spines in a thatched hut. Supposedly, a new building was being built to house them in the future. The "museum" also displayed ornate Ethiopian crosses and antique royal crowns, donated to the monastery by visiting Ethiopian monarchs.

The forested walk between the two monasteries was most enjoyable. Hornbills flew from tree to tree, and monkeys watched us from the branches. The greenery of the jungle was a refreshing change after days spent in urban environments.

On the boat ride back, we got into an intense spiritual discussion with our guide. Tomas was a practicing Orthodox Christian, but he was also a very well read young man with an exceptional intellect, and he was obviously troubled by the contradictions between modern science and the Bible. As we talked, he confessed a moving personal story to us. He had read something that was in direct opposition to the teachings of his church, and it had troubled him as much as it had fascinated him. He was talking about Dan Brown's novel, *The Da Vinci Code*. The idea that Christ might have been married and might have fathered a child was heretical, but he just couldn't put the novel down. He felt so guilty that he turned all of the lights off in his room so the eyes of Jesus couldn't stare at him from the picture on his wall, and he continued to read the story under the covers by flashlight. In the end, he got over some of his compunctions, and he eventually read the book five times. He even went to find an art book with a picture of the "Last Supper" in it, to see the alleged symbolism in the painting. I greatly admired his language skills to have absorbed such a difficult novel in a second language, and I also admired his courage for allowing his mind to explore such uncharted and taboo territory.

We were almost sad to get off the boat! We had just shared a meaningful discussion of what happens when you approach the world with an open mind. Our driver Sisay was not as willing to step away from spiritual orthodoxy. He politely listened when we talked to him about dinosaurs and distant galaxies, but he remained firmly convinced that the world is only 6,000 years old. Still, Sisay was thoughtful in his own way. When we brought up the fact that each star is a sun, and that the potential of millions of planets exists in our neck of the universe, with the high probability of intelligent life somewhere out there, Sisay brought up a good question, noting that in the past couple of decades, U.F.O. sightings have all but disappeared from the news.

"If they were here, then where did they go?" he wondered. "Were we too boring for them, or what? Today, everybody has a cell phone to photograph them, so you would think that they would quickly be caught on film if they were still around. So, why aren't they here now? Why did they leave? Camera shy?"

recommended Google search: Lake Tana Ethiopia Images

DAY THREE; THE "JADUGAR" — BAHIR DAR TO GONDER

It was a pleasant drive through miles of open, rolling (deforested) farmland in the highlands to reach the medieval city of Gonder. Our hotel, the Fasil Lodge, situated right in the shadow of the ancient walled fortress in the center of Gonder, was so charming I almost failed to notice the disaster that had befallen us. We were short one piece of luggage!! And we were now a four-hour drive from the morning's hotel! And this was Africa, a land where my used hiking boots and my ratty old tee shirts were valuable items indeed! The chances were good that my knapsack had already "disappeared."

We called Sisay, our driver, and he came right away, cell phone in hand. The hotel in Bahir Dar had found my luggage! Now, how to get it to Gonder? Sisay was resourceful. He had a friend who was driving a group of tourists along the same route we had just taken, and they were planning an afternoon departure. In less than five minutes, Sisay had fixed everything. We gave him the title of *jadugar*—*"magician"* in Hindi.

In the afternoon, we visited the Debre Birhan Selassie Church. Most Ethiopian churches are round, symbolizing the Alpha and the Omega, but this one was rectangular, symbolizing the Ark of the Covenant. It was originally built in 1694, although most of the paintings inside have been re-done since that time. Once again, I appreciated the simplicity of the church, although Orthodox artwork always seems to focus on scenes of death and the torture of Christ. There was even a picture of Mary being forced to drink poison during the Roman Regent's efforts to murder Hebrew children. Our guide pointed out many Ethiopian saints (all gruesomely martyred) and a picture of Daniel with the lions. The ceiling of the church was famous— it is covered in hand-painted angels, all of whom have Ethiopian features and hair. Their eyes seemed to follow us around, no matter where we stood in the sanctuary.

Next, we visited an unusual place: a miniature castle built right in the middle of a deep man-made swimming pool. It was originally a recreational retreat for the royal family during medieval times. Since then it has been preserved as a monument, and it is still used once a year for the Church ceremony of Epiphany (the baptism of Christ) when huge crowds come to be re-baptized by Orthodox priests. The little castle in the center of the lake was enchanting! Too bad we were not allowed over the bridge to visit it.

Lastly, we went to the castles on the hill in the center of the town. These were once the residences of the kings of Abyssinia. The castles themselves looked great from the outside, but inside, they were lonely, empty places, mostly in ruins, and smelling of bats. Our attention was drawn to what was going on outdoors. Apparently, it was fashionable to photograph wedding parties in front of the castles; this day, two different wedding parties showed up, horns blaring, in the parking lot. They crowded around the bride and groom, and danced and sang their way onto the castle grounds, accompanied by drums and Ethiopian "violins." The music was catchy and fun, and the ladies sometimes ululated (the shrill, trilling sound common in East African and Arab-speaking lands). The wedding parties were all in Western dress, with brightly colored matching bridesmaids' dresses and rented tuxedos. Our guide told us about half of the couples in Ethiopia today wear Western dress, and the other half opt for traditional clothing.

While the bridal parties posed for pictures, the rest of each family danced and sang and got the party started. I got up close to watch, and one teenage girl befriended me. She welcomed me, and taught me how to dance in the traditional style. It requires a peculiar movement of the shoulders, very similar to the American inner-city dance move called "krumping." She dragged me into the center of the circle, and I gave it a try. Dave also wound up joining in, which amused the locals, until one of the ladies started smacking her forehead with her hand. She gave us impatient glances, but we didn't know what she was doing. When we failed to respond the way she wanted us to, she indignantly shooed us away.

Puzzled, we asked our guide. He explained that head smacking was one way of asking for money in Ethiopia. What an odd gesture! We would never have guessed! He also told me the young lady who invited me to dance was, coincidently, his niece. Small town!

That night, we experienced our first Ethiopian Sunday morning. Because it was Lent, the loudspeakers on all the Christian church steeples started prayers at three o'clock in the morning, and they stayed on for the rest of the night. There were at least ten different churches broadcasting. Each had a singer or singers, and the sound they made was unmusical, rambling and just intermittent enough to drive us crazy. It was as if you took ten drunks, put each one in a separate bar so they couldn't hear the others, and let them amplify their drunken diatribes and slurred remnants of half-remembered songs, in a hellish, whiskey-soaked, karaoke marathon "battle of the bands" all over the town, all night long. I'm sorry, I know it's religiously insensitive of me to say so, but I think all religions should be denied the use of outdoor loudspeakers after nightfall. Together, it just sounded like caterwauling, especially when one nearby church turned their P.A. system over to a series of small children at four o'clock in the morning. Honestly, if God is everywhere, does he want to ruin everybody's night's sleep once a week? Does he need loudspeakers to hear our prayers? Is he deaf? The pictures in the churches depict scene after scene of suffering and torture. Is this the twenty-first-century version? (Once again, I apologize to those I may have offended).

recommended Google search: Gonder Ethiopia Images

DAY FOUR: GONDER TO THE SIMIEN MOUNTAINS

The next morning, a bit bleary-eyed, we headed up into the Simien Mountains. The scenery became more and more dramatic, with deep red canyons and towering stone monoliths that occasionally put Monument Valley to shame. Our trip took us to the homely little truck-stop town of Debark, where we got a room at the Giant Lobelia Hotel. The Lobelia was apparently the only hotel option in the whole area, which wasn't saying much. The lobby floor was strewn with cut grass (easier than sweeping it), and the hotel "restaurant" was serving raw meat (an Ethiopian favorite) for lunch. We bought snacks at a local "convenience shack" instead.

In the afternoon, we signed in at the Simien Mountains National Park Office, where we picked up a local guide and a jack-booted camouflage-clad soldier armed with an automatic weapon. Apparently this was required since, as Sisay explained, some locals were a bit hostile to tourists. Technically, the man wasn't a real soldier; he was more of a park ranger and peacekeeper. Our guide was blandly professional, but the soldier was memorable. He was the strong, silent type: tall and fit, with a marvelously rugged, craggy face, the perfect soldier's stance, and deep-set dark eyes that missed nothing. He would have made a great extra in a war movie!

The trail began soon after the park entrance. We walked along the jagged edge of a cliff, gazing straight down at least two hundred meters to the valley below. It was a beautiful day. Hawks circled gracefully overhead, and cliff springer antelope grazed on the next ridge. Wild quail scattered into the bushes as we approached. The gorge itself was very impressive—a gigantic amphitheater with a slender waterfall cascading down into the abyss. Nearby, we found soft, shimmering, white, crystallized stone that crumbled easily underfoot. Could this possibly be non-gem-quality Ethiopian opal? After all, they are finding a lot of opal in this area.

Before we left the park, we encountered a troupe of Gelada baboons, so we stopped to watch them for a while. They were incredibly blasé about having humans nearby. We crept closer and closer until we were only a few feet away, and they accepted our presence fearlessly. Most of the time, they were so intent on grazing on the sparse vegetation they didn't even bother to watch us, even though we were almost close enough to touch them. Each baboon was scrabbling in the dirt and tearing up wild rosemary plants by the roots. The gentle sounds they made were hauntingly human, almost as if they were developing the beginnings of language. Their calls seemed to convey contentment as they ate.

Our guide told us a startling bit of information about the baboons. The local people dislike them because of the damage they do to their grazing land. Occasionally they throw stones at the baboons and chase them away. White people, on the other hand, just gawk at them and take pictures, so the baboons have learned to trust white people more than blacks. Is this a bizarre form of animal racism or simply a culturally learned behavior? Do they regard Caucasians as a different and less dangerous species of human? Anyway, this was the one time on the whole trip when our guides hung back near the car and left us alone. They knew they would scare the baboons away if they got too close.

recommended Google search: Simien Mountains Ethiopia Images

DAY 5 – THE ROAD TO AXUM—MORE LESSONS IN ANIMAL BEHAVIOR

Sisay warned us. The road to Axum was under construction. Virtually all of its 253 kilometers were a choking, dusty, bone-jarring mess. I've never seen so much construction equipment working on one road at one time in my life! The Ethiopian government had hired every local company in the region and supplemented them with foreign companies, including Chinese contractors. The mountains presented the workers with a colossal engineering challenge. Most of the time, the road builders had to dig into the sides of dangerously steep, unstable cliffs, creating series after series of jackknife turns. At one point, we encountered a huge pile of gravel and small boulders entirely blocking the road. We had to wait for a nearby bulldozer to dig it out and create a temporary roadway for us before we could continue.

Luckily, we always found plenty to talk about. We were getting to know our driver Sisay, and jokes and stories constantly flowed back and forth between us. We amused him with our travel stories (especially the racy ones from Thailand), and he recounted an old Ethiopian folktale about how various types of domestic animals deal with roads and traffic. Here's the story: An Ethiopian donkey, a goat, and a dog once got on a bus. The donkey paid the full fare. The goat got on, took his ride, and fled without paying at all. The dog didn't have the correct change, so he overpaid. He had to leave the bus without getting his change. This is why these animals behave as they do. The donkeys have paid the fare, so they act like they own the road. The goats haven't paid, so they always run away. And the dogs chase every bus because they are still looking for their change. After hearing that story, it became a standard joke for us. In restaurants, Dave and I would threaten to behave like goats and run away without paying.

Domestic animals, people, and potholes were a constant hazard on the roads in Ethiopia. I have never seen a country with so much livestock! Large herds of cattle were driven right on or across the road, and Sisay had to brake hard to dodge strays. Heavily-laden donkeys often trotted right down the middle of the road, just like their famous brother on the bus. (Many of the donkeys are tiny; only waist-high to a human.) Sheep and goats flowed around oncoming traffic, and chickens, dogs, and young children appeared out of nowhere, testing Sisay's reflexes and making me thankful for my seatbelt. There were very few horses in the country, but the ones we saw were decorated with red tassels and colorful blankets. The most sensible creatures in the country were the slow-paced camels, the only domesticated animals clever enough to stick to the curb.

The second half of the journey took us through some desolate places. The fields were full of sun-blasted rocks. I cannot understand how they possibly farm this land. How can anything grow out there? No wonder Ethiopia suffers terribly during drought years!

By Diana McLeod

After many hours of bone-grinding bumps and eating our own dust, we finally arrived, tired and gritty, in Axum, the ancient capital of Ethiopia. Sisay looked especially worn out after such a long and challenging drive. That night we stayed in a motel-style place called the Africa Hotel, which was certainly better than the Lobelia. We had dinner in a far fancier place across the street. That evening, a dramatic thunderstorm struck—quite something in such a dry, dusty province. It was a blessed relief to feel the rain, but the soil swallowed it right up, and twenty minutes afterward, it was as if it never happened.

DAY SIX: AXUM—OBELISKS

We met Sisay in the morning, and he drove us a mere two hundred yards up the street for breakfast. He is so used to chauffeuring tourists every minute of the day that I think he forgets that some of us are capable of walking around an Ethiopian town by ourselves! (And there must be plenty of intimidated tourists who are frightened to walk alone, even for the tiniest of distances).

After breakfast, we picked up our local guide and went to visit the famous stone obelisks of Axum. The largest of these carved stone monoliths is the biggest known stone obelisk ever created in the ancient world—even heavier than all the Egyptian ones. They were burial markers, placed over the tombs of ancient Ethiopian kings more than two thousand years ago. Decorations on the stelae indicate the ancients worshiped the sun and the moon. This primordial religion existed in Ethiopia until around 380 A.D., when King Izana converted everyone to Christianity.

Of the many stelae in this sacred royal burial ground, three are truly exceptional. Each has a false door at its base, and levels of false windows in the obelisks indicate how many family members were buried beneath it. The biggest of the three has fallen over and, now in pieces, exposes the tomb below. The tomb is empty but the subterranean rooms are open to the public, and they are nicely preserved. The engineering is impressive, considering that the edge of the tomb chamber had to hold up a block weighing more than 160 tons without collapsing. The second largest obelisk was "borrowed" by the Italians when they briefly colonized Ethiopia, and it was set up in Rome; this national art treasure was returned to its home in 2008.

Inside the museum, we saw many tomb artifacts, including carved elephant ivory, glass chalices, gold coins and more. UNESCO has recently been buying up nearby land because Axum may have many more treasures still hidden beneath its modern neighborhoods! Persistent legends of secret doors and underground tunnels have led to an additional archeological investigation. It has now been determined that several mysterious tunnels exist between the tombs, some of which lead to a new gravesite that has yet to be excavated.

After lunch, we went to the Saint Mary of Zion Church. Behind this modern cathedral is the small (and rather homely) chapel where Ethiopian Orthodox Christians now believe the actual Ark of the Covenant resides. Nobody is allowed to see it except two guardian-priests, who are sworn to remain in the chapel with the ark for their entire lives.

Is it the real deal? Or are they wasting their lives watching over a fake, while the real one molders behind velvet curtains somewhere else? Or is the whole story apocryphal? We will never know...

The church museum displayed a fine collection of royal ceremonial robes, crowns, manuscripts, and antique crosses. One of the crowns supposedly had over 200 diamonds on it (probably all paste, since the crown was donated to the church after the royal visit.) We were also lucky enough to see a major church procession in the afternoon. The priests led the congregation three times around the church, stopping at the end to bless people with their crosses.

After the church service, I shopped for Ethiopian crosses to give as gifts, but frankly, the merchandise was cheap, stamped-out junk in white metal, and the prices were absurd. One shop owner proudly showed us an impressive collection of antique hand-calligraphed and hand-illuminated Bibles on parchment paper. Surprisingly, these were for sale, but of course these precious artifacts should never leave the country.

That night, we spent the evening in the hotel's outdoor bar area, drinking St. George beer and playing backgammon. As I recall, I won.

recommended Google search: Axum Ethiopia Images

DAY 7 - AXUM TO HAWSEIN
PREHISTORIC AFRICA and A SECRET MOUNTAIN
MONASTERY

On this day we drove to the ruins of Yeha, a city dating from the Eighth to the Fifth Centuries B.C. This is the largest and most significant site of Bronze Age Civilization yet found in the Horn of Africa. There were two areas of importance in Yeha: a rambling palace and an imposingly tall structure called "The Great Temple." Archaeologists were restoring the temple walls and excavating the palace foundations. We were able to watch the teams at work, which was exciting to see.

The sites were pretty impressive, considering the fact that Africa has no indigenous animals that can be domesticated (except for guinea fowl). The lack of domesticated livestock really held back African development south of the navigable Nile. People were forced to spread out and remain semi-nomadic in order to hunt wild game. They

278

couldn't cluster in towns because that would have depopulated the wild herds in the area.

In the afternoon, we left the main road. Sisay threw the Land Rover into four-wheel drive, and we entered a rugged area of high cliffs and towering mesas. The imposing terrain reminded me of the stone escarpments of Wadi Rum in Jordan (where many of the epic scenes of the movie *Laurence of Arabia* were filmed). Hardscrabble homesteads of piled stone and thatch clung to a meager existence wherever their inhabitants could find water in the cruel desert. I can't imagine how much labor it must have taken to pile rocks without mortar to build a house, and then to struggle to keep the roof maintained, using only straw.

At last we reached our goal—a tiny village at the end of the dirt road. From it, we climbed up hundreds of sandstone steps carved directly into the bedrock until we reached the base of a large mesa. About a hundred feet above us, atop a nearly vertical cliff, was a wooden doorway. One long hemp rope, and a second rope, made of cured cowhide hung from it. This was the only entrance to an ancient monastery above. The gatekeeper looked down, ready to hold the safety rope so that Dave could scale the rock face.

As a woman, I was forbidden to climb it because of the monastery above. Frankly, I was relieved. Even though I was dying of curiosity, I could never have scaled such a challenging rock face. It was a long way up. Our driver Sisay went up first. They tied the safety line around him, and he used the hemp rope as he struggled to find footholds. His arm muscles were straining, and he slipped a couple of times. Then it was Dave's turn. He got about halfway up, but he couldn't get a grip on the slippery rope, and his sneakers were sliding on the footholds. I think he would have made it if he had been wearing his hiking boots. He turned back, and it was probably just as well. It was too dangerous! But I bet the wizened old monks go up and down just like mountain goats. After all, they've been practicing since childhood. When Sisay got back down, we asked him about the monastery, but he said there wasn't much to see.

That night, we stayed at the exotic Gheralta Lodge. After three days of scruffy hotels, the tour planners thought we would be ready for something special. And they were right. (Anybody contemplating taking the Northern Route in Ethiopia, take this advice: go cheap elsewhere, so that you can book at the Gheralta Lodge!) The Gheralta was a series of luxurious stone villas out in the countryside, stylishly designed by its Italian owners. Chic, clean and charming, it was a treat!

After days of being trapped in funky hotels in the center of large towns, it was delightful to be able to walk around by ourselves in the African countryside. The Western edge of the resort's land provided a magnificent view of red rock cliffs on the far side of the valley. We strolled over to the stone wall and gazed out at the late afternoon sun's golden rays. Of course, the inevitable horde of kids from scattered huts below came running up as soon as they spotted us. Dave quickly made friends with them, and he started a little game of piling small rocks on top of each other. The kids soon set about making little piles of their own, and we got quite a little competition going. They were all pretty good at it. I was the judge, and I gave points for artistry as well as for the number of rocks balanced. It was a lot of fun. I bet some of our little cairns are still there, decorating the stone wall.

When the sun dipped low, we excused ourselves and said goodbye, because we wanted to walk to the top of the hill to take pictures. As we ascended, we found ancient steps carved right into the sandstone. Rock Hyrax scampered around the rocks. Strange animals, they look like a cat-sized rodent, but their closest living animal relative is, believe it or not, the elephant. They seemed intelligent and agile, and communicated with each other using a unique, distinctive language of trills, chirps, and whistles. They even managed to climb into the trees, despite their fat bodies.

Dave and I also climbed a tree! It was a magnificently large bushy tree, with spreading, stair–like branches. It was so easy to climb, we simply couldn't resist. I soon found myself fantasizing about tree-house designs.

Dinner at the Gheralta was an enjoyable affair. Our tablemates were from Slovenia. One of them was the European C.E.O. of the Goodyear Corporation. What a great conversationalist! He'd spent quite a lot of time in the U.S, and his command of the English language was dazzling. Dave and I dove straight into world politics and economics, and the discussion was most enlightening. The cuisine was delicious and mostly organic, grown from the hotel's gardens. We washed it down with Ethiopian honey wine.

That night, we were able to get our first good look at the African night sky out in the countryside. The stars were radiant. It's sad to think that, in the urban northeastern U.S., the light of the stars is so diminished by our electrical excesses, we cannot see them nearly as well as one can in Africa. That night, they lit up the whole sky so brightly they almost created shadows. The Milky Way was a luminous bridal veil woven of starlight gauze and embroidered with diamonds. The familiar stars I've looked at since childhood were all there, although they were turned about at unfamiliar angles. I had to look twice to find the North Star. But we didn't need our flashlights to find our peaceful, cozy bungalow.

recommended Google search: Debre Damo Monastery Images

By Diana McLeod

DAY 8: DON'T LOOK DOWN!
THE CAVE CHURCHES OF MARYAM KORKOR

In the brilliantly sunny morning, we left the Gheralta Lodge and headed east, towards the province of Tigray. Turning off the main road, we headed into rough terrain. A local guide joined us as we drove to the outskirts of a small village, where we encountered a large group of men who were also determined to "guide" us. Sisay had to use both diplomacy and firmness to get them to leave us alone. Dave and I pantomimed our willingness to turn back and go somewhere else if the issue was not resolved. We also demonstrated our refusal to give them money. It took a while, but eventually, they left us alone.

The cliff face went straight up, and I wondered where the trail was until I saw a crack in the rock. At some point in history, an upwelling of lava had forced its way up, splitting the older sedimentary rocks apart. The lava had hardened into a black seam of basalt. Basalt often "crystallizes," making six-sided black crystals as big as logs. In this case, they were turned lengthwise, creating a natural flight of "stairs" inside the chasm. The "staircase" was four to eight feet wide and easy to climb, with natural handholds on both sides. We spotted evidence of ancient sea fossils in the sandstone around us.

Reaching the top of the lower mesa, we enjoyed a commanding view of the surrounding countryside. Nearby, there was a "shepherd's cave." It had been originally hollowed out for use as a dwelling, and later converted into a very primitive church. Now it lay abandoned, but the local goat herders were still using it as a shelter during mountain storms. There was a cozy firepit inside, and even a "picture window" with a stunning view of the canyon. Definitely Flintstones.

Back outside, we looked at the next part of the ascent, finding an incredibly steep section right above a near vertical drop of over two hundred feet. Our guides were urging us to climb, using a series of small handholds and footholds. I thought they were crazy and would have turned back, except for one thing: the stone beneath my feet gripped like sandpaper. Our guide (and one young boy who joined us partway up) both scrambled up the cliff like a pair of mountain goats and held out their hands for me. One spot was intensely scary, with only a single handhold to pull myself up with, and certain death below if I fell, but I finally made it to the rim. I wondered how in hell I was going to get back down again, but I put those thoughts aside to prepare for what was to come.

There were several other challenging spots, but I tried to focus on what a beautiful day it was and on the ancient sites at the top. After being denied access to yesterday's monastery, I was determined not to let this one get away. At last the path leveled off and we saw the stone wall designating sacred ground. The entrance to the cave church was not particularly memorable, but the interior was. It was almost a cathedral! Pillars reared upwards like tree trunks, supporting a carved ceiling nearly three stories above our heads. The sanctuary was quite large, for a hollowed-out cave. It would hold a good-sized congregation on holy days. An elderly priest was inside, and he gladly showed us around, pointing out some niches in the walls that supposedly held the bones of local saints. Dave tipped the old fellow quite well, and he surprised us both by giving Dave a huge hug. He even laid his head on Dave's chest. It was quite touching.

On the other side of the mesa, a breathtakingly narrow trail took us to the other church. It was not easy to look almost straight down at the Land Rover, parked hundreds of feet below us, but the view of the valley was stunning. I was thankful for the lack of wind. There were no railings up there!

The entrance to the second "church" was a mere hole in the cliff through which we had to crawl. Inside, two chambers were hollowed out of the sandstone. One was a simple domed cave, with a mat on the floor and a few crude paintings on the walls. The second chamber held the tomb of a local saint, and we were forbidden to enter it. But the old priest gave us his warm blessing and told us this church dated from the first century A.D. I was skeptical Christianity made it that far south that quickly, but it was possible. Or, maybe the cave was in use by the first century A.D. and had been converted to Christianity a bit later.

We spent the night at the "Hilltop" hotel and bungalows, which, at one time, must have been quite a showplace. It sat atop a ridge and was built so that guests could enjoy the view while dining. Sadly, it showed many signs of decay, especially the defunct swimming pool, which was cracked and crumbling as the jungle quickly reclaimed it. We stayed in one of the hotel bungalows built along a series of winding paths, under trellises weighed down with tangles of overhanging vines. Black ravens squabbled and cawed overhead. The tunnels of vegetation were a bit creepy—like the maze in *Harry Potter*.

recommended Google search: Maryam Korkor Ethiopia Images

DAY 9: ROAD TO LALIBELA

Reviewing my handwritten trip diary of this day, I noticed I made no entries during most of the journey to Lalibela. The reason was that it would have been impossible for me to write during most of the trip. The road was far too rough.

We started off on a boring, modern highway and only one moment was notable. On the road near the Djibouti border, we saw a sight that will soon fade into memory: a salt caravan. Men were bringing salt from the Danakil Desert to markets in Ethiopia. In a long line, heavily-laden camels plodded stoically along the edge of the modern highway, looking sadly out of place among modern trucks and heavy construction vehicles. The caravan's ragtag band of camel drivers walked alongside, heads held high despite the choking dust and diesel exhaust. Sisay told us these historic caravans are rapidly becoming things of the past as the African Horn modernizes. For me, it was a thrill to see these people, who were probably Afar tribesmen, because I had written about them and their salt caravans in the novel I wrote in 2012.

The road south took us up and down several rugged mountain passes. The vegetation was more desert-like in this part of the country, and the cactus plants beside the highway were all in bloom. In the afternoon, we branched off from the main highway and took a dirt road shortcut to Lalibela. It was extremely rough going, with loose gravel sliding beneath our wheels. Sisay didn't talk much. He was concentrating on the road's challenging bumps, twists, and turns. Once again, I was glad we had picked such a good driver and a powerful vehicle, but as we got further and further out into the deserted countryside, I began to wish we had packed extra water in case of vehicle failure or another emergency. We were miles away from any town or village, and we didn't see another car or truck for over an hour. The desert was dead dry, rugged and rocky, and the vegetation was thorny and scraggly. The few homesteads we passed by looked very impoverished, and the cattle were scrawny and unhealthy thanks to the lack of any decent grazing land. I had sympathy for people unlucky enough to be born into such a merciless environment, doomed to battle against incredibly challenging odds for their entire lives. The fact that they can live there at all is a tribute to their skill and determination. I bet an Ethiopian farmer could teach an American some incredible desert survivalist techniques.

The road climbed yet another major mountain pass and then plunged downwards into another deep valley. As we were heading into the series of dog-bone switchbacks down the mountain, we passed a solitary farmstead with a group of kids outside. They immediately put on their best smiles and started doing a little comic dance for us. (Many of the vehicles that take this road are tourist buses or cars, so the kids were accustomed to seeing foreigners). We smiled and waved. The Land Rover took the next hairpin turn down into the next switchback. When we descended to the next level, about eighty feet below, there were those kids again! They had climbed frantically down the steep embankment to meet us. Sure enough, they did their little dance, and then, as soon as we went by, they ran as fast as they could to get down to the next turn. They did this two more times, descending several hundred feet, hoping for a fat tip from us.

Unfortunately for them, we've been conditioned to turn away from roadside beggars overseas. All too often, children in India are forced to beg in heavy traffic at busy intersections or highway interchanges, which exposes them to ungodly levels of pollution and sudden death by automobile or truck. We turn a cold shoulder to this kind of exploitation because it endangers children needlessly. Our first reaction to these kids was, therefore, an automatic "no." As we drove off down the mountain, I began to have second thoughts. Their little dance routine was clever and amusing, and I knew they had quite a long, thirsty, empty-handed hike back up the big hill to get home.

Ah well, I thought, the money would be better spent on donations to a real charity. I could then assure myself it would not be wasted on sweets or junk food, especially when these things make children sick if they're not used to the sugar and chemicals. On the other hand, were we depriving these kids of a chance to earn their keep and help their mom? These issues always weigh heavily on my heart when I'm abroad. Of course, we must help, but there is a right way and a wrong way to do so, yet it's not always easy to know which is which. No matter how careful I try to be, there are times when there is no right answer, and I feel I'm doing harm no matter what I do. I just wish I could feed the whole country.

And then I thought, *Hey, these kids were the lucky ones.* Their home was right at the viewpoint at the top of the valley where most tourist cars stopped for pictures. They had the perfect location to rake in tips. I bet they were making plenty. I've seen tourists tip children much more than the equivalent of a working man's daily salary. I told myself to stop feeling so badly for these kids, and instead, feel sorry for the kids who *don't* live right on the main road. I planned to make it up to those kids with charitable giving.

We kept descending until we hit the valley floor, crossed it, and started back up the other side to the town of Lalibela, which we could see perched on cliffs above. It was an interesting looking city, with an eclectic mix of modern hotels, concrete houses, and traditional wooden huts, all jumbled together at the edge of the mesa.

EVENING OF DAY 9: BIRDWATCHING IN LALIBELA

Throughout the whole Northern trip, we had driven through miles of open, deforested land, cleared for agriculture. Except for the Simien Mountains National Park, we'd had virtually no chance to experience African wildlife at all. That's why I was so delighted with our little hotel in Lalibela. It was a small hotel, situated almost on the edge of town, and our room was on the second story in the back, with a porch facing some trees. We settled in, purchased some cold beer to enjoy on our balcony, and discovered we had ringside seats to some excellent birding!

One of the trees was covered in sprays of purple flowers, and little sunbirds flitted around them, sipping at the nectar with long, curved beaks. Sunbirds are very small, not dissimilar to hummingbirds, with feathers that flash iridescent green or blue when the light hits them just right. High in the eucalyptus tree, a raucous flock of brown hornbills ruled the roost until a flock of ravens bullied them out. At another fruit-bearing tree, a noisy flock of seed-eating birds squabbled over the feast. They looked like cedar waxwings, only with more color: red tufts on top of their heads and stripes along their elegant long tails. Additional songbirds made little cameo appearances in the trees: little finches and wrens, and other colorful African species that I've not been able to identify. I counted over fifteen varieties!

recommended Google search: Lalibela Ethiopia Bird Images

DAY 10: THE FAMOUS STONE CHURCHES OF LALIBELA

In the morning we visited the stone churches of Lalibela, starting with the Northwestern group. They are remarkable, not only for their age (made in the 12th and 13th centuries) but also because they are not actually buildings; they are sculptures. Pious Ethiopian kings commissioned workers to carve them from solid rock. Luckily for the laborers, the rock in the area is compressed volcanic ash, which is far softer than most rock, and it carves relatively easily. Stoneworkers started from the top down, sculpting the multi-storied "buildings" out of pure stone. The most difficult part of the labor was not digging out the churches themselves, but the areas around them. Tons and tons of material had to be removed so the each church could be a freestanding building inside its giant hole. Interiors had to be carefully planned so the remaining pillars could support the weight of the solid stone roofs above. These rock-hewn churches are phenomenal evidence of the religious devotion of generations of religious Ethiopians.

King Lalibela himself was responsible for many of these churches. According to legend, he was poisoned by his half-brother. While comatose, angels supposedly transported King Lalibela to heaven where God told him to re-create Jerusalem in Ethiopia because a pilgrimage to the real city was too dangerous a journey at that time. The King recovered from his near-death experience and started serious work on the new task. He even tried to duplicate the "map" of historic Jerusalem. Names convey this concept today: the river "Jordan" flows through the area, and to get to some of the churches, the pilgrim first has to cross it. There is also a "Tomb of Adam" and "Calvary."

These ancient and monumental holy places are simple inside, with large, open columned halls and little decoration. The tall ceilings and pillars do evoke a calm, meditative state when the daylight filters through the windows in long, slanting beams. Some of these windows are cut in the shape of Maltese crosses, so they illuminate the interior with crosses of golden light when the sun hits them just right. Other windows are a throwback to an earlier age, with Axumite half-moon tops copied from pagan times.

At the back of each church is a curtained-off room called the "holy of holies." Only the priests are allowed to enter because this is where each church's copy of the Ark of the Covenant resides. One persistent rumor is that the "True Ark" was brought to Ethiopia soon after Christ's death, and that it was locked away, and that thousands of false copies were then made, to keep it safely hidden for all time. Every church in Ethiopia has a copy, and any one of them could potentially have the real thing. While this is all highly unlikely, it gives each church in the country a spiritual power and legitimacy most other churches around the world will never have. If there ever were such an Ark in Ethiopia, it is highly likely it would have been brought here, to Lalibela, since it has been the holiest pilgrimage spot in the country for centuries. It is exciting to imagine the Ark still exists and remains hidden in a secret room in one of the stone churches, or in some unknown, windswept monastery on a mountaintop, like the ones we visited earlier.

I felt greatly at peace in these cool, hushed, pillared halls, and I certainly felt a tug on my imagination as I gazed at those curtained rooms. The religious fervor of the priests and visiting Ethiopian pilgrims added to the aura of sanctity within.

The House of Mary Church was by far the most attractive in the group. Ethiopian churches use imagery to teach the gospel, and this was no exception. Even from the outside, the building itself told a story from its windows alone. At the back of the church, there were ten different windows, each with a different meaning. The top three rectangular windows represented the Father, Son, and Holy Ghost. Below them was a cross, representing the crucifixion. Below that, there were two half-moon shaped windows symbolizing Christ in the womb of Mary. At the bottom, there was another row of three windows. The one in the center was another cross for Christ, and the other two were for the two men crucified beside him; they were depicted with swastika-shaped windows. (This was an ancient good luck symbol, which Hitler later bastardized for his own evil purposes.) According to Orthodox teachings, one of these crucified men went to heaven, but the other went to hell. There was one last oddly-shaped, off-center window below, which signified the path the unfortunate bandit took to perdition.

Inside the church, there were ten arches, one for each of the Ten Commandments. The sanctuary was elegantly decorated, with upstairs galleries for noble pilgrims to look down from, and ornate "endless knot" and Greek key designs on the ceiling. The central pillar was covered with cloth because written on it are revelations supposedly unraveling the mystery of the world's beginning and the world's end. Nobody is allowed to see that pillar because they would then know the truth about Judgment Day. Only the head priest of the church is privy to the mysteries, and it is his job to keep the pillar wrapped up tightly.

There were many churches, each with many interesting and unique features. To get to one church, we had to enter an underground passageway and then cross a narrow stone bridge over a carved "chasm" twenty feet deep. There were several dark and spooky tunnels. Inside one of them, I felt the presence of somebody right behind me. When I turned to let them pass, there was nobody there, and the hairs on my arms were standing straight up.

We ate lunch at an inn called "The Seven Olives." The rambling old bungalow hotel was built high up above a small, forested area, and its outdoor dining section was nestled among the trees. One huge birdfeeder was the center of attention. Many interesting and colorful African bird species swooped in to help themselves to the bounty, from the largest hornbills to the smallest wrens, finches, and sparrows. Brilliantly iridescent sunbirds flitted among sprays of purple blossoms. They were brilliantly plumed and fun to watch. It was quite a bird show.

We struck up a conversation with the people at the next table, and it turned out one of them was the head of the Ethiopian chapter of the charity organization Oxfam America. This gentleman was responsible for assisting Ethiopian farmers to attain "Fair Trade" status for most Ethiopian coffee. He had also won a lawsuit preventing the coffee chain Starbucks from trademarking the word "Ethiopian" on coffee marketed in the U.S. and Europe. If the chain had succeeded, no Ethiopian growers would have been able to legally sell coffee with their national name around the world, except to Starbucks!

We enjoyed our conversation with these dedicated people, although we did bemoan the fact that the term "Fair Trade" cannot easily be applied to the jewelry and handicraft business. Most of the people we deal with cannot qualify for legal "Fair Trade" status. (It is an impossible task for most single-family businesses in which the family members work in their own homes; they can't meet international standards for the workplace without a modern factory.) Our new friend shook his head and said that what we were doing—making direct contact with as many family entrepreneurs as possible in many countries—is the true intention of "Fair Trade." It felt good to hear a "Fair Trade" pioneer being supportive of our business model.

After lunch, we had a little time to kill before meeting up with our driver again, so Dave decided to go and get a haircut. (Dave likes to get a haircut in every country we visit, and it's a habit that always makes for a memorable experience.) Dave reasoned that since Ethiopian men all have curly African hair, the Ethiopian barbers would be unfamiliar with his straight Caucasian locks. He thought he would have better luck at a ladies' salon because many Ethiopian girls straighten their hair. There was a beauty parlor right on the corner, so Dave went inside to negotiate a price.

The young lady on duty thought he was crazy. So did the crowd of young men who were tagging along with us. (We were rarely able to walk around town without an entourage of "new friends," most of whom were hoping for a handout of some kind.) I showed the young hairdresser how much hair she should take off the top of Dave's head. She proceeded to get out the oldest, saddest, dullest scissors I have ever seen in my life and began to hack. When the scissors didn't cut well enough, she got annoyed and tried to yank his hair tight so it would cut better. Dave howled in protest whenever she pulled too hard. In the end, I think she tore out as much hair as she cut. The boys pointed and burst into gales of laughter, which only made her angrier.

This made her tug harder, which made Dave squirm and yelp, which only provoked more guffaws.

And the result? Well, I suppose it was an improvement. Dave's hair was shorter and somewhat neater, but some spots looked like he'd been in a dogfight and had lost some of his fur. When Sisay heard what we'd done, he looked carefully at the results, and then laughed so hard he had to pull over and stop the car. His reaction cracked us up. We had to wait several minutes before we all got ourselves under control. Finally, he drove off, wiping tears from his eyes.

That afternoon, we toured the most famous Lalibela church of them all: the Church of St. George. This one is the most photographed because the entire church is shaped like a giant cross. The building is cut straight down, three stories from its cross-shaped roof. Distinctive carved windows and a little portico in the front decorate its exterior. It is an arresting and unique piece of sculpted architecture, enhanced by a subtle reddish color. I wondered if the color was natural or man-made. The church sits in the gigantic hole that forms its courtyard. An access stairway is dug down about a story and a half, which turns into a tunnel linking the church with the outside world. Once inside the courtyard, you can see niches and little caves dug into the cliff. One of them holds the mummified remains of ancient people (priests? pilgrims?) who perished here long ago.

I must confess, I was a bit disappointed by the interior, which was quite plain. It looked as if the builders were weary and eager to finish given the monumental amount of labor it must have taken to carve out the exterior and the courtyard.

We walked back to the Seven Olives for dinner that night, and they served us the best meal we had in Ethiopia. We had succulent lamb stew in a hot clay pot, served with a tomato and chickpea "chipotle" sauce, which gave the stew an aromatic, spicy, smoky flavor. There was also a delicious vegetable dish of spinach and sweet carrots mixed with onions, potatoes, and other goodies, and served in another heated clay pot. (The red carrots in Ethiopia are divine, much better than our carrots back home—they even beat the fancy organic Vermont ones in flavor.)

recommended google search: Lalibela Ethiopia images

DAYS 11 and 12: THE ROAD BACK TO ADDIS

When Sisay picked us up in the morning, he was appalled to find out we had walked all the way to the Seven Olives and back the night before, all by ourselves. He asked why we hadn't called him for a ride. Apparently, most of his guests would never have the nerve to find their way through an Ethiopian town all by themselves, especially at night. Sisay is not used to independent travelers.

By Diana McLeod

Before leaving town, we toured the ancient monastery of Ashetan Maryam. This primitive cloister was built under a dramatic overhanging cliff. The monks showed us their collection of treasures, which included exquisitely illuminated manuscripts, crowns, crosses and ceremonial drums. Part of the sacred enclosure was a natural cavern into which water dripped continuously from the cave roof into a natural limestone pool. Basins carved of limestone were placed along the cave floor to catch the pure drops of holy water, which the monks claimed was endowed with healing powers.

The road back to Addis was not terribly memorable, except for one scenic overlook, but our last hotel before returning to the capital was amusing. Our hosts thoughtfully left some amenities placed on the nightstands for their guests' convenience. On one nightstand was, of course, the Bible. The other nightstand held a selection of colorful condom packets. At least this hotel could not be accused of contributing to AIDS in Africa.

SOUTHERN ETHIOPIA ROAD TRIP:
A JOURNEY TO THE TRIBAL LANDS
- an extended travel diary

DAY ONE: ADDIS ABABA TO ARBA MINCH

After a bit of rest in the capital city, we reunited with our driver, Sisay. We were very glad to see each other again, and our conversation was lively, all the way to Arba Minch.

Along the way, we stopped at an ancient burial site at Tiya. Constructed in approximately 900 BC, it had rows of tall, carved standing stones as grave markers. They were crudely anthropomorphic—the male gravestones had large, flat chests, and the females had big breasts and jewelry. Depictions of swords indicated how many warriors each man had killed in his lifetime.

Our guide told us there were many such sites in the vicinity. One of them, on private land, has over 300 carved standing stones. We spotted other menhir clusters near the main road.

As we hit the hill country, the scenery became very attractive. Perfectly manicured fields of fertile red soil contrasted with green patches of lush jungle between villages. Clusters of conical thatched huts, many with decorative, overturned terracotta pots on top of the thatched peaks, added to the bucolic charm.

I cannot say enough about the quality of Ethiopian homesteads. Pride of place is everywhere. I never saw a messy or disorganized house. The huts were well maintained, often with fanciful decorations painted on them. Yards were freshly swept, gardens were beautifully cultivated, and firewood and animal fodder stacks were always neatly organized. Stone walls were elegantly constructed. There was no untidiness, no garbage, no disharmony anywhere, no matter how impoverished the inhabitants were. I never saw roadside trash or any human-made mess—not ever.

The only problem was that, near the road, the land was all under cultivation. There was never a spot out of sight of a homestead, or two, or three. People were everywhere. For us, this presented some difficulty, because we couldn't find anywhere for a rest stop with privacy. We finally found one clump of bushes with a herd of camels grazing among them, but even that almost failed us as a gang of young boys came running over to see what we were doing. Sisay had to chase them off, earning the nickname, "The Pee Police."

As we got further south, the road became inundated with livestock. Farmers drove herds of cattle, camels, donkeys, sheep, and goats right

By Diana McLeod

down the middle of the highway. Yes, the road was straight and virtually empty of vehicles, but there was still a lot of stop-and-go traffic. At times, the Land Rover was utterly surrounded by cattle.

In the early evening, we reached the town of Sikela, Arba Minch, a very nice looking lakeside community. All along the road, flame trees were in bloom, picturesque in the red sunset. We pulled into a hotel/restaurant complex and settled in for the night. The Paradis Hotel was entertaining. It had a terrific indoor-outdoor restaurant/bar area, set into a wonderfully jungle-like garden. We dined al fresco, with the heavy scent of tropical flowers wafting around our table. Both tourists and locals were mixing nicely. Arba Minch is a university town, and many of the students were out for a big Saturday night. Young couples flirted at the bar, and local families came out for dinner at the restaurant. The firepit at the traditional Ethiopian coffee ceremony area was also busy. (Dave and I never indulged in the coffee ceremony, because it is performed in the afternoons and evenings, and we'd be up all night if we drank the hardcore stuff they serve).

After a delicious dinner, we settled in for our usual St. George beers and an epic backgammon game. We both enjoy this pastime, but David had been on a real losing streak which had lasted for days. The only time he had won consistently was when Sisay was sitting with us. My husband declared Sisay to be his lucky charm and had been buying him beer to keep him nearby. On this particular evening, Sisay was not with us, and I beat Dave so badly he decided to phone Sisay and prank him.

"Sisay!" Dave exclaimed, "you have to come here right away! It's an emergency!"

Sisay's voice sounded alarmed. "What's wrong?" he gasped.

"Diana is kicking my butt at backgammon! You have to come and save me! I can't win without you! You're my good luck! Hurry up and get over here!"

There was a silence on the phone, followed by gales of laughter. "David, you scared me!" Sisay exclaimed. "I thought you were in serious trouble! You're the craziest guy! I should learn not to take you so seriously!"

recommended Google search: Tiya burials Ethiopia images

DAY 2 : WADING WITH CROCODILES

To be honest, neither Dave nor I set foot into the perilous waters of crocodile-infested lake Chamo. But that doesn't mean that risks weren't taken...

Our day started when Sisay came to pick us up in the morning. He waggled his finger at Dave because of the prank Dave had played on him the night before. Dave was undeterred; he couldn't resist joking with Sisay because Sisay made such a natural "straight man." Sisay informed us his company had scheduled a boat ride for us on which we would see crocodiles and hippos in their natural habitat at the lake. Dave immediately put on his serious face and told Sisay that, in fact, scientists had actually interbred the two species, producing the world's first crocopottomus and hippodiles. For a long moment, Sisay was shocked by this news, until he realized Dave was at it yet again. Poor Sisay! He was so used to straight foreigners! For those of you who know Dave well, just imagine being stuck in a car with him for three long weeks, eight hours a day! Between the endless travel stories, ranting about politics, philosophical discussions and constant fooling around, we were driving Sisay crazy.

Luckily, toward the end of the second road trip, Sisay got very skilled at handling Dave. I think he relished the challenge. Sisay said we were much more fun than his regular tourist customers, many of whom never took the time to hang out with him and get to know him at all. He was accustomed to being treated more like a servant than a potential friend, I'm sorry to say.

We stopped to acquire permits before driving deep into the national park. The "road" was extremely boggy and, at times, completely underwater. Baboons scampered alongside as the Land Rover slogged laboriously through the muddy swampland. Finally we reached the boat launch site, which was little more than a thin bamboo bridge out over the mud. The boat was tethered to the far end, and its driver was already there, waiting for us. The man wore a pair of shorts, a torn tee shirt, and an automatic weapon slung over his shoulder as casually as a lady wears a purse. We inquired about the gun, and Sisay said it was for security. *Were there pirates on the lake?* I doubted it. I think the gun was for protection from charging hippos. Hippos look foolish, but they are one of the most dangerous animals in the world, and they can easily swamp a boat and kill humans if provoked.

Our guide started up the outboard motor and headed us out onto the lake. We were relieved because we were suddenly anxious to get moving. Our boatman had the worst body odor either of us had ever encountered, and we've spent plenty of time in countries where people seldom wash. This guy's aroma was so strong that, even out on the lake, in a moving boat, with a brisk breeze, we couldn't avoid his scent even from ten feet away. Dave remarked he must have become a boatman because he could never have made a living as a hunter. Or a waiter, for that matter.

But he turned out to be an excellent (and intrepid) guide. He drove us to an area of the lake where a small stream joined the larger body of water. Over two dozen crocodiles were there! The crocs were either swimming lazily or sunning themselves on the muddy shoreline. Our guide tried to bring us in for a closer look, but the boat soon got stuck on a sandbar. Nonchalantly, he jumped over the side and waded, waist deep, into the crocodile-infested water! I was quite concerned for his safety, especially when a ten-footer moved off the bank and slid into the water, heading right for him! The croc disappeared into the opaquely muddy water, and our guide risked running into him, or even stepping on him as he swam past. The boatman's face showed no concern. I guess the crocs are very used to his feet intruding into their territory. He certainly earned himself a hefty tip, but I hope his love of tourist largesse doesn't lose him a leg someday!

Surprisingly, lots of shorebirds wandered among the crocs. Herons fished in the shallows, and spoonbills waded, moving their odd, spoon-shaped bills from side to side in search of tasty tidbits. Maribou storks stalked along the water's edge, practically stepping over the sleeping crocs. I wondered how often the crocs pretended to snooze, luring the birds into a false sense of complacency...

There were other birds as well. An African fishing eagle preened his wing feathers on a nearby bush. Terns and pelicans hovered in the breeze, while swallows dipped low over the water, looking for flies. In the trees, hornbills and white egrets congregated noisily. Brightly colored songbirds flickered past. It was a birdwatcher's paradise!

On the way back, to my delight, we saw some hippos. They watched us with curiosity. The boatman got close—but not too close—so Dave could get a decent picture that showed more than just a pair of nostrils and funny looking ears sticking out of the water.

As we drove back in the car, Dave chattered excitedly about seeing crocopottomuses for the first time, while Sisay sat stoically behind the wheel, rolling his eyes.

recommended Google search: Lake Chamo Ethiopia

DAY 3: MURSI GIRLS AND BANA BOYS

We had to drive through part of the Omo Valley National Park to reach remote tribal villages near the Kenyan border. Our ride through the park was not particularly scenic, given we were surrounded by thorn trees on either side, but we saw plenty of wildlife. Black and white Calabash monkeys and baboons swung comfortably to and fro among the branches, despite the vicious prickles. Waterbuck antelope grazed nearby. Flocks of wild helmeted guinea hens ran along the roadside, reminding me somewhat of wild turkeys in our country. Tiny Dik-dik deer leapt across the road, startled by our vehicle. These adorable little foragers are only about twelve to eighteen inches tall, and they almost always come in pairs. Our Ranger/guide claimed it is a fact that the adult Dik-dik must mate at least once a day or they will die. (Wikipedia says only that they are monogamous, and couples spend most of their time together. I don't know who to believe.)

The most extraordinary wildlife was also the smallest. We saw dozens of gigantic termite mounds, with crazy looking chimneys and domes soaring fifteen to twenty feet into the air. I posed next to one, and the photo shows me dwarfed by the strange structure. I saw no sign of the mound's tiny inhabitants, but I'm sure they were busy inside, trying to keep up with the neighbors by building their colony even taller than the high-rise next door. What remarkable builders they are! It made me wonder: do termite cities compete for "world's tallest building" like humans do?

As we got farther away from the national park, we began to see people again. Tribal costumes became more and more pronounced. My favorites were the Bana boys. These young men dressed in nothing but very short, tight, striped mini-skirts. Most of these fellows were tall, handsome and muscular, and their skin-tight wraps left little to the imagination. I think Sisay was genuinely scandalized when I remarked (repeatedly) just how hot the Bana boys were. But Dave just teased me, saying I just couldn't resist sweaty, bare-chested males with AK-47s slung over their shoulders. Later, Dave got his revenge when we started seeing bare-chested young Mursi girls. Dave made sure to comment on the scenery while Sisay just shook his head at us both and kept his eyes on the road.

Sisay, the local guide and an armed guard took us to visit two tribal villages. These were pretty impoverished-looking places, and the villages' primary source of income was soon obvious—us. I don't remember the name of the first tribal group, but as soon as we entered the village, we were mobbed by people desperate to have their picture taken for money. It was a bit much for us since we always hope for genuine interaction with people. Most of the tribe turned out as soon we showed up, and they all stood stiffly at attention, posing awkwardly in long rows. To Dave's despair, they all lined up with the sun behind them (making it impossible to get a good picture), and many of them wore ridiculous outfits made just to please tourists. People grabbed pots to put on their heads, or they wore outlandish headdresses that were anything but authentic. We found it impossible to get natural-looking photographs, and, frankly, handing out banknotes for pictures is just not our style. Still, we did succumb to a bit of the local photo prostitution, because there was no choice.

We were more successful at the Mursi village, and we did see tribal life that was real, not just for show. This time, we were invited into one of the huts and belly-crawled through its tiny doorway. The darkened interior held few possessions, only blankets and clothing, a water jar made from a calabash squash, and a ragged bundle of stuff in the corner. The lady of the house had pulled out her giant mouth plate, and you could see the slice below her lower lip. The long loop of her lip hung below her jaw, quivering in the air, as unappetizing as a shiny earthworm. We didn't see her put her plate back in, but she showed it to us, and it was about seven inches in diameter. Similar plates stretched her earlobes.

This custom, according to most sources, was probably developed in response to slavery. When foreigners invaded the area, people started using plates so slavers wouldn't take their women. Eventually, the stretched lips and earlobes became the norm, and today they are regarded as a mark of beauty, along with ritual scarification. Many of the people of this village had long rows of decorative raised scars all over their bodies. The marks are produced by creating a series of small open wounds and then stuffing them with fire ash so they heal as raised bumps. The Ethiopian government is trying to discourage all of these practices because of infections.

I noticed one girl with an open sore on her leg, which was swollen and infected. I went back to the car, dug through my stuff, and got out a tube of Neosporin. Dave suggested I use leaves to distribute it. Word spread through the camp, and I was suddenly "Doctor Diana," distributing medicine to anybody with a scratch. There were quite a few.

We suddenly had a purpose in the village. No longer were we just "photo johns" paying for "photo prostitution." I felt much better about being there, and I could tell that the Mursi did too. Since this was supposedly the most "difficult" tribe to win over, according to our guides and drivers, we were pleased and proud to have broken the tourist ice with them.

(If anyone reading this is considering a trip to Southern Ethiopia, and you wish to avoid the photo-op prostitution situation, there are several other ways to endear yourself to the local population besides cash. #1: Topical medicines like Neosporin, distributed carefully, only one dose per person. NEVER hand out bottles of pills, because the people won't understand the concept of dosage, and they will overdose. #2: Small bars of soap (we were asked for soap in several villages). #3; Cheap cosmetic mirrors with protected edges. These items might be well received. Please do not ever hand out candy or any other items that might cause harm, and please do not distribute plastic goods, because the goats will eat them, and their digestive tracts could become blocked. Be aware that you may need several hundred of any item you choose!)

In the afternoon, we went to a weekly market. The town was teeming with people of various tribes, eager to trade. The field was mobbed with buyers and sellers. Vegetables and produce, meat and skins, cloth goods, tribal jewelry, calabash squash containers, cowrie shells, baskets, pottery, honey, and other items were on display.

Vendors squatted in the noonday sun, bantering and bargaining good-naturedly with their customers.

It was easy for us to romanticize the scene, but market days were challenging for these people. I had to remind myself that many of these folks awakened before dawn to reach the market location in the morning. Many would have to trek throughout another night to reach their homes again. They were all barefoot, and they would be hiking on sharp, hot gravel for hours, without water or shade, in temperatures that often reached a hundred degrees, carrying heavy loads both to and from the market. As they got closer to their homes, they would have to veer off the road and follow foot trails through scrubby underbrush without flashlights where every step could lead to three-inch long spines in their feet, or torn up legs or arms. At night, they would risk dangerous encounters with wildlife, including packs of hyenas and African wild dogs. (Now, imagine yourself taking a shopping expedition to your air-conditioned supermarket by car. The next time you can't find a parking space right near the supermarket door, just think about the Ethiopians before you get too bent out of shape about it.)

recommended Google search: Bana Tribe Ethiopia

Day 4: THE BULL JUMPING CEREMONY

On day four of our journey, we got some fabulous news: we would be able to attend a bull jumping ceremony, as long as we were willing to give a financial donation to the family. Dave and I leapt at the chance, especially when we learned the deal would include unlimited photography of the entire celebration. We would finally be able to get those unposed photos we had been yearning for, with entire Hamar tribal clans decked out in authentic attire, and we would be welcome guests at this spectacular and rare ceremony.

Bull jumping is a once-in-a-lifetime event in a Hamar man's life. If he is successful and jumps the bulls properly, his success indicates to the tribal elders that he is a full-grown man, ready to marry and to assume his place in adult society. If he fails to leap over the cattle three times, he is shamed before the tribe. He is taken by the women into the forest to be whipped, and he must wait months before he can try again.

The ceremony itself is all about the man, but the unsung heroes of the family are the women. In my opinion, their role requires much more bravery than his, and make his bull jumping seem almost easy by comparison. The feats of courage the ladies demonstrated were breathtaking. I will never forget what I saw that day, and I will never forget the Hamar women.

The ladies were gorgeous, not because they were sexy, but because they were strong, and their strength shone radiantly on their beautiful

296

faces. These women all had the bodies of hardcore athletes. Their muscles flexed like bodybuilders, and their calves and thighs were shapely and rock-hard from all the walking and the hard daily work they had to do. They all sported the traditional Hamar hairstyle: a helmet of tight braids covered in a red ochre mud. (This sounds unattractive, but they looked pretty cool). Their costumes were bold as well. Each woman wore handmade skirts of intricately beaded cowhide. The married ones wore side-slit skirts that covered their inner thighs and backsides. The unmarried girls' outfits were slimmer and showed more leg. The women also wore spectacular jewelry: necklaces and headbands of cowrie shells, and rows of chunky metal bracelets. Heavy anklets with large bells jingled as they walked. Some women wore thick metal collar necklaces, and many wore two or even three of these big chokers. Apparently, a first wife had one collar, a second wife had two, and so on. (A Hamar man is allowed to have up to four wives, as long as he can afford them.)

Most of the women wore Western tee shirts, but these were rolled up and tied tightly just below their breasts, and rolled even higher in back, leaving most of the back fully exposed. The tee shirts looked quite out of place, and I wondered about their purpose until I realized what was about to happen, and then I understood why the girls had donned them on this day.

Our guide explained it to me. For the first part of the ceremony, before the party arrived at the bull-jumping place, the young man was involved in a private preparation ritual, conducted by a male elder or shaman. While this was happening, it was the time for the women of the family to assume their traditional role.

Their job was to show their love for the young man who was about to jump, and they proved it by demonstrating their willingness to accept pain on his behalf. At one side of the clearing, there was a group of young men who had already successfully jumped the bulls during the same year. They wore distinctive headdresses, with feathers that stuck up in the air. These men were all given long switches made from young, flexible tree branches. The women taunted them by singing, dancing, and blowing brass horns or cow's horns. I could not understand their spoken language, but their body language made their meaning crystal clear. Their words must have meant something like this: "Come on, I want you to hit me, and hit harder this time. Don't be such a coward." The young man would respond by hitting the woman fiercely with his switch. The woman would taunt him again, telling him he hit like a girl. Angered, he would whip his branch harder across her back.

Most of these blows sounded like the snapping of a horsewhip. They raised six to eight-inch welts across the woman's back, and the welts usually drew blood. I saw women with eight to ten bleeding switch marks on their backs, overlapping other rows of old scars. I watched women approach the men, again and again, demanding more from them, even though each blow rained down on flesh already torn open and raw. I could see, now, that the tee shirts were there to protect their breasts from being sliced open from glancing blows. As it was, blood flowed freely, dripping down their lower backs.

There were about fifteen tourists gathered at this event. The female tourists were strongly affected by this brutal display, and they would flinch and cringe with each crack of the switches. Not so the Hamar women. I studied their faces as the whipping continued. I never saw one flinch. I never even saw one blink or gasp, or even acknowledge the blow at all, even when the whip struck across a freshly opened wound.

The women just kept smiling and heckling the men. Their bravery was stunning. Our guide told me they were all pretty drunk, which must have helped—although they were not drunk enough to stumble or look intoxicated. I wondered if they had discovered some local medicinal plant that eased their pain. If they had, the ladies kept it a secret. Our guide, who was Hamar, and was going to jump the bulls himself that year, had no knowledge of any such medication.

At last the whipping event was over, and the clans hiked a short distance down the road to the jumping area as we trekked alongside. I walked with one group of Hamar women. They were all bleeding, but they paid no attention to their injuries. They were in a festive mood, talking, laughing and blowing their horns enthusiastically. One of the women was, in my opinion, the bravest of them all. She was a beautiful, mature woman of about thirty-five, who had gone back time and time again to face the whip. I deliberately caught her eye and attempted to communicate my respect for her. I smiled at her, pointed at her, indicated my own poorly flexed bicep, and then touched hers. She nodded and flashed me a fabulous smile of understanding.

Dave walked behind the women, documenting the welts and the bleeding on film. The ladies didn't seem to mind being photographed at all—they were proud of their battle scars. Some of their backs showed plenty of evidence of past bull jumping events as well. Dave shook his head and couldn't resist remarking as to how, in the West, girls whine about having to wear ugly bridesmaids' dresses.

The main event took place on a sandy clearing among the thorn trees. The Hamar had driven a large herd of bulls into the open area, and tribesmen were circling around, driving them closer and closer together. When they were ready, the owners of the animals grabbed each bull by the ears, while others pulled their tails. Eventually, each bull was positioned so it couldn't move without causing itself considerable distress. They stood, side by side, in a long line, about fifteen bulls in all. These cattle were of the Brahmin variety, and they are more placid animals than most Western breeds. (Although not always—I have been chased by them before). The Hamar are expert herdsmen, and they certainly accomplished this remarkable task efficiently, but I'm sure there is some personal risk involved.

With the bulls in line, the young man prepared to jump. His task was to leap from the ground to the back of the first bull, and run, barefoot, across the backs of all the bulls in the line, and do this without falling until he had traversed them all. He had to do this three

By Diana McLeod

times. If he succeeded, he would be considered a man, and he would join the ranks of eligible bachelors. If he failed, he would be shamed before the tribe.

Needless to say, the young man looked extremely nervous. He was stark naked, with all of the tribe watching, and the tourist paparazzi was snapping pictures of him as if he was a rock star. His manhood and pride depended on the next five minutes. The pressure on him was tremendous. Everybody held their breath as he made a test run, turning aside at the last second. The next run started well, and he got enough momentum to land on the bull's bony back. Feet flying, he scrambled from one to the next, trying desperately to keep his balance until he was all the way over.

This young man made it—he got in three good runs. There was an audible collective sigh of relief from the whole crowd. I'm sure the ladies were overjoyed, since they would have had to undergo another whipping six months later when the young man tried again. The tribe happily left the jumping ground, heading back to celebrate at their village with a whole day of feasting.

recommended Google search: Ethiopia Bull Jumping Images

(And look for video on youtube)

DAY 5: THE KONSO TRIBAL HIGHLANDS

The Konso highlands are one of the most beautiful areas in Ethiopia. The rich red soil is elegantly terraced, tilled and planted with a variety of healthy-looking crops. According to outside agricultural experts, traditional Konso farming methods have kept their lands productive and self-sustaining for hundreds of years. Behind the farms, the rolling hills held patches of green virgin forest, almost the first surviving jungle we'd seen in the entire country.

The villages were fascinating. Impressive terraced stone walls surrounded ancient villages, some of which are now UNESCO World Heritage sites. Inside the village we visited, each family lived in an elaborately walled homestead, along with their livestock. Charming open arched doorways of woven branches tempted us to peek inside and take a look. When we did, we often saw mothers gazing out of the doorways with small children in tow, or aged grandmothers with wizened faces weaving or making handiwork. Great pride and attention had been given to the care of each compound. Everything was neat, clean and orderly, with every yard freshly swept and each woodpile elegantly stacked.

At the village center, there was a longhouse where all the unmarried young men lived. Nearby was a ceremonial area with a large open courtyard and the tribal "generation pole"—a tall mast of wood

299

with shorter poles bundled around the center pole. Every eighteen years, each generation adds its own pole to the group.

In the middle of the open space was a rounded rock, about fifteen inches in diameter. It is known as the "maturity stone," because young men of the village have to lift it over their heads and toss it backward three times to prove their maturity as men. It was a pretty big rock, and I wondered what might become of boys who were physically incapable of lifting it. Would they still be regarded as boys for their whole lives?

The maturity stone is also known as the "swearing stone." If two people have a disagreement and the truth needs to be determined, they are both required to lay hands on the swearing stone and tell the truth. It is said that any person who lies while touching this stone will die within a week.

The Konso espouse a mixture of Orthodox Christian beliefs and local ones. Traditions regarding their village chiefs are pre-Christian. When a chieftain dies, he is mummified and kept for nine years, nine months, nine days, nine hours and nine minutes. At the end of this time, he is buried in the sacred forest, and only then can a new leader be chosen. A coronation ceremony is a great event. The chieftain is decked out in the finest garments, including phallic jewelry and ivory bracelets. Our guide wouldn't tell us where the old chief's mummy was being kept, but we knew it was in the village somewhere.

recommended Google search: Konso Villages Ethiopia Images

DAY 6: ON THE ROAD TO A DORZE VILLAGE

The next day, we turned off the main road onto a twisting dirt track leading up into the mountains. As Sisay maneuvered the Land Rover through the hairpin turns, he started telling a few stories about some of the tourists he had encountered throughout the years. He mentioned one couple who had arrived in Ethiopia just after one confessed to the other about having an affair outside of wedlock. It was apparently an ice-cold journey! Poor Sisay had to spend ten days in the car with two people who refused to speak to each other!

Another story he told us was humorous. He was driving a group Australian women across the high plains. Several of them had to go to the bathroom, but there was no place to stop. The countryside was wide open, without bushes or cover, and it was a densely populated area. There were no inns or restaurants or anything like that nearby, only endless small villages and open fields. (Ladies, if you are going to Ethiopia, this can be quite a problem. One time, the only cover I could find was a steep embankment. I took quite a tumble down the rocky

By Diana McLeod

slope and was lucky to get out of the experience with small cuts and bruises. A bedsheet kept in the car might serve to solve the modesty problem more safely.) Anyway, back to the Australians... the girls grew increasingly desperate. Finally, they had Sisay ask a woman if they could use her backyard to relieve themselves. The woman nodded, and the girls fled to the rear of her hut. The lady immediately got on her cell phone and summoned the entire neighborhood so they could see if white people's behinds were as white as the rest of their skin. Sisay tried to prevent their embarrassment, but he was ignored, to the mortification of those poor girls!

THE DORZE VILLAGE: The most interesting thing I learned about the Dorze tribe was their traditional house construction. At first glance, the Dorze houses were typical, except that some houses were fifteen to twenty feet tall. Inside, they were impressively large, with a central sitting area, a kitchen fire, and an upstairs sleeping loft. Additional sleeping quarters fitted snugly around the perimeter, and there was even a small area for the family cow, off to one side. The house was warm and cozy, even on the cold, damp morning when we visited. It looked quite comfortable, except for the lack of indoor plumbing.

Back outside, our guide pointed out that the front of the building was supposed to look something like an elephant. Vents on either side of the door did resemble an elephant's eyes. Apparently, generations ago, the Dorze may have kept elephants. Our guide also pointed out the stark difference between the home we visited and the one next door, which was so small it was barely high enough to accommodate humans. The taller house, the guide explained, was a new one, while the short one was at least fifty years older. He then told us that the Dorze build their homes so tall because of shrinkage. Dorze homes shrink by inches each year. The cause? Termites. They can't stop the termites from constantly nibbling away at the base of each hut, so they've learned to build their houses twenty feet tall, and their doorways fifteen feet tall, so that when the house gets old, they can still get inside.

BACK TO ADDIS ABABA: On the way back to the capital, I was surprised by my melancholy mood. After three weeks of driving up to eight bumpy hours a day in the Land Rover, I should have been yearning to get off the road. Not so! I was sad to see the journey ending. I found the Ethiopian countryside endlessly fascinating. I loved the beauty of the land itself—the mountains, the high plains, the grand canyons and harsh deserts. I also greatly enjoyed the human element. Never have I seen so many people make so much out of so little. The determination of the Ethiopians to make the best of what they have, and to strive for something better, was apparent everywhere we went. I felt the country was energetic, ambitious and moving in the right direction. Even the government seemed to be instituting some forward-looking programs, educational advances, and investments in long-term infrastructure for the future.

301

Footsteps of a Nomad

The country has come a long way, especially when one looks back into its past. The next day, just before leaving the country, we visited the National Museum in Addis, and gazed on the actual skeleton of "Lucy." She was a 3.2 million-year-old pre-human ancestor species, discovered in Ethiopia in 1974. She created quite a sensation at the time, and she remains one of the most famous pre-humans ever found. Was Ethiopia the birthplace of humanity? We will probably never know for sure. At any rate, she seems a fitting place to end the last chapter of this book.

By Diana McLeod

FINAL THOUGHTS

People often tell me that I must be very brave to do what I do. Actually, it's not true. It's much easier to travel independently around the world than you might think. I find it more intimidating to find my way around American cities than many other parts of the world. They have fewer guns elsewhere, and that makes a big, big difference. And, unless you are very far out in some tiny village, you can almost always find someone who speaks English. It is rapidly becoming the world's universal language.

If there is a message to this book, it is that you can do this too. It's not that hard. You don't have to sign up for expensive, all-inclusive guided tours. You do need to carefully research where you are going, and you need contingency plans that are well thought out in advance. You will need to bring reference materials with you, and guidebooks and maps. For example, when your taxi driver assures you that he knows where your guesthouse in Cairo is, at one o'clock in the morning, and he drives you halfway into the city, then confesses that he's unsure of the destination, you have to have a backup plan. If you have anticipated this possibility, as we did, you can direct him to take you to a nearby national monument, and then you can guide him from there, because you've already studied the map and you know where you are going. If you've thought out every step (and every possible snafu), you should be fine, as long as you use common sense. Worst case scenario, you wind up back at the airport, in order to try again with a different driver. Today, with cellphone GPS, life is much easier than before. If you get a local SIM card at the airport, or as soon as you can, you'll rarely be truly lost.

"I can't afford it." Maybe not, but you'd be surprised how far you can get on a budget in certain places in the world if you work at it. If you shop for airfares during the "shoulder" seasons, you can find very cheap flights. If you're willing to lower your expectations, you can get clean, functional rooms at bargain rates. If you travel to places in economic hardship, like Nepal, you can score rooms for between $10 to $20 per night. Sure, there's no heat, and only solar hot water, but that's all part of the adventure.

Start with easier countries that have a decent tourist infrastructure, but *do* try countries where English is not the spoken language. Try Italy, or Croatia, or Thailand or Bali or Hong Kong. Then move to more daring places. You only have one life, so throw a little adventure into it. Go see the Himalayas. Explore the cultural craziness of India. Don't play it too safe. Leave the "safe" countries for later in life when you will need more security for health reasons.

Good luck, and happy trails!

ABOUT THE AUTHOR

Diana is a graduate of Phillips Exeter Academy and Middlebury College. She met her husband David while at Middlebury, and they married in 1977. Their import store, Tradewinds, first opened (under the name Himalayan Handicrafts) in Burlington Square Mall in 1990.

Diana and Dave live in Burlington Vermont, where they still run Tradewinds Imports, selling unique items and jewelry from around the world. In 2009, the store moved out of the mall and onto The Church Street Marketplace. For the past few years, David and Diana have produced their own line of handcrafted gemstone jewelry, which can be seen on the store's website, www.tradewindsvt.com.

Her first book, a novel, entitled *Cracks in the Earth: the Mayan Legacy* is also available on Amazon.

By Diana McLeod

Made in the USA
Columbia, SC
19 July 2018